CULINARIA
GREECE

GREEK SPECIALTIES

CULINARIA
GREECE

GREEK SPECIALTIES

MARIANTHI MILONA

EDITOR

WERNER STAPELFELDT

PHOTOGRAPHER

h.f.ullmann

Abbreviations and quantities

1 oz	= 1 ounce = 28 grams	
1 lb	= 1 pound = 16 ounces	
1 cup	= 8 ounces * (see below)	
1 cup	= 8 fluid ounces = 250 milliliters (liquids)	
2 cups	= 1 pint (liquids)	
8 pints	= 4 quarts = 1 gallon (liquids)	
1 g	= 1 gram = $\frac{1}{1000}$ kilogram	
1 kg	= 1 kilogram = 1000 grams = 2 ¼ lb	
1 l	= 1 liter = 1000 milliliters (ml) = approx 34 fluid ounces	
125 milliliters (ml)	= approx 8 tablespoons = ½ cup	
1 tbsp	= 1 level tablespoon = 15–20 g * (see below) = 15 milliliters (liquids)	
1 tsp	= 1 level teaspoon = 3–5 g * (see below) = 5 ml (liquids)	

Where measurements of dry ingredients are given in spoons, this always refers to the dry ingredient as described in the wording immediately following, e.g. 1 tbsp chopped onions BUT: 1 onion, peeled and chopped.

*The weight of dry ingredients varies significantly depending on the density factor, e.g. 1 cup flour weighs less than 1 cup butter.
Quantities in ingredients have been rounded up or down for convenience, where appropriate. Metric conversions may therefore not correspond exactly. It is important to use either American or metric measurements within a recipe.

Quantities in recipes

Recipes serve four people, unless stated otherwise.
Exception: Recipes for drinks (quantities given per person).

© 2004 Tandem Verlag GmbH
h.f.ullmann is an imprint of Tandem Verlag GmbH

Art direction:	Peter Feierabend
Project management:	Franziska Sörgel
Editorial staff:	Andrea Euerle, Andrea Görldt, Christian Heße, Martina Schlagenhaufer
Design & layout:	metzgerei strzelecki_grafikdesign
Food photography:	Heinz Troll
Picture editing:	Silke Haas
Cover design:	Carol Stoffel
Front cover photo:	© Molly Hunter/StockFood
Back cover photo:	© Tandem Verlag GmbH/Werner Stapelfeldt

Original title: *Culinaria Griechenland – Griechische Spezialitäten*
ISBN 978-3-8331-1051-1

© 2008 for this edition: Tandem Verlag GmbH
h.f.ullmann is an imprint of Tandem Verlag GmbH

Special edition

Translated by Susan Ghanouni, Harriet Horsfield, Pat Pailing, and Rae Walter in association with First Edition Translations Ltd., Cambridge UK
Edited by Lin Thomas in association with First Edition Translations Ltd., Cambridge UK
Typesetting: The Write Idea in association with First Edition Translations Ltd., Cambridge UK

Printed in China

ISBN 978-3-8331-4888-0

10 9 8 7 6 5 4 3
X IX VIII VII VI V IV III II I

Based on an idea by Ludwig Könemann

If you would like to be informed about forthcoming h.f.ullmann titles, you can request our newsletter by visiting our website (**www.ullmann-publishing.com**) or by emailing us at: newsletter@ullmann-publishing.com.
h.f.ullmann, Im Mühlenbruch 1, 53639 Königswinter, Germany
Fax: +49(0)2223-2780-708

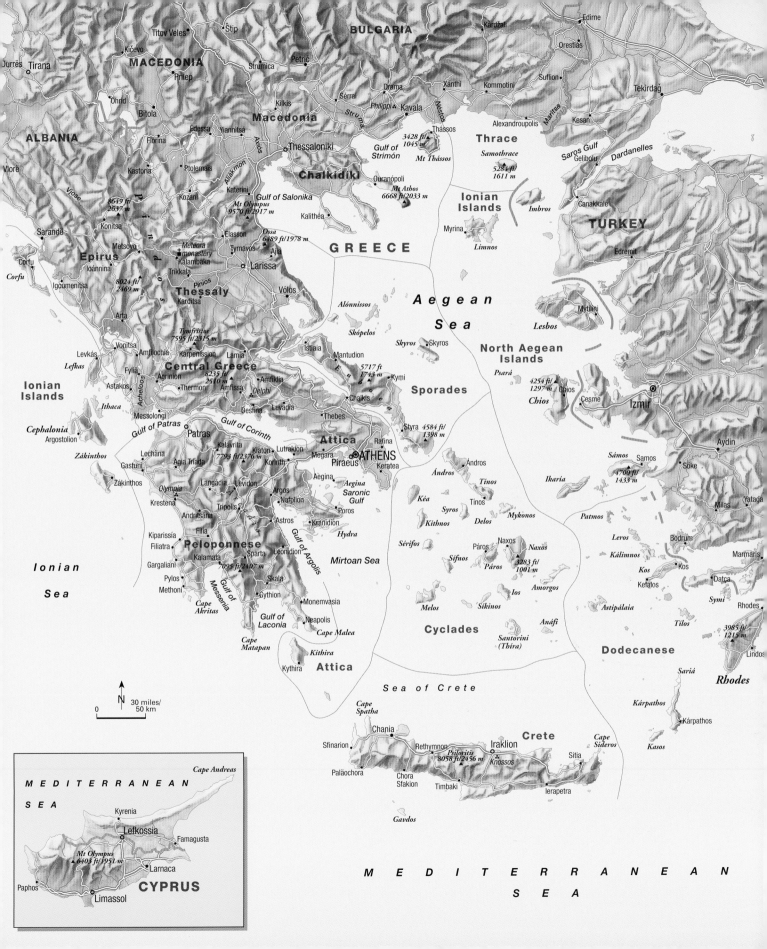

CONTENTS

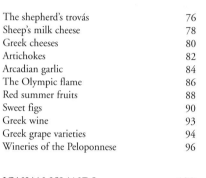

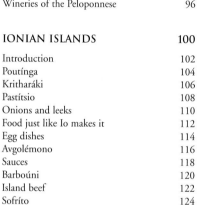
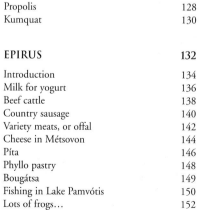

FOREWORD

A Macedonian cook once said that good cooking was simple, colorful, wholesome, and rich. This statement places him firmly in the tradition of his ancient forefathers, as in ancient times the gastronomic art was built on four pillars, which still characterize contemporary Greek cuisine: freshness, richness in vitamins, simplicity, and variety. The ancient Greeks mixed common and newly discovered ingredients together and tried out various possibilities for preparing and combining them. Even in those days pork and fish came together in the cooking pot, or they made fried dishes of fruit, nuts, and vegetables. Now ancient knowledge and refined techniques blend together to make what is perhaps one of the healthiest cuisines in Europe.

Very few people know the true Greek cuisine. This is in large part due to the fact that Greek restaurants abroad offer only a small, regularly recurring selection, which scarcely stretches beyond doner kebabs, souvlákia, or tzatziki.

The aim of this book is to tempt readers to go on a culinary voyage of discovery, which will introduce them to a richly varied cuisine, as diverse as the individual regions of the country. They will find game dishes in the mountains, all kinds of fresh fish in the coastal regions, and vegetable dishes and fruit in the hinterland. Simple, traditional cooking predominates on the islands, using seafood, and peas and beans, that thrive on the arid soils. But Ariadne's guiding thread stretches across all the regions, from Thrace to the Cyclades. People prefer to use fresh products from their own gardens – following the cycle of the seasons. No Greek cook would wish to make white cabbage salad in spring or ask for fresh peaches in December. And this country of many parts is united by one further distinctive feature: whichever region you are in, one thing seems to have remained unchanged since antiquity – the triad of bread, olive oil, and wine. No table would be complete without these three elements. Bread is served at any time of the day or night; baking, roasting, and seasoning is done with only the finest olive oil; and in many regions Greek wines are still made from the variety of grapes that Plato knew and loved.

In spite of the strong influence of foreign cultures, which held sway in Greece throughout the whole of the Middle Ages, the country has preserved its culinary heritage and blended it with new, exotic influences. Nowadays, nobody cares any more which elements were originally Ottoman, Jewish, Italian, or Greek. New combinations are constantly being created, exemplifying the success of multicultural Mediterranean cooking. Greek food reminds you of warm summer evenings, the gentle sound of lapping waves, the seductive scent of jasmine – impressions which combine with the aroma of hot olive oil to give the restaurants an exotic touch. This book is intended to arouse the reader's curiosity and whet the appetite for learning more about this wonderful food.

Marianthi Milona

9

ΑΘΗΝΑ

Above: guards in national costume parade outside the Greek Parliament building.
Background: the courtyard hall of the Grechthion – a famous view of the Acropolis.

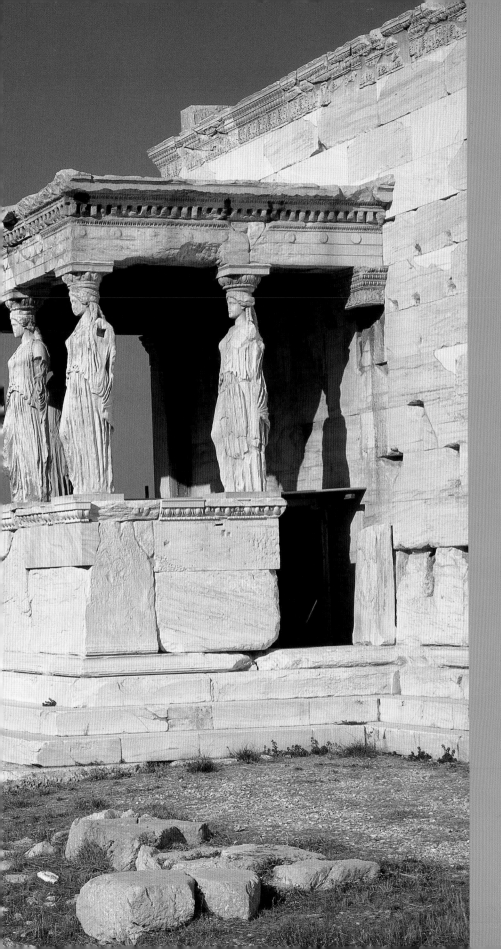

ATHENS

An Athenian andrón

Restaurants in Athens

Lobster with everything

Down at the harbor

Metaxa

With music and dance

Selection of mezédes

Appetizer culture

Made to order

Sweet temptation

In the Pláka

Athens has a history in itself. Almost everyone visiting the capital of Greece will have in mind that they are entering a city that is considered to be the birthplace of Western culture and the cradle of democracy. But nobody will find such a city, or at least not right away. Visitors expecting a place with a firm, unbroken link to its own glorious past find themselves instead in an artificial creation, which in fact owes its very existence to this classic image. This is because the decision taken in 1834 to proclaim the unimportant provincial town, which Athens had become, the new capital of Greece, was substantially influenced by foreign philhellenes. The time when Athens was everything that the name still conjures up for us today lies about 2500 years in the past, when the city reached its peak in economic and political terms.

The whole of Greece was divided into hundreds of small *poleis* – independent, self-governing communities run by the aristocratic elite, whose ordinary rural people were certainly free, but not equal – with the great city of Athens at their head. In Athens the aristocracy was prevented by law from reigning supreme, and the free population (*demos*) was guaranteed a large measure of participation and a rise in status. Cleisthenes' reforms of 510 B.C. laid the foundations for all later democracies. Soon afterward the Athenians themselves created the myth that the city had always been the center of civilization. Though it lost its economic and political importance in the 4th cen-

tury B.C., for some 500 years it still remained the exclusive home of learning and the art of sophisticated living (and cooking), until it began to lose this status too, starting in the 2nd century A.D. What has survived is its fame. Under these circumstances, present-day, rapidly growing Athens, with its five million inhabitants, the seat of parliament, the most enormous bureaucratic machine, a thriving media industry, and the greatest concentration of capital in the country, was bound to have problems with its powerful reputation. But now the links with its former political, economic, and intellectual importance cannot be overlooked, and as far as the people's way of life is concerned, there are probably few grounds for dissatisfaction. Exclusive restaurants, all well patronized, have opened up in the midst of the ancient columns. Athens has armed itself for the culinary fight.

A city with a – not uninterrupted – culinary past, in recent years Athens has again begun to feel it has a duty to its heritage, and as a result has also kept up the noble art of distilling.

The *Archaeon Gevsis*, which roughly means "antique taste," is an attempt to recreate the look and taste of ancient Greek cuisine.

Whichever way you approach Athens, the first thing you see is the Acropolis, which dominates the city. Like many of Athens' buildings, the Parthenon has undergone various changes of use: first the temple of the city's patron Athena, then a church, and later a mosque. It has been cannibalized for building projects and has suffered bombardment.

AN ATHENIAN ANDRÓN

Around 400 B.C. every prosperous Athenian citizen's house had a special room called the *andrón*, literally "men's room," which served as a dining room. It was the place where the master of the house entertained his male guests, and while they were there, the women of his household were absolutely forbidden to enter. As a rule, the men and women did not have their meals together. Even if they did eat in the same room, the men were served first. The dimensions of the *andrón* were usually sufficient to allow seven couches with tables in front of them to be set up. When guests were invited to a meal, the courses consisted of *propómata*, appetizers, followed by *sítos* (things to fill you up) and *ópson* (things to eat with bread).

PALLAS ATHENA

The birth of Athena is one of the most miraculous events in classical mythology. Her father Zeus was once told by a prophet that, after bearing him a daughter who would be his equal, his first wife Metis would bear a son who would be his superior. As Zeus had overthrown his own father and did not want to suffer the same fate, he devoured the pregnant Metis. But as the time when the child would have been born approached, he realized he had acted rashly, and called on Hephaestus or Prometheus, the god of fire, to help him. Hephaestus split open Zeus' head with an ax and out sprang the goddess Athena in full armor! As the goddess of defensive war, she was opposed to Ares, the god of aggressive war. She was the special protector of all the Greeks and sided with such heroes as Odysseus in her role as the

goddess of wisdom. She owes her virginal, Amazonian image to the epithet Pallas, which means "the maiden." She competed with Poseidon, the god of the sea and earthquakes, to become the patron of Attica and the city of Athens. When Poseidon struck one of the rocks of the Acropolis with his trident and caused a horse to come forth – or, in another version, caused a salt spring to flow from it – Athena made an olive tree spring up close by. The gods and the citizens of Athens recognized the olive tree as the more valuable gift and accorded her the patronage of the city, which for this reason has borne her name ever since. That is why the owls that lived on the Acropolis, those wise birds with far-seeing eyes, became what is probably the best-known symbol of Athena, goddess of wisdom.

After that, they had the tables carried out and cleaned, before they were brought back into the room with all the utensils needed for *oínos* (wine), and *tragémata* (things to eat with wine). Then either a harmless drinking session (*pótos*), a formal banquet (*sympósion*), or a drunken orgy (*kómos*) ensued. But back to the *deipnon*, the dinner, and its courses. As well as olives, appetizers could be anything fairly spicy and also juicy, slightly tart fruit such as apples or plums. *Sítos* were any dishes based mainly on the traditional staple foods of lentils, barley and wheat prepared in a variety of ways. *Ópson* included vegetables, cheese, eggs, fish, and seafood, as well as meat, poultry and game. By way of vegetables, they had celery, asparagus, Swiss chard, nettles, various kinds of cabbage, cardoon hearts (closely related to artichokes), fennel, onions, leeks, mushrooms, and lettuce. Cucumbers and pumpkins were probably still relatively new to Athenian markets. They did not eat the roots of carrots, and there were no tomatoes yet. The selection of herbs left virtually nothing to be desired. There was a vast selection of fish, meat, poultry and game. Cakes, fresh fruit, dried fruits such as raisins and figs, and also nuts could be served for *tragémata* (dessert).
The quality of all the ingredients was strictly controlled. Products from particular regions were highly valued and imported to Athens. Cooks became famous. The importance of the art of cooking as a way of enriching everyday

life was much discussed, but they also saw a close link between diet and healing, with the result that more of the recipes which survive today come from ancient medical texts than from "cookbooks." Buying food, preparing meals, and the food itself were considered so worthy of mention in classical Athens that such scenes were frequently portrayed in comedies, and always led to the same conclusion: good food is to be taken seriously.

What an ancient Greek dessert might have looked like: nuts, fruit, and raisins with honey, accompanied by a beaker of honey wine.

KHIRINÓ ME DAMÁSKINA
Pork tenderloin with prunes

4 pork tenderloins, 8 oz/250 g each
20 sulfur-free prunes, pitted
1 can (16 oz/500 g) peas, drained
Greek extra virgin olive oil
4 oz/100 g garlic, crushed
14 oz/400 g artichoke hearts, simmered until tender
1 scant cup/200 ml white or red wine vinegar
1 scant cup/200 ml balsamic vinegar
1 cup/400 g pine tree honey
Salt
Freshly ground black pepper

Cut the meat lengthways two thirds of the way through, open each out and flatten slightly with a rolling pin. Season with salt and pepper. Place 5 prunes on each piece, roll the meat up and tie tightly with kitchen string. Grill over charcoal for 10–15 minutes. In the meantime, purée the peas in a blender with some of the olive oil, add salt, pepper and a little vinegar, and set aside. When the meat is cooked, cover with foil and rest for 5 minutes. Heat some olive oil in a pan and add the garlic and artichoke hearts. Season with salt and pepper and sauté briefly, stirring continuously. When cooked, divide the hearts between the plates. Remove the string, cut the meat in slices and arrange on the plates with some of the purée. Bring both kinds of vinegar and the honey to a boil in a small saucepan. As soon as the sauce thickens, remove from the heat and pour over the pork. Serve with a medium-dry white wine.

Giant shrimp on a bed of salad is a good, simple, timeless recipe.

RESTAURANTS IN ATHENS

In recent years, the city of Athens has reacted to the steadily increasing influence of European cuisine in Greece by offering a wide diversity of foods that has amazed both local customers and visitors. A colorful selection of restaurants has sprung up, from Indian and Japanese to French and Italian. The cuisine of countries all over the world is represented in Athens, the showpiece of Greece, promising gourmets culinary delights that will carry them off on a new world tour every day. At the same time, ambitious Greek chefs have made it their goal to prepare traditional local dishes according to all the rules of gastronomy and in exclusive surroundings. It has paid off. The Athens restaurant scene is now the most varied and innovative in the whole of Greece. For many years now, it has not been the world famous remains of its past greatness which leaves the most lasting impression on visitors to the city; they are at least as deeply impressed by an array of cooking styles and restaurants aiming specifically at pleasure and enjoyment. A stay in Athens can become an unforgettable cultural and gastronomic experience.

"Dafnis," with its luxurious murals and apricot-colored décor, is undoubtedly one of the top restaurants. Statesmen and bohemians are equally welcome here.

Below: musical entertainment is standard in all the best restaurants. Good Greek folk music is as much a part of Greek gastronomy as good taste and atmosphere.

Above: a visit to the renowned fish restaurant "Varoulko," where Chef Lefteris serves his famous fish creations, is easily combined with a short trip to Piraeus.

Left: the "Maritsa" represents the restaurant culture of young Athens. High-class traditional cuisine is served in surroundings with modern décor.

Below: every self-respecting restaurant employs a host or hostess who greets the guests as they come in, and invites them to study the menu.

LOBSTER WITH EVERYTHING

Lobsters still have a special place in Greek cuisine, because they are not common enough in Greek waters to have ever become an everyday food. This flavor of exclusivity is just fine for Athenian chefs, who have put a lot of effort into polishing their city's gastronomic reputation. To make certain there is no shortage of lobsters here, lobster farms have spread along the coast of Attica, but the best lobsters are still caught off the island of Alónnisos in the Sporades. Athenian high society is ready to accept anything exotic that might blend with the taste of Greek food. This includes the many varieties of lobster, which chefs Nikos Sarantos and Sotiris Evangelou met on their travels through Europe and from which they drew inspiration when they got home. The individual elements of the lobster menus put together here by Sarantos have been widely praised and are frequently ordered as the specialty of the Athens Plaza Hotel.

MENU

Lobster salad on new potatoes
Astakóssalata me mikrés fréskies patátes

Medaillons of lobster on vegetable spaghetti
with lemongrass dressing
Fetoúles astakoú me spagéto prásino kai sáltsa lemonókhortou

Crêpes filled with sautéed lobster
on a bed of saffron sauce
Krépes me astakó sotarisméno se kroko

Creamed lobster, flavored with Metaxa
Kréma astakoú, aromatisméni me Metaxa

Lobster Thermidor with wild rice and julienne of vegetables
Astakós Thermidor me ágrio rízi kai lakhaniká à la Julienne

Chocolate mousse with caramelized William pears
Mousse sokoláta me akhladia karamelisé

Coffee or tea
Kafés i tsái

Fruit Delight
Froutolikhoudiés

DOWN AT THE HARBOR

Often a favorite subject for song, Piraeus attracts a large number of visitors. Many of them visit the fish restaurants and tavernas that line the shore of the "Turkolimano" – the Turkish Harbor, as one of the three bays is known – to enjoy the view of the boats and the sea. And that is not the only reason they visit. After all, a look at what is in the pot is just as worthwhile since the fishermen deliver fish and seafood daily that are quickly made into tasty delicacies. For Athenians, Piraeus is the point of departure for boats to the Greek islands and to Western Europe, but much more often for short pleasure trips on warm evenings or weekends.

SARDÉLES LEMONÁTES
Sardines in lemon sauce

Olive oil for frying
5 large potatoes, peeled and sliced
3 cloves of garlic, thinly sliced
½ hot chili pepper
6 cups/1.5 liters cold water
2 lbs/1 kg sardines, filleted
½ cup/125 ml olive oil
2 tbsp/30 g butter
Juice of 2 lemons
1 bunch flat-leaved parsley, finely chopped
Salt

Lightly brown the potatoes, garlic and pepper in a little oil, pour in the cold water and boil for about 30 minutes. Reduce the temperature, skim any foam, and boil for a further 10 minutes, adding the sardines. Finally add the butter, lemon juice, parsley, and salt.

BAKALIÁROS ME SPANÁKI
Hake with spinach

1¼ lbs/600 g spinach
2 tbsp/30 g butter
2 tsp red pepper
1 pinch cumin
Juice of 1 lemon
4 hake fillets
4 cups/1 liter fish stock

Steam the spinach in a little salted water for about 12 minutes, drain, and toss in melted butter with the red pepper and cumin. For the sauce, make a sauce mousseline (see page 444) using the fish stock, and flavor with retsina. Clean the fish fillets, pour over the lemon juice and leave to steep. Place the fillets in the sauce, which should be brought carefully almost to a boil but on no account be allowed to boil. As soon as the sauce begins to simmer, leave to stand for about 10 minutes until the fish is cooked. Carefully remove the fillets and serve immediately on warmed plates with some of the sauce. Decorate with ground red pepper.

GARÍDES SAGANÁKI
Baked shrimp in tomato sauce

3 tbsp olive oil for frying
1 lb /500 g tomatoes, peeled and diced
3 garlic cloves, thinly sliced
½ pimento, finely chopped
1½ lbs/750 g large shrimp, shelled
1 bunch flat-leaved parsley, finely chopped
4 oz/100 g mild sheep's cheese, crumbled
Salt

Preheat the oven to 350 °F (180 °C).
Heat the olive oil in a saucepan. Add the tomatoes, garlic, pimento, shrimp and parsley, and cook gently over medium heat for 15 minutes. Stir in the sheep's cheese, cook for a further 2 minutes, and transfer to an earthenware casserole. Place the casserole in the oven and bake for 10 minutes. Serve hot.

METAXA

Metaxa is more than just a brandy, it has almost become a legend. In 1880, Spyros Metaxas settled in Piraeus, and shortly afterwards acquired extensive vineyards in the south of Attica. Here he combined various wines from which, using traditional methods, he distilled his first brandy, made in his own factory and sold under his name from 1888 onward. His first customers came from the upper strata of Greek society at the court of King George I, in Serbia, Russia and Ethiopia. Success came so quickly that he was able to open a second distillery in Odessa as early as 1890. Five years later, when Sultan Abdul Hamid also gave his approval to Metaxa, all doors were open to its creator, even in Istanbul.

Metaxa brandy is still produced in the same way, using Spyros Metaxas' method. The raw materials are wines made from the Savatiano, Sultanina, and Korinthiaki varieties of grape. From these a brandy of 82–86% vol. is distilled in two processes which do justice to the different characters of the wines. This basic brandy matures for a number of years in barrels of Limousin oak. Distillers call the annual loss of alcohol from the barrels the "tribute to the angels." This first distillation already produces the delicate taste so characteristic of Metaxa, and its golden color. Before the next stage of the process, it is passed through a mixture of herbs, which still remains a well-kept trade secret, except that it involves rose petals. Then the distillation is blended or "married" with mature Muscat wine from Limnos and Samos and matured again in oak barrels, until it has fully developed its unmistakable bouquet and achieved the desired quality.

Above (left to right: the number of stars indicates the minimum age):
Metaxa 7 Star Amphora; Metaxa 5 Star Classic; Metaxa Grande Fine (15 years) in handmade porcelain carafe.
Below left: Private Reserve 25 years (only in Greece).

Metaxa is more or less born in this copper distillation equipment.

The maturity of the Metaxa that is stored in the huge barrels is regularly checked.

On each barrel is a board on which the precise date it was filled must be noted.

The annual test glass is offered to the gods of Olympus as a symbolic gesture.

WITH MUSIC...

The word "music" comes from Greek, and originally applied not only to music in the narrow sense but also meant all the musical arts, and therefore included dance, which is one of the oldest forms of human expression. Young men dance in Homer's *Odyssey*; Sirens sing, or at any rate emit sounds; Pan plays his pipes and Athena, briefly, the double flute; Apollo plucks the lyre – no wonder songs and dances with traditional connections still have a firm foothold in Greek daily life. Even in the cities it is not unusual to see young people dancing step sequences, parts of which may be hundreds of years old, and Greek children still learn some of their country's best-known folk dances at school.

When people talk about Greek music today, they usually mean songs written in the 19th century, which have a historical or political significance. Many of them were protest or resistance songs, with which people could identify.

The most important Greek musical genre of the last century is the *rembétiko*, which originated in the poor quarters of Athens at the time when the first Greek refugees from Asia Minor, who had lost everything they owned, settled there around 1923. With no money, no jobs, and pushed to the margins of society, they met in the evenings in the simplest restaurants to give musical expression to their melancholy. Today people compare the *rembétiko* to the American blues, which arose in similar circumstances. This kind of music, which has become socially acceptable since the 1950s, has hardly changed, although the conditions in which it is performed have. What was once the lament of the homeless has now become entertainment for relaxing evenings, when there is not only singing and dancing but also a great deal of eating and drinking.

Tambouri, the classical drum, is beaten hard and makes a muffled sound.

Modeled on the ancient *lyra*, this three-stringed instrument is played like a violin.

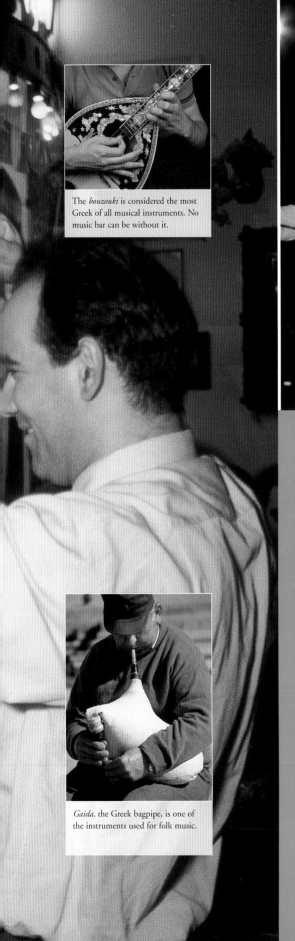

The *bouzouki* is considered the most Greek of all musical instruments. No music bar can be without it.

Gaida, the Greek bagpipe, is one of the instruments used for folk music.

...AND DANCE

Among round dances of rural origin, two basic groups can be distinguished according to their tempo and type of steps. *Sirtós* are slow round dances with sliding, shuffling steps. *Pidiktós* are faster; the dancers hop, skip, stamp, and jump. Round dances are always danced in a counter-clockwise direction.

Among the five best-known of the 150 Greek dances are two centuries-old peasant dances, *kalamatianós* and *tsámikos,* and three dances, *seibékikos, khasápikos* and *tsiftetéli,* belonging to 20th-century urban popular culture.

Kalamatianós: this dance, which comes from Kalamata in the Peloponnese, is danced by a number of people holding hands in a line. The leader dances variations on the basic long-short-short step.

Tsámikos: this dance from Epirus is also known as the "handkerchief" dance, because the leader and the second dancer hold opposite corners of a handkerchief. This round dance in three-four time is danced mainly by men. At the time of the war of independence, it was thought of as the dance of the mountain fighters. At the climax of the *tsámikos,* the leader executes complicated, truly acrobatic leaps.

Seibékikos: this was originally a dance for men, but is now also danced by women. This improvisatory dance is led by one person, or by two people who circle round one another. In the world-famous film *Zorba the Greek,* Anthony Quinn danced something resembling a *seibékikos.* This dance is considered difficult, because it has no set sequences of movements. It relies entirely on the dancer's individual interpretation.

Khasápikos: in this "butcher's dance," men and women hold each other by the shoulders with outstretched arms. The basic pattern of the step sequence is three side-steps to the right, three to the left and two cross-steps forwards. The movements of the *khasápikos* are slow and dignified. The origin of this dance is uncertain, but people have tried to find a connection with the Byzantine *makellárikos* (*makellaris* as in butcher). The *sirtáki* is actually a simplified version of the *khasápikos* and was specially created to the music of Míkis Theodorakis for Anthony Quinn in the role of Zorba. Nobody could have foreseen at the time that this compromise solution would become the most famous of Greek dances. Where the *khasápikos* is tense and concentrated, the *sirtáki* is relaxed, but lively, and speeds up toward the end.

Tsiftetéli: this dance of Turkish origin, with its circling, markedly sensual movements, used to be the all-female equivalent of the *khasápikos.* It is another dance that is no longer danced separately by the two sexes.

APPETIZER CULTURE

For a Greek restaurant, its appetizers, or starters, *mezédes*, are a kind of visiting card. Through its *mezés*, the restaurant demonstrates just what its kitchen can do. After all, the whole range of foodstuffs – meat, fish, vegetables, and dairy products – is available for use in Greek appetizers. They range from the simple and refined to the brilliantly creative, and quite often reflect the main courses. They can be eaten hot or cold and may be just the introduction or the main course itself – whatever the customer chooses.

In the cities especially, around midday the great army of office workers is drawn in little groups to the countless small restaurants that have opened up in recent years, hidden among the rows of houses, and that have now become sought-after addresses. In the *mezedopolio*, a shop selling nothing but *mezés* as far as the eye can see, there will certainly be something to suit every taste. Ouzo, the Greek anise-flavored schnapps, is a constant accompaniment to all *mezédes*. Drunk with ice, water, or straight, its task is to reinforce the appetizing sensation aroused by the *mezédes*. "Appetite making" is, after all, the meaning of the word *mezés*, which comes from Turkish. Appetizers certainly do that, but if you are not careful, they manage to do something else as well; they make you feel much too full much too quickly, just because you are longing to try a bit of everything. You can always tell experienced connoisseurs of *mezédes* by the restrained way their forks pick up, say, a piece of squid, then a potato, perhaps an olive next or maybe a small meatball. In between people chat, break off a piece of bread, sip their glass of ouzo, have a drink of water, and generally take their time. Where people dine in groups, all selecting uninhibitedly from the dishes, something of the original rural Greece has obviously survived, as in the past whole villages would demonstrate and renew their social solidarity through similar forms of communal eating.

The different regions of Greece reveal the characteristics of their cuisine not least in the selection and preparation of the typical local *mezédes*. So the *mezés* must definitely be seen as a kind of ambassador. For example, in the areas which were once strongly Ottoman, oriental influences predominate, while a western fragrance permeates those parts of the country which were formerly under Venetian sovereignty. On the Greek islands, the selection of *mezédes* is still determined by what is produced on each island, and on the mainland, appetizers have a stronger taste than in the south of Greece. The whole variety of Greek *mezédes* can be seen gathered together in the big cities, where the host's origins and the preferences of his regular customers are the deciding factors. And they are available from morning till night, because Greek appetizer culture is a round-the-clock affair. *Mezédes* will be available at any time of day, even if you arrive at 11 p.m.

TZATZÍKI
Yogurt with cucumber and garlic

1 small, firm salad cucumber, peeled and
coarsely grated
2 cups/500 g yogurt
3 cloves garlic, crushed
2 tbsp chopped mint
2 tbsp Greek extra virgin olive oil
1 tbsp white wine vinegar
Salt
Chopped mint for garnishing

Salt the grated cucumber, allow to stand in water for a few minutes, then gently press out the water. Mix the yogurt and the grated cucumber in a bowl. Crush the garlic and add to the mixture. Mix in the mint, olive oil and white wine vinegar and add salt to taste. Refrigerate for at least 30 minutes, or until it is time to eat. Before serving, sprinkle with a little chopped mint. *Tzatzíki* is usually just served with bread as an appetizer, but it also goes well with any roast or grilled food.

MELITZANOSALÁTA
Eggplant purée

2 lb/1 kg eggplant
3 cloves garlic, crushed
4 tbsp/60 ml Greek extra virgin olive oil
Wine vinegar to taste
1 bunch flat-leaved parsley, finely chopped
½ pimento, finely diced
1 small tomato, quartered
Salt

Preheat the oven to 350 °F (180 °C). Wash the eggplants, dry well, and place on a rack in the oven. Bake until the skin is slightly burnt and the inside is quite soft, turning frequently. Remove the eggplants from the oven, rinse with cold water and peel immediately. Cut the eggplant into small pieces, place in a bowl, and stir in the crushed garlic. Add salt and stir in the olive oil, a drop at a time. Add wine vinegar to taste and the parsley, stirring continuously. If the purée is not yet fine enough, work over it again briefly with a masher. Add salt to taste. Arrange the purée on a plate and decorate with the diced pimento and tomato quarters. Eggplant purée is usually served with other appetizers – and with freshly baked white bread and a glass of ouzo! Tip: Lemon juice can be used instead of wine vinegar.

The full glory of the colorful array of Greek appetizers is set out on a series of small tables, so the individual dishes can easily be reached from all sides.

EATING HABITS

As far as meals are concerned, the Greek day does not actually begin until midday, as instead of the "classic" leisurely breakfast of boiled eggs, there are little cookies and pastries – sweet or savory according to taste – to be eaten with coffee on the run, so to speak. By contrast, when it gets to midday, the big warm or cold buffet opens up, offering countless possibilities: fresh salads; boiled, pickled, or puréed vegetables; grilled meat or baked fish. In spite of all this variety, the individual portions remain pleasantly modest in size. Usually it is a question of *étima fagitá*, food which has been cooked earlier in the morning and has therefore more or less cooled down, as distinct from *tis óras*, freshly prepared dishes. The main meal of the day is not eaten until late at night, as people do not go out until 10 or 11 p.m. This then completes the cycle, and the almost nonexistent breakfast does make sense; after all, the time that has elapsed between it and the last meal of the day is relatively short.

No matter whether the plates contain pasta or salad, bread is an indispensable part of every meal, and you can always order more. It is still customary to eat fruit and vegetables in, not out, of season, which is one of the great merits of Greek cuisine. Another is that packaged ready-made meals and frozen foods are relatively new phenomena, and confined almost exclusively to the cities, where working women are happy to take advantage of them.

Eating is more than just the intake of food, it is also consciously used as a way of fostering social contacts. This is particularly obvious when you look at the fruits in syrup and the sweet pastries that the Greeks like to eat, preferably in company and with great relish, in the afternoon with mocha and a glass of wine. Devout Greeks have very strict customs about what they do not eat, as well as what they do. Following the teachings of the Orthodox Church, they give up certain foods, in various combinations, for different lengths of time over the course of the year.

SELECTION OF MEZÉDES

Soupiá mayireftí: boiled squid is considered a delicacy throughout the whole of Greece. Prepared squid is boiled slowly until tender, and served hot in a thick tomato sauce.

Fasólia piaz: medium-sized, not too soft-boiled navy beans, fresh scallions and parsley are covered in a dressing of olive oil, vinegar or lemon, salt and pepper, and served cold.

Koliós: salted mackerel fillets, which have bones you scarcely notice, are fried well in plenty of olive oil, served hot, and not complete without a glass of ouzo.

Kopanistí: very finely chopped peas, carrots, potatoes, and pickled cucumbers, stirred into a spreadable blue cheese made from ewe's milk, are prepared beforehand to allow everything to blend well.

Gávros foúrnou: unlike grilled sardines, anchovies cooked in the enclosed heat of the oven develop more of a special flavor, not overlaid by the taste of charring.

Revíthia: chickpeas (garbanzo beans) in tomato sauce, cooked with herbs, are mostly served as a hot appetizer. As a variation, you can also have boiled chickpeas served cold and prepared like a salad.

Khtapódi: finely chopped octopus tentacles, stewed with olive oil and tomatoes for a long time over a low heat until really tender, are a perfect combination with noodles.

Soupiá spanáki: diced, stewed squid with leaf spinach makes an interesting hot appetizer, which can be enhanced by the addition of sheep's cheese.

Tsirossaláta: dried, salted herrings are made into a smooth purée and mixed with plenty of olive oil and fresh herbs. You can go easy on the spices.

Antzoúyes: a whole plateful of small, grilled sardines in salt and vinegar, which can be eaten whole, heads and fins included. This appetizer is also served hot.

Lakérda polítiki: thin slices of marinated tuna are served in plenty of good quality olive oil, and with lemon, which can be drizzled over the fish according to taste.

Gávros tiganitós: grilled anchovies must be well browned and should be served as hot as possible. They can be used as an alternative to salted sardines.

Garídes saganáki: shrimp are braised in an ovenproof dish with olive oil, puréed tomatoes, herbs, and roasted garlic, and served very hot.

Loukániko khoriátiko: homemade Greek sausages are considered a specialty all over the country. They have a hot, spicy taste and are served with potato wedges (or with scrambled eggs).

Souvláki khirinó: diced pork is first tossed in a mixture of salt, pepper, and oregano, before being put on skewers and very well roasted.

Fáva: lentil puree can be coarse or smooth in texture. The dash of vinegar for flavoring is important. Combining it with fresh, slightly sweet onions can be recommended.

Tzatzíki: this salad of grated cucumber with plenty of pressed garlic in a yogurt sauce must be left to draw for several hours to develop its unmistakable flavor.

Flórinis: long red peppers are grilled for a few minutes, so they can be skinned, then steeped in olive oil and vinegar and seasoned with salt, pepper and garlic.

MADE TO ORDER

This is a purely urban phenomenon, which goes on almost unnoticed in the streets. In the heart of the busy commercial districts you can nearly always see people standing at the counters of little stalls, choosing the various ingredients for their sandwiches. Rolls are cut in half and filled with meat or sausage, eggplant purée or *tzatzíki*, eggs, tomatoes, cucumber or even *patátes*, fried potatoes, then quickly toasted, wrapped in thin paper or a napkin, and held in the hand to be eaten while still warm. The one thing you can be sure of with these Greek snacks is that the ingredients used are absolutely fresh. Athenians enjoy this kind of sandwich at any hour of the day or night, whenever they are hungry enough, even if it happens to be immediately before lunch or dinner. Greece had its own fast-food culture long before the familiar international competition made its appearance. And it is much more easily digestible than the imported fashion for meals that are quickly made, quickly packed, and too quickly consumed.

Above: looking at food makes you hungry. With this in mind, modest restaurants display various kinds of food in glass cabinets.

Top right: whether they sit down with a small plate of food or take a sandwich in their hands – the lunch break is short and the customers constantly changing.

Bottom right: *kantines*, snack stalls, are a welcome sight everywhere, and in the city you will always find some that are open.

Döner kebabs cooked on an upright spit have now become a firmly established tourist favourite. Kebabs have had no trouble keeping their place on the fast food menu.

If it's well prepared, it's quick: first a piece of paper, on which goes the pita bread…

…a portion of kebabs, lots of onion rings and sliced tomatoes, then…

…a little *tzatzíki* on top, fold it over, and that's it!

SWEET TEMPTATION

Getting to know the world of Greek cakes and candies is an adventure in itself. Innumerable patisseries, *zakharoplastía,* offer an abundance of creamy temptations and heavenly fruit delights, which the eye alone cannot do justice to. However, a little taster confirms what you already suspected. All Greek cakes are victims of a hopeless passion for sugar. They are sweet in the most sugary sense of the word, and are never served without a glass of water. Athens can offer something to suit every taste, from traditional Greek cakes served in old-fashioned coffee houses with character to Belgian and French pastries in bright, air-conditioned surroundings.

In the old days, people simply went to the dairy on the corner when they fancied something sweet, because you could buy not only fresh milk and cocoa there but also rice pudding, blancmange, *galaktoboúreko, kadéfi* and much, much more. Since it became illegal for these "milkmen" to sell milk ladled straight from the churn, they have gone over to making sweet milk products in the widest sense including the traditional Greek rice pudding.

RIZÓGALO
Rice pudding

1 cup/200 g round grain rice
4 cups/1 liter milk
1 scant cup/200 g sugar
2 tbsp potato flour
2 egg yolks
Seeds of 1 vanilla bean
1 tbsp ground cinnamon

In a saucepan, bring 1⅗ cups/400 ml water to a boil, add the rice and stir in the milk. When the rice begins to soften, add the sugar. Mix the

potato flour with a little water and stir into the rice. Whisk the egg yolks with the vanilla seeds, and stir into the rice. Continue stirring, and as soon as the rice mixture starts to become creamy, remove from the heat. Spoon onto plates, keep in a cool place, and sprinkle with cinnamon before serving.

PÁSTA SOKOLATÍNA
Chocolate torte

For the dough:
3 cups/350 g all-purpose flour
1 tsp baking powder
1½ cups/350 g sugar
1 scant cup/200 g margarine
2¼ cups/250 g cocoa
1½ tsp baking soda
3 tbsp/50 ml milk
6 eggs
¼ tsp almond extract
Seeds of 1 vanilla bean

For the filling:
3 egg yolks
3 tbsp brandy
3 tbsp butter
2 tbsp milk
8 oz/200 g chocolate cake glaze, melted
3 generous cups/350 g confectioner's sugar
2 cups/500 ml heavy cream, whipped until firm

For decoration:
Grated chocolate and chocolate leaves

Preheat the oven to 345 °F (175 °C). Mix all the dough ingredients. Put the mixture into a greased and floured cake pan about 12 inches/30 cm in diameter. Bake for about 1 hour. Meanwhile melt the chocolate glaze in a bain-marie or according to maker's instructions. Mix the egg yolks, brandy, butter, and milk, and add to the chocolate. Sift over the confectioner's sugar and work the ingredients into a smooth paste. Remove from the bain-marie and allow to cool. Remove the cake from the oven, place on a wire rack to cool, then cut horizontally into three rounds of equal thickness. Place one on a serving plate and spread on half the chocolate cream. Put on the second round and cover with the whipped cream. Put on the third round, and spread the rest of the chocolate cream on top and down the sides. Sprinkle with grated chocolate and decorate with the leaves. Keep cool until serving.

CANDY COLORS

Next to eating chocolate, the Greeks' greatest passion is sucking candies. They love them in all sizes and flavors, but when it comes down to it, the more colorful the better. And if the wrappings also shimmer in every color of the rainbow, the contents must be simply delicious. On hot summer days, they suck candies for refreshment, especially those with a lemon or orange flavor. Only a few years ago you could still buy a single candy from the corner kiosk for one dekáta – less than one cent – and children would stand in front of the displays, unable to make up their minds. Perhaps the desire for candies is a survival of the old oriental forms of hospitality, when it was considered polite to offer sweetmeats, and also to eat them. And once the addiction has you in its grasp…

IN THE PLÁKA

There are two essential items that must be on the agenda for any stay in Athens: a visit to the Acropolis and a stroll through the Pláka. Depending on what kind of entertainment you are looking for, the latter can be undertaken in the daytime or in the evening and at night.

Laid out like a semicircular terrace around the Acropolis, the old town is actually the only part of Athens that existed in the centuries of relative unimportance between the great city of the ancient past and the present-day capital of modern Greece. Fortunately it was saved in the nick of time from the modern craze for demolishing and rebuilding. It would have been a pity to lose a prime example of completely unrestrained contact between the multifarious building styles that have accompanied and succeeded one another over the centuries. If you stroll through the narrow streets in the daytime, you will continually

come across signs of how past generations reused building materials that were already a part of history. However, your attention will very likely be captured by the street theater, as the Pláka is now the entertainment district and evening meeting-place for young and old, foreigners and locals alike. Most of those who make their way to the Pláka in the evening have food in mind, even including those who may not succumb right away, after just a short walk, to the enticing scents of grilled meat and fish wafting through the streets and alleyways. For most of the year you can sit and eat outside here and keep an eye on the hustle and bustle in the street over the rim of your glass. After the meal, you can filter back into the stream and let yourself be carried along, perhaps into a cocktail bar, the next ice cream parlor, or wherever the fancy takes you. For those who work in the Pláka, the evening streets really are paved with gold, and anyone still on their feet at four in the morning might well believe that the Pláka never sleeps.

Top: the street traders selling *salepi*, a pale hot drink made with an extract of orchids, are part of a long-standing tradition. In 17th-century Istanbul street traders were already extolling the virtues of a similar drink, which was said to strengthen, stimulate, and improve the sight. Its modern descendant is drunk out of plastic cups and has a sweet, creamy taste.

Left, and below: the Pláka – to the hungry it seems like one huge street café, but on a closer look it becomes clear that the bars and restaurants are divided according to the type of food and drink served, giving you the chance to weigh up the competition. Many of the old buildings could not be preserved without the income from the trade in the Pláka.

PAGOTÓ ME FROÚTA
Vanilla ice cream with fresh fruits

2 eggs, separated
4 tbsp superfine sugar
1 tsp vanilla extract
1 scant cup/200 ml whipping cream
½ lb/250 g fresh fruits in season, at least 4 different kinds, peeled and sliced
1 generous cup/250 ml sweet white wine
8 tbsp honey
Chopped walnuts
Ground cinnamon

Whisk the egg yolks with 1 teaspoon sugar and the vanilla extract until the sugar has dissolved. Whisk the egg whites with 2 tablespoons sugar until stiff. Fold into the beaten egg yolks. Whip the cream with the remaining sugar until peaks form, adding more sugar to taste. Combine with the egg mixture. Pour into a plastic container and allow to set in the freezer. Place the fruit in a bowl, pour over the wine and allow to steep for 30 minutes. Divide the ice cream into 4 dessert dishes, put some of the marinated fruit into each one, and glaze each portion with 2 tablespoons of honey. Sprinkle with walnuts and cinnamon and serve immediately.

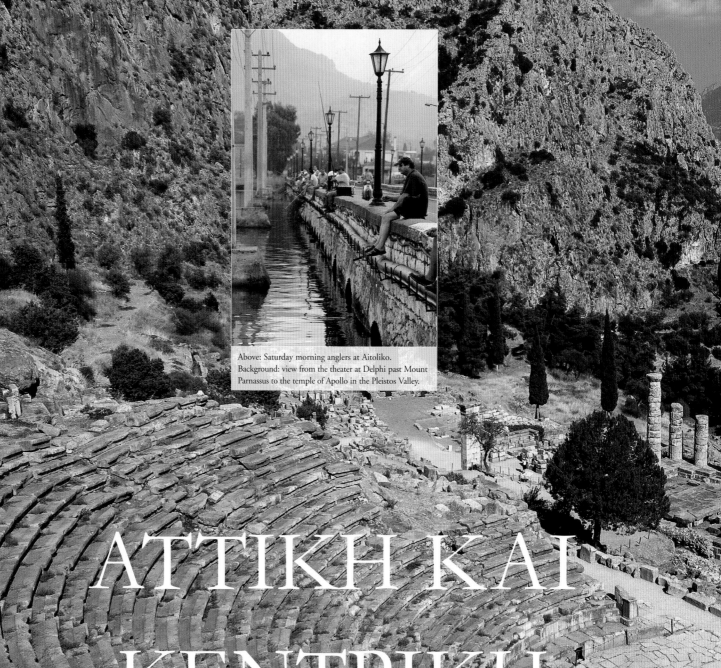

Above: Saturday morning anglers at Aitoliko.
Background: view from the theater at Delphi past Mount
Parnassus to the temple of Apollo in the Pleistos Valley.

ΑΤΤΙΚΗ ΚΑΙ
ΚΕΝΤΡΙΚΗ
ΕΛΛΑΔΑ

ATTICA AND CENTRAL GREECE

Pistachios

Kadéfi

Galaktoboúreko

Khilopítes

Attic wine

Retsina

Savories

The salt in the soup

Sea urchins

Shellfish

Eels and more

Tsípouro

When they hear the name "Attica," connoisseurs of Greece and lovers of wine will immediately think of the classic wine area. After all, retsina, the famous resin-flavored Greek wine, comes from here and has conquered the whole of the (tourist) world. But Attica has another face. Together with Athens, the region is now the most densely populated area of Greece. This last tip of mainland Greece, stretching southeastward into the sea, has developed into an important industrial area. One of the biggest airports in southeast Europe is being built here, as an intersection point for flights to and from destinations in Asia and the Arab States.

Central Greece lies to the west of Attica, extending along the Gulfs of Corinth and Pátrai, and bordered by the Amvrakian Gulf, Epirus, and Thessaly to the north. Here the frontier of modern Greece follows its old historic line. The regions of Aitolia, Akarnania, Boeotia, Lokris, and Phokis managed to retain their autonomy until the 4th century B.C. In 370 B.C., the Lokrians, Phokrians, and Aitolians joined the Boeotian League; Euboeia and Akarnania followed.

Central Greece is not an area of outstanding economic or political importance. Tobacco is grown in the west, cotton in the east, plus the ever-present olive groves. By way of compensation, the region was one of the first to encounter the dubious pleasure of man's overwhelming urge to travel. Back in ancient times, the temple of Apollo at Delphi at the foot of Mount Parnassus, with its famous oracle, was already one of the most visited places in the Greek world, and in the centuries that followed, it attracted archaeologists as well as crowds of foreign travelers. By contrast, the hilly, sometimes wild and rugged landscape of central Greece offered a welcome refuge to bandits, freedom fighters, and adventurers, while throughout history the towns along the coast became important centers for the Romans, Spanish, Venetians, and Turks. In Boeotia there are the healing springs of Thermopylae, which have been famous since ancient times. In 1571, one of the biggest sea battles fought against the Turks by an alliance of Venetians, Spanish, Genoese, and the Knights of Malta took place off Náfpaktos, known to the Venetians as Lepanto. Missolonghi, now the country's salt mining area, was a military headquarter around 1820 during the Greek war of independence. Lord Byron, who had joined in the fight for freedom from the Turks, died at this location in 1824.

In the harbors of Attica – such as Piraeus – big barges and proud seafarers are still a common sight.

PISTACHIOS

The island of Aegina may be small, but it has two claims to fame: the Temple of Aphaia, one of the best preserved Doric buildings in the whole of Greece, and *fistíki aegínis*, the pistachio. Some 150 years ago hardly anyone on the island knew of this plant, but there has been a radical change as *Pistacia vera* now covers almost a quarter of the 32-square-mile (84-square-kilometer) island.

The deciduous trees with their dense crowns grow up to 30 feet (10 meters) high and can live for a hundred years. The male and female flowers grow on separate trees, so care must be taken to plant the correct proportion of male to female trees. This is usually one to seven, planted 25 feet (7 meters) apart. From about the fifth year, the female plants start the biennial rhythm of producing clusters of 30–50 inconspicuous white flower buds, which open in February the following year. After successful pollination by the wind, they ripen into about 1¼-inch (3 centimeters) long, narrow stone fruits comprising a thin fleshy exterior that gradually dries and the stony seeds inside. (Like walnuts or almonds, in botanical terms, pistachios are not nuts as the fruit flesh does not completely lignify like that of the hazelnut). About one month before they are fully ripe, the seeds should begin to split, starting at the tip, so that the "nuts" inside can be seen. This stage is called the "laughing" fruit.

Immediately after the harvest in August/September, the fruit is first dried in the sun, then stirred continuously in water, so the dried fruit

As with the olive harvest, the ripe pistachios are first knocked down from the branches.

They fall on to tarpaulins spread out on the ground where they are easily collected.

After harvesting, the fruits are spread out in the sun for 24 hours so the flesh completely dries out.

Separating in water: the flesh and unopened fruits float; the salable goods collect at the bottom.

Of the 50 or so fruits in a cluster, 20 may have formed empty seeds or ones that fail to open, and these must be sorted out after harvesting.

Many women on Aegina make and sell the regional specialty, pistachio *glikó*.

To make it, unripe candied fruits and ripe pistachios are tightly packed in a jar.

In time, the honey used to fill each jar acquires a delicate pistachio flavor.

The mingled tastes of unripe fruits and sun-roasted nuts are deliciously sweet.

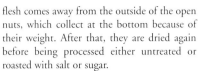

flesh comes away from the outside of the open nuts, which collect at the bottom because of their weight. After that, they are dried again before being processed either untreated or roasted with salt or sugar.

Greece produces 4960 US tons (4500 tonnes) of pistachios, about 1.5 percent of the world harvest, almost two thirds of which is produced by Iran. Of course biennial fruiting means that only half the trees yield up to 66 pounds (30 kilos) of pistachios each per year, but even so, the farmers of Aegina in their organized cooperatives have no reason to be unhappy about their laughing fruit.

Roasted, salted "laughing" pistachios. Quality produce should contain few unopened nuts.

On Aegina and throughout Attica, pistachio bread is seen everywhere.

Sweet or strong-flavored pistachio products are welcome gifts.

KADÉFI

Extra-thin spaghetti? Finely spun wool? A special filler for restoring upholstery? Just looking at it may not be enough to sweep away the last doubts. Many people must have had to pick up the thin white wooly threads in their hand, before they could believe that they came out of a baking dish. And anyone who is still not convinced that you can use them in baking can only be persuaded by trying it for themselves. At any rate, it is worth the small amount of effort. Thankfully the days are past when women had to make *kadéfi* dough by hand, using their own skill and effort. Instead of rolling thinner and thinner strings of dough for hours between the palms of your hands, in many Greek and Turkish delicatessens you can now buy foil-wrapped, ready-made *kadéfi* dough, which owes its hair-like texture to the untiring power of modern machinery. In bigger towns you can actually still (or once again) find specialist *kadéfi* shops or obliging bakeries, where you can buy the dough freshly made. When handling the fragile, fine spun dough, as with ready-made phyllo pastry, you must take care not to let it dry out, as otherwise it loses its essential malleability. To avoid this, place the dough between two dry cloths, which you then additionally cover with a damp (but well wrung out) cloth. This means the dough remains protected, even while you are working, and unpracticed *kadéfi* rollers, who have to manage without having acquired the dexterity of the seasoned expert, can easily allow themselves a little more time.

Like *revaní* and *baklavás*, cooked *kadéfi* is saturated with syrup, softening the crisply baked surface. And as if *kadéfi* were not already pure sweetness, in Greece they love to top it off with a scoop of soft vanilla ice cream.

KADÉFI
Syrup and nut rolls
Makes about 30–35

4 cups/400 g chopped walnuts
2 tsp ground cinnamon
½ tsp ground cloves
Butter (or oil)
2 lbs/1 kg kadéfi dough (available from Greek or Turkish delicatessens)

For the syrup:
4 lbs/2 kg sugar
Juice of ½ lemon

Mix the chopped walnuts and spices in a bowl. Grease a deep rectangular baking pan (about 12 × 14 inches/30 × 35 centimeters) with butter. Preheat the oven to 350 °F (180 °C). Spread out the *kadéfi* dough, carefully disentangle, and divide into thick strips about 8 inches (20 centimeters) long. Place some walnut filling on one end of a strip and roll up carefully, starting at this end. As you do this, guide the strings of dough at the edges of the strip with your fingers so they do not "fray." Place the roll with the "seam" downward in the bottom of the baking pan. Do the same with the rest of the dough and place the rolls close together in the pan so they support each other. Melt some butter in a pan and moisten each roll with about 1 tablespoonful. Bake the *kadéfi* in the preheated oven for about 40 minutes until the top is golden brown. Remove from the oven and leave to cool. Heat about 4 cups (1 liter) of water in a pan and dissolve the sugar in it. Add the lemon juice and boil briefly, stirring continuously, then remove the syrup from the heat, pour evenly over the *kadéfi* and set aside for 12 hours.

Tip: the lemon juice in the syrup prevents sugar crystals from forming. Allow the *kadéfi* to cool thoroughly before saturating them with syrup, otherwise the dough will become too soft.

ION CHOCOLATE

There is only one name for chocolate in Greece: ION. The company was founded in 1930 in the south of the country under the name "Violet." Soon afterward they put their first almond chocolate on the market, wrapped in the characteristic red paper adorned with a white violet. At that time there was only one kind with chopped almonds. Today the range includes one with whole almonds, as well as many other flavors. Although the Greek "Pavlidis" chocolate had already been in existence since 1841, no other before or since "ION ALMOND" has been able to capture so many children's hearts so completely. It cannot have anything to do with the production process – there is very little difference between that of "ION ALMOND" and any other European chocolate. Roast and grind cocoa beans, mix with sugar, milk, and cocoa butter, heat, and slowly mix in all the other ingredients, which create the magic of chocolate.

But throughout the years, the special thing about it has always been the taste of fresh Greek almonds. A 4 oz (100 g) bar means 30 squares of chocolate heaven. At the small shops on every street you can also have tailor-made 2½, 1½, or 1 oz (70, 45, or 30 g) bars and, at granny's house there will still be a little china dish of ION chocolate candies… At the beginning of the 1980s, when Greek supermarkets began filling their shelves with a colorful array of foreign chocolate products, many a child stood hesitating before the enticing surfeit. Greek chocolate is virtually unknown abroad, where ignorance about it is only exceeded by ignorance about Greek wine. But in Greece itself, the profits from "ION ALMOND" break all records, despite the competition.

Sugar, melted butter or oil, walnut filling, and ready-made *kadéfi* dough are all you need.

Spread out a handful of strings as evenly and parallel as possible and place the filling on one end.

Smooth the edges with your fingers as you roll them up, and direct the all too mobile strings toward the middle.

A portion of *kadéfi* with soft ice cream. And it all started so easily.

Arrange the *kadéfi* roll in the tin so that the "seam" is underneath.

In the tightly packed tin, each roll has a tablespoonful of melted butter poured over it.

The golden brown *kadéfi* must cool completely before being saturated with syrup.

First line the baking pan with floured baking parchment, then with individual sheets of phyllo pastry.

The base must overlap the sides of the pan all round. Brush the pastry with butter before putting in the cream.

Cover with the remaining pastry, fold the edges of the base over it, and brush it all with butter.

Cut in pieces with a thin, sharp knife, without using too much pressure.

Pour the prepared vanilla syrup over the baked cake, allowing it to be absorbed as much as possible.

GALAKTO-BOÚREKO

When Greeks visit friends on the mainland or the islands, they do not often take flowers as a present. Instead, they take one of those mysterious cardboard boxes, whose contents never remain secret for long. The bottom of the box soon gives way to a sweet stickiness, especially if it is filled with syrup cakes. Among the choicest of syrup cakes is *galaktoboúreko*, a delicious confection of puff pastry, filled with a custard made of milk, semolina, sugar, and eggs, known to every child in Greece. As with all puff pastry cakes, *galaktoboúreko* can either be served while still warm or chilled, with coffee or a refreshing drink as the high point of a summer afternoon – whether you interrupt a stroll around town to buy one in a cake shop, seek out one of the traditional dairies on a nearby corner, or just go into your own kitchen. *Galaktoboúreko* is a marvelous sweet for in between meals, but it is so rich, it is not really to be recommended as a dessert.

GALAKTOBOÚREKO
Milk cake

1⅔ cups/400 ml milk
10 oz/300 g phyllo pastry (from supermarkets or Greek or Turkish delicatessens)
1 cup/200 g melted butter
3 eggs
2 egg yolks
A scant ½ cup/100 g sugar
A generous ½ cup/75 g (wheat) semolina
Seeds of one vanilla bean

For the syrup:
1⅓ cups/300 g sugar
1 scant cup/200 ml water
1 tbsp lemon juice
½ tsp vanilla extract

Preheat the oven to 375 °F (190 °C). Bring the milk to a boil and allow to cool. Line a baking pan about 8 × 12 inches (20 × 30 centimeters) with baking parchment and dust with flour. Arrange half the pastry in the tin, allowing plenty of overlap all round. Brush this base generously with melted butter.

In a pan, beat the eggs, egg yolks, and sugar to a foam, and gradually add the semolina, vanilla seeds, and the milk. Heat the mixture just enough for it to begin to go creamy, while stirring continuously. Remove from the heat immediately, and mix in ½ cup (100 g) butter. Pour the filling into the prepared pan, cover with the remaining sheets of pastry, fold the overlap from the base down onto it, and brush this lid with butter as before. With a sharp knife (if possible without pressing), cut into portions and place the tin in the preheated oven. After 15 minutes, reduce the temperature to 320 ºF (160 ºC) and bake for a further 30 minutes, until the cake begins to turn a golden brown color.

Meantime, boil up the syrup of sugar, water, lemon juice and vanilla extract, stirring continuously. Drizzle over the milk cake while this is still warm.

Tip: phyllo pastry dries out very quickly, so while you are working, lay the sheets you are not using between two kitchen towels, and cover with a third towel that has been previously moistened and well wrung out.

The finished cake must not be covered, otherwise the flaky pastry will not remain crisp!

Only dedicated calorie-counters will be able to resist a piece of *galaktoboúreko*.

KHILOPÍTES

Khilopítes, distinctive homemade noodles, are one of the specialties of Greek cuisine. They are broad, short, and thin, sometimes a little uneven, and no two are alike. They are particularly appreciated in the west of the country, which is also the home of puff pastry, but in reality they are eaten in all those parts of Greece where people make their living mainly from agriculture and grow sufficient cereal crops. It may be confusing that, though the ingredients and methods remain the same or at least similar, the names may vary from region to region. For instance, homemade noodles in Macedonia and Thrace are called *petoúra*, which also means "crumbs."

Greek *khilopítes* are not difficult to make; only handling the thin rolling pin perhaps needs a little practice. It is important that the noodles be allowed to dry for several days in a warm, dry, airy place, as this is what makes it possible to keep them for several months.

Khilopítes feel moister on the tongue than ordinary noodles, as they are cooked in only a little water, so that, if possible, you do not have to strain them. They can be used in many ways: as a side dish, or simply sprinkled with a little grated sheep's cheese and enjoyed as a really hearty meal.

Form the flour into a dough trough, make a well with your hand, and break the eggs into it.

Pour in the milk with the presoaked semolina. The liquid must not leak out of the well in the flour.

Using both hands, knead all the ingredients into a malleable dough, working from the edges to the middle.

Above: the dough is rolled out in portions.
Below: cutting the noodles is judged by eye.

Above: religion in everyday life – many Greek women cross themselves when making noodles, baking bread, or before meals.

KHILOPÍTES

Greek noodles
Makes about 4 lbs (2 kg) noodles.

1 generous cup/250 ml milk
1 generous cup/200 g fine wheat semolina
2 tbsp salt
8 eggs
13 cups/1½ kg wheat flour

Mix the milk with the semolina and salt, cover, and leave for 1 hour. Pour the flour into a dough trough, make a well with your hand, and break the eggs into it. Pour in the semolina milk and work all the ingredients into a malleable dough (adding water if necessary). Cover, and leave for 1 hour.

Divide the dough into smaller pieces and roll one out very thin, using a thin rolling pin. Leave to dry for a few minutes, then cut evenly into thin strips with a knife, and cut these into pieces. Do the same with the remainder of the dough. Alternatively: roll the dried dough out on the rolling pin, cut through to the wood along the pin, and peel off the dough. Cut the resulting pile of strips into *khilopítes* about ½ inch (1 centimeter) wide. Lay the noodles out on a cotton cloth and leave to dry for 4–5 days in a warm, dry, airy place. Tie the cotton cloth round them and hang the bundle in the cellar or in the pantry.

KHILOPÍTES ME MELITZÁNES

Noodles with eggplants

2 lbs/1 kg eggplants
½ cup/125 ml Greek extra virgin olive oil
2 cloves garlic, finely chopped
1 lb/500 g tomatoes, peeled and puréed
1 lb/500 g khilopítes
3 tbsp butter
½ lb/250 g kefalotíri cheese, grated
Salt
Freshly ground black pepper

Peel the eggplants, wash, and slice thinly lengthways. Sprinkle with salt, leave to draw for 1 hour, and gently squeeze out the slices. Heat some olive oil in a pan and sauté the garlic. Add the tomatoes, season with salt and pepper, and cook gently over medium heat for 10 minutes. Add the eggplant, reduce the heat, and simmer for 40 minutes. Cook the *khilopítes* in not too much boiling water (so that you do not have to strain them, if possible) and toss in butter. Serve with the sauce and the grated kefalotíri cheese.

Above: the dried *khilopítes* can either be hung up in the pantry in a knotted cloth, as in grandmother's day, or sealed in jars.

Below: nowadays you no longer have to be able to make *khilopítes* yourself, even if homemade is definitely best – you go to the delicatessen.

ATTIC WINE

One of the grapes most frequently grown in Attica, indeed in the whole of Greece, is the excellent white wine grape Savatiano, which can produce wines that are moderately alcoholic, but distinctly robust and full of character. It is perfectly adapted to the hot climate and very dry soils of Attica. Savatiano is not only extensively made into the resin-flavored retsina. Kantza, Château Matsa, and the white Cava Cambas also owe a lot to it.

Savatiano is the favorite, but not the only variety of grape growing in Attic soil. The estate of Château Matsa is experimenting with Assyrtiko and Athiri, which originally had their home in the stony Cycladean soil of Santorini. The Malagousia grape, an aromatic variety with a scent of lemon, which first reached northern Greece in 1960, is also being tried out here. The Rhoditis grape from the Ionian islands is being grown by the estate of La Reine Tour. George Pachys set up his wine business in 1908 on an estate previously belonging to Queen Amalia. In 1919 it was taken over by Lavria Serpieri, who has exported her highly respected wine to France, Egypt, and even the United States. Today, under the management of the Serpieri grandson, the estate may have shrunk to one third of its original size but, among others, it produces Pyrgos Vassilissis, which is considered to be one of Attica's best red wines.

In addition, there are a number of other estates, which have recently succeeded in acquiring a good reputation by means of good vintages and sundry international prizes: the Hatzimichalis, Fragou, Vassiliou, Strofila, Semeli, and Megapanos wine companies. By harvesting early and using modern winemaking methods, they have recently succeeded in making good dry *vins ordinaires* with surprisingly fresh orange and peach bouquets.

HATZIMICHALIS

Close to Mount Parnassus, Dimitris Hatzimichalis has planted traditional Greek and French grape varieties. This man has cellars that house the best wines in central Greece and has now risen to become one of the most famous winegrowers in Greece. The first Hatzimichalis Cabernet came onto the market in 1982 and was a great success.

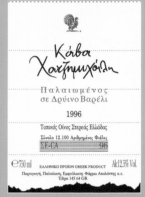

Ktima Hatzimichalis: Hatzimichalis Sauvignon Blanc is a dry, fruity, aromatic white wine, which is popular served with fish, at about 46–50 ºF (8–10 ºC). It should not be kept for too long.

Erythros Hatzimichalis: This strong red wine is made from Cabernet Sauvignon, Syrah, Carignan, and Grenache. It tastes slightly fruity and is an ideal accompaniment to meat, sausages, and cheese.

Cava Hatzimichalis: The dry Cabernet Sauvignon from this estate has a wonderful deep red color. It has a scent of red berries, a spicy, velvety taste, and is best served with game dishes and with cheese.

There are treasures stored in the cellars (background) of the Hatzimichalis estate.

SEMELI

Anne and Georges Kokoros run this small family business in Attica, founded in 1977, and set about extending into producing international style wines. The jewel among their wines is Château Semeli.

Château Semeli: for this dry red, grown on 25 acres (10 hectares) of land, 90% Cabernet Sauvignon is mixed with 10% Merlot. After two years maturing in new French oak barrels, it finally matures for a further year in the bottle. It tastes its full-bodied best at around 65 °F (18 °C) and is drunk with meat, game, and cheese.

Semeli Nemea: this 12% vol. red wine is made from a single variety, the high quality, aromatic Agiorgitiko grape from Nemea, which is grown on a Semeli estate on the Peloponnese. It is ruby red and bears traces of vanilla scents. Preferably, it is served with meat in light sauces and with soft cheeses.

Semeli: this simple red table wine is made from 75% Agiorgitiko from the Nemea region (appellation contrôlée) in the eastern Peloponnese and 25% Cabernet Sauvignon. Its strong bouquet develops best served at 65 °F (18 °C). It also stores well. Of course the Semeli estate also grows the local Savatiano grape. The clean white wine that is made from it reaches an alcohol content of 11.5% vol.

FRAGOU

Assiminia Fragou literally had to rescue her historic 18th-century vineyard from ruin and, in the process, she developed a successful concept combining local winemaking tradition with innovative marketing.

Savatiano Fragou: Savatiano from the Fragou vineyard is a light Attic white wine with a very fresh, flowery taste. It is one of the best-loved vins ordinaires of the region and is recommended for serving with fish and seafood dishes at a temperature of 50 °F (10 °C). This wine is Assiminia Fragou's great pride. The success of wines from the Fragou vineyards, especially on American buying trips, is also due to the expertise of head oenologist Yannis Allageorgiou.

Cava Fragou: the red Cava is made from 100% Cabernet Sauvignon. It matures for one year in oak barrels, and a second in the bottle. Served at a temperature of 65–68 °F (18–20 °C), it develops an aroma of dark berries. Cava Fragou is only available in a very limited number of bottles.

Chardonnay Fragou: this fresh Chardonnay from the Fragou vineyard develops a delicate aroma with a hint of fruit. At the recommended serving temperature of 50 °F (10 °C), it makes a harmonious accompaniment to lobster, salmon, and white meat.

VASSILIOU

The centerpiece of this business, which has been in the Vassiliou family since 1905, is 3700 acres (1500 hectares) of the finest grape-growing land, planted with 35-year-old Savatiano grape vines.

Erythros Vassiliou: from 60% Agiorgitiko and 40% Cabernet Sauvignon, the firm of Vassiliou produces a fragrant vin ordinaire, which goes well with red meat and game birds. A serving temperature of 65 °F (18 °C) is recommended for this wine, which can age for up to five years. Since the 1980s one of the declared aims of the company has been to help Greek wine to gain more respect abroad through organized wine tours.

Fumé Vassiliou: This three-year-old white wine is made entirely from Savatiano grapes and matured in oak barrels, which are later used for red wine production. It has delicate scents of vanilla, chestnut, and butter. This is an interesting wine that goes surprisingly well with some of the specialties of Epirus, such as eels, trout, or Metsovo cheese.

Ampelonas Vassiliou: this dry vin ordinaire is made from 85% Savatiano and 15% Moscofilero grapes. At a temperature of 50 °F (10 °C), it goes well with fresh salmon and seafood. This very fruity wine is not recommended for long storage. Only a limited quantity of this wine comes onto the market each year.

RETSINA

The Greeks, and at first the Romans too, stored wine in earthenware vessels, as they did almost all foodstuffs. However, the material was porous, so when amphorae were intended to hold liquids, they were sealed with pitch or the resin of the Aleppo pine *Pinus halepensis*. It was probably by this roundabout route that residue from this resin first found its way into the wine, and the first resinated wine into the cup. This accident, if it was an accident, not only meant the wine would keep longer, but also gave it that unmistakable spicy taste, which has acquired greater importance as the number of enthusiasts has increased. So, for example, Pliny the Elder recommends in his *Historia Naturalis* that for preference the resin of pines from mountainous regions should be mixed with the fermenting must, because it had a more pleasant taste. When the Roman wine producers changed over to lighter, more easily transportable wooden barrels, which no longer needed to be sealed, resinating wine went out of fashion, at least in the western part of the Roman Empire. By contrast, in the area of Byzantine influence the preference for resinated wines remained undiminished. Where East and West met, the travel literature often contains evidence of a clear lack of understanding. For instance, the Irish archaeologist and artist Edward Dodwell, who traveled through Greece between 1801 and 1806, crowned his disparaging remarks on the poor food in the house of the Bishop of Salona by observing that the wine was unspeakable and had so much resin mixed in with it that it almost stripped the skin from their lips.

Until about 1960, retsina was drunk only in Greece. It was not exported until modern tourism developed, when tourists wanted to enjoy the drink they had gotten to know on vacation at home as well, and almost overnight it was vying with ouzo for its position as *the* Greek national drink. The European Union eventually assigned this wine to the "traditional description" category, meaning that commercial production of retsina is only permitted in Greece. Best retsina, which is nowadays stored in barrels of cypress wood, is mostly made from Attic Savatiano, or more rarely from Rhoditis and occasionally from Assyrtiko grapes. The production method for retsina is as simple as possible: Small pieces of the resin of the Aleppo pine (Greek: *retsíni*) are added to the must of the otherwise traditionally made wine up to a maximum of 2 pounds per 25 gallons (1 kilo per hectoliter), and left in the wine during the fermentation process until it is drawn from the barrel.

Ritinitis: retsina from the firm of Gea in Attica has a mild, dry taste.

Thivi: a stronger retsina comes from the Thívon Wine Company.

Kekhrimbari: retsina that is made from Macedonian grapes and sold as a table wine.

Retsina Olympias: a dry white wine is also made into retsina on the island of Crete.

A viscous fluid, which is insoluble in water, oozes from a wound in the bark of the Aleppo pine…

…and solidifies in the air. It is said that more than 3300 US tons (3000 tonnes) per year are added to the wine.

Above: retsina's intensity also depends on how much resin is added to the wine and for how long – a decision made by the oenologist.
Background: in summer, the heavy scent of the Aleppo pines hangs over the land.

This produces a drink that certainly goes well with dishes containing a lot of olive oil, small fried sardines, or food that is strongly garlic flavored, but which can still split wine lovers into two camps. The market leader among retsina producers is Kourtakis. Rightly or wrongly, his bottles with their yellow labels have now become the epitome of good resinated wine all over the world. Efforts have been made in recent years to improve the image of retsina abroad. The wines are being produced in smaller quantities, contain less alcohol, and the resin content is reduced to 4 ounces per 25 gallons (100 grams per hectoliter).

PSÁRIA XIDÁTA
Fish cooked in vinegar

2 lbs/1 kg gopes (bogue) or small sardines, cleaned and prepared
1 generous cup/250 ml Greek extra virgin olive oil
1 lb/500 g onions, cut in rings
1 generous cup/250 ml vinegar
Peppercorns
Whole allspice berries
1 bay leaf
Salt

Rub the fish inside and outside with salt. Heat some olive oil in a pan and sauté the onions in it. Add the vinegar and spices and bring to a boil. Turn off the heat and allow the liquid to cool before adding the fish. Let the fish draw the liquid for about 30 minutes, then transfer to a glass jar and store in a cool place (will keep for a few days in the refrigerator). Serve cold, accompanied by a glass of retsina. Variation: Add a selection of smoked and pickled fish to make a fish platter.

SAVORIES

Savory crackers are just as popular in Greece as the sweet *koulourákia*, the cookies that are served with mocha. A good hostess will always have both at hand, and offer them as required in two different dishes, separated according to taste. Savory crackers are nibbled any time, at every opportunity. In the country, you will find them on the table with the appetizers or as an alternative to bread. It is almost impossible to distinguish the savory crackers from the sweet cookies on outward appearance alone, as the commonly sold shapes and sizes are very similar. You can also have trouble when buying them, especially if the baker displays sweet and savory right next to each other. If you want to arrive home with the right plaits, rings, or cookies, you should ask the experts in the shop. That way you will be sure that your choice of cookies and crackers is what you wanted, and you can safely leave the shop carrying one or more high piles of neatly packed little cartons. As soon as you get home and transfer the contents to glass or earthenware containers, the savory crackers and sweet cookies reveal that they have something else in common – not only do they look alike; neither of them will be around very long.

ALMIRÉS BOUKÍTSES
Savory crackers

½ cup/125 ml Greek extra virgin olive oil
½ cup/125 g butter, at room temperature
2 tsp sugar
2 tsp salt
½ cup/125 ml milk
2 tsp baking powder
1¾ cups/125 g kefalotíri cheese, grated
2 lbs/1 kg all-purpose flour
1 egg yolk
1 cup/100 g whole filberts

Beat together the olive oil, butter, sugar, and salt using an electric hand mixer. Pour the milk into a bowl with the baking powder and, one at a time, stir in the cheese, flour, and the oil and butter mixture until a smooth dough is formed. Knead thoroughly and leave in a cool place for 1 hour. Divide up the dough, form into thin rolls and weave three at a time into little plaits. Preheat the oven to 400 °F (200 °C). Cover a baking sheet with baking parchment and arrange the plaits on it. Mix the egg yolk with a little water, brush the plaits with it, and decorate each with a filbert. Bake the plaits in the preheated oven for about 15–20 minutes until brown.

BISKOTÁKIA ME FÉTA
Feta cheese crackers
(Illustration top right)

4½ cups/500 g all-purpose flour
1 tbsp baking powder
¼ tsp salt
1 tbsp sugar
4 tbsp/60 ml milk
½ lb/250 g féta, crumbled
6 tbsp/80 g butter
1 egg yolk

Sift the flour and baking powder into a bowl and mix in the salt and sugar. Pour in the milk, add the crumbled *féta* and the butter, and work into a smooth dough. Wrap the dough in foil and leave in a cool place for 1 hour. On a floured work surface, roll out the dough to a thickness of about ¼ inch/5 mm. Using a small glass or cookie cutter, cut small rounds out of the dough.
Preheat the oven to 400 °F (200 °C). Cover a baking sheet with baking parchment and arrange the crackers on it. Mix the egg yolk with a little water and brush the crackers with it. Bake in the preheated oven for about 15 minutes until brown.

LORD BYRON

When George Gordon Noel, 6th Baron Byron (1788–1824), the great English poet of the Romantic period, best known as Lord Byron, left Italy for Greece on August 2 or 3 1823, it was not the first time he had set off for the land of the ancient gods. Between 1809 and 1811, he had already visited Greece during a two-year tour of the Mediterranean and the Orient and described this as the happiest time of his life. Now the Greek Committee of London, a philhellenic association formed to support the Greeks' struggle for independence from the Turks, had entrusted him with the task of accompanying a consignment of weapons, munitions, medicines, and money to Greece.
In his verse epic *Childe Harold's Pilgrimage* (1812), Byron had created an idealistic picture of Greece and the Greeks, which had fired the enthusiasm of Europe's liberal and revolutionary intellectuals for the Greek war of independence – especially since many of their liberal ideals could not be realized in Europe, because the period of restoration had begun. They were all the more ready to idolize an image of Greece that had been molded by their classical humanistic education, even if it bore little resemblance to reality. Greece was no longer a land of gods and heroes. Byron wrote that he felt surrounded by thieves and robbers, the freedom fighters were quarreling among themselves and in complete disagreement over their strategy, there was no

unified leadership, and each man wanted to claim the biggest share of the consignment of aid for himself. Byron was in doubt as to which one he should support. He financed small individual actions and groups of mercenaries, until he finally broke through into Missolonghi, which was under siege by the Turks. He died there of malaria on April 19, 1824, without ever having taken part in the fighting.

KOULOURÁKIA ALMIRÁ
Savory twists
(Illustration bottom right)

6½ cups/750 g all-purpose flour
1 tbsp baking powder
1 tsp salt
2 tsp sugar
½ cup/125 g butter, at room temperature
⅓ cup/80 ml Greek extra virgin olive oil
½ cup/125 g yogurt

Mix together the flour, baking powder, salt, and sugar. Using an electric hand mixer (lowest speed), beat the butter, olive oil and yogurt in a bowl, and slowly stir in the flour mixture until it forms a workable but firm dough (adding a little flour or water if necessary). Cover the bowl, and let stand in a cool place for 2 hours. Divide the dough into small portions, make into thin rolls and form two at a time into small twists. Preheat the oven to 375° F (190 °C).
Cover a baking sheet with parchment paper and arrange the twists on it. Bake the twists in the preheated oven for about 15–20 minutes until they are a golden brown color.

AVGOTÁRAKHO

The mullet (*Mugil cephalus*), which is farmed in the salt pans of Missolonghi, reaches a weight of up to 18 oz (500 g) and prefers lagoons or brackish water close to the shore. It is to this fish that Greek cuisine owes a product that is one of the least well known outside Greece: *avgotárakho*, the oriental caviar. Made from the roe of the mullet, this delicious appetizer has been considered a delicacy in Greece since Byzantine days. The salted, compressed roe is coated with wax, and can be kept for several months.

The way *avgotárakho* is obtained is even more spectacular than its preparation. Between August and December, when more and more female mullet are about to spawn, things start to get interesting. Experienced fishermen can remove the entire roe from a fish with one quick, accurate stroke of their knives, without piercing the membrane surrounding the egg sack. The roes that have been removed are washed in seawater and laid in Missolonghi salt until dry, i.e. most of the water has been drawn off. The roes are paired, pressed in round wooden molds, and stored in a well-ventilated place until the *avgotárakho* has acquired its distinctive honey color. After being coated with beeswax, the finished product can be cut and served with a slice of lemon and a little parsley as an exclusive appetizer with champagne. Though there are no preservatives in *avgotárakho*, it still contains 28% water and an impressive 35.8% fat. In Missolonghi, up to 4 US tons (3.5 tonnes) of *avgotárakho* are produced each year, commanding top prices on world markets. In the catalog of Petrossian Stores in New York, where Greek *avgotárakho* is given a prominent position as a luxury delicacy, 8 oz (200 g) will cost you close to $100.

THE SALT IN
THE SOUP

In ancient times, salt was already indispensable for seasoning. At first it was evidently less often used just to flavor food, but more as a way of preserving fish and meat – there are countless sources containing references praising salted tuna fish. Salt was also important in the production of a strong, spicy fish sauce (*igáros*, Roman *igarum*), which formed part of many dishes in which you would not expect to find it today. Various kinds of fish and fish waste were mixed with salt and fermented in the sun in large earthenware pots for three or four months, while being constantly stirred. After being strained, flavored with herbs, and transferred to more manageable clay jars, *igáros* would keep for a relatively long time. You have to imagine a product something like the Asian fish sauce.

It is unnecessary to stress the importance of salt in modern Greek cooking. But salt production is inextricably linked to one of the unforgettable names in Greek history, which will never lose its importance for Greek national feeling. The modern day salt center of the country lies very close to the town of Missolonghi, which is situated on the Gulf of Patras in the southwest of central Greece and was a center of Greek resistance at the beginning of the 19th century. The major Greek salt companies are located here. As in the other salt producing regions of the world, salt is produced by channeling seawater into big, shallow evaporating pans, in which the first pollutants can settle to the bottom, and the salt content of the water can be increased by repeatedly letting in new seawater. These pans feed the salt gardens, where the water finally evaporates in the sun until the crystallized salt remains. About one third of the world demand for salt is produced from the sea in Greece and France. Unlike rock salt, sea salt contains very small amounts of additional minerals such as bromine or iodine. The latter regulates the metabolism and the functioning of the thyroid gland, so sea salt can prevent iodine deficiency and the symptoms connected with it. High quality sea salt is sold unrefined, unbleached, and without anti-caking agents. It is pale gray and lumpy.

The salt pans of Missolonghi are also home to a huge variety of birds. Avocets, great white herons, and stilts are as much at home here as calandra, crested, and short-toed larks. There are plenty of fish here for them.

Above: good sea salt should not be bleached and should feel slightly moist. The biggest salt suppliers get their salt from central Greece.
Background: the white surface of the salt lake lies just outside the gates of Missolonghi.

BAKALIÁROS ME SKORDALIÁ
Deep-fried stockfish with garlic cream sauce

1 lb/500 g stockfish
1 scant cup/100 g all-purpose flour
1⅔ cups/415 ml Greek extra virgin olive oil
1 egg white, beaten stiff
1½ lb/750 g stale white bread, with the crust
*   removed, soaked in water, and squeezed out*
4 cloves garlic
3 lemons
Salt and freshly ground black pepper

Soak the stockfish for 24 hours, changing the water several times. Remove the skin and bones from the stockfish and cut into strips 2 inches (5 centimeters) wide. Mix the flour with salt, pepper, 1 tbsp olive oil, and ⅔ cup/150 ml warm water, then cover the batter and set aside for 1 hour. Carefully fold in the beaten egg white. Heat ¾ cup/200 ml olive oil in a deep pan, dip the pieces of fish in the batter, fry for 5–7 minutes until crisp, and drain off the fat on paper towels. Arrange on a serving dish, garnish with slices of lemon, and serve with *skordaliá*.
For the *skordaliá*: purée the white bread with the garlic in a blender, slowly adding ¾ cup/200 ml olive oil and the juice of 1 lemon. Add salt to taste.

When fish are dried as stockfish, the heads, tails, and entrails are removed.

Sea urchins can protect themselves effectively by using their spines. One touch can have painful consequences even for humans, especially if the spines break off in your skin.

SEA URCHINS

"A Spartan was invited to a banquet and during the meal he was offered sea urchins. He took one, but he did not know how to deal with it and did not notice how the other guests were managing. He put its hard shell to his mouth and tried to bite it open with his teeth. As he was making no progress and did not want to admit that the hard shell was resisting him, he shouted: 'Horrible food! I will not give up and let you go, but I will not take any more of your kind!'" From this anecdote, told by Athenaeus of Naucratis at the end of the second century A.D. in his *Deipnosophistae* ("The Banquet of the Learned" or "The Gastronomers"), we can at least learn to avoid making over-hasty promises. Sea urchins are among the secret delicacies that are well worth making the effort to deal with, even though they have one of the lowest proportions of edible parts in relation to their body size. The only eatable parts of these hermaphrodites are the ovaries or gonads, which are attached to the wall of the shell and glow orange red in the face of anyone who has breached the creature's natural defense mechanism and penetrated to the inside. You can watch Greek children on the coast as they, successfully if somewhat in-

elegantly, manage this task with a stone. Anyone not practiced at this is recommended to use a napkin and a strong pair of scissors. You hold the sea urchin in your hand with the concave side (belly side) up and cut a hole, not too small, in its armor around the mouth opening. With a bit of luck, you will have found a female with roe, which is considered particularly delicious.

On the coast of Greece, you mostly encounter stony (or purple) sea urchins (*Paracentrotus lividus*), which are found all over the Mediterranean region and in the warmer parts of the European Atlantic. Their shells can grow to a diameter of up to 3 inches (8 centimeters) and they are considered the tastiest. They inhabit (obligingly, in the opinion of those who catch them) the shore and coastline by the thousands, so real clean-up operations are carried out before the start of the tourist season. Although these sea urchins, which occur in shallow water up to a depth of 30 inches (80 centimeters), are comparatively useful creatures because they graze on the algae, "swimming with sea urchins" is rather a mixed pleasure. Bathers who do not aspire to be gourmets could well do without it, as too close an acquaintance with echinoderms is one of the less pleasant experiences of a seaside vacation. They would certainly be surprised to learn that in his *Historia Naturalis*, Pliny the Elder actually emphasized the medicinal properties of sea urchins as a remedy for eczema. From his observations that some kinds camouflage themselves with shellfish and stones, he concluded that they were trying to increase their weight in order to have a better grip when a storm was approaching and considered sea urchins to be an early warning system.

However, if you learned how to deal with them as a child, sea urchins do not stand much chance.

The fresh, raw ovaries or gonads of these echinoderms are a much-prized delicacy.

AKHINÓS YEMISTÓS
Stuffed sea urchin
(Illustration opposite)

12 sea urchins
⅔ cup/150 ml Greek extra virgin olive oil
1 onion, finely chopped
2 tomatoes, peeled and diced small
½ bunch flat-leaved parsley, finely chopped
1 cup/200 g rice
Salt and freshly ground black pepper

With a pair of scissors, cut the spines as short as possible and make a circular cut in the underside to remove the mouth parts and entrails.
With a spoon, remove the red ovaries or gonads

(also called tongues) and set aside. Strain the juice into a bowl and set aside. Clean the sea urchin shells thoroughly inside and out, then put the gonads back into the shells. Heat half the olive oil and sauté the onions in it. Add the tomatoes and parsley, season with salt and pepper, and boil briefly. Mix in the rice, bring to a boil, and remove from the heat. Divide the filling into the shells, so that they are only about two thirds full, as the rice will swell. Arrange the filled shells in a shallow pan, so that they cover the base. Mix the juice from the sea urchins with the remaining olive oil and carefully pour it from the edge into the pan. Add water until the liquid is about ⅜ inch (1 centimeter) above the tops of the shells. Bring to a boil, reduce the temperature, cover, and simmer for about 1 hour. Add boiling water if necessary. Arrange on plates and serve while still hot.

BEER

If the Greek gods on Olympus had any reason to envy their Germanic colleagues, it would certainly have been their early successes in the art of brewing beer, as beer was unknown in ancient Greece. So it is not surprising that the first brewery on Greek soil was set up by the Bavarian Johannes Fuchs during the reign of Otto of Bavaria (1832/35–1862) as king of Greece. The beer produced there was named "Fix." Although Henninger and Heineken later captured the Greek beer market, Fix beer managed to hold its own until 1987. Nowadays, beer is a respected drink to find on the Greek table and has its enthusiasts, particularly as an accompaniment for roast meat or fried potatoes. Because Greece is trying to get a little closer to Europe, Greek beers with exotic brand names are pushing their way onto the European market, just as many international brands are great favorites in Greece, especially German beers such as Löwenbräu. The latest Greek beer has been brewed since 1989, by the northern Greek Boutari Group, which actually makes wine. It is called Myrthos, and has now captured the entire Greek beer market. The Atlanti Brewery in the south of the country markets Löwenbräu alongside Myrthos. Among the 20 brands of Greek beer now in existence, Athenian, Marathon, Sparta, and Vergina are the firm favorites.

SHELLFISH

There is a large selection of bivalves to be found in Greek fish markets, so it is all the more surprising that only mussels have succeeded in becoming generally accepted in the tavernas along the coast. Prices have something to do with it, as the offshore mussel beds in many places on the coast keep prices low. You have to dig deeper into your pocket for other species, however, because they are imported. In spite of this, in recent years many restaurants have widened the selection of shellfish on their menus and offer imaginative dishes. Despite the cost, a taste is well worthwhile; after all, shellfish were on the menu in Greece as long ago as the 3rd century B.C. and probably a lot earlier. It is possible to distinguish at least ten different genera and various species. It was generally thought that shellfish were difficult to digest, not very nutritious, and had a laxative and diuretic effect, yet raw oysters were much appreciated. Shellfish were often discussed in dietary and pharmaceutical texts, such as the works of the doctor Xenocrates from around the turn of the 3rd to 2nd century B.C. He wrote that scallops and venus shells were opened, drained, and flavored with brine, vinegar, or fresh mint, and with sweet wine. And what sounds like an appetizer was probably just a medicine.

Above: many shellfish can be found in extravagant quantities in Greece, and they are equally common on the menu in private homes.

Below: hidden in a bay, the town of Galaxidi is a favorite weekend destination for Athenians. And where there are good restaurants, seafood is not far away.

MÍDIA SAGANÁKI
Mussels au gratin
(Illustration opposite)

2 lbs/1 kg mussels
½ cup + 2 tbsp/150 g butter
1 lb/500 g tomatoes, peeled and diced
1 cup/150 g sheep's cheese, crumbled
1 tbsp vinegar
½ tsp sugar
Salt and freshly ground black pepper

Thoroughly scrub the unopened mussels under running water. Put in a pan, add a little water, and boil briefly, until the mussels open. Discard any unopened mussels. Strain the stock, remove the mussels from their shells, wash well again, and drain. Preheat the oven to 350 °F (180 °C). Melt the butter in a pan and sauté the diced tomatoes. Season with salt and pepper, add the mussel stock and boil down to thicken. Add the vinegar and sugar, and as soon as the sauce thickens, remove from the heat. Pour the tomato sauce into a buttered ovenproof dish, stir in the mussels, and cook for 15 minutes in the preheated oven. Sprinkle over the cheese and grill for a further 10–15 minutes. Serve in the ovenproof dish, with freshly baked white bread. Can be served as an appetizer or as a main course.

Not as aristocratic as the common oyster, but still sought-after: the elongated Portuguese oyster.

Mussels are the main ingredient in the Greeks' favorite shellfish dish: *Mídia saganáki.*

The striped venus clam is very common in the Mediterranean. For preference it is eaten grilled.

Warty venus clams are often eaten raw, or prepared in the same way as mussels.

The brown or hard clam is the biggest and tastiest of all the venus clams.

EELS AND MORE

While conger eels (*Conger conger*) live mainly in coastal waters, common eels (*Anguilla anguilla*) in Europe live in almost all coastal and inland waters. All American and European eels have their spawning grounds in the Sargasso Sea, in the Atlantic. There the females lay 10 to 20 million eggs at a depth of 20,000 feet (6000 meters) and then die. The larvae of the North American eels reach the North American shelf in the same year, while those of European eels take two and a half years to reach the European continental shelf. There they make the transformation from the white, willow leaf shaped larvae to the still transparent "glass eels." Only when they reach brackish or fresh water do they develop dark pigment and scales. These nocturnally active edible eels grow at varying rates. They feed on small fish and crayfish and spend the cold season buried in sand or mud. Their firm, dark skin and glistening silver belly form gradually. Their slimy skin and concealed gill openings enable eels to survive quite a long time out of water, so that during the night they can cross over wet grass from one stretch of water to another. Nowadays, fresh water stocks increasingly have to be replenished by putting in young eels.

To prepare eels for cooking: First rub the eel with salt to remove the slime. Leave for a while to take effect, then rinse the salt off under running water. To clean the fish, cut the eel open along its stomach from the vent toward the head and for 2 inches (5 centimeters) toward the tail. Pull the entrails out toward the head and detach close to the gills. Remove all internal organs and viscera. Now remove the skin, and cut off the fins in the opposite direction to which they lie. (The traditional way of removing the skin is to nail the head of the eel to a board so that both hands can get a better grip.)

KHÉLI ME SÁLTSA DOMÁTA
Eel in tomato sauce
(Illustration right)

1 eel, weighing about 2½ lbs/1.2 kg, already prepared
Juice of 1 lemon
1 tbsp capers
1 scant cup/200 ml Greek extra virgin olive oil
1 onion, finely chopped
1 clove garlic, crushed
3 large tomatoes, peeled and puréed
½ bunch flat-leaved parsley, finely chopped
1 bunch chervil, finely chopped
1 tsp dried oregano
1 scant cup/200 ml dry white wine
2 oz/50 g butter
Fresh dill to garnish
Salt
Freshly ground black pepper

Cut the prepared eel (see left) into big pieces. Make a marinade from lemon juice, capers, and salt and marinate the pieces of eel in it for 30 minutes. Heat the olive oil in a pan and sauté the onion and garlic. Drain the pieces of eel, add to the pan, and brown well. Add the puréed tomato and herbs, and pour in the wine. Reduce the temperature and leave the eel to steep for 15 minutes. Now arrange the fish in a serving dish, stir the butter into the sauce, bring briefly to a boil and pour over the eel. Garnish with the dill, and serve with freshly baked white bread.

KHÉLI ME SÁLTSA APÓ VATÓMOURA
Eel in blackberry sauce
(Illustration below)

4 carrots
2 small zucchini
4 small white turnips
8–10 blackberries, washed
⅔ cup/150 ml red wine
1 eel, weighing about 2 lbs/1 kg, ready for cooking
⅔ cup/150 ml dry white wine
½ tsp dried oregano
2 tbsp honey
1 tbsp vinegar
1 tbsp butter
1 tsp cornstarch, mixed with a little water
Salt and freshly ground black pepper

Peel and cut the vegetables into pieces of similar size and shape (see illustration below), and set aside for later use in water to which a little

TÓNNOS ME REVÍTHIA
Tuna fish and chickpea salad
(Illustration below)

2 lbs/1 kg tuna fish, sliced
½ lb/250 g dried chickpeas or garbanzo beans
4 scallions, cut in thin rings
1 stick celery, thinly sliced
Juice and grated zest of 1 lemon
a scant ½ cup/100 ml Greek extra virgin olive oil
1 bunch flat-leaved parsley, finely chopped
½ bunch dill, finely chopped
2 cloves garlic, crushed
¼ tsp mustard powder
Dill and parsley for garnishing
Salt and freshly ground black pepper

Soak the chickpeas overnight. The next day, drain, rinse, and cover with water. Add a little salt and cook until soft. Wash the tuna fish, pat dry and rub with salt and pepper. Heat the olive oil in a pan and fry the slices of fish. Reduce the temperature, add water, and cook until tender. Remove from the heat and cut into small pieces. Mix together the chickpeas, tuna fish, scallions, and celery. Mix the lemon zest and juice, parsley, dill, garlic, mustard powder, salt, and pepper together in a bowl. Pour the sauce over the tuna and chickpea mixture, stir in carefully, and let stand in a cool place for a few hours. Garnish with parsley and dill, and serve with freshly baked white bread.

lemon juice has been added. Heat the blackberries and the red wine in a pan. Cut the prepared eel (see previous page) in pieces and poach in white wine with oregano, salt, and pepper. Remove the eel and keep warm, add the white wine to the blackberries, bring to a boil, then reduce the temperature. Stir in the honey and vinegar, and simmer the sauce for 10–15 minutes. Meanwhile, blanch the vegetables (starting with the carrots) and toss in salted butter shortly before serving. Pass the sauce through a strainer, thicken with the cornstarch mixed with a little water, and season with salt and pepper. Fillet the pieces of eel and arrange on warmed plates. Place a selection of vegetables next to the eel, and pour over a little blackberry sauce. Serve while still warm.

LAVRAKÍ PLAKÍ
Sea bass cooked in wine
(Illustration above)

2 lbs/1 kg sea bass fillets, skinned
1 onion, cut in rings
2 sticks celery, sliced
2 scallions, cut into rings
a scant ½ cup/100 ml Greek extra virgin olive oil
1 bunch flat-leaved parsley, finely chopped
2 tomatoes, sliced
2 cloves garlic, crushed
2 tsp dried oregano
3 tbsp lemon juice
2 unwaxed lemons, sliced
1 generous cup/250 ml dry white wine
1 scant cup/50 g fresh breadcrumbs
Flat-leaved parsley, finely chopped
Bay leaves and rosemary sprigs for garnishing
Salt
Freshly ground white pepper

Preheat the oven to 350 °F (180 °C). Heat the olive oil in a pan and sauté the onions. Add the celery, scallions, parsley, tomatoes, and garlic, season with salt and pepper, and simmer for 5 minutes over a medium heat.
Brush an ovenproof dish with a little oil, and arrange the fish fillets side by side. Season with salt and pepper, sprinkle with oregano, and pour over the lemon juice. Spread the mixed vegetables over the fish, and put the lemon slices on top. Pour over the wine and sprinkle over the breadcrumbs. Cook for about 45 minutes in the preheated oven. Arrange on plates, sprinkle with chopped parsley, and garnish with the bay leaves and rosemary sprigs.

In a big distillery or in a farmer's barn, the procedure is the same: fermented must…

…consisting of grape skins, seeds and stalks, and any residual grape juice…

…is poured into a copper boiler to be distilled. The top is tightly closed and…

…the must inside is then gently heated over a gas burner. The alcohol, which rises in the form of steam, is channeled through a pipe…

…into a container of cold water, where it quickly cools, condenses to a liquid, and…

…drips on to a cotton filter as distilled tsípouro. The whole distillation process is monitored by experienced distillers.

TSÍPOURO

While ouzo has been on its way to becoming a national drink and finding new fans all over the world, you have the impression that the Greeks themselves prefer to drink tsípouro. This is a strong marc brandy, up to 60% vol., distilled from the remains of the grapes after the must has been pressed, which may be flavored with aniseed. You can find a marc brandy without the aniseed flavor in Epirus and also in the south of Greece, and there are generally different local names for the schnapps that almost every winemaker produces himself. The characteristic appearance of both tsípouro with aniseed and ouzo is the milky clouding that occurs when you add water or ice. This causes the ethereal oils dissolved in the alcohol, which are not readily soluble in water, to crystallize. The strength of the clouding also depends on the amount of aniseed used. Both ouzo and tsípouro can be drunk after meals, but people prefer to serve them with strong-flavored appetizers, which they complement well. Apparently the only distinction between ouzo and tsípouro is that tsípouro has to be distilled from marc and may be flavored with aniseed; with ouzo it is the other way round.

ΠΕΛΟΠΟΝΗΣΣΟΣ

The defensive towers, also home to the defiant Maniot pirates, are an emblem of the Mani peninsula. The rugged west coast of Mani rarely looks so inviting.

THE PELOPONNESE

It is almost sheer coincidence that the Peloponnese region, the "Island of Pelops," now forms the southernmost part of the Greek mainland, attached by the Isthmus of Corinth, and is not the largest Greek island. Throughout the history of the earth, geological movements have repeatedly separated it from and linked it to the landmass to its northeast, just as they have also shaped the peninsula's topography, creating its diverse and scenic landscape of mountain ranges, plateaus, and coastal lowlands. These testify to the region's varied history. Whereas the conquest of the peninsula by the eponymous hero, Pelops, lies far back in the mythological mists of time, traces of the very advanced Bronze-Age culture of the Mycenae are easy to find and date. Centuries later, Sparta attained fearsome importance here, drawing its rival, Athens, into the Peloponnesian Wars. In Olympia, athletes competed in honor of Zeus, the Father of the Gods, as well as for their own glory, and the Hellenic "health resort" of Epidauros was famed beyond the region's boundaries as the center of the cult of Asclepius. After the Roman conquest, the Peloponnese joined forces with the area that is now central Greece to become the province of Achaea. It was administered by Corinth, which from the 13th century onward acted for the succession of rulers from the Frankish, Florentine, Byzantine, Venetian, and Ottoman occupying forces in many other parts of the peninsula. The bellicose Maniots in the south of the Peloponnese, those fearsome pirates whose reign of terror continued on the high seas of the Aegean right up to the 19th century, were the only people never to be conquered in these constant struggles for power. The peninsula again came to the fore during the modern Greek resistance, Nauplia being the first capital city of liberated Greece from 1829 to 1834. Since antiquity, the Peloponnese peninsula has been fought over not least for its fertile soils, and perhaps it is no coincidence that food repeatedly plays an important role in the myth of Pelops. Pelops' father, Tantalus, sinned against the gods, not only by stealing ambrosia and nectar from their table, but also by killing his son and trying to serve his flesh to them. But the gods were aware of Pelops' murder, restored him to life, and punished his father with the proverbial torments of Tantalus. For all eternity, he had to suffer the torment of seeing water and fruits within his reach, yet being unable to grasp hold of them. Such tantalizing fruits doubtless included grapes from Corinth, citrus fruits from Argolida, garlic from Arkadhía, olives from Lakonía, figs from Messinía, and melons from Ilía…

Greece is Europe's main fig producer. However, only kalamata figs are suitable for drying.

It goes without saying that a lot of the meat from a pig is made into sausages.
Top layer (from left to right): *loukániko prasáto* (pork and leek sausage), *loukániko soutsoúki* (blood sausage with *krithári* =barley), *loukániko kafteró* (spicy sausage).
Bottom layer: *loukániko khoriátoko* (country sausage).

PIGS RULE

There is no misplaced sentimentality about the Greeks' relationship with their suckling pigs. They usually view the stages of development of the "cute little piglet" in a rather down-to-earth way, seeing it for what it is: an animal that is easy to keep and can always be made into a worthy delicacy. Animal rights activists expecting to see pigs living in fields would find hardly any, but they would also not find great numbers living under the horrendous conditions of intensive pig production. Large pig-breeding concerns with several hundred animals are the exception in Greece, which is why pig meat can be in short supply if you are too far from the nearest abattoir. A medium-sized concern seldom slaughters more than 90 animals per week and these are either processed directly on the farm or at the nearest pork butchers. All the meat and sausage products also come highly recommended because the animals are fed corn, wheat, soybean, pasta, vitamins, and powdered milk.

Only a century ago in Greece, anyone who could call a sizable herd of pigs his own was still considered to be wealthy, prosperous, and a good catch. If we trace the high regard in which pork was held even further back, we might find ourselves in the 5th century B.C. at a banquet in Athens. Here we could listen to people discussing the advantages of *galathenoí* (suckling pig) over *délphakes* (full-grown young pigs) and discover that Sicilian pigs are absolutely the best, but that pigs in general are at their worst between spring and autumn. That should come as no surprise, because pork was highly valued in the Athens of ancient Greece. It was cured, prepared in various ways, even sacrificed – and people knew sufficient special terms to be able to converse about all aspects of pig rearing and processing for hours on end.

Below: many pig breeders plant large clover fields in a wide area around their farm, enabling them to retain control over the quality and type of food they feed to their animals.

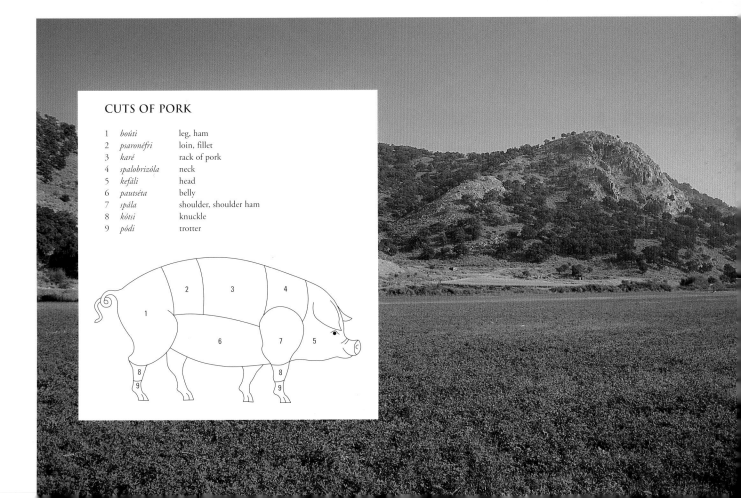

CUTS OF PORK

1	*boúti*	leg, ham
2	*psaronéfri*	loin, fillet
3	*karé*	rack of pork
4	*spalobrizóla*	neck
5	*kefáli*	head
6	*pautséta*	belly
7	*spála*	shoulder, shoulder ham
8	*kótsi*	knuckle
9	*pódi*	trotter

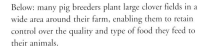

GOUROUNÓPOULO PSITÓ
Roast suckling pig
(Illustration left)
Serves 6

1 young suckling pig, oven-ready
Olive oil
Oregano
Lemon juice
Lemon wedges
Salt
Freshly ground black pepper

Preheat the oven to 350 °F (180 °C). Combine the oregano, salt, pepper, olive oil, and lemon juice, and rub well into the suckling pig. Place the pig over a roasting tin on a shelf in the oven. Roast for 2½–3½ hours, basting with the roasting juices every 20 minutes, and turning at least twice during the cooking time. Arrange on a platter, drizzle with lemon juice and garnish with lemon wedges. Serve with baked potatoes and salad.

VEGETARIANS BEWARE!

KEFTÉDES
Meatballs

2 tbsp butter
2 small onions, finely chopped
2 cloves of garlic, finely chopped
1 lb/500 g ground pork
1 stale bread roll, soaked and squeezed
1 egg
1 tsp sweet paprika
2 tsp salt
Freshly ground black pepper
Olive oil for frying
½ cup/125 ml dry red wine

Heat the butter in a skillet, add the onions and garlic, soften, then leave to cool. Put the ground pork in a bowl with the contents of the skillet, combine with the bread roll, egg, and paprika. Season with salt and pepper and knead well. Heat the oil in a skillet. Shape the mixture into walnut-sized balls and fry until crispy all over. Arrange the meatballs on a platter, then add the red wine to the frying juices and pour over the *keftédes*. Serve warm with a fresh green salad.

SOUTZOUKÁKIA
Ground meat rolls in tomato sauce

1 lb/500 g ground pork
1 stale bread roll, soaked and squeezed
2 cloves of garlic, finely chopped
½ tsp ground cumin
All-purpose flour for coating
Olive oil for frying

1 lb/500 g tomatoes, skinned and finely diced
Salt
Freshly ground black pepper

Put the ground pork in a bowl with the bread roll, garlic, cumin, salt and pepper and knead well. Form the mixture into small rolls, 1 inch/2 centimeters wide and 3 inches/8 centimeters long. Heat the oil in a skillet, toss the rolls in flour, and fry in the hot olive oil until crispy all over. Remove from the skillet, add the tomatoes and braise. Reduce the heat, season the tomatoes with salt and pepper, and simmer gently for 5 minutes. Add the *soutzoukákia* and leave for 5 minutes to heat through. Serve with salad and freshly baked white bread.

KHIRINÓ KRASÁTO
Pork in wine

1 scant cup/200 ml Greek extra virgin olive oil
2 lbs/1 kg diced pork
2 cups/500 ml dry white wine
1 bay leaf
Sprigs of fresh rosemary to garnish
Salt
Freshly ground black pepper

Heat the olive oil in a pan, add the meat, and brown all over. Pour in the wine, add the bay leaf, and season with salt and pepper. Pour in enough water to cover the meat, cover, and braise over moderate heat until the meat is tender. To serve, transfer the meat and its juice to a bowl and sprinkle with fresh rosemary. Baked potatoes or rice are a good accompaniment.

KHRINÉS BRIZÓLES SKHÁRAS
Grilled pork chops

4 pork chops
A scant ½ cup/100 ml Greek extra virgin olive oil
3 cloves of garlic, crushed
Juice of 2 lemons
Oregano
Salt
Freshly ground black pepper

Put the chops in a bowl. Combine the juice of 1 lemon with the olive oil, garlic, oregano, salt and pepper, and pour over the chops. Leave the meat to marinate in a refrigerator for several hours.
Place the chops on the barbecue and grill, turning frequently. Season with salt, pepper, and oregano, then pour over the remaining lemon juice. Serve hot with baked potatoes, rice, or salad.

Opposite: It is important that meat is cooked through before being eaten. As in many other regions of Greece, pink or bloody meat is not considered a delicacy in the Peloponnese.
Clockwise: *Khirinó krasáto* – pork in wine; *souvlákia* – meat kebabs, shown with *khirinés brizóles skháras* – grilled pork chops; *soutzoukákia* – ground meat rolls in tomato sauce; *keftédes* – meatballs.

SOUVLÁKIA
Meat kebabs

2 lbs/1 kg marbled pork
¼ cup/50 ml Greek extra virgin olive oil
Juice of 1 lemon
Oregano, lemons, and tomatoes to garnish
Salt
Freshly ground black pepper

Cut the meat into 1 inch/2.5 centimeter pieces and put in a bowl. Combine the olive oil, lemon juice, oregano, salt and pepper, pour over the meat, and mix until the meat is thoroughly coated. Leave the meat pieces to marinate in a refrigerator for several hours, then thread them onto wooden or metal skewers. Cook on the barbecue, turning frequently. Sprinkle the kebabs with oregano and serve with lemon and tomato wedges. Rice, baked potatoes, or fresh salad are good accompaniments.

POTATOES

Nowadays, potatoes are an essential part of Greek cuisine and are just as popular an appetizer as they are a main dish, whether fried, baked, or boiled. However, when this "new-fangled" food was first introduced about 150 years ago, it caused such controversy that Ioannes Antonios Capodistrias (1776–1831), the first government chef of the young Greek state, allegedly had to resort to a cunning ploy to get his extremely suspicious countrymen to accept this unknown food. Thus, instead of handing potatoes out freely, as he had intended, he ordered his soldiers to appear to guard them. This immediately aroused the curiosity of the farmers, who promptly stole them!

The best potatoes come from Arkadhía, where they are sold straight from the fields as early as March. But they can be found in every greengrocer's store throughout Greece, because despite heavy competition, Arcadian potatoes are still considered the best.

Anyone who considers American french fries to be the best way of preparing potatoes has probably not had the chance to try homemade Greek *patátes tiganités*. To make this dish, aromatic potatoes fresh from the soil are fried in top-quality olive oil. Despite the incredible amount of work involved, Greek mothers willingly prepare large quantities of them, as they are a firm favorite with their children.

PATÁTES LEMONÁTES
Lemon potatoes

*2 lbs/1 kg waxy potatoes, peeled and cut
into fingers
1 tbsp oregano
Greek extra virgin olive oil
Juice of 2 lemons
Salt*

Preheat the oven to 400 °F (200 °C). Arrange the potato fingers over the bottom of an oven-proof dish, season with salt and oregano, add the olive oil and lemon juice, then pour over sufficient water to just cover the potatoes. Bake in the preheated oven until the water has evaporated. To brown the top, drizzle with more olive oil. When brown, turn off the oven and leave the potatoes in the oven to stand for a few minutes longer.

Lemon potatoes are an ideal accompaniment to meat or fish.

In Greece, it is not so important to have a wide range of potato varieties on display in the market. As in almost all northern Mediterranean countries, the favorite variety is the "Spunta," which originated from Holland.

The market traders sell the oval, white-fleshed, waxy "Spunta" by size, depending on whether they are to be baked or roasted.

As well as potatoes from Arkadhía, products from the Achaea region or from Amaliáda in the Ilía region also find their way to the marketplaces. The first new potatoes in the middle of July are immediately snapped up.

Cut the peeled waxy potatoes lengthways into narrow fingers of roughly the same size so that they all cook at the same rate.

Arrange the potatoes as flat as possible and drizzle with olive oil. The oil is important for the roasting process, but the amount can vary according to taste.

Lemon juice not only adds a fresh flavor to the baked potatoes, but also hardens their surface, giving a much crispier texture.

Pour over sufficient water to just cover the potatoes. Left: golden-brown lemon potatoes are a versatile accompaniment.

CARNIVAL

The Greek word for Carnival is *apokriá*. This is derived from *apokreos*, which in turn means abstaining from meat, because Carnival is followed by a period of fasting. The Carnival period, or *Triodio*, begins three weeks before Shrove Monday. In these three weeks, you really must make the most of all the celebrations, because for the following 40 days of fasting leading up to Easter, going by the Julian calendar, the Orthodox Church allows no festivities. The first and second Sundays are Meat Sundays (*Kreofágou*), and the third Sunday is Cheese Sunday (*Tirofágou*). The main focus of the Carnival celebrations starts on the Thursday (*Tsiknopémpti* in Greek) before Shrove Sunday (*Kiriakí tis Apokrías*).

In the north, people don goatskins and bells and go from house to house, wishing everyone a prosperous year and successful harvest. But the real celebrations take place in the Peloponnese region. In Pátras, they celebrate the legendary "white ball." All the principles of a centuries-old orthodox tradition seem to be suddenly forgotten. Everyone, even the women, feels free to make fools of themselves. Clad from top to toe in black, groups of women walk through the streets, flirting with every man they like the look of, and dreaming of liberty and equality. The Pátras Carnival celebration lasts four weeks and ends on Shrove Monday, known as "Clean Monday." This is followed by a period of inner and outer purification. Another equally attractive custom practiced throughout the country on Shrove Monday is kite flying.

A bowl of hot cuttlefish soup is just the thing to revive you after the excesses of Carnival. It is served hot with plenty of white bread and a dash of lemon juice.

Greece's biggest Carnival celebration takes place in Pátras with processions and dancing in the streets.
Background: Carnival in Sohos, East Macedonia.

ON SKYROS

Skyros, an island in the Sporades, is famous throughout Greece for its Carnival celebrations. These go back to the story of a herdsman who lost his entire flock in a snowstorm. Beside himself with grief, the *yéros* (old man) took the skins from his animals, hung their bells about his body, and returned to the village. Ever since, the men of the island have dressed up in skins, bells, and masks once a year in his memory to perform the "Struggle of the Yéri." According to how the clothes are worn, the *yéros* is a herdsman from the waist down and a goat from the waist up. On Shrove Monday, the islanders gather in the streets, dance, roar, and fight with each other, ringing their bells, which weigh up to 88 pounds (40 kilograms).

THE SHEPHERD'S TROVÁS

Just as his crook, jacket, and a dark cap, to shade him from the sun's glaring rays are essential to any Greek shepherd, so too is the *trovás*, the deep shoulder bag made of tightly woven coarse wool. It can hold everything a shepherd will need in the mountains, where he will often stay for many weeks: a large piece of sheep's milk cheese, *paximádia* (Greek biscuit), hard sausage, tomatoes, fruit, a water bottle, the shepherd's knife that sits so comfortably in the hand, and finally a hard-wearing cotton handkerchief. The shepherds of the past certainly did not go without a hearty meat meal if they had to rely on themselves for days at a time "in the wilderness" far away from their home villages, because one of the animals under his care could always be "found." That it might possibly not be one from the shepherd's own flock was in a way an unwritten rule, by which the men of a village community could live out their ideas of freedom of will, independence, and also resistance while "sheep rustling due to hunger."

Just as unrealistic as this heroic image is the idyllic one of the shepherd, characterized by the representation of Christ as the good shepherd who returns his lost sheep to the safety of the fold. Never will he be taken from this tranquillity, he is totally free, and is at one with the natural world that surrounds him, with only

his trusty sheepdogs to share this tranquil mountain solitude. He pays careful attention to his sheep and goats, and his job ensures that the community has food, because it is thanks to his painstaking efforts that they have milk, cheese, and wool.

In reality, shepherding is one of those disappearing occupations, and recruitment has become increasingly difficult in the last several years. Shepherds' wages and pensions have to be subsidized by the state, and the European Union pays the shepherds and farmers 5,000 drachma (about 15 Euro/US dollars) for every animal purchased.

PANIC ALARM

The Arcadian god of the shepherds, Pan, was the son of the god Hermes and a nymph, who was perhaps the daughter of the Arcadian Dryops. It is said that his mother ran away in shock when she saw her son's hirsute body, goat's legs, and horns. Much to the pleasure of the assembled gods, however, Hermes proudly presented his son on Mount Olympus. Dionysus was particularly fond of Pan. Once, Pan was pursuing the nymph Syrinx. She, however, wanted to remain a virgin huntress, so while fleeing Pan she asked nearby nymphs in the river Ladon to change her into a reed. Pan made this reed into his famous panpipes, the *syrinx*, on which he made music with great dexterity at the feasts of Dionysus. He also loved to gambol through the woods and accompany the nymphs' dance on his pipes. In Arca-

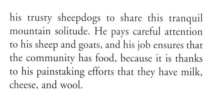

dia, he was worshiped by the herdsmen as a god of fertility. Taking the form of a male goat, he would mount the female goats, thereby guaranteeing the survival of the flock. But he was also thought of as an unpredictable, fearsome ally, as he would suddenly and unexpectedly appear in the oppressive midday heat, panicking both resting animals and herdsmen and sending them on a scrambled run.

When the Athenians asked the Spartans for help in the battle against the Persians, their messenger reported that Pan had met him on Mount Parthenios and wanted to know why the Athenians did not worship him, even though he had helped them before, and would continue to do so. After their victory over the Persians, the grateful Athenians erected a shrine to the god beneath the Acropolis and worshiped him with sacrifices and torch races.

PAXIMÁDIA
Greek biscuits

8½/1 kg all-purpose flour
3 tsp baking powder
¼ tsp salt
1¾ cups/400 g sugar
1 cup/250 ml vegetable oil
5 eggs, beaten
1 tsp vanilla sugar
½ tsp ground aniseed
2½ cups/250 g chopped walnuts
1 egg yolk, beaten with 1 tbsp water
1 tbsp sesame seeds

Preheat the oven to 350 °F (175 °C). Combine the flour, baking powder, and salt in a bowl. Make a well in the center, add the sugar, oil, eggs, vanilla sugar, and aniseed, and work into a smooth dough. Roll half the dough out thinly, cover with half the walnuts, and roll up tightly. Repeat the process with the remaining dough. Place the rolls on a buttered baking sheet, brush with the beaten egg yolk, sprinkle with the sesame seeds, and bake for 30 minutes. Leave to cool, then cut into slices. Return the slices to the oven and bake for a further 15 minutes until the biscuits begin to color. Leave to cool. If kept in an airtight container, *paximádia* will stay fresh for about one month.

Above and left: So that the shepherd does not go without a good meal during his days away from home, his solicitous wife packs him his *trovás*.

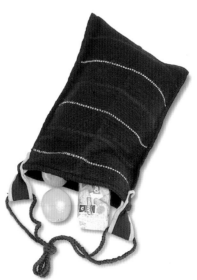

As well as fruit and *paximádia*, the shepherd's shoulder bag typically contains cheese, sausage, tomatoes, and a knife.

FLOKATI

In the 1970s, the shaggy shepherd's rug was an obligatory souvenir of a Greek holiday. There was hardly a living room or bedroom where it was not laid out on the floor or on the bed, or so it seemed at any rate. For the Greeks, on the other hand, the *flokati* was the embodiment of poverty, and the first thing any Greek did when he became more prosperous was to distance himself from this symbol. It is said that the *flokati* originally came into existence out of necessity. In the mountain regions where the winters are harsh, the farmers collected the wool caught in the branches and spun it into short-fiber yarns, that could be skillfully woven together. If they then washed and fulled these blankets in the mountain streams, the material compacted to create a durable, felt-like fabric, which could be dyed different colors and provided a warming carpet or blanket. The *flokati* is now making a surprise comeback and can be seen in all the fashionable clubs.

Any impurities in the fresh sheep's milk are filtered out through a thick cotton cloth.

Even just a small amount of powdered rennet is enough to curdle over 2½ gallons (10 liters) of milk.

After the rennet has been stirred in, the milk is covered and left to stand for 1 hour until it has thickened.

Above: the separated whey flows off. Below: the curds are cut into thin slices with a knife.

The *feta* cheese is kept in airtight tin-plate containers that have stood the test of time. It will keep for about two years if stored in a cool place.

FETA CHEESE QUALITY

SHEEP'S MILK CHEESE

Hardly a day goes by without a piece of sheep's milk cheese appearing in some form or other on a Greek dinner table. Sheep's milk cheese is a staple food and a Greek family enjoys tucking into an average 220 pounds (100 kilograms) of it each year. As a result there are many small concerns throughout the country meeting local demand. As is typical of Greece, the flavor of the sheep's milk cheese varies from region to region, but each producer swears by his own product and has his loyal customers, who will buy the large quantities of the cheese they need from no one else. The word *féta* means a slice or a piece and refers to the way the curds are treated during the manufacturing process. *Féta* is not associated with any specific type of sheep's milk.

HOMEMADE FÉTA CHEESE

In the countryside, you can still find housewives who make their own sheep's milk cheese, albeit in smaller quantities. Two and a half gallons (10 liters) of non-pasteurized milk are poured into a bowl through a closely woven cotton cloth. The temperature of the milk should be between 61 °F (16 °C) and 64° F (18 °C). Although lactic acid bacteria on their own would separate the milk proteins, the process is accelerated and improved by adding rennet (from calves' stomachs). For two and a half gallons (10 liters) of milk you will need no more than one teaspoon of rennet, mixed with a little milk before being added to the bowl and carefully stirred. Cover the bowl with a cloth and leave the milk to stand for about one hour.

Line a strainer with a cheesecloth, and then pour in the thickened milk, the curds, allowing the whey to drain off.

After about four hours, slice the curds remaining in the cloth to release more whey, then place the slices in layers in a large, airtight container, sprinkling each layer of cheese with sufficient salt. People reckon on about 1 pound (450 grams) of salt to 18 pounds (8 kilograms) of cheese. The cheese can be eaten even in this soft, fresh condition, but as time goes by the salt continues to draw out more liquid, making the cheese more compact. After about 60 days, the cheese will have completed the first maturing stage. Freshly prepared sheep's milk cheese can be stored in a cool place for about two years. The older it is, the more advisable it is to rinse it under running water before eating.

Typical Greek cheese shops sell many different local types of cheese, made from sheep's, goat's or cow's milk. Here *féta* is still stored in the traditional wooden barrels.

BARREL MANUFACTURE

As a place for storing foodstuffs, the wooden barrel has superceded the ancient ceramic pitcher in Greece, because it also keeps its contents fresh for a long time. The tradition of making barrels for storing sheep's milk cheese is still carried on in the Epriot mountain village of Métsovon. The open barrels (vats) are made of local timber, usually oak, but softwoods can also be used. The planks (staves) are planed to the right shape, smoothed at the ends, and a groove (chine) is hammered into the edges, in which the lid or base is fitted. Circular metal rings hold the timber planks together. The brine in which the cheese is placed to prevent oxidation makes the timbers expand slightly, so that the pores in the wood become saturated and the barrel remains watertight.

GREEK CHEESES

NAME	BRIEF DESCRIPTION	ORIGIN
Anthótiros (4)	Similar to *mizíthra*; soft and unsalted with a full fat content	Crete
Bátzos (15)	Sweet-sour, semihard cheese made from sheep's or goat's milk	Náousa
Halloumi	Spicy, high fat content hard cheese	Cyprus
Khloró (6, 13)	Soft cheese from sheep's or goat's milk; *khloró vinsanto* (13) is preserved in wine	Santorini
Féta (10)	Soft or slightly crumbly white sheep's milk cheese	Various regions
Formaélla	Strong, cylindrical hard cheese made from sheep's milk	Parnassos
Galotíri	Very strong, white, spreadable soft cheese	Thessaly
Graviéra (14)	Aromatic hard cheese made from cow's milk, similar to Swiss cheese	Various regions
Kasséri (17)	Semihard, slightly tangy, yellow-white sheep's milk cheese	Various regions
Kathoúra	Soft goat's milk cheese similar to mozzarella	Ikaría
Kefalograviéra (7)	Tangy, pale yellow hard cheese made from cow's or sheep's milk	Various regions
Kefalotíri (12)	Tangy, salty hard cheese made from sheep's or goat's milk	Various regions
Kopanistí	Tangy, spreadable, blue-veined sheep's milk cheese	Cyclades
Krasotíri/Giloméno	Hard sheep's milk cheese preserved in wine	Dodecanese
Ladotíri (2)	Hard cheese matured in oil	Zákinthos
Manoúri (9)	Mild, soft sheep's milk cheese	Various regions
Metsovóne (5)	Smoked hard cheese	Métsovon
Mizíthra (8)	Soft sheep's milk cheese similar to *manoúri*	Chios
Petroto (18)	Hard cow's milk cheese pressed between two stones	Tínos
Pretza	Creamy, very strong soft cheese	Zákinthos
San Micháli (3)	Tangy hard cheese made from cow's milk	Syros
Sféla	Strong cheese made from sheep's or goat's milk	Peloponnese
Telemés	Like *féta*, but made from cow's milk	Various regions
Tirí Tirakí (11)	Cow's milk cheese; a specialty of Tínos	Tínos
Touloumotíri	Strong soft cheese made from goat's milk	East Aegean
Xinomizithra (16)	A type of high fat cottage cheese, usually tangy and salty	Cyclades
Xinótiri (1)	Goat's milk cheese	Naxos

1 2 3 4 5

10 11 12 13 14

ARTICHOKES

The artichoke (*Cynara scolymus*), like cauliflower and broccoli, is grown for its flower heads, in other words it is the closed flower bud that is eaten, either whole or in part. It is usually the flower head base and the fleshy parts of the scales, which overlap each other like roof tiles and surround the base, that are eaten. This means that barely 20 percent of the flower head is edible. When preparing artichokes, the woody stalk should be completely removed. The artichoke buds are then totally immersed in boiling salted water and cooked in a covered pan.

Artichokes, which are sensitive to frost, thrive primarily in the warm climate of the Mediterranean region. All plantings of this thistle-like herbaceous plant, which grows nearly 7 feet (2 meters) tall, need to be rejuvenated roughly every four years, as yield declines with age. The artichoke in its modern form is a comparatively new vegetable in Greece, arriving there via Italy only in the late 15th century, although it originates from Iran or Arabia. Not many people know that the fields of the Peloponnese region produce many thousands of tons of artichokes for the international market, and Greece is the world's seventh largest producer. The main areas where artichokes have managed to make their way into Greek cuisine are the Dodecanese and the Ionian Islands. They are usually served with olive oil, plenty of lemon juice, fresh herbs, and also with asparagus.

Not many people know that artichokes are widely grown in Greece.

ARNÁKI ME ANGINÁRES
Lamb with artichokes

⅔ cup/150 ml Greek extra virgin olive oil
2 lbs/1 kg shoulder lamb, diced
5 cups finely chopped onion
8 small artichokes
2 eggs
Juice of 1 lemon
1 bunch dill, finely chopped
Salt
Freshly ground white pepper

Heat the olive oil in a pan. First brown the meat, then add the onions and soften. Season with salt and pepper, then add a generous 2¾ cups/700 ml water. Lower the heat and braise the meat until tender. Cut back the artichoke stems to ¾ in (2 cm). Remove the tough outer leaves and cut off the tips of the inner leaves. Rub all cut surfaces with lemon juice. Leave for 25–30 minutes, then place the artichokes, stem up, in the pan, adding more hot water if necessary, and cook for 10–15 minutes over a constant low heat. Remove from the heat and leave to cool slightly.

Break the eggs into a bowl and beat until frothy. Add the lemon juice and some of the cooking liquid, beating continuously. Add the egg and lemon sauce to the braised meat, stir, sprinkle with dill, and serve with freshly baked white bread.

Angináres à la polita – artichoke hearts in olive oil and lemon juice with tender vegetables and fresh herbs is the most popular Greek recipe for artichokes – and with good reason, because all the flavors complement each other wonderfully.

Its flower may be beautiful, but when an artichoke begins to flower it has ceased to be of any interest to the gourmet.

ANGINÁRES YEMISTÉS
Stuffed artichoke hearts

4 large artichokes
Juice of 1 lemon
1 tsp all-purpose flour, combined with a little water
½ cup/125 ml Greek extra virgin olive oil
2 tbsp vinegar
Salt
1 egg, hard-cooked
4 green olives

For the filling:
½ lb/200 g fish of your choice, filleted, poached, and finely chopped
1 tbsp brandy
2 tomatoes, skinned and finely chopped
2 anchovy fillets, finely chopped
⅔ cup/150 g mayonnaise
1 tsp capers, finely chopped

Remove the stalks, outer leaves, and top two thirds of the artichokes. Peel the bases (removing all the dark green parts), place in a bowl, sprinkle with lemon juice, cover with water, and leave to stand for 15 minutes. Pour some water in a pan, add the salt and the flour and water mixture, and bring to the boil. Add the artichoke bases and cook until the inner leaves come away easily. Leave to cool, then, using a spoon, remove the inner leaves together with the choke. Beat together the olive oil and vinegar and pour over the bases. Drizzle the brandy over the fish fillet. Combine the chopped tomatoes and anchovies with the mayonnaise and capers, add the fish, then season with salt and pepper. Fill the artichoke hearts with this mixture and garnish with egg slices and olives.

Remove the stalk and outer leaves and cut off the top two thirds of the flower.

Peel the bases and cut off all the dark green parts, removing any remaining outer leaves if necessary.

When cool, use a spoon to remove the inner leaves together with the choke.

MEDICINAL AND CULINARY

The first garlic recipes are recorded in one of the oldest Egyptian medicinal guides dating from the 15th century B.C. Even then, garlic was known as a cure for headaches and hemorrhoids. In the famous Hippocratic School on Kos, garlic was prescribed in the 4th century B.C. for constipation and uterine tumors. In Rome in the 4th century A.D., Pliny the Elder was advocating the use of garlic for high blood pressure. As in classical times, garlic is either crushed in a press or very finely chopped, because only when the cells are damaged can the organic sulfur compound alliin, contained in the essential oil, be broken down by an enzyme to form the pungent smelling allicin. Unfortunately, the smell is inextricably linked to the antibacterial and fungicide agents, which is why attempts to breed it out have failed.

ARCADIAN GARLIC

How did garlic, the smell of which even the gods found so unbearable that no believer was allowed to enter their temple after eating garlic, reach Arcadia, that musical kingdom of the art of pastoral singing? Quite simply – it didn't! The idyllic Arcadia, where cultured shepherds whiled away the time waiting for the return of the Golden Age by means of noble poetic competition, is purely a fiction of Virgil created around 40 B.C. in imitation of the pastoral poetry written a good 250 years earlier by the Greek poet, Theocritus. It exists only in books and in paintings. Nor does its name have anything to do with the plateau in the center of the Peloponnese area, which the traveler and historian Pausanias still described as rough and impassable even around A.D. 170. At the shrine on the top of Mount Lycaeus he issued dark intimations about the human sacrifices that had been made in the past in honor of the god worshiped there, Zeus Lycaeus, Zeus the wolf god. The view from here far into the region of Arkadhía is still worth the climb today. This real Arcadia, however, is the main growing region for Greek garlic. Here *Allium sativum* finds its preferred growing conditions: lots of sun and an extremely dry climate. The long, narrow, gray-green leaves and the white to pink sterile flowers of the spherical inflorescence of this hardy plant that grow to a height

of about 3 feet (1 meter) must have died away completely before a start can be made on harvesting the garlic bulbs under the soil. About 2.7 million US tons (2.5 million tonnes) of garlic are produced each year all over the world, and if properly stored (dry and well ventilated) it can keep for months.

An appetizer of fresh young garlic preserved in oil and vinegar is an Arcadian specialty.

SKORDALIÁ
Garlic cream

1 lb /500 g stale white bread
4 cloves of garlic
1 scant cup/200 ml Greek extra virgin olive oil
Juice of 1 lemon
Salt

Soak the white bread, then squeeze out well. Blend the bread and garlic cloves in a mixer at the lowest setting, gradually adding the olive oil and lemon juice. Arrange on a plate and serve as an appetizer or as an accompaniment to fish and meat dishes. Mashed potato can also be used instead of bread as the basic ingredient for this dish.

Tip: *Skordaliá* tastes best if left for a day. If made in large quantities it will keep for a few days if stored in a refrigerator.

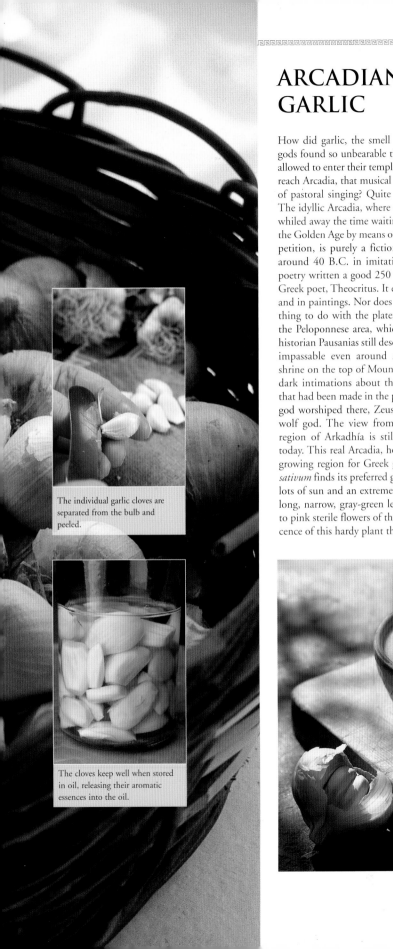

The individual garlic cloves are separated from the bulb and peeled.

The cloves keep well when stored in oil, releasing their aromatic essences into the oil.

STIFÁDO
Braised beef or veal with onions

¼ cup/50 g butter
2 lbs/1 kg veal or beef, roughly diced
1 lb/500 g tomatoes, peeled and diced
2 lbs/1 kg small onions or shallots, peeled
1 generous cup/250 ml mavrodaphne (red liqueur wine)
2 bay leaves
½ tsp cinnamon
1 tsp sweet paprika
Salt
Freshly ground black pepper

Melt the butter in a pan, then brown the meat well on all sides. Add the tomatoes, quickly bring to the boil, then add the onions. Soften for a few minutes, then pour in the wine. Add the bay leaves, cinnamon, paprika, salt and pepper, and enough water to cover well. Cover the pan, lower the heat and simmer for about 1 hour until the meat is cooked, checking from time to time that it does not need to be topped up with boiling water. As soon as the meat is cooked and the liquid has thickened, remove from the heat, arrange on plates, and serve with freshly baked white bread and salad.

Tip: Any meat (pork, beef, veal, hare, rabbit, goat, lamb) can be used to make *stifádo*, as can fish, such as octopus or cuttlefish. The important thing is that the onions are small (in Greece, you can buy special *stifádo* onions) and that it melts in the mouth when cooked. The wine used should also be very sweet and full-bodied in order to produce the characteristic *stifádo* flavor.

THE OLYMPIC FLAME

Once the Olympic flame was lit, all acts of war had to cease and once the participants had vowed to abide by the rules, the games could begin. Olympia is situated in the heart of the green hill country, surrounded by magnificent acacia woods, splendid plane trees, and fragrant eucalyptus groves in the region of Ilía, where the Kládhios

River flows into the Alfiós. Even in Mycenaean times there was a settlement at the foot of the Hill of Cronos. Finds indicate a cult of Hippodameia and Pelops, who won his beloved here with the help of Poseidon in a chariot race against her murderous father, Œnomaus. Greek newcomers to the region at the end of the 2nd millennium B.C. brought with them a cult of Zeus. Offerings from as far back as 1000 B.C. refer to games where spreading branches and tripods were awarded as trophies for the winners. Pausanias reported two versions of the legend of how the ancient games were founded in Olympia. According to one version, Zeus first organized the games between the gods in Olympia after his victory over his father, Cronos. At these games, Apollo won the pentathlon among other things. Other sources state that Heracles, the son of Zeus, restarted the games, located the site for the first games of the gods, and challenged his brother to a competition. Thus Zeus as ruler of Olympus was linked with the games from a very early stage.

The Olympic Games are documented historically in the first recorded list of victors in a competition in 776 B.C. In the middle of the 7th century B.C., the shrine of Olympia began to be developed, and the games began to be extended.

The Olympic Games ran in a four-year cycle. Only free Greek men could take part, and married

Above: the symbolic flame is now lit once again for the modern Olympic Games.
Left: the Games in Olympia were the largest, but games were also held in other parts of Greece. Athens always celebrated its athletes the year before the games in Olympia, honoring the victors with "pan-Athenian prize amphorae" like the one shown here.

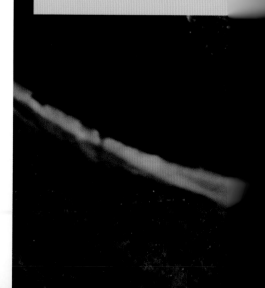

women were not allowed to watch. Over time the games were extended to include more and more competitions, and from the 5th century B.C. there were also cultural performances such as poetry readings. When the Olympic Flame was lit in 393 A.D., it was to be for the last time. A year later, the Christian emperor Theodosius banned the games as heathen. Flames, earthquakes, and floods meant that shrines and any thoughts of the Olympics sank to oblivion under the sand and rubble until the 19th century.

BAY LEAVES IN OLYMPIA?

Legend has it that Apollo fell in love with the nymph, Daphne, who, however, energetically rejected his advances. Pursued through the woods by the stubborn god, who refused to accept rejection, Daphne sought the help of Gaea, the goddess of the earth, who turned the nymph into a laurel or bay tree (the Greek word for such a tree being *dáfni*). All Apollo could then do was to break off a branch, which he wore in his hair from that moment on. Hence laurel groves were planted in shrines to Apollo, Apollo's muses wore laurel branches, and Pythia, the chief priestess who ascended the laurel-bedecked seat of the oracle of Apollo at Delphi, chewed bay leaves. In both musical and athletic competitions held at shrines to Apollo, the victors received laurel wreaths, underlining the use of laurel as a token of victory and honor. In modern times, however, the separate uses of the laurel and olive wreath led to confusion. The winners of the Olympic Games held in Zeus' honor, the most important pan-Hellenic games, were rewarded with a branch from the wild olive tree in the holy temple grove at Olympia, just as the victors of the pan-Athenian games in Athens, held in honor of Athena, received olive branches from the grove there.

Apollo's tree, the evergreen laurel that grows to a height of about 40 feet (12 meters), is found primarily in the Azores and in the Mediterranean region, where it prefers low copses and rocky sites. The bay laurel (*Laurus nobilis*) is particularly valued as a culinary plant for its shiny dark green, aromatic leaves.

RED SUMMER FRUITS

The heat of summer and ice-cold watermelons complement each other perfectly, because there is nothing so refreshing on a baking hot sunny day as a slice of this pleasantly sweet, very juicy red fruit. Nowadays, the refrigerator in almost every Greek home seems to contain a watermelon just waiting to be eaten. And so that people never have to go without, in many places the melon seller regularly drives his truck through the streets obligingly bringing the fruits, which weigh up to 33 pounds (15 kilograms), and which in purely botanical terms are actually berries, to every door.

A slice of watermelon is all you need to enter the local long-distance seed spitting championships, junior class.

With each watermelon weighing as much as 33 pounds (15 kilograms), the traveling melon seller is a welcome sight at the house door.

The biggest area in Greece for growing watermelons (*Citrullus lanatus*) is in the northwest Peloponnese, in the area around Pírgos. Many farmers have specialized solely in this product. Many years of monoculture drain the soil of essential minerals, and yet watermelons rely on important nutrients such as lime and magnesium, so suitable preparations have to be applied during the growing season. In the last few years, farmers have been experimenting increasingly with crosses between watermelons (*Citrullus*) and pumpkins (*Cucurbita*). The resultant plants are more resistant to pests and any slight change in flavor is merely viewed as another plus.

Apart from that, the large berries need only water, and lots of it, because they have a 90

ALL WITH A KNIFE

Melon sellers go from house to house throughout the summer, weighing out heavy watermelons on their improvised scales and usually selling several at a time. A lucrative business! But when the melon seller shouts from his truck through his dented megaphone: "Fresh melons and all with a knife," he doesn't mean that as a special promotion each watermelon comes with a free knife. "With a knife" actually means: "I'll cut open a watermelon for you and you can try it. Then you can decide whether you want to buy it or not."

KOLOKÍTHA GLIKÓ
Pumpkin in syrup

2 lbs/1 kg pumpkin
6½ cups/1.5 kg sugar
2 cups/500 g glucose
Juice of 1 lemon
2½ cups/600 ml water

Peel the piece of pumpkin, remove the fibrous parts on the inside, and dice the remaining flesh. Put the pumpkin pieces in a pan with a little water, quickly bring to a boil, and remove from the heat. Boil the water, sugar, glucose, and lemon juice together to form a syrup. Fill sterilized preserving jars with the pumpkin pieces, top up with syrup, and seal tightly. The pumpkin will keep for many months. Serve on small plates as a dessert or with a glass of water with mocha coffee.
Tip: glucose and lemon juice prevent the formation of sugar crystals.

percent water content when fully ripe. Some experience is required to tell how ripe a watermelon is "blind," in other words without cutting it open and checking the color of its flesh or its taste. Farmers tap on the fruit with their finger or the palm of their hand and can hear how ripe it is. According to them, unripe fruits have an almost metallic ring to them, whereas overripe ones sound hollow and flat, and only melons that are just right produce a dull, vibrating sound. If you don't trust your ears, then you can also use your eyes to look at the "surface markings." Provided it has not been moved while ripening, the place where the melon was in contact with the ground should not be white but cream colored to pale yellow. The most popular melon in Greece is the sweet melon (*Cucumis melo*). It is grown primarily in the southwest Peloponnese. Although its water content is actually only 5 percent lower than that of the watermelon, they each have a very distinct role to play when planning a menu.

You don't have to buy all of this magnificent pumpkin – the market trader will be happy to cut you off a piece the size you want.

Like watermelons, sweet melons should be harvested only when fully ripe.

Whereas the watermelon can be eaten at any time almost as a refreshing "drink," the sweet melon is used more as a summer desert.
The giant or edible pumpkin (*Cucurbita maxima*) is a distant relative of the watermelon and the sweet melon. It too has a water content of about 90 percent, but its flesh is firm and not at all juicy. It is therefore not eaten raw, but is prepared in several ways hardly suitable for fully ripe melons. One such way is to preserve it in syrup. This way it can be enjoyed throughout the year, providing a little taste of late summer sunshine well into those gloomy winter days.

89

The Greeks have appreciated dried (wild) figs for their sweetness, storability, and ease of transport for over 8000 years. No one knows for sure when figs were first cultivated.

SWEET FIGS

The Mediterranean region produces about 1.6 million U.S. tons (1.5 million tonnes) of figs each year. Greece is the second largest fig-producing country after Turkey. However, with most varieties of *Ficus carica*, pollination is so hazardous that the fact that they have survived this long is bordering on a miracle. Over the centuries, two cultivated varieties have developed from the wild fig. According to an intricate system these two varieties depend on each other and on a particular type of gall wasp (*Blastophaga psenes*). The edible fig bears only female flowers with long styles, whereas the (inedible) male fig develops female flowers with short styles (gall flowers) and male flowers (and lignified fruits). Both varieties flower three times a year at the same times. The gall wasp larvae grow in the ovaries of the gall flowers. The female wasps leave the wooden-like fruits, already fertilized and laden with pollen, at exactly the time when the next generation of flowers has already opened. In their search for a suitable ovary in which to lay their eggs, the

| Kalamata | Totato | Mission | Kimi |

In botanical terms, the fig as we know it is a collection of stone fruits. Within the pear-shaped skin grow vast numbers of tiny stone fruits on fleshy oval stems. Of the four varieties, only *Kalamata* figs are dried, the rest being eaten fresh.

Dried *Kalamata* figs are rinsed under running water to remove any impurities.

The cleaned, dried figs are placed on a conveyor belt, where any remaining substandard ones are removed.

Only perfect fruits are put into their commercial packaging by hand.

only flowers available to them are the gall flowers with their short styles, because their egg-laying pipe is too short for the long styles of the edible fig flowers. In their attempts to lay eggs here too, however, they pollinate the edible fig, without damaging it with their eggs.

Figs are sensitive, yields fluctuate, and their harvesting and processing requires intensive manual labour, all of which are reasons why many farmers have already given up growing them. The fruits thrive only in southern countries.

SIKOMÉDA (SIKÓPITA)
Fig cakes

1½ lbs/750 g fresh figs
1 scant cup/200 ml grape must
1 tbsp + 1 tsp/20 ml ouzo
1 tsp ground cinnamon
½ tsp ground cloves
½ tsp ground nutmeg
Zest of 2 unwaxed, or well-scrubbed, oranges, grated
1 tsp chopped fennel
Freshly ground black pepper
1½ cups/150 g finely chopped walnuts or almonds
Walnut leaves

Cut the figs in half and leave to dry in the sun. When dry, chop finely, then thoroughly combine all the ingredients. Shape the mixture into a small cakes and leave to dry in the sun. Wrap the individual cakes in walnut leaves and tie securely together. Serve as an appetizer with ouzo or wine.

THE FIG LEAF

In the 3rd century B.C., fig leaves, *thríon*, were used as wrapping material. In the same way as grape leaves are used today, they were preserved in salt to reduce their bitter elements, so that tasty morsels could be wrapped up in them and eaten. The fig leaf became an important symbol of the loss of Paradise, its use betraying to God the Father how Adam and Eve had fallen from grace: "And the eyes of them both were opened, and they knew that they were naked; and they sewed fig leaves together, and made themselves aprons." (Gen. 3:7.) Artists could not avoid using the fig leaf when portraying this theme, and as a consequence Adam and Eve were never seen without hiding their modesty in this way.

These little fig cakes are a delicious, but very substantial, specialty from Corfu.

GREEK WINE

The winegrowing regions in Greece today are characterized by various climatic conditions and geological features. Since vines were first grown back in classical times, many of the total 326,728 acres (132,225 hectares) of vineyards, about half of which are used for dessert grapes and raisins, have been in the coastal regions. In contrast to the constant, cooling wind found here, the great summer heat of the plains and the islands means that the grapes have to be harvested early. Winegrowing is made even more difficult by the fact that artificial irrigation is possible only with recently planted rows of vines. In contrast, the low temperatures in the highlands mean that grapes have to be picked there before they are fully ripe. The limestone and volcanic soils, and the Mediterranean climate with its hot summers and mild winters, generally create such favorable conditions that the grapes can thrive even at altitudes of up to 3300 feet (1000 meters) above sea level. That is why it has even been possible to turn the land in the north extending into the rugged mountains over to winegrowing. Agriculture is predominantly mixed, which is why Greek viticulture is widely dispersed in terms of area and there are fewer of the consolidated vineyards so common in the winegrowing regions overseas and in central Europe. Given the country's southern situation, it is equally remarkable that most of the wine produced – about 60 percent – is white, in no small part due to the world-famous retsina.

Greece now has an applicable wine law in common with the rest of Europe. It was created on its entry to the European Community in 1981, after introducing the controlled origin appellations as long ago as 1971. The categorization system of the Greek wine law (see box) follows the European decree defining the "quality wines from specific growing regions." The striking feature of Greece as a wine-producing country is the great number of its grape varieties. There are about 300 varieties in total. Of these, barely two dozen are of any great significance, producing wines in the various winegrowing regions for the international wine market.

White wine is produced from the Assyrtiko grape on Santoríni and Athos, from the Vilana on Crete, and primarily from the Robola grape on Cephalonia. In the regions of Macedonia, Thrace, and the Peloponnese, on the other hand, the white Rhoditis grape is used. The retsina wines are also white, as is the well-known aperitif and dessert muscatel wine from Samos. One of the most important red wine grapes, the Xinomavro, is grown in the Goumenissa and Náousa regions of Macedonia and Thrace. Meanwhile, on the Peloponnese the Agiorgitiko and the Mavrodaphne are used in the area around Pátras and also on Cephalonia. The Mandelaria grape defines red wine production on Páros, Crete, and Rhodes. Another very old and important red grape variety is Limnio. On the island of Cyprus, which has a wine tradition of its own, the indigenous red grapes of Mavro and Ophthalmo and the white Xynisteri are used, as is Muscatel of Alexandria.

Of the international grape varieties, the red Cabernet Sauvignon, Cabernet Franc, Grenache, Merlot, and Syrah are used and/or grown in Greece for blending or sometimes also as single-varietal wines; Chardonnay is the main white wine grape.

THE PELOPONNESE

The Peloponnese region is of particular significance among Greece's winegrowing areas. This area produces the grapes for raisins as well as the grapes for a quarter of all Greek wines. With 149,295 acres (60,419 hectares), the region has the largest area under vine. Ranging from the lowlands to mountains of up to 2640 feet (800 meters), the landscape is as variable as the climate, which produces heavy rainfall in the west and extreme drought in the east. The Peloponnese is predominantly red wine country. In Neméa, a spicy, well-structured red wine going by the name of "Blood of Hercules" is produced from the Agiorgitiko grape. The highly prized Mavrodaphne from Pátras is a dark, oily fortified wine. Although Pátras also produces the sweet white Muscatel and a dry, white version from the Rhoditis grape, the Mantinea region with its fruity Moscofilero is the only major white wine producer.

The Peloponnese is associated with one grape in particular. Monemvasia, a strategically important access point on the eastern side of the Peloponnese, saw its golden age in the 13th century, with one wine being an important commodity, subsequently called Malvasia by the Venetians. This was the legendary and also mythical "nectar of the gods," a sweet liqueur that was once boiled in cauldrons on Crete in the palace of King Minos to preserve it in a way, and was then able to find its way in the Middle Ages via Monemvasia, the hub of sea trade, to Italy, France, and England.

WINE GLOSSARY

Afródes: sparkling wine
Ágouro krasí: immature, in other words young wine
Ambelónas: vineyard
Drίinio varéli: oak barrel/cask
Elafrí krasí: light wine
Epitrapézio: table wine
Erithró or *kókkino:* red
Géfsi: taste
Inapothíki: wine cellar
Inopíisi: wine production
Inopiós: wine producer
Inopolío: wine bar, wine merchant's store
Isoropiiméno krasí: well-balanced wine
Khróma: color
Kivótio: wooden box
Krási me polí sóma: full-bodied wine
Krasí: modern Greek for wine
Ktima: winery
Lefkó: white
Oínos: classical Greek for wine
Paleó krasí: old wine
Potíri: glass
Varí krasí: heavy wine
Xirós: dry

GREEK WINE CATEGORIES

Epitrapézios oínos: table wine
Cava: table wine that must be stored in wooden barrels and bottles for two years in the case of white wine, three for red.
Topikós Oínos: country wine
O.P.A.P. (Onomasia Proelefsis Anoteris Piotitas): equivalent to the V.Q.P.R.D. *(Vin de Qualité Produit dans une Région Déterminée)* EU quality mark: to date 22 appellations of this quality have been defined.

Wines matured in wooden barrels can also use the following descriptions:
Epilegménos (Réserve): white wine for two, red wine for three years, each with one year in the bottle
Idiká Epilegménos (Grande Réserve): one year more
O.P.E. (Onomasia Proelefsis Elenkhomenis): denotes relevant quality, liqueur, or dessert wines; 13 appellations have been defined.
Retsina: a "traditional appellation" awarded to Greece by the EU.

GREEK GRAPE VARIETIES

Moscofilero: grape of the Peloponnese, similar to Muscatel. The dry white wine develops a floral, rose-scented bouquet.

Xinomavro: grape of the north with a high acid content, marked berry flavor and mild tannins for full-bodied wines such as Naousa.

Agiorgitiko: quality aromatic variety from Neméa with strong color and mild tannins; produces fruity, sometimes only slightly acidic wines.

Limnio: distinctive, spicy grape from Límnos, called limnia as far back as Aristotle's time. Produces full-bodied and acidic wines.

Savatiano: the most cultivated grape in Greece; classic base for retsina, but also produces fruity, well-balanced white wines.

Rhoditis: complex, old Peloponnesian variety with low sugar content and high acidity. This young wine, best served chilled, has a spicy flavor.

Moscato: the famous sweet dessert wine from Samos is produced from this Muscatel grape. It is also grown in the Pátras region.

Assyrtiko: very high quality white grape variety that thrives particularly well on the volcanic soils of Santoríni. Develops good acidity.

Mavrodaphne: the aromatic "Black Laurel" grows in the Pátras area and on Cephalonia. Used as a base for sweet, heavy dessert wines.

Kotsifali: grape grown on Crete with a spicy aroma, high sugar content, and low tannin levels. Often blended with Mandelaria.

Mandelaria: an old grape from the Cyclades and Crete with a high tannin content. Produces wines with strong color and a relatively low alcohol volume.

Robola: this grape, grown mainly on Cephalonia, produces particularly strong, dry white wines with delicate citrus hints.

Malagousia: this grape, indigenous to the southwestern mainland, produces aromatic, well-rounded white wines with cedar, mint, and pepper notes.

Vilana: this old-Cretan white, very aromatic grape variety produces wines that taste of fresh flowers and green apples.

George Papaioannou is an ambitious winegrower, whose early attempts at marketing his own wine met with great success. At the heart of the ancient Neméa region, he experiments with 30 different types of wine and is now one of Greece's best-known winegrowers.

PAPAIOANNOU WINERY

This splendid 124-acre (50 hectare) winery lies in Neméa – one of the two wine regions of the Peloponnese not directly on the coast – and is run with passion by the independent winegrower Anthanassios Papaioannou and his son, George, a trained enologist. Papaioannou' Greek colleagues say that he is so closely attached to the soil of his home country in spirit that it is really only his body that roams around the world. Although the winery was founded as early as 1867, its current owner was brave enough to be one of the first winegrowers in Greece to take the step of marketing his product himself. The Papaioannou winery is now one of the best known in all

Pinot Noir is a dark, dry red wine with distinctive character traits.

Fumé Papaioannou is a tempting proposition with its slightly smoky spice notes.

Agiorgitiko is a dry country wine, displaying all the merits of this region.

Neméa, some of which are very old. One of its distinctive features is that it displays a dense red color and has sufficient structure to make it a wine that stores particularly well.

The Papaioannou family also grows international grape varieties including Chardonnay, Cabernet Sauvignon, and the big Burgundy Pinot Noir grape from the French Cote d'Or with its peerless bouquet. They are sold as country and table wines. The Papaioannous are also experimenting with Riesling and Sauvignon Blanc.

of Greece. Anthanassios and George Papaioannou have specialized totally in dry wines. They make a good, earthy red Neméa AOC, a classic "Blood of Hercules," using Agiorgitiko vines which grow at between 825 and 2640 feet (250–800 meters) above sea level here in

ACHAIA CLAUSS WINERY

When the Bavarian wine dealer Gustav Clauss traveled through the Achaea region in the northern Peloponnese in 1859, he immediately felt at home in its hilly landscape with its fertile vineyards around the harbor town of Pátras and decided to settle there. He bought some land and in 1861 set up his own winery. The original main building of the winery, which looked like a small fortress complete with tower, still stands today. The owner's idea was that the apartments for the people working on his estate, who were of many different nationalities, should be grouped around this tower rather like a small wine village. As early as 1880, there were Greeks and Italians working here in wine production, Germans on the administrative side, and Maltese barrel makers. Clauss also had a school and even a Catholic and a Greek Orthodox church built for his workers.

His products were of such high quality that Clauss was able to export the wines throughout Europe, and as far back as 1873 his Muscatel of Pátras and the Mavrodaphne won their creator his first international awards. 1901 saw

White Demestica is a light, fruity wine with a hint of peach.

Ruby red Demestica is firm-bodied and is best served at 61 °F (16 °C).

Sweet Mavrodaphne dessert wine of Pátras is Achaia Clauss' traditional wine.

the first bottling of the Demestica from the mountain village of Demestíkha.

After Clauss' death, the Greek entrepreneur and raisin exporter Vlassis Antonopoulos acquired the Achaia Clauss winery in 1919, continuing the wine tradition established by Gustav Clauss. In the exhibition rooms on the history of the estate, you can see a bust of the second owner.

As a visitor, you can see not only the historical buildings and sections, but also practically all the rooms of the winery, which even after six generations still looks like a Tuscan winery or a Spanish bodega. In one of the exhibition rooms you can find appreciative letters written by the great and the good, including letters from Queen Elisabeth of Austria, Queen Victoria of England, Bismarck, Franz Liszt, Charles Montgomery, Neil Armstrong, and several American presidents.

In 1983, the winery underwent a thorough modernization program. Since then it has become one of Greece's largest winery businesses, producing 25 million bottles each year, with a distribution network extending beyond Greece to 37 other countries.

The internationally best-known table wine produced by Achaia Clauss has to be the Demestica (white, red, and rosé). But they also produce other respectable V.Q.P.R.D. quality wines, such as the Nemea, Inokastro, and Mantinea white wines. The Cava Clauss quality wine also deserves to be mentioned, of course, as do the famous sweet dessert wines (AOC): the red Mavrodaphne from Pátras and the white Muscatel of Pátras. The winery also produces retsina and ouzo.

The fortress-like winery of Achaia Clauss, with its model social institutions, is one of the largest in the Peloponnese. Huge old barrels of the sweet Mavrodaphne wine of Pátras are stored in its cellars.

ANTONO-POULOS WINERY

Konstantinos Antonopoulos – a wine expert well versed in the ways of the world – turned his long-standing dream of having his own winery into reality in the 1980s. In 1987, on the outskirts of Pátras, Greece's third largest city, he founded his modern winery and planted 27 acres (11 hectares) with his own grapes. Increasingly, grapes harvested from other winegrowing regions such as Neméa and Mantinea are also brought in to make the renowned red and white wines. Antonopoulos successfully created one of the first really great Greek red wines, and his tragic death in 1994 in an automobile accident was an irreplaceable loss to the whole of

Chardonnay is stored for two years in new oak casks, releasing its aroma when served at a temperature of 50 °F (10 °C).

Cabernet-Nea Dris is a medium- to full-bodied red wine with subtle cedar and mint notes. A good accompaniment to hearty dishes.

Cabernet Franc Ampelochora is reminiscent of a spicy Loire wine with a slightly fruity and fresh berry taste.

Greece's wine industry. In the words of his colleague, Thanassis Parparoussis, who has just as much pioneering spirit, with the death of Konstantinos Antonopoulos, Greece lost a "spearhead that led Greek wines out of obscurity." Happily, his wife and his cousins, Yiannis and Nikos Chalikias, are carrying on his legacy, successfully developing it even further.

Particularly important products from the Antonopoulos winery are the Cabernet-Nea Dris, the Private Collection Red (Agiorgitiko, Cabernet Sauvignon), and White (Chardonnay). Other important products include the white Adoli Ghis blend of indigenous varieties and Chardonnay, as well as a white Mantinea.

THE VINE OF PAUSANIAS

The Greek historian Pausanias traveled through the Peloponnese in the year A.D.176. Although he made no mention in his journals of the wild grapevine of Arcadia, this vine now bears his name. It is not clear how this description came about, but what is certain is that this wild grapevine can now be viewed as one of the few surviving original Greek vines. Wine researchers have rediscovered it in Arkadhía. It is a strong vine and although it has now become far too old to bear fruit, its stem still carries the original gene of today's top quality vines. It was one of the many wild wine grapes that grew throughout Greece in classical times, and was used to make the first Greek wines, which rapidly became popular beyond the country's boundaries and which were praised over many centuries by philosophers and historians. Not only Homer, Herodotus, Xenophon, Aristotle, and Theophrastus, but also the Romans Cato and Virgil, extolled them in their writings. The wild grapevine of Greece survived well into the 19th century between Thrace and the Peloponnese, precisely in the regions where even today Greece's many grape varieties still thrive. Only the phylloxera outbreak of 1898 destroyed most Greek vines. Two of the most important Greek wine regions, Mantinea and Neméa, have developed where until recently the few surviving Pausanias' wild vines grew.

The Antonopoulos winery is one of the largest and most ambitious on the Peloponnese. It was founded in 1987 by Konstantinos Antonopoulos. After his tragic death, his wife and his cousins Yiannis and Nikos Chalikias have continued to put heart and soul into the art of wine producing that he had started with such success.

OENOFOROS WINERY

This winery has spectacular vineyards above the Bay of Corinth. Its vineyards are laid out over five levels on the northern slopes of the climatically favorable region of Egion, at altitudes of between 960 and 2880 feet (300–900 meters). The central mountain range of the Peloponnese to the south protects the grapes from hot winds, while the fresh marine climate of the Gulf of Corinth guarantees fertile growth. A feature of the company is that the winegrowers have successfully introduced foreign grape varieties such as Chardonnay and Cabernet Sauvignon, while at the same time reviving the old Lagorthi and Volitsa grape varieties that had all but disappeared, having been destroyed by a devastating phylloxera outbreak. The winegrowers showed great perseverance, spending a lot of time replanting them. The winery marries modern technology with the values of traditional wine production. Great pleasure is taken in producing wine from the grapes, which are picked on the estate, then fermented and laid down in oak barrels or in modern stainless steel tanks.

In the Oenoforos winery (Greek for wine bearer), local specialists use Greek and European references to create interesting blends from indigenous and international grape varieties and occasionally single-varietal wines. The grapes they process include Rhoditis, Moscofilero, Mantinea, and Agiorgitiko.

White Asprolithi wine made from Rhoditis grapes has a clear, fruity aroma (10–12 ºC).

Esperitis is a light rosé wine made from the Agiorgitiko grape, and tastes of roses.

A single-varietal wine, made from the red Volitsa grape grown in only a few areas.

SPIROPOULOS WINERY

Ode Panos sparkling wine made from Moscofilero, the best grape for such wine, best drunk when four years old.

White Orino should be drunk up to two years after it is made.

The deep red Porfyros blend has a complex and powerful aroma.

The Spiropoulos family has been involved in winegrowing and wine production since 1860. The family now owns 100 acres (40 hectares) of vineyards in the Appellation Mantinea, a plateau 2080 feet (650 meters) above sea level, and the modernized winery with its successful architectural design is situated among the vineyards. In 1993, the progressive winegrowers switched to organic winegrowing as part of an EU program, and in 1999 this was rewarded with the ISO quality mark. The symbiosis between biological cultivation, technically perfected wine production, and the production of quality products has thus finally become a philosophy of life for the family. The wines have won numerous international prizes and awards, and around 20 percent is now exported. The Mantinea from Moscofilero is a specialty wine.

The Spiropoulos winery sets very high, exemplary standards in organic wine growing.

ΕΠΤΑΝΗΣΑ

Above: Campiello, the old town of Corfu, doesn't look typically Greek.
Background: view of the former residence of the English Lord High Commissioner with the Church of St. George built in the Greek style.

IONIAN ISLANDS

Poutínga

Kritharáki

Pastítsio

Onions and leeks

Food just like Io makes it

Egg dishes

Avgolémono

Sauces

Barboúni

Island beef

Sofríto

Robola

Propolis

Kumquat

It may be true that the Ionians, the tribe that once occupied the northern Peloponnese, gave these islands their name, but there is also an ancient myth that provides a much better known explanation. Io, one of Hera's priestesses, was pursued by Zeus and changed into a cow. Tormented by a gadfly unleashed on her by his jealous wife, Io's only means of escape was to leap bravely into the very sea that now still bears her name. If you approach Greece from the west, the scenery that unfolds is totally different from the picture of Greek islands you may have in your mind. This is due not only to the extremely impressive, dramatic natural surroundings that the 13 inhabited islands of the Ionian Sea have to offer, but also to the unusually lush, green vegetation, this coast of Greece enjoying a higher rainfall than the Aegean coast. When crossing from the Mediterranean to the Adriatic, the northernmost Ionian Islands are only a few miles from the Italian coast. This explains their cultural affinity with Western Europe, heightened by the fact that, with the exception of the Levkás peninsula, they never came under Turkish rule. Venice, which saw the opportunities these islands presented as a stepping stone to the eastern Mediterranean, and also to Russia, France, and England, was able to exert a greater influence. The effects of Venetian rule, which began in the 13th century, can be seen not only in the architecture, but also in its decidedly Western history of art and literature. Thus the Ionian Islands offered many Greek intellectuals and scholars a place of exile still within Greece, yet where they could escape the influence of Constantinople. In the 19th century, Empress Elisabeth of Austria had a palace built on Corfu, subsequently acquired by Emperor Wilhelm II. The Greek royal family frequently stayed here, and the British prince consort of Queen Elizabeth II, Philip, Duke of Edinburgh, was actually born on Corfu. The inhabitants of the Ionian Islands being inclined more toward the West than to their own mother country, they experienced fewer difficulties with the idea of European integration. And it should come as no surprise if a Venetian way of life, English tradition, and French *esprit* all combine to make Ionian cuisine one of the tastiest in Greece.

Ionian Island beef comes from animals that are reared totally naturally. That makes the butcher happy too.

POUTÍNGA

Tracking down this little known specialty may require some effort, because it is found only on the western islands. Attempts to find it throughout the rest of Greece will be in vain, from which you can perhaps conclude that English recipe books were behind the creation of this sweet dessert. *Poutínga* was originally a bread pudding served only in winter, when there was no fresh fruit. Now restaurants that are once again turning their attention to the local cuisine include *poutínga* in their menus all year round, and it meets with great success.

POUTÍNGA
Corfu bread pudding

1 tbsp butter
1 generous cup/250 g sugar
All-purpose flour
6–8 slices white bread
5 eggs
5 tsp vanilla sugar
3 generous cups/750 ml milk
1½ cups/200 g chopped walnuts
1¼ cups/200 g raisins
20 prunes, pitted and chopped
Grated zest of 1 unwaxed or well-scrubbed orange
Apricot jelly
Juice of ½ lemon

Preheat the oven to 350 ºF (180 ºC). Grease a loaf pan with butter, then sprinkle with sugar, then with flour. Line the base of the pan with half the white bread.
Beat the eggs in a bowl with the remaining sugar and the vanilla sugar until frothy. Stir in the milk, then add the raisins, prunes, grated orange zest, and half the chopped walnuts, and mix well.

First beat the eggs in a bowl with the sugar and vanilla sugar until frothy.

Then stir in the milk and add the raisins along with the pitted prunes.

Finally stir in half the chopped walnuts and the grated orange zest.

Pour the mixture into the loaf pan and cover with the remaining bread. Fill a large baking pan two-thirds of the way with boiling water, place the loaf pan in the water, and bake in a preheated oven for about 1 hour, until the creamy egg mixture has set and the bread is golden. Remove from the oven, leave to cool, cover, and place in a refrigerator overnight.

The next day, heat the apricot jelly with the lemon juice. Carefully turn the pudding out of the pan onto a large plate. Cover with the hot jelly and sprinkle with the remaining chopped walnuts. To serve, place a slice of bread pudding on a plate with a little apricot sauce.

Sprinkle the buttered loaf pan with sugar, then line the base with white bread.

Pour in the creamy egg and milk mixture and cover with a second layer of white bread.

When baked, turn the *poutinga* out onto a large plate, brush with apricot jelly, and sprinkle with chopped walnuts.

KRITHARÁKI

Your first taste of the Greek pasta called *Kritharáki* or *orzo* can be somewhat disconcerting: are you eating what you're seeing or what it tastes like? Do you have rice or pasta on your plate? As far as their ingredients are concerned, *kritharáki* are definitely pasta, because they are made of fine durum wheat semolina and water, kneaded to form a smooth dough. To make the pasta into its typical rice grain shape, the dough is pressed into specially made molds and dried for between eight and ten hours. They are carefully checked to make sure they are properly dry before being turned out, because it is vitally important that the pasta has lost every trace of moisture if they are to store well.

When it comes to cooking orzo, however, the method bears a much closer resemblance to that used for rice, because the pasta is boiled in exactly the amount of water that they are able to absorb. As a rule of thumb, put three parts water in a pan, salt it lightly and add the rice noodles as soon as it comes to a boil. Then simmer gently over a low heat until all the water has been absorbed. To make sure that they are correctly cooked, it is not so much the timing that is crucial, but rather the quantity of water and the cooking temperature – the Greeks think *kritharáki* is quite tricky to cook, and with good reason.

YOUVÉTSI ME ARNÁKI

Baked orzo with lamb
(Not illustrated)

½ cup + 1 tbsp/125 g butter
2 lbs/1 kg lamb, diced
1 large onion, finely chopped
4–5 tomatoes, skinned and puréed
½ tsp sugar
2½ cups/500 g kritharáki
1½ cups/100 g grated kefalotíri cheese
Salt
Freshly ground black pepper

Preheat the oven to 350 ºF (180 ºC). Melt the butter in a pan, fry the meat, then brown the onion. Add the tomatoes and sugar, then season with salt and pepper. Lower the heat, cover, and braise the meat for 1 hour. Remove from the heat and stir in the *kritharáki*. Half fill individual high-sided, flameproof dishes with this mixture, top up with hot water, and stir. Bake in the oven for 30–40 minutes. Shortly before the end of the cooking time, sprinkle with the cheese and bake until browned on top. Serve hot in the baking dishes.

YOUVÉTSI ME THALASSINÁ

Baked orzo with seafood
(Illustration opposite, above)
Serves 4–6

1 lb/500 g mussels
½ lb/250 g raw shrimp
½ cup + 1 tbsp/125 g butter
1 large onion, finely chopped
2 cloves of garlic, crushed
4–5 tomatoes, skinned and puréed
½ tsp sugar
2½ cups/500 g kritharáki
1¾ cups/200 g crumbled sheep's milk cheese
Salt
Freshly ground black pepper

Preheat the oven to 350 ºF (180 ºC). Wash and scrub the mussels, then boil in a little water until they open. Drain the mussels, collecting the juice, and set to one side. Discard any mussels that have not opened. Remove the mussel flesh and rinse carefully under running water. Wash the shrimp. Melt the butter in a skillet and fry the shrimp over a low heat until they turn pink. Add the onions and garlic, and fry until slightly softened. Add the tomatoes, mussels, and a little mussel juice; season with salt, pepper, and sugar, and braise for 10 minutes. Remove from the heat and stir in the *kritharáki*. Half fill individual high-sided, flameproof dishes with this mixture, top up with hot water, and stir. Bake in a preheated oven for 30–40 minutes. Shortly before the end of the cooking time, sprinkle the sheep's milk cheese evenly over the dishes and bake until browned on top. Serve in the baking dishes while still hot.

YOUVÉTSI ME LAKHANIKÁ
Baked orzo with vegetables
(Illustration right, below)
Serves 4–6

1 generous cup/250 ml Greek extra virgin olive oil
1 large onion, finely chopped
3 tomatoes, skinned and finely diced
1 stick celery, finely sliced
1 red bell pepper, seeded and finely chopped
2 cloves of garlic, finely sliced
4 cups/500 g kritharáki
8–12 keftedákia (see recipe on p. 111)
1¾ cups/200 g crumbled sheep's milk cheese
Salt
Freshly ground black pepper

Preheat the oven to 350 ºF (180 ºC). Heat the olive oil in a pan and fry the onions and garlic until softened. Add the tomatoes, celery, and bell pepper, then season with salt and pepper. Reduce the heat and cook the vegetables for 5 minutes. Remove from the heat and stir in the orzo. Half fill a high-sided flameproof dish with the vegetable and noodle mixture, top up with hot water, and stir. Bake in a preheated oven for about 1 hour. Shortly before the end of the cooking time, top with the *keftédes* and the crumbled sheep's milk cheese and leave in the oven for a few minutes to brown. Serve straight from the dish while still hot.

Cook the macaroni until *al dente*, then spread out half of it evenly in a baking pan and sprinkle with the grated *kefalotíri*.

Pour the prepared ground meat mixture evenly over the noodles and cheese to form the next layer. Cover with another layer of noodles and cheese.

For the béchamel sauce, make a roux and stir in warm milk. Remove the pan from the heat and stir in the eggs, cheese, nutmeg, and seasoning.

While still hot, pour the creamy sauce over the macaroni and bake in a preheated oven for 20–30 minutes until the top is browned.

PASTÍTSIO

Pasta dishes are firmly established in the cuisine of the Ionian Islands as part of their Italian heritage. That is why *pastítsio*, the most popular Greek noodle dish, is made particularly well here, with its macaroni shapes alternating with layers of ground meat, various vegetables, and grated cheese, all covered in a rich béchamel sauce. To the tourist, *pastítsio*, baked in the oven until golden brown and served hot, seems to stand apart from other Greek specialties such as *mousakás* (moussaka or eggplant bake) and *souvláki* (meat kebabs). Because it is more time-consuming to prepare than many other Greek recipes, this dish usually features in domestic menus only at the weekend, when people have more time to devote to cooking. And because *pastítsio* is undisputedly one of those dishes that become ever more flavourful each time they are reheated, the ingredients are usually measured to make enough to last for several days.

PASTÍTSIO
Ground meat and macaroni bake
Serves 4–6

1 scant cup/200 ml Greek extra virgin olive oil
2 large onions, finely chopped
1 lb/500 g ground beef
2–3 tomatoes, skinned, seeded, and diced
1 bay leaf
1 lb/500 g macaroni
1½ cups/150 of grated kefalotíri cheese
Salt
Freshly ground black pepper
Chopped fresh basil

For the béchamel sauce:
¼ cup/60 g butter
½ cup/60 g all-purpose flour
3 cups/750 ml warm milk
3 eggs, beaten
1 cup/100 g grated kefalotíri cheese
Grated nutmeg to taste
Salt
Freshly ground black pepper

Heat half the olive oil, soften the onions in it, then brown the meat. Add the tomatoes and bay leaf, together with some water. Season with salt and pepper and simmer for about 30 minutes. Cook the macaroni in boiling salted water until *al dente*, drain, and leave to cool. Combine the macaroni with the remaining oil, and spread half in a baking pan. Sprinkle with grated cheese, spread the meat sauce over the top, and cover with the remaining macaroni. Preheat the oven to 400 °F (200 °C). For the sauce, make a roux with the butter and flour, then gradually add the heated milk, stirring constantly. Remove the pan from the heat and stir in the eggs, grated cheese, leaving some for topping and season with nutmeg, salt and pepper, adding more warm milk if necessary. Pour the sauce over the macaroni and sprinkle with the remaining cheese. Bake in a preheated oven for about 20–30 minutes until browned on top. Remove from the oven, leave to cool slightly, and serve garnished with chopped basil.

Leeks are also a favorite vegetable on the Ionian Islands. They are grown in kitchen gardens as well as on an agricultural scale.

ONIONS AND LEEKS

In botanical terms, onions and leeks both belong to the same genus (*Allium*). Add to them garlic, and you have a trio that occupied the minds of numerous authors in classical times, who gave deep thought to their cultivation, propagation, uses, curative effects, and their differences, because onions are one of the first plants that human beings cultivated. There is evidence of different species of the plant that originated in the Middle East dating from about 5000 years ago. In Homer's time, leeks, *prasia*, were clearly such a common garden vegetable that in his *Odyssey*, the poet could speak of *prasia* when he meant a vegetable garden in general, and his listeners would understand him.

As for the onion rings that add flavor to so many dishes, hardly anyone gives a thought to the fact that another wonderful aspect of the plant is sacrificed for its culinary value. If left to grow into the summer, onions would produce flowers about 3 feet (1 meter) tall, the narrow stems bearing large, spherical umbels made up of numerous individual soft white or bright purple flowers. There is good reason why the onion belongs to the lily family. Leeks (*práso*) and onions (*kremídi*) are so closely related in Greek cuisine that they can be substituted for each other as desired, as fillings for phyllo dough, for example. Both are available throughout the year, and are easy to grow in the islands' moderate climate, because they make barely any demands on the soil; although

they appreciate having enough water, they can get by without it. But it is onions that are the most commonly found ingredient, because, unlike leeks, they serve two purposes at once: as a vegetable and as flavoring. In summer, onions appear fresh each day in the Greek country salad. They are present in vegetable stews, and they form a flavourful base for many sauces; Greek meatballs owe their texture in large part to puréed onions, and *stifádo*, a Greek national dish, would be unimaginable without onions. The piquant local dishes of the Ionian Islands get their characteristic spiciness from allicin, the essential oil contained in both onions and garlic. Apart from that, up to 8 percent of the edible parts of an onion is made up of sugar, and the higher the sugar content, the longer they can be stored. In this respect, this is a great advantage over the leek, which quickly withers, losing a large proportion of its vitamins, and is therefore best eaten soon after picking. Like onions, leeks contain numerous minerals and, most importantly of all, those antibacterial, sulfurous essential oils that also give the onion its infamously strong "bite," as well as its reputation as a natural antibiotic. These elements are believed to act as an expectorant when treating coughs, lung infections, and bronchial illnesses. Thus there could be some reason behind the rumors that Byzantine monks ate leeks to clear their vocal cords before a religious service, although the same effect would probably have been achieved if they had bitten into an onion.

Onions are so important in Greek cuisine that it would never cross anyone's mind to buy just a pound of them. They just don't bother with such small quantities.

MOSKHÁRI ME PRÁSA
Veal with leeks
(Illustration left)

1 scant cup/200 ml Greek extra virgin olive oil
2 lbs/1 kg lean veal, diced
1 large onion, finely chopped
1 scant cup/200 ml dry white wine
1 stick celery, finely chopped
2 lbs/1 kg leeks, cleaned and cut into pieces
2 eggs, beaten
1 tsp cornstarch, combined with 2 tbsp water
Juice of 1 lemon
Salt and freshly ground black pepper

Fry the meat and soften the onions in the olive oil. Add the wine and season with salt and pepper. Add a scant cup of water and simmer for 25 minutes. Remove the meat and set aside. Add the vegetables and season with salt and pepper. Add a scant cup of water and simmer for 20 minutes, then add the meat and simmer for a further 20 minutes. Combine the cornstarch and water mixture with the eggs, then stir in the lemon juice and meat stock alternately. Add this sauce to the pan, stirring constantly. Leave to stand for a few minutes and serve while still hot with freshly baked white bread.

PRASOSALÁTA
Leek salad
(Illustration center)

8 leeks, cleaned and cut into pieces
4 tbsp olive oil
2 cloves of garlic, finely sliced
4 tomatoes, finely diced
1 tsp chopped fresh thyme
6 tbsp dry white wine
Fresh thyme to garnish
Salt and freshly ground black pepper

Boil some salted water in a pan and simmer the leeks for 15 minutes until soft. Pour the water off and leave the leeks to drain. Heat the olive oil in a skillet and soften the garlic. Add the tomatoes, thyme, and white wine, reduce the heat, and simmer the sauce for 10 minutes until creamy, stirring constantly. Season with salt and pepper.
Arrange the leek pieces on a large plate, pour over the sauce, and garnish with fresh thyme. Serve while still warm with an accompaniment of freshly baked white bread.

KEFTEDÁKIA
Small meatballs
(Illustration bottom left)

¾ lb/400 g onions, peeled and quartered
4 slices of stale white bread, crusts removed
2 lbs/1 kg ground beef
4 tbsp Greek extra virgin olive oil
3 tbsp finely chopped mint
1 tbsp vinegar
1 tsp oregano
All-purpose flour
Oil for frying
Salt
Freshly ground black pepper

Purée the onions in a blender, add salt, leave to stand for a while to release water, then squeeze out well. Soften the bread in water, again squeeze out well, and knead briefly. Combine the onions and bread in a bowl together with the ground meat, olive oil, mint, vinegar, and oregano. Season with salt and pepper and knead thoroughly. Cover the bowl and leave to stand in a cool place. Heat some oil in a skillet, shape the meat mixture into small, round balls, coat in flour, and fry quickly. Serve with tomato sauce (see recipe on p. 119), rice, or baked potatoes.

FOOD JUST LIKE IO MAKES IT

KÓTSI YEMISTÓ
Pork knuckles with garlic

4 pork knuckles, skin removed
3 cloves of garlic, quartered
½ bunch of flat-leaved parsley
Butter
1 scant cup/200 ml Greek extra virgin olive oil
Salt
Freshly ground black pepper

Preheat the oven to 480 ºF (250 ºC). Wash the knuckles, pat dry, and score the meat deeply using a knife. Into each incision, insert a piece of garlic wrapped in a leaf of parsley, together with a little butter. Rub plenty of salt and pepper into the knuckles and place in a roasting pan with high sides. Pour the olive oil over the knuckles, put the pan in the oven, and fill two-thirds with water. Turn the oven down to 400 ºF (200 °C) and bake the knuckles for about 2–3 hours until the meat is cooked.

BOURDÉTO
Scorpion fish in tomato and paprika sauce

1 scant cup/200 ml Greek extra virgin olive oil
2 onions, peeled and grated
3 cloves of garlic, crushed
1 tsp sweet paprika
1 tsp ground red pepper
1 tbsp tomato paste
2 lbs/1 kg skórpios (scorpion fish)
Juice of ½ lemon
Salt

BOURDÉTO

Bourdéto is the name of this special sauce made from tomatoes and paprika, in which fish or some other main ingredient is braised. It is possibly a corruption of the Venetian word *brodetto*, meaning soup or stock. Corfu and Paxi are home to this type of dish.

Heat the olive oil, fry the garlic and onions until softened, and add the paprika and ground red pepper. Reduce the heat and stir in the tomato paste. Add a little water and bring to a boil. Add the fish, season with salt, cover with water, and simmer for 30 minutes. Transfer the fish to a large plate, and pour over it the sauce seasoned with salt and lemon juice.

TSOUKÁLI
Corfu pea purée

2 lbs/1 kg lathíri (tuberous bitter vetch peas: Lathyrus tuberosus)
1¼ cups/300 ml Greek extra virgin olive oil
3–4 large onions, finely chopped
Juice of 1 lemon
Salt

Soak the nut-sized dried tubers overnight. The next day, drain and boil with water in a covered pan until all the water has been absorbed. Do not add any salt until they are almost cooked. Purée the peas in a blender. Heat a scant ½ cup/100 ml olive oil in a skillet and fry the onions until softened. Add a scant cup of water and quickly bring to a boil. Stir the purée in with the onions and gradually incorporate the remaining olive oil. Season with salt and lemon juice.

Tsoukáli comes from southern Corfu and is eaten warm as well as cold. It can be served with meat and fish dishes, or more simply with white bread.

PASTITSÁDA VASILIKÍ
Ragout of pork with spaghetti

1 scant cup/200 ml Greek extra virgin olive oil
2 lbs/1 kg diced pork leg
6 large onions, finely chopped
10 cloves of garlic, finely chopped
1¼ cups/250 g tomatoes, skinned and diced
1 scant cup/200 ml dry white wine
1 bay leaf
2 cinnamon sticks
¼ tsp grated nutmeg
2 cloves
½ bunch flat-leaved parsley, finely chopped
3 sprigs basil
1 lb/500 g spaghetti
1½ cups/100 g grated kefalotíri cheese
Salt and freshly ground black pepper

Heat the olive oil in a pan, fry the meat, and soften the onions and garlic. Add the tomatoes and wine. Add the spices and pour in sufficient water to cover the meat well. Bring to a boil, reduce the heat, and simmer for about 1 hour until the meat is cooked. Meanwhile, cook the spaghetti, drain well, and toss in butter. Arrange the pasta on a large plate with the meat and sauce, sprinkle with the grated cheese and chopped parsley. Serve hot garnished with the basil sprigs.

BAKALIÁROS A BIANCO
Whiting with potato and garlic sauce

1 scant cup/200 ml Greek extra virgin olive oil
1 large onion, finely chopped
10 cloves of garlic, crushed
½ lb/200 g potatoes, grated
1 tsp oregano
1 bay leaf
1 whiting, about 3¼ lbs/1.5 kg, ready-prepared
Juice of 1 lemon
Lemon slices to garnish
Flat-leaved parsley to garnish
Salt
Freshly ground white pepper

Heat the olive oil in a fish pan, add the onions, and soften. Remove from the heat, add the garlic and grated potatoes, together with sufficient water to cover the mixture. Add the oregano and bay leaf and season with salt and pepper. Quickly bring to a boil, place the fish in the pan, then simmer for about 30 minutes. Transfer the fish to a large plate, add the lemon juice to the sauce, and pour over the fish. Garnish with the lemon slices and parsley, and serve immediately.

EGG DISHES

Although not eaten so much for breakfast, sliced hard-cooked eggs with a sprinkling of salt and pepper served on a slice of freshly baked white bread makes a simple, quick and satisfying snack in Greece. The omelet and scrambled egg recipes, which are served as a light lunch, garnished with bell peppers, parsley, tomatoes, sausage, bacon, or sometimes shrimp and other seafood, are slightly more complex. But no egg dish is complete without white bread, broken into pieces and dunked in olive oil.

OMELÉTA ME GARÍDES
Shrimp omelet

½ lb/250 g raw shrimp
½ cup/100 g butter
6 eggs
Flat-leaved parsley to garnish
Salt
Freshly ground black pepper

Wash the shrimp. Heat a little water in a pan, add salt, and boil the shrimp until they turn pink, then peel them and cut into pieces. Melt half the butter in a skillet, quickly fry the shrimp pieces, then remove from the heat. Melt the remaining butter in a second skillet. Beat the eggs in a bowl, season with salt and pepper, and pour into the skillet. Draw the flat side of a fork through the egg mixture several times and then leave to set. Scatter the shrimp pieces over the omelet and serve warm.

OMELÉTA KHORIÁTIKI
Country omelet

1 scant cup/200 ml Greek extra virgin olive oil
2 large onions, chopped
Salami type sausage, sliced
¼ lb/100 g olives, pitted and sliced
8 eggs
1¾ cups/200 g crumbled sheep's milk cheese
Salt
Freshly ground black pepper

Heat half the olive oil in a skillet and fry the onions, sausage slices, and olives. Season with salt and pepper, remove from the heat, and set aside. Beat the eggs in a bowl and season with salt and pepper. Heat the remaining olive oil in the skillet and pour in the beaten eggs. Draw the flat side of a fork through the egg mixture several times. Scatter with the onions, sausage, olives, and crumbled sheep's milk cheese. Serve as soon as the eggs have set and the cheese has melted.

STRAPATSÁDA
Scrambled eggs with bell pepper sauce

½ cup/100 g butter
8 eggs
A generous ⅔ cup/100 g crumbled sheep's milk cheese
1 tbsp finely chopped flat-leaved parsley
½ cup/125 ml bell pepper sauce (see recipe on p. 119)
Freshly ground black pepper

Melt the butter in a skillet. Beat the eggs in a bowl and stir in the cheese, parsley, and bell pepper sauce. Pour into the skillet and cook, stirring slowly with a wooden spoon. When the scrambled egg attains the desired consistency, sprinkle with freshly ground black pepper and serve.

OMELÉTA MIALÓ MOSKHARÍSIO
Calf's brain omelet

1 calf's brain
1 scant cup/200 ml Greek extra virgin olive oil
5 eggs
Flat-leaved parsley to garnish
Salt
Freshly ground black pepper

Remove the membranes from the brain, wash thoroughly, and leave to stand in cold water for 2 hours. Rinse again, pat dry, and cut into small pieces. Heat some of the olive oil in a skillet and fry the brain pieces for 3–4 minutes. Beat the eggs in a bowl and season with salt and pepper. Heat the remaining olive oil in the skillet, and pour in the beaten eggs. Draw the flat side of a fork through the egg mixture several times. Arrange the fried brain pieces on top and remove from the heat as soon as the eggs set. Transfer to plates, sprinkle with parsley, and serve hot.

From top to bottom: *Omeléta me garídes* – Shrimp omelet; *Omeléta khoriátiki* – Country omelet; *Strapatsáda* – Scrambled eggs with bell pepper sauce; *Omeléta mialó moskharísio* – Calf's brain omelet

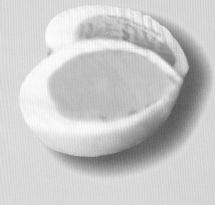

AVGOLÉMONO

As its name suggests, this sauce, which always comes as a surprise to non-Greeks, is made from nothing but fresh eggs and lemons, with the occasional addition of a little sour cream. But do not underestimate its importance. For the Greeks, *avgolémono* is more than just a sauce. It is used to thicken soups and gives dishes a refreshing, decidedly lemony flavor.

AVGOLÉMONO 1
Egg and lemon sauce

2 eggs, separated
Juice of 2 lemons
2 generous cups warm stock from the main dish

Beat the egg whites with a pinch of salt until stiff. Beat in the egg yolks and add the lemon juice and stock, stirring constantly. Add the sauce to the slightly cooled dish and fold in carefully. Do not allow to cook any further!

AVGOLÉMONO 2

2 egg yolks
2 tbsp cornstarch
Juice of 2 lemons
2 generous cups warm stock from the main dish
1 tbsp cold butter

First combine the egg yolks, cornstarch, and lemon juice with a little of the stock in a bowl suspended over a pan of barely simmering water. Gradually add the remaining stock, stirring constantly. Add the pieces of cold butter one by one. Do not allow the water to boil, as this will make the sauce curdle.

KRÉMA AVGOLÉMONO
Egg and lemon sauce with cream

3 egg yolks
3½ tbsp/50 ml lemon juice
2 tbsp cornstarch, combined with water
2 generous cups warm stock from the main dish
½ cup sour cream

Beat the egg yolks, gradually pour in the lemon juice, and stir in the cornstarch and stock. Add the sour cream and stir well, then pour the sauce into the dish and fold in carefully.

Left: Ingredients for *avgolémono* (clockwise around the finished sauce): beaten egg whites, lemon juice, egg yolk, stock.

SAUCES

Two basic ingredients stand out in Greek sauces: lemons and eggs. No other European cuisine embraces this combination as enthusiastically as Greek cuisine. However, garlic and olive oil come a close second in the pop charts of sauce dishes. Vinegar, on the other hand, is treated rather unkindly, and is generally served only in a few Greek soups, usually those containing leguminous vegetables. Lemon juice is without peer. It not only gives summer salads their freshness and additional vitamin C, but also neutralizes the fat in dishes, making them easier to digest. The Greeks just love pure lemon juice in sauces, and simply on grilled fish or meat. *Avgolémono*, egg and lemon sauce, and *ladolémono*, oil and lemon sauce, are standard Greek favorites. There are many variations, especially of *avgolémono*, because it is not a finished sauce in the true sense, but is used as a thickening agent, and the final result varies depending on the liquid it is being used to thicken. One common permutation of the egg-lemon sauce even includes chopped green peppercorns (see illustration 5, right).

CORFU OLIVES

The oldest living "inhabitants" of the Ionian Islands are the olive trees. Many of them were planted as long ago as the Venetian era and still tirelessly bear fruit, which is then pressed to produce valuable olive oil throughout the year. Nearly all the green groves on Corfu are planted with olive trees, which have a somewhat melancholy air with their slender, trailing branches.

SÁLTSA DOMÁTA ME KIMÁ
Tomato and ground meat sauce (1)

⅓ cup/80 ml Greek extra virgin olive oil
1 onion, grated
2 cloves of garlic, finely chopped
1 lb/500 g ground meat (beef, pork, or lamb)
2 lbs/1 kg tomatoes, peeled, seeded, and finely diced
1 tsp oregano
1 tsp sugar
1 bunch flat-leaved parsley, finely chopped
3 sprigs mint, finely chopped
Salt
Freshly ground black pepper

Heat the olive oil in a pan. Add the onion, garlic, and ground meat, and fry, pressing down on the ground meat with the back of a large spoon. Add the tomatoes, oregano, and sugar, and season with salt and pepper. Reduce the heat, cover, and simmer the sauce for about 1 hour. Finally, stir in the chopped parsley and mint, and season again with salt and pepper. The sauce goes well with pasta and rice, but is also good for baked dishes such as *pastítsio* and *mousakás*.

LADOLÉMONO
Oil and lemon sauce (2)

2 parts Greek extra virgin olive oil
1 part lemon juice
Finely chopped flat-leaved parsley (optional)
Salt
Freshly ground black pepper

Beat together the olive oil and lemon juice (add the parsley if using), and season with salt and pepper.
Ladolémono is used as a sauce for boiled vegetables, grilled fish, and seafood.

SÁLTSA DOMÁTA
Tomato sauce (3)

⅓ cup/80 ml Greek extra virgin olive oil
1 small onion, grated
1–2 cloves of garlic, crushed
2 lbs/1 kg tomatoes, peeled, seeded, and
finely diced
1 tbsp vinegar
½ tsp sugar
½ bunch flat-leaved parsley, finely chopped
Salt
Freshly ground black pepper

Heat the olive oil in a pan and fry the onion and garlic until softened. Add the tomatoes, vinegar, and sugar, and season with salt and pepper. Reduce the heat, cover, and leave the sauce to cook until it has thickened and taken on a smooth consistency. Finally stir in the parsley.

This sauce will keep for a long time in a refrigerator if poured into preserving jars, topped with a little olive oil, and sealed. It is good for pasta and baked dishes, but also for many meat and fish dishes.

SÁLTSA PIPERIÁS
Bell pepper sauce (4)

2 lbs/1 kg red bell peppers
1 scant cup/200 ml Greek extra virgin olive oil
Generous 4 lbs/2 kg tomatoes, skinned, seeded,
and finely diced
8 cloves of garlic, finely chopped
½ bunch flat-leaved parsley, finely chopped
¼ tsp ground red pepper
Salt
Freshly ground black pepper

Preheat the oven to 480 °F (250 °C). Wash and dry the peppers, then place on a shelf in the oven. Roast until the skin blisters and turns black in places. Take the peppers out of the oven and remove the skin, stem, seeds, and white membranes, then cut into thin strips. Heat the olive oil in a pan and fry the tomatoes until softened. Stir in the garlic and parsley, and season with salt and pepper. Reduce the heat, cover, and cook the sauce until it takes on a smooth consistency. Add the strips of pepper and season with the ground red pepper, salt, and black pepper. Remove from the heat and leave to stand for a few minutes, then pour into large preserving jars. The sauce will keep for a reasonably long time if stored in a refrigerator. It goes well with pasta or can be used as a base for various braised dishes.

AN ANCIENT RECIPE FOR CUMIN SAUCE (5)

⅔ cup/150 ml white wine vinegar
⅔ cup/150 ml white wine
2 tbsp/30 ml fish sauce (available from
Asian delicatessens)
4 tbsp clear honey
1 tsp ground cumin
1 tsp finely chopped mint
2 tsp finely chopped parsley
1 tsp finely chopped lovage (or celery leaves)
1 bay leaf
Freshly ground black pepper

Put all the ingredients in a skillet and repeatedly bring to a boil. The sauce is ready when it has thickened slightly. It can be served with fish and meat dishes, but also goes very well with potatoes, dumplings, and pasta.

YAOÚRTI ME SKÓRDO
Yogurt and garlic sauce (6)

1 cup/250 g yogurt
2 cloves of garlic, crushed
2 tbsp Greek extra virgin olive oil
2 tbsp finely chopped dill or parsley
Salt
Freshly ground black pepper

First place the yogurt in a cloth, leave to drain, and then squeeze out any residual liquid. Combine the yogurt with the garlic and olive oil in a bowl. Season with salt and pepper and leave to stand in a cool place. Just before serving, stir in dill or parsley. This sauce is good with fried vegetables (for example eggplant and zucchini), but is also a popular accompaniment to roast meat or fish dishes.

BARBOÚNI

It has become just as expensive as it is rare, but every summer broiled *barboúni* still makes an appearance on the menus of Greece's seaside tavernas. Like all fish, no matter how it is cooked, whether fried or baked, the Greek red mullet (*Mullus barbatus*) tastes best fresh from the sea. The Greeks prefer it just lightly or well broiled and drizzled with lemon juice. It is served with all types of salad and the compulsory freshly baked bread.

Red mullet can be up to 12 inches (30 centimeters) long and weigh about four and a half pounds (2 kilograms), but fish this size are seldom caught. The fish that makes it to a plate in a restaurant is rarely bigger than 8 inches (20 centimeters). All along the Mediterranean coast, the delicate white, almost boneless flesh of this tasty fish makes a popular light summer meal. For this is precisely the season when mullet, who live in small shoals, spend more time on the seabed beneath the shallow waters near the coast. Here they grub through the seabed looking for invertebrate sea creatures, sucking the sand into their mouths like a vacuum cleaner, filtering their food out, before expelling the waste through their gills. The two forked barbs on the fish's "chin" are an essential tool in this quest for food, as they are equipped with sensory and taste organs to seek out the buried prey.

BARBOÚNI PSITÓ
Grilled red mullet
(Illustration right)

8 large red mullet
Juice of 2 lemons
1 scant cup/200 ml Greek extra virgin olive oil
1 bunch flat-leaved parsley, freshly chopped
½ tsp oregano
Salt
Freshly ground black pepper

Scale, clean, and thoroughly wash the fish, then leave to drain. Rub the fish inside and out with salt and pepper. Combine the lemon juice and olive oil, and brush some over the fish. Grill the fish on both sides on a barbecue until cooked. Combine the remaining oil and lemon dressing with the chopped parsley and a little oregano and serve with the fish, together with a salad and freshly baked white bread.

MORE MEMBERS OF THE MULLET FAMILY

Striped red mullet (*Mullus surmuletus*): This fish is found in the Black Sea, the English Channel, and as far away as Senegal, the Azores, Madeira, and the Canary Islands, as well as the Mediterranean, thus sharing its habitat with the red mullet. It is very tasty, especially the smaller fish.

West African Goatfish (*Pseudopeneus prayensis*): Unlike the real mullets, this fish, called spiny mullet in some languages, lives solely in the western Mediterranean. Its flesh is tougher and is best fried.

BARBOÚNIA ME DOMÁTA
Red mullet in tomato sauce

8 large red mullet
All-purpose flour seasoned with salt and pepper
1 generous cup/250 ml Greek extra virgin olive oil
4 tomatoes, skinned and passed through a sieve
1 clove garlic, finely chopped
A generous ½ cup/125 ml dry white wine
Juice of 1 lemon
Salt
Freshly ground black pepper

Scale, clean, and thoroughly wash the fish, then leave to drain. Rub the inside with salt. Toss the fish in the seasoned flour. Heat half the olive oil in a skillet, fry the fish, and remove from the heat. Heat the remaining olive oil in a pan and fry the garlic until softened. Add the sieved tomatoes, bring to a boil, and pour in the wine. Season with salt and pepper, and simmer over a low heat for about 30 minutes. Preheat the oven to 350 °F (180 °C). Place the fish in a roasting pan, pour over the tomato sauce, and bake in the oven for about 15 minutes. Transfer to a large plate, drizzle with lemon juice, and serve with freshly baked white bread.

BARBOÚNIA MARINÁTA
Marinated red mullet
(Illustration below)

8 large red mullet
All-purpose flour
1 generous cup/250 ml Greek extra virgin olive oil
1 sprig fresh rosemary
8 cloves of garlic, crushed
1 tsp sugar
½ bunch flat-leaved parsley, finely chopped
Salt
Freshly ground black pepper

For the egg and lemon sauce:
2 eggs
Juice of 2 lemons

Scale, clean, and thoroughly wash the fish, then leave to drain. Rub the fish inside and out with salt and toss in flour. Heat the olive oil in a skillet, and fry the fish. Remove from the skillet, pass the frying oil through a fine strainer, then return the oil to the skillet. Beat the eggs, stir in the lemon juice, and combine with the slightly cooled oil. Add the rosemary and garlic, season with salt and pepper, and do not allow the sauce to cook further. Stir in the sugar, place the fried fish in the sauce, and leave to rest for just a few minutes. Transfer to a large plate and sprinkle with parsley. Serve slightly cooled with freshly baked white bread.

Meat near at hand that can be inspected by the customer will be of the best quality. That is why throughout opening hours, every available piece of meat hangs from large hooks in full view or right at the entrance to the butcher's store.

ISLAND BEEF

Beef is undeniably the favorite in Ionian Island cuisine. Influenced by the Italian roasting tradition, unusual beef dishes have developed here with a surprisingly spicy, sometimes even cinnamon flavor. At the same time, the cattle on the Ionian Islands seem to lead a very secluded life. They are seldom seen even in the higher pastures in the heart of the mountains, where the farmers prefer to raise their cattle. It is therefore all the more surprising to find the copious supply of beef that you can admire every day at the butcher's store, because, as far as beef goes, the Ionians are thoroughly spoiled. It has to be hung exactly right and should be slightly marbled with fat before homemakers or restaurant owners will even look at it. Here on this Greek archipelago, large ranches are quite rare, and the beef cattle are basically fed a natural diet, its basic ingredients being thoroughly safe: ground corn, ground sugar beet, soy flour, barley, wheat, and *pitíri*, which is the residue from grinding wheat. Apart from that, the beef cattle on the Ionian Islands are left to grow for eighteen months longer and are not "fed" any hormones whatsoever. The proof is in the eating, with traditional dishes often being prepared even in the restaurants: succulent meat with a distinctive flavor, powerful, but not in the least tough.

Butchers on the Ionian Islands are housed rather inconspicuously in the narrow alleyways. They are usually small, with the entire supply being squeezed into the small space. The range is not as extensive as in the major Greek cities, but in exchange you know exactly which farm the slaughtered animal comes from and the conditions in which it was reared.

SOFRÍTO

The delicious aroma of braised meat seems to pervade every taverna in the Ionian Islands, because the dish with the Italian sounding name *sofríto*, which has become a trademark of Corfu, is now a specialty famed well beyond its regional boundaries. Every restaurant of any standing includes it on its menu, and every chef swears by his own recipe. One thing everyone does agree on, however, is the meat: to make the best *sofríto*, you must use rump beef or veal, and it is critical that it is cooked to perfection. It goes without saying that the chefs on Corfu are totally convinced that only genuine Corfu people can prepare good *sofríto*.

SOFRÍTO
Veal in garlic and wine sauce

4 slices rump veal, each ¾-in/2-cm thick
All-purpose flour
1 scant cup/200 ml Greek extra virgin olive oil
4 cloves of garlic, thinly sliced
½ bunch flat-leaved parsley, finely chopped
2 bay leaves
1 scant cup/200 ml dry white wine
Salt
Freshly ground black pepper

Pound the meat and coat in flour. Heat the olive oil in a heavy-bottomed pan and fry the meat. Add the garlic, parsley, and bay leaves, and season with salt and pepper. Increase the heat and fry for a few minutes, then add the white wine. Add sufficient water to cover all the ingredients, reduce the heat, cover, and simmer until the meat is tender. Serve with baked or mashed potatoes, or rice.

Good *sofríto* requires relatively few ingredients, but they must be of top quality: meat, wine, olive oil, garlic, and spices.

First the slices of meat, initially ¾-inch (2 cm) thick, are patiently pounded until they are half as thick.

Quickly coat the thin slices of veal in flour before frying to prevent them from sticking or drying out too quickly.

As soon as the olive oil is really hot, add the flour-coated meat slices and quickly brown on both sides.

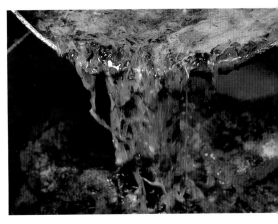

To serve, arrange the meat and accompaniment, in this case rice, on a plate (left), and pour over the white wine, herb, and spice sauce (above).

CULT OF THE SNAKE

In Arginia, a small hill village on Cephalonia, a spectacle shrouded in mystery takes place on August 15 each year at the feast of the Ascension of the Blessed Virgin Mary: the return of the "snakes of the mother of God." Each year everyone impatiently awaits their coming, because their arrival is a good omen, and if they do not come, it is said that something terrible will happen. The snakes are there during the mass in the church and are passed from hand to hand, to protect people against disease and evil. No one is afraid of them, and the animals seem to sense that and have no fear of the people. But by August 16 each year, all the snakes – which in mythology are viewed with ambivalence, just think of the Asclepian snake or the snake of paradise that was vanquished by Mary – have vanished as if by magic…

Arethousa Spring: fruity Agiorgitiko red wine.

Robola Metaxas: dry, yellow-green white wine.

Gentilini Robola: white wine from Cosmetatos winery.

Gentilini Classico: light, refreshing country wine.

Gentilini fumé: white wine with a slightly smoky note.

Gentilini cuvée exceptionelle: top quality white wine

The best growing area for the white Robola grape lies at the foot of Mount Enos, 5340 feet/1628 meters high. The head office of the Cephalonia winegrowers' cooperative is at the nearby monastery of Agios Gerassimos.

ROBOLA

It is considered the best, but also the most beautiful grape in Greece, because the Robola grape is a rapid grower and forms large, plump, pale yellow berries. The fresh fruity citrus aroma of the full-bodied straw-colored wine they produce is described as peerless. The origins of the Robola grape do not lie as far back in the past as the other Greek grapes. It is probably the same as the Gialla Ribolla of the Italian region of Friuli, or the Slovenian Rebula or their antecedents, and was introduced to the Ionian Islands by the Venetians at the end of the 13th century.

The main growing area for this grape is on the island of Cephalonia, but it is also found in smaller vineyards on the other Ionian Islands such as Corfu, Levkás, and Zákinthos. Like all Greek vines, which can thrive only in special soil conditions, the beautiful Robola grape seems to have taken a liking to the conditions found on the Ionian Islands. The winegrowers on Cephalonia devote about 750 acres (300 hectares) to the Robola grape, which thrives best on dry, less fertile mountain slopes with low rainfall. Each year, these grapes produce 264,000 gallons (10,000 hectoliters) of wine, which says something for the extremely high yield of the grape. Three wines have the O.P.A.P. protected mark of origin, the equivalent of the French A.O.C. Robola wines are usually sold under the name "Robola of Cephalonia."

When the harvested grapes are delivered to the winery, everyone has to help unload them, because the grapes need to be pressed with some urgency.

All the juice quickly flows from the plump green Robola grapes. The skins are left behind, as they would darken the wine.

This is still grape juice, but it is soon to be wine: this picture shows the must flowing into the barrel.

PROPOLIS

Propolis (or bee glue), which a beekeeper on Ithaca has been producing for years, is one of the oldest remedies in the world, and even now no harmful side effects have been discovered. The people of eastern and southern Europe have long known the benefits of *propolis*, and it enjoys greater respect there than it does in the West. The actual work of obtaining *propolis* is done by the bees. They collect resins from pine trees, but also from the buds of birch, alder, and poplar trees, and ferment them using their own bodily secretions to form a hard, brown, antiseptic mass. Plants also secrete these resins to seal wounds and to protect themselves against bacterial infections and fungal infestations, and even the bees use its antimicrobial properties. They use it to compact the beeswax produced from digesting flower nectar, and then use the beeswax to construct the honeycombs for rearing their young. The walls of the honeycombs where the queen lays her eggs are sometimes painted with *propolis* inside and even sealed with it. This protects the breeding colony against disease and guarantees survival. There is also extraneous matter that can harm the swarm, so it is used to coat defective points, preventing leaks and acting like heat insulation in winter. It is thus a useful tool for the bee state: *pro polis.*

WHAT PROPOLIS CONTAINS

Iron, copper, calcium, aluminum, vanadium, silicon, strontium, manganese, zinc, vitamin B1, vitamin B5, pro-vitamin A, resins, wax, essential oils, honey pollen, and tanning agents in various proportions

Removing the hard bee glue from the honeycombs set in wooden frames is a time-consuming task. At 61–66 °F (16–19 °C), *propolis* is brittle and is easy to grind. It does not regain its elasticity until it reaches a temperature of 97–100 °F (36–38 °C). In antiquity, *propolis* was used only in ointments to heal wounds and bruising, but today it is available in powder, tablet, and granular form, as a paste and as a tincture. Its uses have increased too. *Propolis* strengthens the immune system, reduces inflammation, especially of the gums or in various skin complaints, and acts as an analgesic. In the case of infections, it is a proven detoxifier and can increase the antimicrobial effect of all known antibiotics. It has a regenerative effect on bones, muscles, and nerves.

Propolis is often confused with royal jelly. But whereas the former is a "raw material" obtained from nature, the other is a substance secreted by nurse bees and used to raise the queen bees.

Above: It is a long journey from the plants that secrete the resin, via the bees who collect it and whose secretions transform it into *propolis*, to the beekeeper, who has the troublesome task of removing it from the honeycombs (right).

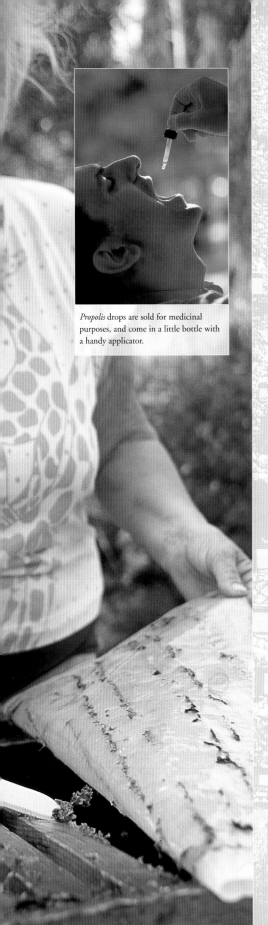

Propolis drops are sold for medicinal purposes, and come in a little bottle with a handy applicator.

ROYAL JELLY

Really miraculous qualities are attributed to the queen bee's nutritious juice or royal jelly, because it turns an ordinary bee larva into a queen bee. The so-called nurse bees produce it in their food glands, mixing it with a little of the secretion from the glands in their upper jaw. It is fed to some bee larvae by the nurse bees, while the larvae from other beehives are fed nutritious liquid from the worker and drone bees. The queen larvae get royal jelly throughout their entire development period, and the fully-grown queen needs it all her life. Perhaps it is just the quality and quantity of the wonder juice that they are fed —a queen bee cell has 200–400 mg as opposed to 2–4 mg in a worker bee cell – that turns a larva into a queen, or there may be an extra juvenile hormone. However that may be, royal jelly has always fired the human imagination, and people have attributed health promoting effects that must be related to the proportions of trace elements and the vitamins it contains. Royal jelly is obtained by using the bee swarm's instinct to attract a new queen when it has lost the old one. The first thing to do is to produce as many new queen bee cells as possible, from which the valuable substance can then be extracted using a pipette.

Right: *Propolis* is mixed with alcohol in a jar, which is then shaken repeatedly until the *propolis* eventually dissolves. The alcohol extract is poured off, filtered, and diluted before being sold as a remedy.

HONEY IN ANTIQUITY

The earliest definite evidence of beekeeping in Greece was found in Akrotíri on Santorini, the Thera of classical times. This town was destroyed and buried by the volcanic eruption around 1600 B.C. Excavations there unearthed the remains of a beehive. In classical times, Aristotle's zoological writings contain detailed descriptions of how the flavor of honey depends on the flowers the bees visit and prefer. In antiquity, honey was first and foremost a luxury culinary item. It was used to sweeten foods and drinks, but also to preserve fruit and vegetables. Dishes involving sauces sweetened with honey were considered a delicacy. Honey was combined with grape must and then diluted with water. Another specialty was mulse, a wine, usually an old one, sweetened with

honey. It was a popular aperitif, as well as a remedy, because honey was thought to have a general prophylactic effect. It was also used in the preparation of ointments and various medicines.

Honey played a major role in mythology and various cults. On Crete, bees are said to have brought food to the young Zeus. Honey was sacrificed to the gods of the underworld, Hades and Persephone, and was included in graves as a burial good, being viewed as a symbol for crossing over to another world. It was also a symbol of the Golden Age, a future full of promise. Beeswax was used to make small figurines for the sculptural metal-casting technique as well as in the manufacture of writing tablets.

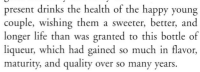

The sweet syrup in kumquat *glikó* creates an interesting contrast with the slightly bitter fruits.

Above: the dwarf orange is one of many examples of botanic colonialism throughout the entire world, because without human intervention this plant, indigenous to China, would never have reached Corfu.

Below: the "wedding liqueur" is associated with a custom that spans the generations.

KUMQUAT

If on Corfu you come across red, yellow, green, or blue bottles of liqueur, then you are on the trail of a plant (and its fruit and a traditional liqueur process) that is extremely rare to Europe, for with the exception of Corfu, it is found only in Asia. The kumquat, also called dwarf orange, better known as a small ornamental tree, is an evergreen, slightly prickly shrub. It thrives in conditions similar to those required for growing oranges (which belong to the same genus within the citrus fruit family). They tolerate stony soil and like sun in summer and rain in winter.

In 1846, the English botanist, Robert Fortune, who gave the kumquat its Latin name, *Fortunella*, brought the plant, originally indigenous to southeast China and Indochina, to Europe as an ornamental shrub. The British soon brought it to Corfu, where it became happily established. Since then, these attractive fruits, which now grow primarily in the subtropical regions of China and Japan, but also in Africa and America, have also grown in Corfu. Greek kumquats are known only in western Greece, and are only readily available fresh on the markets of the Ionian Islands.

Greek kumquat fruits, which should be eaten as fresh as possible, are about the size of small

THE AKHÍLLION

When Elisabeth, Empress of Austria and Queen of Hungary, visited Corfu for the first time in 1861, she was so enchanted by the landscape with its olive, lemon, and orange groves that she stayed on the island for more than a month. Yet she did not make a second trip to Corfu until 1885. In the interim, her mind had been much occupied with antiquity, and she had learned ancient and modern Greek. When she was shown the old Venetian Villa Braila at Gasturi, which was for sale, she was instantly inspired. Two years later she bought the villa and had it converted into a mini-castle based on the architecture of Pompeii. She named it after her favorite classical hero, Achilles. Until her violent death, the empress came regularly to the *Akhíllion* that she had thought of as her retirement home. In 1907, Emperor Wilhelm II acquired the estate. Today visitors can see the garden, the imperial chapel, and a small museum with memorabilia belonging to the two rulers.

mandarin oranges, and have a thin, golden-yellow to reddish-orange edible rind. They do not store well, and are therefore usually preserved by being candied or made into jelly. These bitter, acidic fruits are also used as the base for various spirits and liqueurs from Corfu. The pure kumquat essence distilled from the fruit juice is colorless, but the product is dyed all sorts of wonderful colors. On Corfu there is another tradition that is associated with kumquat liquor: It is thought of as the drink for newlyweds, but it is also the custom to buy a bottle on the occasion of the birth of the first child and to keep it until that child's marriage. Only then is it opened with great ceremony and every one present drinks the health of the happy young couple, wishing them a sweeter, better, and longer life than was granted to this bottle of liqueur, which had gained so much in flavor, maturity, and quality over so many years.

Above: one of the manufacturer's ideas to promote sales is to allow sugar crystals to develop in the liqueur.

Background: kumquat distillate is color-less, but the liqueur comes in many colors.

ΗΠΕΙΡΟΣ

Above: Métsovon, a charming small mountain village famous for its cheese.
Background: Epirus is still considered a rather impregnable region of Greece.

EPIRUS

Milk for yogurt

Beef cattle

Country sausage

Variety meats, or offal

Cheese in Métsovon

Píta

Phyllo pastry

Fishing in Lake Pamvótis

Lots of frogs…

Shrimp

The hunting season

Epirus in northwestern Greece is still one of the lesser known regions that has not yet opened its doors wide to industry or tourism. Bounded on the west by Albania and the Ionian Sea, yet having no economically important port there, and on the east by the high Píndos mountain range, Epirus has always been an isolated, almost impregnable region. Corinthian settlers on the Ionian Islands simply called the unknown land over the water Epirus, meaning nothing more than "mainland." Epirus made its first appearance on the stage of ancient history when the Epriot king's daughter Olympia married the Macedonian king, Philip II, in 357 B.C. In the Middle Ages, Wallachian shepherd tribes came over the Píndos mountains and on into Epirus. There was even some migration between Greece and Albania. Under Ottoman rule, many Albanians made out they were pro-Islamic. Yet it was actually the Albanian provincial governor, Ali Pasha, who, from his palace in Ioánnina, allegedly tried to set up an area under joint Albanian–Greek rule and independent of Istanbul between 1788 and 1822. In the Ottoman era, Greek freedom fighters withdrew to Epirus, attracted by its impenetrability, although this did nothing to hasten independence, which was achieved in 1913. The inward-looking attitude necessitated by the region's geography has always helped the population to be self-sufficient, even when times were hard. The wealth of game in the mountains was a great help. Today, Epirus has the largest association of hunting clubs in Greece – and with good reason. The region's numerous lakes and the Ionian Sea also guarantee plentiful supplies of fresh fish, and there are few important agricultural products that do not thrive on the fertile soils of the small valleys in the heart of the region. In addition, Epirus has a superbly organized dairy industry and, unlike elsewhere in Greece, livestock farming is not restricted to sheep and goats. Indeed, pig and beef cattle farming take priority. A quick glance at a few recipes of the mountain dwellers or the culinary customs at the annual folk and fishing festivals is enough to prove that, like its people, the cuisine has retained its independence.

The brightly colored costumes and headdresses remind the older Epirus women of their own past. For young women, they represent at best a bit of tradition worth hanging on to.

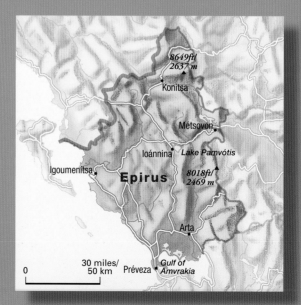

8649ft/
2637 m

Konitsa

Métsovon

Ioánnina   Lake Pamvótis

Igoumenítsa

Epirus   8018ft/
2469 m

Arta

0   30 miles/
50 km   Préveza   Gulf of
Amvrakia

MILK FOR YOGURT

In Greece, it is only relatively recently that yogurt has become readily available in supermarkets, prepackaged in small cartons. In the towns, you used to be able to buy it from the local dairy in the same way as milk, whereas in the country, people preferred to get their milk straight from the farmer and make their own yogurt at home. The advantage of this milk was that it had all the lactic acid bacteria needed to make good yogurt. Although pasteurized milk, in other words milk that has been heated to a maximum temperature of 165 ºF (74 ºC), does keep, it is no longer suitable for making yogurt, unless coagulants are added. As far as the spontaneous souring of the milk is concerned, the Greeks had in some ways always been in just the right place, because one of the bases of yogurt is *Lactobazillus bulgaricus*, a special lactic acid culture that, as its name implies, is found not far away. It has the special quality of curdling only certain milk proteins, thus having a beneficial effect on the flavor and acid content of the yogurt. With milk fresh from the cow, the right spores in the air, a warm day, and sufficient time, you would be hard pushed not to make perfect yogurt. Today, even in the rural regions of Greece, when making homemade yogurt, people still think it advisable to boil up the milk first and then leave it to cool, before stirring in some of the previous batch of yogurt as a starter culture, and leaving the pan to stand in a warm place.

As milk producers, cows are undisputedly one of the most important domestic animals in Greece, but the systematic farming of dairy cows on any large scale is still very recent here. The countryside has always been home to some farmers who kept dairy cows for their own consumption. But even just a generation ago, Greece used to import a large part of its total milk requirement from Holland. In the last few years, the Greek government has set about a better organization of the regional dairy industry by developing or supporting it with state incentive programs. A region such as Epirus would seem particularly well suited to this plan. Half of its pastures are in mountain areas and provide nutritious, healthy fodder, while its many streams provide clear, clean water. The climatic conditions are also ideal for keeping cows outdoors. As a result, Epirus is now home to the largest milk processing company in Greece. "Dodoni" now exports its products to 18 countries and is one of the most successful companies of its kind in the entire country.

Above: milk products from Epirus have a reputation throughout Greece for being the tastiest. They are successfully marketed both at home and abroad by one of the biggest companies in the country. Background: when combined with the yogurt cultures, the milk must be left to stand "undisturbed" at a constant temperature for at least 12 hours if it is to set.

The first thing to do when making homemade yogurt is to heat the fresh milk.

A glass "magic disc" is placed on the base of the pan to prevent the milk from boiling over.

With a little practice, you no longer need a thermometer to tell when the milk has cooled sufficiently.

A small amount of yogurt from a previous batch is added to the tepid milk as a starter culture.

Everyone knows yogurt with muesli and honey is nourishing, but in Greece it is mainly eaten during the fasting period. In summer, yogurt and honey are usually mixed with fresh fruit.

BEEF CATTLE

In ancient Greek cuisine, beef was used with restraint, which is odd, as it was not only prized, but also readily available. Like all the old advanced civilizations, the Greeks knew how to rear beef cattle, and owning large herds guaranteed a community's survival. Beef cattle were also easy to keep, because, like other domesticated animals, they grazed on the meadows, having only the protection of the herdsmen and the gods. And they needed it too, because time and again, whole herds of cattle are mentioned as war booty. Beef cattle were used as working animals, as can be seen from Greek vase pictures, where oxen appear yoked to the plow.

Oxen had a special role in cult worship and sacrifices often began with the slaughter of an ox. In the *Odyssey*, all the rituals surrounding such a sacrifice are described in detail. Red wine was poured over the best piece, the leg, which was wrapped in fat and burnt on an open wood fire as an offering to the gods. The entrails, however, and the remaining pieces of meat were cut up, threaded on skewers, roasted on the fire, and eaten almost picnic-fashion. If an urban family found an excuse to sacrifice an animal, it could hire a specialist (*mageiros*), who would not only expertly slaughter and sacrifice the creature, but also prepare its meat for the celebrations. The reason behind beef's rare appearance in recipes perhaps lies in the amount of fresh meat obtained from a fully-grown slaughtered ox. In 400 B.C. you did not have the option of freezing it, so it had to be dealt with all at once.

Today, the rising number of aspiring, government-subsidized cattle farms is in stark contrast to the falling number of self-sufficient small farms and smallholdings in rural areas. But despite this, the sight of cattle grazing peacefully and confidently on lush meadows, knowing no electric fences, and standing directly in front of you in isolated country lanes is still typical of Greek beef farming, especially in Epirus.

This region has a wealth of interesting recipes that suggest ways of using every part of a steer. The favorite way of cooking meat in the rather isolated mountain villages of Epirus is to braise it in a large pan with the addition of a variety of herbs and spices.

MOSKHÁRI ME ELIÉS
Beef with olives
(Illustration opposite left)

1 scant cup/200 ml Greek extra virgin olive oil
2 lbs/1 kg beef, cut into large cubes
1 onion, finely chopped
1 scant cup/200 ml red wine
2 tomatoes, finely diced
2 cloves of garlic, finely chopped
1 bay leaf
1 lb/500 g green olives, pitted and soaked in
hot water
Salt
Freshly ground black pepper

Heat the olive oil and soften the onion. Add the meat and fry all over. Add the red wine, followed by the tomatoes, garlic, bay leaf, salt, pepper, and olives. Braise over moderate heat for 2 hours, adding hot water if necessary. Serve warm with white bread.

MOSKHÁRI ME MELITZANOPOURÉ
Veal with eggplant purée
(Illustration opposite right)

1 scant cup/200 ml olive oil
1 onion, finely chopped
2 lbs/1 kg veal, cut into large cubes
1 scant cup/200 ml dry red wine
1 lb/500 g tomatoes, peeled and puréed
1 tsp sugar
Salt
Freshly ground black pepper

For the purée:
6 large eggplants, pricked all over with a fork
A generous ½ cup/125 g butter
A generous ½ cup/125 ml milk

Heat the olive oil, soften the onion in it, and fry the meat all over. Add the wine and sufficient water to cover the meat. Braise over moderate heat for 2 hours, adding hot water if necessary. When the meat is almost cooked, add the tomatoes and sugar, and season with salt and pepper. Continue cooking until the meat is cooked and the sauce has thickened. Preheat the oven to 400 ºF (200ºC). Roast the eggplants, leave to cool, and remove the skin. Purée the eggplant flesh. Melt the butter in a pan, gently fry the purée, then add salt, and slowly stir in the milk. As soon as the purée has thickened, spread it out in a greased baking pan. Arrange the meat with its sauce in the middle. Bake at 350 ºF (180 ºC) for about 20 minutes and serve while still warm.

Epirus cattle are still put out to pasture on fields and meadows, which is why their meat has a more distinctive flavor than that of animals from other regions.

CUTS OF BEEF

NO.	GREEK	ENGLISH
1	*kilóto*	rump
2	*filéto ke*	
	kóutra filéto	sirloin
3	*brizolíki*	short loin
4	*spalobrizóla*	rib
5	*kapáki spálas*	chuck eye roast
6	*nouá*	bottom round roast
7	*kapáki*	round
8	*strongiló*	tip steak
9	*trans*	tip steak
10	*stithoplevrés*	short ribs
11	*spála*	shoulder, chuck
12	*poutíki*	hock, shank
13	*kótsi*	shin
14	*lápa*	flank steak
15	*stíthos*	brisket
16	*stíthos*	topside
17	*eliá*	neck
18	*lemós*	neck
19	*kefáli*	head

COUNTRY SAUSAGE

Greek country sausage is a dark, hard, air-dried sausage with a decidedly spicy flavor. Although it can be made from either pure beef or pure pork, a mixture of the two is more common, the proportions being a matter of personal taste and varying from region to region. The sausages are usually up to 80 percent beef and about 20 percent pork. The higher the proportion of beef, the harder the country sausage will be when dried. Meat from the forequarters, with the tendons removed, is also processed, as is marbled meat, sometimes even meat full of connective tissue, including stewing beef from the breast and flank. The meat is usually chopped up small when frozen, or coarsely ground in a meat grinder. That way it contains more water, which is beneficial during the slow process of drying out the sausage later on. Salt, pepper, garlic, paprika, cloves, caraway, and all sorts of other spices, all trade secrets of course, are mixed together and carefully stirred into the meat mixture. Cleaned beef intestines are filled with the sausage meat using a special funnel and a tablespoon. The filled intestines are twisted round at regular intervals. This process is much simpler when done by machine. When filled, the sausages are hung out to dry and rinsed in brine every 10–14 days. This acts as an antibacterial agent and also extracts water from the sausage. The old Greek houses in the country look as though they were just built to dry sausages. Their mud rendering stores moisture, releasing it again as required, thus attaining a constant ambient climate and temperature. Greek country sausage is ready after about four weeks. The finished dried sausage can now be smoked over a beechwood fire. The art of smoking is really a matter of intuition. In theory, too little smoke will not achieve the desired effect, while too much makes the outside of the sausage too dark, which does not appeal to the consumer. Homemade Epirus country sausage is a culinary experience. People like to fry it in a skillet with eggs or even serve it cold as an appetizer.

Opposite: Country sausage is hung up to dry for about four weeks and can then be smoked over beechwood if desired.

Spices are thoroughly combined with the raw meat so that they are evenly distributed throughout the sausage.

It is quicker, and the end result looks much more professional, if you use modern technology.

Above: the farmer's wife decides where each sausage begins and ends. Below: much sausage, much respect!

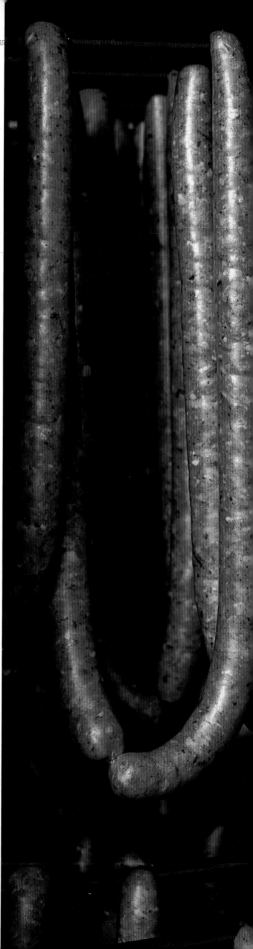

In Epirus you can still find the old "communal ovens" with their large open fireplaces. There, following ancient tradition, large quantities of meat can be left to braise *sti gástra*, in a pot with a lid, originally made of clay.

GÁSTRA

If we ignore the much older idea of the trench dug in the ground, then the first cooking pot of all was definitely a large, communal boiler that could hold enough food for the entire group. This idea continued into times when, although it was usual to have your own hut, it was still uncommon to have a hearth of your own. Even when it became the norm to have your own hearth, this custom was still revived perhaps when there was insufficient help, because everyone was employed for harvesting. In this case, you took meat that you had slaughtered to the oven house, where you could leave it until the evening, cooking slowly and gently, and even fairly safely over an open fire, even though you were not there to supervise. Nowadays, these institutions are maintained in the country not so much out of necessity as for pleasure, because it is mainly for religious anniversaries and weddings that people cook *sti gástra*, with a zinc baking pan often taking the place of the ceramic pot. What is essential, however, is that the cover can take the hot ashes laid on top of it to provide the dish with heat from above.

The circular baking pan is made so that with a little skill all the parts of a whole lamb will fit inside it.

The pans, which are practically surrounded by the flames, are fitted with a lid, which is then covered with hot ashes to provide heat from above.

Greeks have no fear of touching meat, as you can easily see in the larger markets, where fresh variety meats are laid out for inspection like any other goods.

VARIETY MEATS, OR OFFAL

Anyone who has a passion for heart, stomach, tongue, or liver from beef, pigs, goats, or sheep will generally find themselves well looked after in the special Greek tavernas known as *patsatzídika*, which serve nothing but *patsás* and other tripe specialties. Variety meats must be prepared with great care and attention to hygiene, which is why a local *patsatzídiko* comes highly recommended. Allegedly, after a heavy night on the bottle, *patsás* can get your stomach back to rights, and can provide wholesome sustenance for people who have worked through the night, which is why you can always find a motley crew of lorry drivers and party goers at a *patsatzídiko* in the early hours of the morning.

With the exception of the *patsatzídika*, restaurants rarely include variety meats on their menu, but they are considered a delicacy in domestic kitchens. Originally this meat was served on major feast days, when an animal was slaughtered. The parts that spoiled most quickly were rapidly eaten, with enough of the animal left over for the feast. Today, you find a good selection of such meats at any weekly market. Like most dishes, the preferred way of cooking them is to fry them in olive oil. For soups, they are lightly braised before being cut up and puréed. The most famous tripe soup is *mayirítsa*, the traditional Easter soup made from goat's or sheep's offal (see page 191).

PATSÁS
Tripe soup

3 cloves of garlic
1 scant cup/200 ml red wine vinegar
1 goat's or lamb's stomach
A scant ½ cup/100 ml Greek extra virgin olive oil
2 onions, finely chopped
Salt
Freshly ground black pepper

Place the garlic cloves and red wine vinegar in a glass bottle with a cork stopper. Bore a small hole in the cork to allow the liquid to trickle out. The garlic and vinegar produce the *skordostoúmbi*, which must be left to stand for at least 1 day before being drizzled over the finished soup. Wash the stomach well, place in the pan in one piece, fill the pan with water, and boil for 1 hour. Leave to drain, then wash again, and scrape out the inside of the stomach thoroughly using a tablespoon. Wash the stomach out well again, and chop up small. Heat some olive oil in a pan, and soften the onions. Add the finely

chopped stomach, quickly fry, and add enough water to come up at least 4 inches (10 centimeters) over the ingredients. Cook over moderate heat for several hours, until the tripe is soft. Pour into bowls, drizzle with *skordostoúmbi*, and serve with freshly baked white bread.

Intestine pieces left over from slaughtering an animal or calf's feet can also go in the soup.

GARDOÚMBA
Stuffed lamb's intestines

1 lamb's intestines
2 lbs/1 kg lamb's organ meat (lights, liver, heart etc.)
6–8 onions, finely chopped
1 bunch flat-leaved parsley, finely chopped
1 bunch dill, finely chopped
1 scant cup/200 ml olive oil
White wine vinegar
Salt
Freshly ground black pepper

Preheat the oven to 350 °F (180 °C). Wash all the meats well and pat dry. Cut the intestine into 4–6-in (10–15 cm) long pieces. Cut everything else into strips. Combine the meats with half the parsley and dill, and salt and pepper. Fill the pieces of intestine with this mixture and place on a high-sided baking sheet. Sprinkle with the onions, oil, wine vinegar, salt, pepper, and the remaining parsley and dill. Add water to a depth of about 1 inch (2 cm). Cook in the oven, turning repeatedly, until the pieces are brown all over. Serve with freshly baked white bread and a salad.

SIKOTÁKIA MOSKHARÍSIA STI SKHÁRA
Grilled calf's liver

4 calf's livers, split in the middle
8 tbsp Greek extra virgin olive oil
Juice of 1 lemon
4 sprigs basil, finely chopped
½ bunch flat-leaved parsley, finely chopped
Salt
Freshly ground black pepper

Wash the livers and pat dry. Combine the olive oil, lemon juice, and basil, and brush over the liver. Place the liver on a barbecue and grill for 3–5 minutes each side, brushing with the marinade from time to time. Remove the livers from the barbecue, season with salt and pepper, sprinkle with parsley, and pour the remaining oil and lemon sauce over them. Serve with rice and a country salad.

Patsás, the classic tripe soup made from a lamb's or cow's stomach, is still prepared in a huge cooking pot in special *patsatzídika* as it was in earlier times.

The congealed and soured curds must be broken up again before the crucial process of scalding them in hot water.

When the broken curds have been scalded in hot water, the fibrous mixture becomes elastic and can be drawn into threads.

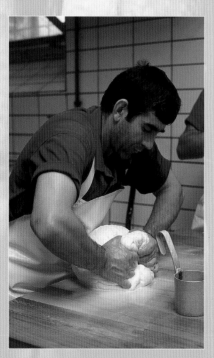

The cheesemaker kneads the scalded, drawn, and hence elastic mixture into the customary shape, almost as though it were bread dough.

CHEESE IN MÉTSOVON

It is now a good 40 years ago that Greek cheesemakers from sleepy Métsovon set out for northern Italy, where they were welcomed by Baron Tositsas, a descendent of an old established Walachian family from Métsovon. He took them under his wing until they had mastered the manufacturing process of the famous Italian *filata* cheeses such as Mozzarella and Provolone, a process that involves scalding and kneading the cheese mixture until it can be pulled into "elastic threads." It did not take them long, and the young Greek cheesemakers returned to Greece with their newly acquired expertise and began to make their own cheese using local milk. And that was when *Metsovóne* was born, a semisoft, smoked cheese made the Italian way.

Metsovóne has a distinctive shape – a sausage roughly 16 inches (40 centimeters) long, with its ends of varying thickness. It is firmly bound with cords so that it can be hung up for smoking. When cut, it reveals holes and hollows. It is mainly made from cow's milk, and the proportion of sheep's or goat's milk may not exceed 20 percent. With 42 percent water, a good 27 percent protein, 26 percent fat when dried, and 2.8 percent salt, *Metsovóne* is a decidedly salty cheese, better served as an appetizer than a sandwich filler.

Initially, the manufacturing process barely differs from that of other types of cheese. The milk is thickened with rennet and the curds chopped up small to release more whey. The pea-sized lumps of curds are then left to form a cohesive mass and to sour, after which the mass is cut up once again. It is then scalded with hot water (167–176 °F, 75–80 °C), drawn out, and kneaded thoroughly. This makes it into an elastic and malleable mass, which can be formed into the characteristic *Metsovóne* shape, either by hand or using special containers. The cheese is then salted and matured at a very low temperature for a period of five months. Once matured, *Metsovóne* cheese is smoked to achieve its distinctive flavor. The cheese is served in slices or broiled, but can also be used grated.

Whole cheeses by the hundred hang in the temperature-controlled ripening rooms of the large cheese-making concerns, waiting to ripen and then be smoked.

Katogi Metsovon: This red wine from the Katogi winery is made from Carbernet Sauvignon and Agiorgitiko grapes. It has a distinctive ruby-red color and a velvety smooth taste.

Métsovon has devoted itself entirely to the cheese business. Particularly at weekends and on holidays, many travelers are happy to make a small detour, desert the high street, and drive down into the valley for some quick cheese shopping. The cheese sellers have adapted to this and now sell a wide range of Greek cheeses in addition to their local cheese.

FÍLLO YA PÍTA
Phyllo pastry

4 cups/500 g all-purpose flour
1 tbsp + 2 tsp/25 ml white wine vinegar
3½ tbsp/50 ml Greek extra virgin olive oil
1 tsp salt
A generous cup/300 ml water
Fine cornstarch

Place the flour, vinegar, olive oil, and salt in a bowl and knead until it forms a soft, elastic dough, adding a little more water or flour as necessary. Cover the bowl with plastic wrap and leave the dough to rest in a refrigerator for 1 hour. Divide the mixture into six equal portions and knead each one into a ball. Dredge the work surface with cornstarch, and roll out one pastry ball using a thin rolling pin. Turn the pastry around 90º and roll out more thinly. Sprinkle cornstarch on the pastry and, pressing gently, roll it right round the rolling pin. While rolling slowly, use your hands to press the pastry from the center of the rolling pin to the outside. Then repeat this process after turning the pastry around 90º until the pastry is the correct size. Repeat the process with the remaining portions of pastry.

STEPS 1–4
1. Roll the pastry out using a long, thin wooden rolling pin. This takes a lot of practice, as you do not just roll the pastry out, as you do with a pasta rolling pin with handles, you also roll it up on the rolling pin.
2. Place several of the thinly rolled out pastry sheets on a greased baking sheet so that they overlap the edges.
3. Spread the filling over the base. Egg is the main source of liquid, so it sets when baked.
4. Place the remaining pastry sheets on top as a lid and press together firmly at the edge with the overhanging pastry from the base.

Kotópita – chicken *píta*

Milópita – apple *píta*

Spanakópita – spinach *píta*

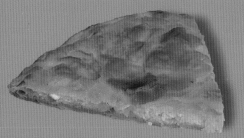

Tirópita – sheep's milk cheese *píta*

Tirópita me féta – *féta píta*

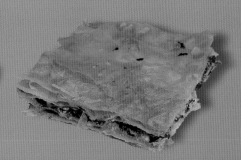

Spanakotirópita – spinach and cheese *píta*

PÍTA

The flat flaky pastry pasties with a thousand and one fillings are a Greek national dish and are made throughout the mainland. The main differences lie in the number of pastry sheets that puff up in the oven, giving *pita* its characteristic crispiness. Making *pita* involves a great deal of work and used to be left mostly to the skilled hands of Greek grandmothers. They often got up with the sun to knead the required pastry mixture by hand. They then kneaded individual portions of dough before rolling them out with a thin wooden rolling pin, turning them, and rolling them out again, until the whole table was covered with a paper-thin layer of pastry. That layer was folded together, and the rolling process would start all over again. It was hours before all the ingredients were ready, and the baking sheet, (which was usually extremely large), could be taken to the nearest baker. In the countryside, this ritual still hasn't quite died out (and no one is sure whether that's something to be welcomed or regretted). No one knows why Epirus in particular became so famous for its *pita*. But anyone who has tried a *pita* here will vouch for its distinctive appearance and taste. In the towns, guesthouses with a sense of tradition have made an even better name for themselves with homemade *pita*. There you can recognize a good host by the various types of *pita* on the menu. The fascinating thing about *pita* is the imagination that their fillings can inspire, because there is nothing that would not taste even better when baked in the paper-thin flaky pastry. As with anything made with *fillo* pastry, the same applies for *pita*: it must never be covered when taken out of the oven, as this would make the softly crisp layers collapse in on themselves, and all that effort would have been in vain. Apart from that, they can be enjoyed either warm or cold, as a meal or as a snack, at any time of the day or night.

PÍTA LEXIKON

bakaliarópita	stockfish *pita*
khortópita	wild herb *pita*
kasópita	cheese *pita*
kolokithópita	zucchini *pita*
kotópita	chicken *pita*
kreatópita	ground meat *pita*
kremmidópita	onion *pita*
ladópita	oil *pita*
milópita	apple *pita*
pita me moskharísio ke khirinó kréas	*pita* with beef and pork
pita yaniótiki	Ioannina *pita* (with *kefalograviéra* cheese)
prasópita	leek *pita*
spanakópita	spinach *pita*
spanakotirópita	spinach and cheese *pita*
tirópita	sheep's milk cheese *pita*

Píta doesn't necessarily have to be rolled out in layers on a baking sheet. Anyone sufficiently experienced …

… in dealing with the paper-thin pastry can also fill individual sheets with the desired filling …

… roll them up into "flutes" and bake them. A final tip: Ask a friend to come over to help.

PHYLLO PASTRY

If you think that you can translate the Greek word *fillo*, derived from the ancient Greek word *phyllo* (a leaf) as "puff pastry," then you're close, but not quite correct. Whereas puff pastry contains eggs and its individual layers are separated by cold butter, (which then melts in the oven and helps it puff up nicely), *fillo* pastry relies on more stability. Its basic ingredients are nothing special. Flour, water, fat, and salt are kneaded until the dough attains the correct consistency: light, but tear-resistant, like strudel pastry. The thin layers are separated with oil instead of butter. The secret of rolling it out lies not only in the skill of the master *fillo*-pastry maker, but also in the thin wooden rolling pin, which is about 20 inches (50 centimeters) long and perfectly straight, having no handles. These rods guarantee good contact with the pastry and the even pressure that is essential if the *fillo* is to attain its leaf-like delicacy.

The slightly sparkling, medium dry aromatic white wine from Zitsa is made from the indigenous Debina grape and goes well with sweet dishes.

The first thin sheet of pastry is laid on the baking pan, so that it overlaps the edge. The excess will be pressed together with the lid to form a secure seal and when baked creates a crispy pastry edge, lending stability to the filled *píta*.

Using your hands, combine the flour, vinegar, oil, salt, and water, and knead to form a smooth dough.

Then sprinkle the *píta* dough with flour, cover, and place in a refrigerator for at least 1 hour.

It would be impossible to roll out the pastry thin enough without the special, long, thin, wooden rolling pin.

The prepared pastry can be rolled out again in the greased baking pan. The individual layers are brushed with butter.

Pour the prepared cream filling onto the layers of pastry forming the base.

Place the cover on the cream filling, building it up gradually layer by layer, and press the excess pastry firmly together.

While still warm, dredge the *bougátsa* with confectioner's sugar and cinnamon, and serve immediately.

The next day, all *bougátsa* needs to make it taste almost oven-fresh is another sprinkling of confectioner's sugar.

BOUGÁTSA

Along with *tirópita* (sheep's milk cheese *píta*) and *spanakópita* (spinach *píta*), sweet *bougátsa* is another phyllo pastry delicacy more usually found in the *píta* stalls than in the bakeries with their syrup cakes. The cream filling makes the pastry rich, so that it is served as a snack in its own right rather than as a dessert, and as such it can take the addition of cinnamon and sugar.

BOUGÁTSA
Fíllo pastry with cream filling

1½ cups/250 g fine semolina
1½ generous cups/350 g sugar
3 eggs
6 cups/1½ liters milk
Grated zest of 1 unwaxed or well-scrubbed lemon
½ cup + 2 tbsp/150 g butter
1 lb/500 g phyllo pastry (see recipe on p. 146)
Confectioner's sugar
Ground cinnamon

Beat the semolina, sugar, and eggs until frothy. Transfer the mixture to a pan and add the milk, stirring constantly. Bring to a boil several times and then stir in the grated lemon zest. Leave to cool. Preheat the oven to 350 °F (180 °C). Melt the butter and brush over the individual sheets of pastry. Place half the pastry on a greased baking sheet, spread the creamy mixture out evenly on top, and cover with the remaining pastry. Bake in a preheated oven for about 20 minutes until the pastry is golden brown and crispy on top and the filling has set. Leave the *bougátsa* to cool slightly, then sprinkle with confectioner's sugar and cinnamon and cut into slices. *Bougátsa* is best eaten while still warm.
In Ioánnina, each slice of *bougátsa* is served with a sweet roll and a glass of water.

POLISPÓRI
Sweet grain soup

¾ cup/150 g dried sweetcorn kernels
¾ cup/150 g dried wheat grains
Olive oil
Salt
Sugar
½ cup/50 g chopped walnuts
½ cup/50 g chopped hazelnuts
½ cup chopped almonds
⅓ cup/50 g raisins
⅓ cup/50 g coarsely chopped dried apricots
⅓ cup/50 g coarsely chopped dried figs
All-purpose flour

Soak the dried sweetcorn kernels in water overnight. The next day, pour off the water and wash the sweetcorn well. Transfer to a pan together with the wheat, add copious water, followed by olive oil, sugar to taste, and a pinch of salt. Cook over a moderate heat until both types of grain are almost soft. Then add the nuts and dried fruits, and cook until the grains are done, stirring repeatedly. Dissolve a little flour in a little warm water and use to thicken the juices. Transfer to plates and serve warm. The soup can be kept for several days in a refrigerator.

In Epriot villages, this soup is made in large quantities for harvest thanksgiving. Several families get together, and there is dancing and singing. The ingredients used, which can be extended to include other items, reflect the produce that has been gained from the soil in the previous year. Having cooked the soup together, the families then sit down together to eat it.

FISHING IN LAKE PAMVÓTIS

The coastal harbors are not the only places where you would expect the Greeks to be on good terms with fish. There are just as many fish – and anglers – inland, and this is especially true of Epirus. The rich fish stocks of Lake Pamvótis near Ioánnina are almost legendary. In times of crisis, such as during the Second World War, when hunting in the mountains was banned, the stocks of the 8.5-square-mile (22 square kilometer) lake were always a reliable and constant source of food for the region's inhabitants. As well as acting as a pantry, in the period before extensive road construction it was a very important transit route. Today it is a popular recreation area for the major town of Ioánnina.

In the tranquil reed beds of the lake, you can catch all sorts of nonpredatory fish: bream, tench, and especially carp, which find their food in the muddy banks. Many fishermen choose to fish here with a pole (above): a fixed line with a hook attached to the end of it, or a

What skill: to keep an eye on four poles at once without missing a single twitch of the hook!

series of hooks at intervals, runs the length of a long pole. The hook with the bait rests on the mud until a fish bites. Now the fisherman has to jerk the pole upward, otherwise the bait will be nibbled away and the evening meal lost. Once cast, the skill lies in watching the pole with the utmost attention to see if the line – or the float – moves. Using two poles at the same time, which is not allowed in many countries, is one of the great arts of fishing.

Before the neighboring lake dried up, the fish stock used to include eels, because Lake

Pamvótis was a stop-off point on their way to the sea. However, for almost 30 years, the lake has been home to a new guest. In the 1960s, the grass carp, originally indigenous to China, was thought to be a wonder weapon against unwanted aquatic plants. It was used here on a large scale to keep the lake clean. The grass carp has not yet become fully established as an edible fish, although its flesh is tasty and nowhere near as fatty as that of other carp.

If you fish in deeper water, you can hope to catch predatory fish: pike, perch, or trout. So-called spin fishermen (below) use an artificial bait or spoon that moves and thus attracts the predatory fish. In this case, there is no danger of the bait being assiduously nibbled away – these fish immediately snap their jaws firmly shut and are so strong that anglers do not like to risk landing them by hand. That is why a landing net is just as essential a piece of tackle in a boat as the rod. The angler uses the rod to draw the prey toward the boat and then catches it securely from below in the landing net to lift it on board.

In the numerous tributaries of Lake Pamvótis there are lots of trout, which – in the same way

Too strong to be landed by hand – a landing net helps stop the fish from getting away.

Kiprina (*Cyprinus carpio*) common carp

Grass (*Ctenopharyngodon idella*) grass carp

Petaloúda (*Alburnus alburnus*) bleak

as salmon – swim upriver in winter to lay their eggs in the smaller, sheltered streams. It is almost two years before the little fish are ready to be eaten. But you no longer have to wait that long, because trout farms have long been established, either in ponds or small enclosures (above). Trout can be reared all year round and in such quantities that all it takes is one swoop of the landing net for an easy catch. It's not surprising, therefore, that Epirus is famous for its delicious trout recipes!

Trout ponds must have a good supply of fresh water so that the water is always sufficiently oxygenated. Then they can accommodate large numbers of fish.

Preheat the oven to 350 ºF (180 ºF). Clean and wash the trout. Rub the fish inside and out with salt, pepper, and lemon juice. Brush 4 pieces of aluminum foil with olive oil, place the fish on top, and arrange the vegetables and dill around the fish. Season with salt and pepper, seal the foil, and bake in the oven for about 30–40 minutes.

PÉSTROFA TIS ÁNIXIS
Springtime trout

4 medium trout
Juice of 1 lemon
Olive oil
2 carrots, finely diced
2 cloves of garlic, finely chopped
2 sticks white celery, sliced
A little fresh dill
Salt
Freshly ground black pepper

PÉSTROFES ME VOÚTIRO
Trout with herbs and butter

4 medium trout
A little all-purpose flour
1½ cups/300 g butter
8 sage leaves
1 scant cup/200 ml dry white wine
1 tomato, sliced
1 lemon, sliced
1 bunch flat-leaved parsley, finely chopped
Salt
Freshly ground black pepper

Cut the trout along the underside, clean and wash them thoroughly, and toss in flour. Melt the butter in a skillet, add the fish, and fry on both sides until golden brown. Season with salt and pepper, and place the sage leaves on top of the fish. Add the white wine and leave the trout to braise over a low heat until they are cooked. Then transfer them to a large plate, pour over the juice, and garnish with the tomatoes, lemon slices, and parsley.
Boiled potatoes and vegetables go well with this dish.

VATRÁKHIA ME SÁLTSA DOMÁTA
Frogs' legs in tomato sauce

1 scant cup/200 ml Greek extra virgin olive oil
1 clove of garlic, finely sliced
Frogs' legs, cut into pieces
1 scant cup/200 ml dry white wine
½ lb/250 g tomatoes, skinned and finely diced
½ bunch flat-leaved parsley, chopped
Salt
Freshly ground black pepper

Heat the olive oil in a skillet and fry the garlic until softened, removing it from the skillet just before it begins to brown. Add the frogs' legs and fry in the olive oil. As soon as they turn white, add the white wine and tomatoes. Season with salt and pepper, and add a few leaves of parsley. Simmer over a moderate heat until the sauce thickens.

ALI PASHA

One of the most colorful figures in the history of Epirus is Ali Pasha, the Albanian prince of Ioánnina. He came from an Arnaut family, as the Greeks called the Albanians, from Tepelini in southern Albania. At the age of 47, through murder and intrigue, he had risen to become governor of Trikala and had managed to seize Ioánnina, where he built his palace. As the Ottoman Empire began to falter at the end of the 18th century, he used this opportunity to build up his own power base independent of Istanbul. By 1800, this encompassed all of Epirus, southern Albania, as well as parts of Thessaly and Macedonia. Under Ali Pasha's rule, the Epiriot economy and finances flourished. Because he himself was often described as Greek, he was able to win over the freedom-loving Greeks and to incite them to join him in his struggle against the Ottoman Empire. He had long understood how to retain the trust of Istanbul while at the same time encouraging prominent people in Western Europe, such as Lord Byron, to take an interest in him and entertaining them as guests in his palace. Even today, the lakeside bars still name some dishes for the prince.

Ali Pasha promoted the visual arts and founded many schools in Ioánnina, yet he proved to be a cruel ruler. Although he later married a Christian Greek woman named Kyrá Vassiliki, he did not tolerate the association of Muslims and Christians. When he found out that his son was involved with a Greek woman named Frosini, he had the young woman drowned in the lake, together with 17 of her friends. In 1820, he earned his just reward, as the sultan declared Ali Pasha to be guilty of high treason and had him besieged by a strong army in Ioánnina. He died of gunshot wounds in 1822. His body was decapitated and his head sent to Istanbul.

LOTS OF FROGS...

For a long time, the frogs of Lake Pamvótis led a peaceful life. Until, that is, word got round that they were tasty. Then not only were they exported to France (a practice which has been banned), but they also increasingly appeared on Greek plates (which is also no longer allowed now). Whereas in Germany, Austria, and Switzerland practically all types of frog are on their respective red lists of protected species, and people are concerned about protecting spawning grounds and footpaths, Greece is not the only place where frogs are considered to be a gourmet's secret recommendation. Although people know how the water frogs (*Rana esculenta*), which grow up to 8 inches (20 centimeters) in length, are caught and killed, they do not like to talk about it. Suffice it to say that the muscular legs are skinned and are a delicacy no matter how they are prepared. Around Lake Pamvótis, frogs are caught in May and June, mostly at night, by dazzling them with large flashlights, so that they can be picked up by hand, or sometimes with nets.

VATRÁKHIA PANÉ
Breaded frogs' legs

Frogs' legs
Fine semolina
Greek extra virgin olive oil for frying
1 egg, beaten
Chopped flat-leaved parsley
Cloves of garlic
Salt

Sprinkle the frogs' legs with salt and coat with the semolina. Heat the olive oil in a skillet, dip the frog's legs in the egg, and deep fry in the hot oil. Transfer to a plate and garnish with the parsley and garlic cloves.

Above: *Vatrákhia me sáltsa domáta*, frogs' legs in tomato sauce, is rarely found in Ioánnina, yet it is a typical Lake Pamvótis dish.

Right: *Vatrákhia pané*, breaded frogs' legs, are served with lots of lemon juice.

KHÉLI SE KERAMÍDI
Eel in a clay tile

1 large cooking tile
1 eel weighing approx. 2½ lbs/1.2 kg
¼ tsp dried oregano
All-purpose flour
A scant ½ cup/100 ml dry white wine
A scant ½ cup/100 ml olive oil
Bay leaves
Salt

First rub the eel with salt to remove the slime. Leave for a while to take effect, then rinse the salt off under running water. To clean the fish, cut the eel open along its stomach from the vent toward the head and 2 inches/5 cm toward the tail. Pull the entrails out toward the head and detach close to the gills. Remove all internal organs and viscera. Now remove the skin and cut off the fins in the opposite direction to which they lie. The traditional method to remove the skin is to nail the head of the eel to a board so that both hands can get a better grip. Preheat the oven to 400 ºF (200 ºC). Cut the eel into pieces and place on a large cooking tile. Sprinkle with oregano and salt. Make a flour-and-water dough, divide the dough in half and press each piece firmly into the end of the tile to seal it. Pour the wine and olive oil over the eel and place the tile in the oven. Bake until the eel is almost cooked, then make small incisions in the flesh and insert the bay leaves. Cover the eel with aluminum foil and bake for a further 5–10 minutes. Serve in the hot tile.

Below: eel simply fried in olive oil, then either threaded on a wooden skewer or just eaten with the fingers, is probably the best eel recipe of all.

SHRIMP

In the coastal villages of Epirus, especially those near the Ambracian Gulf, there is frantic activity among the fishermen on clear spring nights when the moon is full. This is the center of shrimp fishing, and here lie the main fishing beds for Greek shrimp. Even back in the times of Ancient Greece, Athenaeus of Naucratis, in his work *Deipnosophistae* or "The Gastronomers," described *karis*, as shrimp was called in those times, as a popular delicacy, adding "… but the very best dish of all is shrimp in fig leaf." Today, the best places to get fresh shrimp in Greece are the fish markets in major cities, or direct locally on the coast, where they can be enjoyed in the small harbor inns fresh from the sea. This is because shrimp are a culinary delight only when absolutely fresh, and they are truly fresh only when the shell is still firm and the antennae are intact. Shrimp, which are known as prawns in many countries, can be found in all seas all over the world and nearly all species are heavily fished. In the Mediterranean Sea, the most common species are the pink deep sea shrimp (*Aristeus antennatus*) and the red deep sea shrimp (*Aristaeomorpha foliaceae*), which bear a superficial resemblance to each other, but are different in color. Common to both is that they display a red coloration before they are cooked.

You rarely catch just one shrimp. Because shrimp always swim in shoals, the fishermen are either very successful or go away empty-handed.

GARÍDES ME MÉLI
Honey-glazed shrimp

2 tbsp Greek extra virgin olive oil
1 lb/500 g shrimp, boiled and peeled
4 tbsp fish sauce (available from Asian delicatessen stores)
2 tsp fresh oregano, finely chopped
2 tbsp clear honey
Freshly ground black pepper

Heat the olive oil, fish sauce, and honey in a pan, add the shrimp, and sauté gently for 5 minutes until soft. Remove the shrimp from the pan and leave in a warm place. Reduce the juice and add the oregano. Now pour the sauce over the shrimp and sprinkle with pepper. Serve as an appetizer with freshly baked bread and a salad.

GÁVROS PLAKÍ
Anchovies with tomatoes

1 lb/500 g anchovies
2 tomatoes, skinned and diced
1 bunch flat-leaved parsley, finely chopped
1 finely sliced garlic
A generous ½ cup/125 ml Greek extra virgin olive oil
Salt
Freshly ground black pepper

Preheat the oven to 350 ºF (180 ºC). Clean the anchovies, remove the heads, and wash. Place in a fireproof dish, season with salt and pepper, add the parsley, garlic, and olive oil, together with a scant cup/200 ml of water. Bake in the preheated oven for 40–50 minutes. Serve hot with freshly baked white bread and a salad.

Tip: As an alternative, you can dispense with the tomatoes and parsley and use the juice of 2 lemons with lots of oregano.

SARDINE FESTIVAL

The coast of Epirus is the place to celebrate the sardine festival in summer. This is not in the least unusual for Greece, because this festival enjoys great popularity throughout the country. One of the best sardine festivals takes place on the first weekend in August in the port of Préveza. People come from all around to enjoy the clarinet music, inexpensive grilled sardines and cheap wine, and to meet up with friends and family. Many onlookers even claim that the Préveza sardine festival is one of the few occasions when the mountain people of Epirus enjoy a trip to the coast.

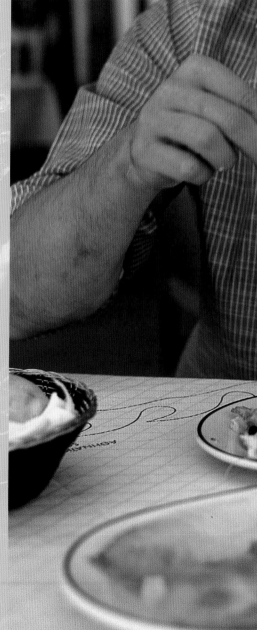

River crayfish are a local specialty of Epirus. These crustaceans, with olive-green to gray-black shells, prefer clean, well-oxygenated, alkaline water where the riverbed is not too slimy.

KARAVÍDES SAGANÁKI
Crayfish in tomato sauce

4 live crayfish
A generous ½ cup/125 ml Greek extra virgin olive oil
1 scant cup/200 ml dry white wine
½ lb/250 g tomatoes, skinned and finely diced
5 sprigs basil, finely chopped
Salt

Fill a pan with plenty of water and bring to a boil. Add salt, followed by the live crayfish. Boil for about 5 minutes, then take out the crayfish and remove their shells. Heat olive oil in a skillet, quickly brown the crayfish flesh, and add the wine. Add the tomatoes and basil, and season with salt. Lower the heat, and leave the sauce to reduce for a few minutes. Transfer to plates and serve with freshly baked white bread.

KARAVÍDES ME LADOLÉMONO
Crayfish in oil and lemon sauce

1 onion, finely chopped
½ bunch dill, finely chopped
1 tsp dried oregano
4 live crayfish
1 scant cup/200 ml Greek extra virgin olive oil
Juice of 1–2 lemons
Salt

Fill a pan with plenty of water and bring to a boil. Add the onion, dill, oregano, and a little salt. Add the live crayfish to the boiling water and cook for 5 minutes. Take out the crayfish, loosen their shells (damaging them as little as possible), and arrange with the meat in the shell on a plate. Beat together the olive oil and lemon juice, pour over the crayfish flesh, and serve with a green salad and freshly baked white bread.

THE HUNTING SEASON

Hunting has a particularly long tradition in the hilly, yet densely wooded regions of Epirus. People hunted here as long ago as 10,000 B.C., as is proven by the bones of red deer, bears, and wild boar that archaeologists have found in the caves occupied by people in this region at that time.

In antiquity, although hunting was theoretically free to all, even on private land, in actual fact some types of animal were reserved for the ruling classes. There was hardly any need for a firm "closed season", at the very least hunting stopped for the major religious festivals, and it was of course forbidden in sacred places. Greece has inherited no special game reserves, such as those laid out by oriental rulers. The oldest surviving hunting book is Xenophon's *Kynegetikos* with its wealth of information on hunting for hare, stag, and wild boar, as well as dog breeding and dressage. But Xenophon also emphasizes the educational value of hunting as a way of training men for war, and thus seizes on an analogy between hunting and war that is expressed in Homer's epics. Hunting victim and hunting trophies were offered to Artemis, the goddess of hunting.

Today, the Greeks are still passionate hunters and many are enrolled in the country's hunting associations, because hunting is not allowed in the Greek forests without a compulsory permit. This law is intended to put a stop to the numerous poachers for whom the impenetrable areas of Epirus offer the perfect opportunity to carry out their illicit deeds. The well-organized hunting association of Epirus is one of the largest in Greece. As in all countries where protecting the environment is taken seriously, one of its tasks is to care for the rich flora and fauna. To that end, hunting quotas now have to be set. The hunting season lasts from August 20 to February 29, but the period during which a particular animal can be hunted varies and is laid down each year to take into account the game population. Another of the association's tasks is to register the game animals that are found only in Epirus.

Above: hunters prepare for the wild boar hunt, but the wild boar have obviously got something better to do.
Background: not much of a bag for four valiant hunters.

AGRIOGOÚROUNO SALMÍ
Salmí-style wild boar

2 lbs/1 kg wild boar from the haunch/leg
½ cup/100 g butter
1 carrot, sliced
¼ celeriac, diced
4 large tomatoes, skinned and strained
3½ tbsp/50 ml brandy
All-purpose flour combined with a little water
Salt and freshly ground black pepper

For the marinade:
2 generous cups/500 ml red wine
1 carrot, sliced
1 bay leaf
Rosemary, thyme, peppercorns
Note: Marinate for 2 days!

Cut the meat into fairly large chunks, place in a bowl, add the ingredients for the marinade, cover, and leave in a cool place for 2 days. Turn the meat each day so that it marinates evenly. Melt the butter in a skillet and brown the marinated meat. Add a little of the marinade, followed by the carrots, celeriac, and strained tomatoes. Season with salt and pepper, and braise gently for 1½ hours. Transfer the meat to a large plate. Pass the sauce through a strainer and thicken with the flour-and-water mixture. Pour over the meat and serve with vegetables and potatoes.

ORTÍKIA ME RÍZI
Quails with rice

4 quails, oven ready
1 scant cup/200 ml Greek extra virgin olive oil
2 onions, finely chopped
1 clove of garlic, coarsely chopped
2 tomatoes, skinned and diced
½ tsp ground cinnamon
1¼ cups/250 g rice
Salt
Freshly ground black pepper

Wash the cleaned quail well and rub with salt and pepper. Heat the olive oil in a pan and brown the birds all over. Then add the onions, garlic, tomatoes, and cinnamon, and sauté gently until softened. Season with salt and pepper and add sufficient water to cover the quail well. Lower the heat, cover, and braise the quail over a low heat for about 1 hour. Then add 2 generous cups/500 ml hot water and stir in the rinsed rice. Cook over a moderate heat for a further 15–20 minutes until the rice has absorbed most of the liquid. Serve hot with freshly baked white bread.

ARTEMIS, THE GODDESS OF HUNTING

Some myths report that Artemis, the goddess of wild animals and all unborn life, daughter of Leto and Zeus and twin sister of Apollo, was born on Delos. The twins remained close and often went hunting together. They killed nearly all of Niobe's

children, because she thought herself superior to Leto, who had fewer children. Artemis spent most of her time armed with a bow and arrow and was accompanied by nymphs on her hunting trips through the woods. She remained chaste and demanded the same of her companions. When the young hunter Actaeon surprised her and her nymphs while bathing, she turned him into a stag, whereupon he was torn to pieces by his own dogs. In response to Agamemnon's boast that he was just as good a hunter as she was, Artemis conjured up unfavorable winds, thus preventing the entire Greek fleet from putting to sea. She is frequently depicted with the mythical golden-horned Ceryneian Hind that, with her permission, Heracles had captured alive as his third labor.

ΘΕΣΣΑΛΙΑ

The Meteora cliffs were carved out of the rock during the ice ages over millions of years by the Piniós River and sculpted by erosion into bizarre shapes.

THESSALY

Greek water

Apples

Medicinal herbs

A taste of the Pílion

Hare and rabbit

The cabbage plain

Chestnuts

Sweet hospitality

Baklavás

With the fairly impenetrable Epirus mountain range rising behind them, the Píndos mountains give way to the broad expanse of the Thessalian plain, which is enclosed on every side by other mountain ranges: the Kamvoúnia mountains to the north, the Ossa massif and Pílion mountains to the east, and the Othrys mountains to the south. The Thessalian basin was a vast sea up until the end of the last ice age, but is now a lowland area with a pronounced continental climate. It constitutes Greece's largest "cereal basket" with just a few scattered olive plantations thriving in sheltered places. While winters in this sparsely populated region frequently experience temperatures dropping to below freezing together with heavy snowfalls, temperatures at the height of summer are among the highest in northern Greece. Over the years, the combined action of the Piniós River and the effects of erosion have carved deep gorges out of the soft rock of the Píndos foothills, leaving bizarre pinnacles of rock, on which are now perched the Meteora monasteries. To the east, the region is bordered by the densely forested and abundantly irrigated Pílion mountains. This range rises up to 5280 feet (1610 meters) in places and functions as the green lungs of the region, the shape of which resembles a hooked forefinger protruding into the sea. Under Ottoman rule, Greek people from other parts of the country sought refuge in the remote villages of the Pílion mountains, where their skills as craftsmen provided them with a modest living. Since the rulers in Istanbul had no choice but to acknowledge that this region was difficult to control, it was granted special privileges and a certain degree of autonomy. Textile production and the manufacture of leather goods and silk flourished, as did oil and wine production and fruit-growing. The resulting export trade drew merchants as far as the coast of Asia Minor and exposed them to influences that may well have inspired their cuisine. In addition to grains, apples are the region's other main commodity. These are either shipped from the commercial center of Vólos, which boasts Greece's third largest cargo port, or are processed here in the region's largest food industry.

The wealth of medicinal plants and herbs to be found in the Pílion mountains has been associated since antiquity with Chiron, the centaur. In contrast to his barbaric contemporaries, this mythical being, half horse, half man, was a wise scholar who was entrusted with the task of teaching Achilles. He later passed on his skills in the art of healing to Asclepius.

Ancient hand-operated water pumps, called *touloúmba*, can still be found on many Greek farms. The quality of the water is well worth the extra effort as far as the residents are concerned.

GREEK WATER

Natural Greek mineral water, which Greek people prize as highly as their wine, is of very good quality and easily bears comparison with its European counterparts. Even in ancient times, the purity of water was something people took very seriously. It was customary in those days to drink wine mixed with water, whereby the respective proportions were sometimes the subject of intense debate.

Even in the summer months, there is such an abundance of water in the Pílion mountains that it is hard to believe you are in Greece. Even so, many of the springs still remain commercially untapped. While the valley bakes in the summer heat, temperatures are quite tolerable at higher altitudes. Many residents of nearby Vólos drive up into the mountains several times a week to fill up large containers with their own supply of spring water. No table is complete without a pitcher of ice-cold water. In Greece, however, a glass of water is an accepted accompaniment to every other beverage. Whether you order ouzo, wine, or fruit juice, or even a bottle of mineral water, you will often find a complimentary glass of water being served along with it, for water is regarded as a mark of hospitality.

Other significant drinking water springs can be found on Mount Olympus as well as in the Píndos, Ossa, Geránia, and Psilorítis mountains. Greece's best known mineral water comes from the small town of Flórina in northern Greece.

Women carrying amphorae at the spring is a popular motif on hydriae, ancient three-handled water jars.

THE CAVE OF THEÓPETRA

The Theópetra cave, situated between Tríkkala and Kalambáka in Thessaly, has been the site of archaeological excavations since 1987. Up until then, shepherds still used the cave as a shelter for their flocks. Radiocarbon dating techniques (C-14 method) have been able to verify that this cave is so far the only known site of its kind in Greece to have remained in continuous use as a place of human habitation from the middle Palaeolithic Age (around 100,000 B.C.) right through to the end of the Neolithic period (around 3000 B.C.) In 1999, human footprints found in the cave were shown to date from the Palaeolithic period. Up until then, the only evidence of such finds had been in East Africa. In addition to the footprints, two skeletons were also discovered dating to 15,000 B.C. and 7000 B.C. Stone tools dating back to all the different periods of settlement have also been found, as well as shells and bones, which indicate that wild, or possibly even domesticated, animals were dismembered and eaten here. Fragments of Neolithic pottery suggest that either the people of that time were familiar with ceramic techniques, or else that the different tribes of the eastern Mediterranean engaged in a brisk trade with each other.

APPLES

In the middle of the Pílion mountains at an altitude of 650–2625 feet (200–800 meters) is the largest apple-growing area in Greece. In spring, this part of the Magnisía region turns into a sea of apple blossom. The region's oldest cooperative, founded in 1916, harvests 27,500 tons (25,000 tonnes) of apples each year and exports them all over the world. Since the terraces drop steeply down toward the sea, nearly all the work has to be done by hand. Heavy rainfall, occasional snow in winter, and moderate temperatures with high humidity in summer provide ideal growing conditions for the "Starkin Delicious" variety with its strong red coloring, firm flesh and the ability to keep well. The Zagorá cooperative harvests around 40 million top-quality apples a year, its soft soil and good pH-values of 4-5 providing perfect growing conditions. Forty per cent of the crop is destined for export from Vólos.

Apples are known to have formed part of the Stone Age diet and are consequently one of the oldest fruits known to man. Even if the first evidence of the systematic cultivation of fruit trees dates from Roman times, we can still assume that it existed even before then. Odysseus, after all, on entering the palace of Alcinous, sees "a great orchard" … "In it grow trees tall and luxuriant, pears and pomegranates, and apple trees with their bright fruit, and sweet figs, and luxuriant olives." (*Odyssey*, Book 7). The *Enquiry into Plants* written in 300 BC by Theophrastus, a pupil of Aristotle, documents that the ancient Greeks were well aware of the importance of a good range and supply of fruit and vegetables. Sources from classical times might, however, be somewhat misleading when it comes to the word "apple." The term did not apply exclusively to what we now call an apple – you only have to recall that the pomegranate was also classed as an apple. It was a more general name, which could apply to any fresh, red-cheeked fruit. Fruit, sweet and refreshingly juicy, it was served during a meal both as an appetizer and as dessert, as well as being a frequent accompaniment to meat dishes.

The apple featured prominently in ancient mythology. At the western end of the world, the Hesperides guarded the golden apples given by Gaea to Hera, on her marriage to Zeus. Angry that she was left off the guest list, Eris, the goddess of discord, flings a golden apple with the words "For the fairest" written on it among the guests at a celebration. The story is well known: three goddesses each lay claim to the apple and Paris is given the task of judging, and in so doing, triggers the Trojan War.

Red Chief: a good sweet dessert apple with a strong aroma and fairly firm flesh.

Iberia: a variety introduced from Spain, fairly tart with rather a soft texture.

Starkinson: a good, slightly tart dessert apple with a firm texture.

Starkin Delicious: a sweet dessert apple with a melon-like aroma.

Golden Delicious: a sweet, fragrant dessert apple.

Firiki: a small, rare variety of apple for the Greek home market.

Ozark Gold: crisp and juicy, similar to *Golden Delicious*.

Renata: slightly tart with a fairly firm texture.

SIKOTÁKIA POULIÓN
Fried chicken livers

½ cup/100 g butter
6 small onions, finely diced
2 lbs/1 kg chicken livers
1 generous cup/250 ml dry white wine
2 apples, peeled and sliced
4 small zucchini, cut into slices
All-purpose flour
Olive oil
1 tbsp finely chopped chervil
Salt and freshly ground black pepper

Melt the butter in a skillet and sauté the onions
until transparent. Add the livers and fry gently.
Pour in the wine and add the sliced apple. Simmer until the liquid is reduced by half, then
remove the skillet from the heat. Sprinkle salt
and pepper over the zucchini slices before tossing them in flour. Heat a little olive oil in
another skillet, brown the zucchini slices on
both sides, then add to the livers. Continue to
cook gently for a few more minutes, then serve
hot, garnished with chopped chervil.

KHIRINÉS BRIZÓLES ME MÍLA
Pork chops with apples

4 large pork chops
½ cup + 2 tbsp/150 g butter
1 scant cup/200 ml dry white wine
2 apples, peeled, cored and sliced in rings
ground cinnamon
salt and freshly ground pepper

Season the chops with salt and pepper. Melt
half the butter and sauté the chops for 10 minutes on each side. Add the wine and set aside.
In another skillet, fry the apple rings in the
remaining butter. Sprinkle with cinnamon and
add to the chops. Leave to simmer for 5 minutes and serve hot.

MEDICINAL HERBS

According to mythology, the original birthplace of all magic and medicinal herbs is not Crete, as is often wrongly claimed, but the Pílion mountain chain in eastern Thessaly. This was the home of Chiron the centaur, son of Cronos and Philyra, half-brother of Zeus and, unlike other centaurs, blessed with immortality. Although he was indeed one of these reputedly wild and unruly creatures, he differed from them not only in origin but also in nature. He was regarded as just, gentle, pious, and very wise and, consequently, the highest gods entrusted him with the task of educating their children. Asclepius, who later became the god of healing, originally gained his knowledge of the healing properties of plants and how to treat various diseases from Chiron.

Even in ancient times, powerful healing properties were attributed to the medicinal herbs growing wild in the Pílion mountains, but they were mainly used externally to heal wounds. More often than not, the healing power of the herbs and plants was attributed to magical properties. In those days, the medicinal and pharmaceutical factors behind the efficacy of a plant were as yet unknown. It was simply experience that dictated the areas of application. In Asclepieia, the priests prescribed mystical measures as therapeutic treatment, such as sleeping in a temple.

A more scientifically based form of medicine did not begin to emerge until Hippocrates (460–ca. 375 B.C.), Theophrastus (372–287 B.C.) and, more significantly, Dioscorides (around A.D. 50). Research began to take place into the causes of illness and into the curative effects of plants. In his reference work on medicines, Dioscorides names 500 different herbs, cataloged according to their usage, which he used in the treatment of around 50 different human ailments.

During the 19th century, Theodor von Heldreich carried out a study on the abundant flora of Greece, including that of the Pílion area, which was published in 1862 in his book entitled *Die Nutzpflanzen Griechenlands (Beneficial Plants of Greece)*. Many of these plants have disappeared as a result of modern urbanization and intensive farming. Nevertheless, the Pílion is still regarded as having an inexhaustible abundance of plants and herbs. Many herbs are used in traditional cuisine.

Centaury *(Centaurium erythraea)*
Good for digestive ailments and fever.

Lemon balm *(Melissa officinalis)*
Helps relieve nervous tension and insomnia.

Mint *(Mentha)*
An infusion of mint leaves in tea relieves nausea.

Common yarrow *(Achillea millefolium)*
Relieves symptoms of feverishness, arthritis.

Camomile *(Matricaria recutita, M. chamomilla)*
Relieves stress-related digestive problems.

Scented geranium *(Pelargonium)*
Leaves can be added to *glikó* and fruit in syrup.

Rosemary *(Rosmarinus officinalis)*
Helps against depression and nervous exhaustion.

Basilikum *(Ocimum basilicum)*
Soothes feverishness, relieves nausea.

(*Salvia officinalis*)
...ves bloatedness and is good for liver problems.

Oregano (*Origanum vulgare*)
Relieves feverish colds and stomach upsets.

St. John's Wort (*Hypericum*)
Used externally for burns and wounds.

Wild mallow (*Malva silvestris*)
Useful against bronchitis and throat infections.

...nder (*Coriandrum sativum*)
...externally for hemorrhoids.

Lime blossom (*Tilia platyphyllos*)
Good against colds and migraine.

Thyme (*Thymus vulgaris*)
Soothes tickly coughs and inflamed gums.

Dill (*Anethum graveolens*)
Stimulates appetite and aids digestive problems.

A TASTE OF THE PÍLION

MOSKHÁRI ME KIDÓNIA
Veal with quinces
(Illustration top left)

2 lbs/1 kg veal
1 scant cup/200 ml Greek extra virgin olive oil
4 cinnamon sticks
6 medium quinces, peeled and sliced
2 tsp sugar
Salt
Freshly ground black pepper

Cut the meat into medium-sized pieces. Heat the olive oil in a saucepan and sear the meat quickly on all sides. Add a generous cup of water along with the cinnamon sticks, and season with salt and pepper. Reduce the heat to moderate, cover, and leave to simmer for 1½ hours. Then, add the quinces to the meat, sprinkle with the sugar and add enough water to cover. Continue to simmer until the fruit is soft and most of the water has been absorbed. Serve warm accompanied by freshly baked white bread.

SPETZOFÁI
Sausages with bell peppers
(Illustration bottom left)

A scant ½ cup/100 ml extra virgin olive oil
2 onions, sliced into rings
2 lbs/1 kg coarse, spicy sausage (from a Greek or
*   Turkish delicatessen)*
2 red bell peppers, cored and cut into strips
2 yellow bell peppers, cored and cut into strips
1 tomato, diced
Salt
Freshly ground black pepper

Heat the olive oil in a saucepan and sauté the onions until transparent. Cut up the sausage into medium-sized pieces and add to the onions. Add the peppers and diced tomato. Season with a little salt and pepper, then cook gently over a medium heat for about 15 minutes. Serve hot with freshly baked white bread.

KAPAMÁS
Meatballs in egg and lemon sauce
(Illustration top right)

1 lb/500 g ground beef
3 slices of day-old white bread with the crusts
  removed, softened in a little milk
3 eggs
1 onion, finely diced
1 bunch flat-leaved parsley, finely chopped
¼ tsp oregano
1¾ cups/450 ml Greek extra virgin olive oil
2 tbsp all-purpose flour
Juice of 1 lemon
Salt
Freshly ground black pepper

Place the ground beef in a bowl. Squeeze the
liquid out of the softened bread before adding
it to the meat. Add one egg, the onions, parsley,
oregano, salt and pepper and knead the ingredients together thoroughly. Heat a scant cup/
200 ml of olive oil in a skillet. Shape the meat
mixture into medium-sized meatballs, sauté
briefly, and set aside. Heat ⅔ cup/150 ml of olive
oil in a saucepan and brown the flour. Pour in
2 cups/500 ml of water and bring to a boil. Add
the meatballs and leave to simmer for 30 minutes. Heat the remaining oil, add a generous seasoning of pepper and pour this over the
meatballs. Lightly beat the remaining two eggs
with a fork, slowly adding the lemon juice at
the same time. Pour this lemon and egg sauce
over the meatballs and serve hot with rice and
freshly baked white bread.

BOURÁNI
Rice with vegetables
(Illustration bottom right)

A scant ½ cup/100 ml Greek extra virgin olive oil
1 onion, finely chopped
2 cloves of garlic, finely minced
2 cups/400 g rice
1 bunch flat-leaved parsley, finely chopped
1 red bell pepper, cored and cut into strips
3 tomatoes, skinned and puréed
Salt
Freshly ground black pepper

Heat the olive oil in a saucepan and sauté the
onions and garlic. Stir in the rice and parsley,
add the bell pepper and tomatoes and cover
with about 4 cups/1 liter of water. Season with
salt and pepper. Simmer over a medium heat
until the water has been absorbed and the rice
is cooked. Serve hot. *Bouráni* can be served as
a main course with white bread or as an accompaniment to meat dishes.

169

HARE AND RABBIT

In ancient times, *lagós*, or hare, was much prized by hunters in the Mediterranean region as a favorite type of game. It was very common, even on the islands, and wherever there were no foxes. Only Odysseus had to forego the pleasure of eating a delicious rack of hare since Ithaca was apparently devoid of hares in antiquity. By far the best description of the hare and its behavior, as well as how to hunt it, is contained in the treatise on hunting entitled *Kynegetikos* by Xenophon (ca.430–354 B.C.). The life of a hare in those days was constantly under threat, not just from eagles and foxes, but above all from man who found it such a delicious dish for the table: "There are many methods and numerous rules regarding the preparation of hare. The following is the best one: the meat should be cooked over a fire and served to each person while he is still drinking. It should be served hot, sprinkled only with salt and removed from the spit before it is completely cooked through. Do not worry if you see blood still dripping from the meat, just eat with relish!" (Athenaeus, *Deipnosophistai*, "The Gastronomers").

Hare or rabbit dishes still feature strongly in contemporary Greek cuisine. Whereas the long-eared field hare produces dark meat with a pronounced gamey aroma and lends itself to traditional marinades for game dishes, the

Like goats and sheep on the pastures, rabbits are part of the Greek backyard scene, where they are kept in small hutches.

leaner meat of the smaller rabbit, be it farmed or wild, is better suited to braising, one of Greece's most favored methods of food preparation. The meat from farmed rabbits is lighter and more delicate, similar to chicken, and requires care in preparation. Hares that live near the sea are said to have a particularly good flavor as they often feed on salt grass.

KOUNÉLI TIRAVGOULÓ
Rabbit with egg and cheese sauce
(not illustrated)

1 oven-ready rabbit weighing about 2 lbs/1 kg
1¼ cups/300 ml dry white wine
1 scant cup/200 ml Greek extra virgin olive oil
2 onions, coarsely diced
½ tsp oregano
Salt and freshly ground black pepper

For the sauce:
1 onion, finely diced
1 carrot, finely diced
⅛ celeriac, finely diced
2 garlic cloves, minced
3 eggs, lightly beaten
7 oz/200 g goat cheese, grated or crumbled

Joint the rabbit: Remove all skin, lower parts of front legs and ribs and any protruding bones and set them aside. Using a meat cleaver, chop the rabbit into three sections: hind legs, back, and front section with ribs. Separate the two hind and front legs, and cut the back into 2–3 pieces. Marinate the rabbit pieces in the wine, oil, onions and herbs.

Place the discarded pieces of rabbit into a saucepan with all the sauce ingredients (apart from the eggs and cheese). Cover with water and simmer for about two hours. Drain the stock and return it to the saucepan. Combine the eggs with the cheese, slowly stir the mixture into the broth and simmer gently until the sauce thickens. Remove the rabbit portions from the marinade and pat dry. Cook over a charcoal fire. Arrange the rabbit pieces on a plate and pour over the egg and cheese sauce.

LAGÓS STIFÁDO
Ragout of hare with olives

1 oven-ready hare, approx. 2–2½ lbs/1–1.2 kg
   in weight
Juice of 1–2 lemons
All-purpose flour
3 tbsp/50 ml Greek extra virgin olive oil
4 sage leaves
1 sprig of thyme
1½ cups/150 g chopped walnuts
1 generous cup/250 ml dry white wine
1 scant cup/200 ml meat stock
1 cup/150 g black olives, stoned
Salt
Freshly ground black pepper

Divide the hare into 6–7 pieces and marinate in
lemon juice for several hours. Remove from marinade and pat dry, season with salt and pepper and
sprinkle with flour. Heat the olive oil, add the
sage and thyme, and sauté the meat until lightly
browned. Add the walnuts and sauté briefly. Pour
in the wine, cover and simmer gently for about
1 hour, adding a little meat stock from time to
time. Add the olives for the last 15 minutes.

LAGÓS ME KARÍDIA
Hare in walnut sauce

1 oven-ready hare, about 2–2½ lbs/1–1.2 kg
   in weight
2 cups/500 ml red wine vinegar
1 tsp oregano
1 carrot, sliced
1 stick of celery, sliced
½ cup/125 ml Greek extra virgin olive oil
Juice of ½ lemon
Ground cinnamon
1 bay leaf
1 cup/100 g chopped walnuts
2 tbsp flour, mixed with water
Salt and freshly ground black pepper

Leave the hare to steep overnight in a cool place
in a marinade of vinegar, oregano, carrot, and
celery mixed with 2 cups/500 ml water. Remove
the hare from the marinade, pat dry with paper
towels, and divide into 6–7 portions. Season the
individual pieces with salt and pepper and sauté
well in hot olive oil. Pour in 2 cups/500 ml
water and the lemon juice and cook. Season
with cinnamon, salt and pepper, and add the
bay leaf. Cover and simmer gently for 1–1½
hours (adding more hot water as necessary).
Add the walnuts for the last 10 minutes of cooking time. Remove the hare pieces from the
saucepan. Remove the bay leaf and thicken the
walnut sauce with flour and pour over the meat.

THE CABBAGE PLAIN

The area between Tríkkala and Kalambáka on the Thessalian plain is where Greece's favorite cabbage (*Brassica oleracea*) is grown. Up to 1655 tons (1500 tonnes) are harvested here between October and January. The heads are cut off in the fields and stored in cool-rooms or sent to market for sale as winter vegetables. White cabbage is a vital ingredient of Greek cuisine. Finely grated and dressed in oil with lemon or vinegar, it forms the ever-present Greek-style white cabbage salad which, when freshly prepared, provides an extremely delicious accompaniment to grilled meat dishes. Cabbage leaves pickled in brine are another specialty. Provided these are carefully prepared, they are not even difficult to digest. Cabbage (*crambe*) and other looser-leaved varieties like curly-leaved cabbage (*rhaphanos*) already existed in ancient Greece. Even in those days, white cabbage had an important role to play and was regarded as a simple but healthy foodstuff. It was even thought to be good for treating a whole range of ailments. Its high vitamin C content undoubtedly gives it an advantage over other varieties of cabbage and a further point in its favor is its ascorbic acid content, which turns into vitamin C on heating. This means that fewer vitamins than usual are lost during the cooking process.

LAKHANODOLMÁDES
Stuffed cabbage leaves in egg and lemon sauce

Serves 4–6
1 white cabbage, about 2 lbs/1 kg in weight
¼ cup/200 g ground beef
¼ cup/200 g ground pork
1¼ packed cups/200 g cooked rice
2 tomatoes, diced

1 onion, grated
½ bunch flat-leaved parsley, finely chopped
½ bunch dill, finely chopped
2 sprigs of mint, finely chopped
1 scant cup/200 ml Greek extra virgin olive oil
Salt
Freshly ground black pepper

For the sauce:
2 tbsp/30 g butter
2 tbsp all-purpose flour
2 eggs
Juice of 2 lemons

Wash the cabbage and place whole in a saucepan filled with water. Add a pinch of salt and blanch for 5 minutes. Then separate into individual leaves and cut out the thick bit of stalk. Place the ground meats in a bowl and mix thoroughly with the rice, tomatoes, onions, parsley, dill, mint, olive oil, salt and pepper. Place a tablespoonful of the mixture at a time on a cabbage leaf, tuck in the ends and roll up firmly. Lay the rolls in a saucepan tightly packed together and cover with an upturned plate. Fill the pan with water and simmer for 40 minutes over a low heat. Drain, reserving the liquid, and keep the *dolmádes* warm. To make the sauce, melt the butter in a small saucepan and lightly brown the flour. Pour in just under 1 cup/200 ml of the reserved liquid and bring to a boil for a moment. Lightly beat the eggs in a bowl, then slowly add the lemon juice, stirring constantly. Stir this mixture into the melted butter and flour. Heat slowly (do not allow to boil), stirring constantly until the sauce thickens. Pour over the rolled-up cabbage leaves and allow to stand for a few minutes. Serve hot with freshly baked white bread.

LAKHANOSALÁTA
White cabbage salad

Serves 4–6
1 small white cabbage, cleaned and very
* finely grated*
1 carrot, cleaned and finely grated
3 cloves of garlic
Juice of 1 lemon
A scant ½ cup/100 ml Greek extra virgin olive oil
Salt
Freshly ground white pepper to taste

Place the cabbage and grated carrot in a bowl and mix well. Put the garlic cloves, lemon juice, olive oil, and salt in a mixer and blend into a sauce. Pour this dressing over the cabbage, mix well and serve.

THE MONASTERIES OF METEORA

As you approach Kalambáka from the Thessalian plain, in the distance you will see the impressive panorama of the bizarre rock pillars of Meteora, rising to almost 1000 feet (300 meters) in places. These pinnacles of rock were carved out millions of years ago by the Piniós River during the last Ice Age and have been eroded into their present strange shapes. The first settlers are thought to have arrived here in the 9th century to occupy small caves in the cliffs. During times of political unrest, more and more men arrived, trying to escape the temptations of the profane world and get closer to God. In the mid-14th century, a monk named Athanasios Meteoritis from Mount Athos founded the first monastery. Further monasteries followed in quick succession, as well as smaller buildings perched perilously on the tiniest pinnacles. Some of these boasted splendid frescoes (including some by Theophanes, a Byzantine artist). Several of the rocky eyries are so inaccessible that the monks get visitors and necessary food supplies to the top by winching them up in nets. Of the 24 original monasteries, only five are still inhabited today.

White cabbage to be used in a Greek raw salad must be very finely grated.

It is seasoned with salt, a lot of lemon juice and white pepper to taste.

A generous measure of olive oil makes the raw cabbage easier to digest.

VODINÓ ME LÁKHANO
Beef with white cabbage

2 lbs/1 kg beef
1 onion, peeled
3 potatoes, peeled
3 carrots, peeled
4 bay leaves
10 peppercorns
½ cup/125 g butter
2 onions, finely diced
2 beets, peeled and diced
1 lb/500 g cabbage, finely sliced
1 stick of celery, thinly sliced
1 bunch flat-leaved parsley, finely chopped
1 bunch dill, finely chopped
1⅔ cups/400 ml tomato juice
Juice of 1 lemon
1 cup/200 g yogurt
Salt

Cut up the meat and place in a saucepan. Cover with water and bring to a boil, then reduce heat and cook for 20 minutes, occasionally skimming off any scum that forms on the surface. Reduce the heat and add the whole onion, 2 potatoes, 2 carrots, the bay leaves, and peppercorns. Simmer for 1 hour. Remove the vegetables from the pan and set aside. Melt the butter in a skillet, add the diced onions and sauté until transparent, then add to the meat. Add the beets and cabbage. Dice the remaining potato and carrot and add to saucepan, along with the celery, parsley, and dill. Cover with water and simmer for 1 hour. Using a blender, purée the vegetables cooked earlier with the tomato and lemon juice. Stir the resulting purée into the meat mixture and simmer for another 15 minutes. Serve hot on deep plates, with a tablespoon of yogurt for garnish.

CHESTNUTS

Chestnuts (*Castanea sativa*), sometimes referred to as "sweet chestnuts," originally come from Asia Minor, but spread very early on in history through Greece into southern Europe. Even so, ancient Greece still imported vast quantities of nuts and chestnuts from Asia Minor. A fine distinction was not always made in classical literature between these different tree fruits. Chestnuts, for example, were often known as "Castanian nuts" after their place of origin, the town of Castanea on the coast of Asia Minor, but occasionally also as "Zeus acorns." Around 300 B.C. Theophrastus wrote in his *Enquiry into Plants* that the chestnut was most widespread in Macedonia, on Euboea, and in the Thessalian Pílion region, where extensive forests of chestnut trees still exist to this day. Herodotus tells of various settlements bearing the name Castanea. Even today, there are many villages, whose names stem from this meaning. They refer to the chestnut forests, which must have existed all over the country. Sweet chestnuts, not to be confused with the horse chestnut that can be found all over Europe, are the fruit of a widely spreading tree which grows up to a height of 100 feet (30 meters). The nuts develop in a shell bristling with long thin thorns which bursts open when the chestnut is ripe. The shell contains two or three flat-sided nuts covered with a brown, woody, leathery

Top and above: The prickly chestnut cases usually contain two nuts, which must be removed first from the hard outer skin, then from their soft, protective inner skin. This is done by making a crosswise cut in the flat side of the chestnuts. They can then be either boiled briefly and rinsed in cold water or alternatively roasted in the oven.

skin which pops open on roasting. This process can be facilitated by making a small cut in the skin with a sharp knife. During the colder months of the year, street sellers can be found all over the world roasting marrons, a variety of chestnut that keeps well. If chestnuts are among the ingredients in a recipe for a meat dish, they will give it a nutty, slightly sweet flavor. The Pílion region is known for a dessert specialty which is made from chestnuts, honey, and orange blossom essence. Chestnuts are also popular in this region as an accompaniment to, or stuffing, in game dishes.

Although chestnuts were used in ancient times for medical purposes, and instructions as to their areas of application and how they should be administered have come down through the ages, they are no longer used in this way and are of no significance to the pharmaceutical industry. The horse chestnut, on the other hand, which is not specifically mentioned in classical literature, has been used in various ways during the course of history both in the pharmaceutical and the cosmetic industry.

MOSKHÁRI ME KÁSTANA
Beef with chestnuts

2 lbs/1 kg beef
1 scant cup/200 ml Greek extra virgin olive oil
1 scant cup/200 ml dry white wine
2 onions, sliced into rings
4 carrots, sliced
3 sticks of celery, cut into short lengths
About 1 lb/400 g chestnuts, roasted and peeled
½ lb/200 g broccoli
½ lb/200 g small potatoes, peeled
1 sprig of rosemary
2 tbsp all-purpose flour
Salt
Freshly ground black pepper

Bind the meat with kitchen string. Heat the olive oil in a saucepan and brown the meat on all sides. Pour in the wine and add the onions, carrots, and celery. Season with salt and pepper. Add enough water to cover the ingredients and bring to a boil. Then reduce the heat and simmer the meat over a medium heat for 1½ hours. Add the chestnuts, broccoli, potatoes, and rosemary and cook for a further 30 minutes. Remove the meat from the saucepan and discard the kitchen string, cut the meat into slices and arrange on a plate with the vegetables. Dissolve the flour in a little water and use this to thicken the stock. Season with salt and pepper and pour over the sliced meat. Serve hot.

The chestnut woman is a common sight on the streets of Greek towns in the fall.

Sometimes, she sells pistachio nuts and roasted corn cobs as well as chestnuts.

SWEET HOSPITALITY

Anyone exploring the land of the Greeks with their taste buds alert will sooner or later encounter the sweet side of life. Not only are sweet treats allowed as a matter of course during fasting periods, they also play a major role in all aspects of daily life, both within one's own family and neighboring families. Fruit, and even some vegetable varieties, feature very prominently in this respect, preserved in sugar or honey syrup according to the same basic recipe. These *gliká koutalioú* were traditionally served in a silver bowl, a *glikotíki*, and sucked, rather than eaten, in small amounts from dainty little spoons. They are typically served at private get togethers with neighbors, for instance, at a birthday celebration, or a house-warming party. *Glikó* usually gets these afternoon celebrations underway and is a sweet accompaniment to coffee. The strict sequence of fruit in syrup, followed by coffee, served with the ritual glass of water, is still upheld to this day. This threesome can then be followed by various types of cake, chocolates, and liqueurs.

Many different ingredients can form the basis of a *glikó*. Oranges, chestnuts, lemons, apples, pears, quince, grapes, figs, and young eggplant are especially popular. Although flavor is very important, every hostess is equally concerned with the visual effect achieved by the bottled fruit. The Zagorá Women's Cooperative is renowned throughout Thessaly for its skill in this art. In their small café in the village square, the women offer a large selection of their preserves in a variety of colors and bottle shapes.

The Zagorá Women's Cooperative is just as renowned for its liqueurs as it is for its fruits in syrup. Their range also includes medicinal and culinary herbs.

No get together is complete without a little spoonful of something sweet.

Morello cherry liqueur has a fresh and rather exotic taste.

You will not find this kiwi fruit liqueur anywhere else in Greece.

BAKLAVÁS

Relations between the Greeks and the Turks have by no means always been harmonious – to put it mildly. Even so, there are certain things on which sweet consensus exists, like *baklavás* for example. And it is not only between these two peoples that this syrup-steeped confection serves as a unifying influence: it is widely known and popular far beyond the Balkans and the East. In the original Turkish version, so-called *yufka*-leaves, from which *börek* (pastry pockets) and *katmer* (puff pastry dainties) were made, formed the basic pastry. The Greeks use *fillo* pastry which is rolled out as thinly as you could possibly imagine and filled, according to preference, with finely chopped walnuts, pistachio nuts, or almonds. This type of confectionery now occupies a firm place in traditional Greek cuisine, not just as a dessert but as a little nourishing snack to go with a coffee and water. *Baklavás* is a must whenever you want to spoil your guests, but at the same time it is a popular gift to bring to your hosts.

BAKLAVÁS

½ cup/50 g chopped walnuts or almonds
4 tbsp breadcrumbs
4 tbsp sugar
1 tsp cinnamon
1 cup/250 g butter
10 oz/300 g phyllo pastry (see recipe p. 146)

For the syrup:
1 generous cup/250 g sugar
7 tbsp/200 g honey
2 cloves
1 cinnamon stick
Juice of 1 lemon

Mix the walnuts or almonds with the breadcrumbs, sugar, and cinnamon. Melt the butter. Preheat the oven to 350 °F (180 °C).

Grease a shallow baking pan large enough to accommodate the sheets of pastry. Brush the pastry sheets with butter and place the first two into the baking pan. Cover the upper layer with nut filling. Lay another buttered sheet on top and cover with filling. Repeat until you have completed eight layers. Once you have added the ninth layer, cut off any excess pastry from around the edge of the *baklavás*. Place one final buttered layer on top and cut a diamond-shaped pattern into it. Sprinkle with water and bake in the center of a preheated oven for 30–40 minutes until golden brown.

To make the syrup, boil the sugar in 6 cups/ 1½ liters of water for 5 minutes. Add the honey, cloves, and cinnamon and continue to simmer. Remove the cloves and cinnamon and stir in the lemon juice. Bring the syrup to a boil, then leave to cool. Remove the confectionery from the oven and pour the syrup over it. For this stage, either the pastry should have cooled and the syrup be warm, or else the pastry should be warm and the syrup cool so that the *baklavás* do not become too soft. Cut into diamond shapes and serve.

Tip: you can buy ready-made *fillo* pastry from a Greek or Turkish delicatessen or from supermarkets. (In the United States it can be found as phyllo or filo pastry in supermarkets.) While you are working, any unused sheets of pastry should be stored between damp tea towels as it dries out very quickly.

Making *baklavás* is a lot of work so it is a good idea to have some help. Sharing the work obviously makes the job easier. While the first pan is ready for the oven and just being brushed with melted butter as a final touch at one end of the table, the second batch is being started at the other end.

The nuts are crushed in a mortar. They do not have to be ground evenly.

Mix together the nuts, breadcrumbs, cinnamon, and sugar to taste.

Brush the first two wafer-thin sheets of phyllo pastry on the baking pan with melted butter.

Make a second layer with 1 buttered sheet and cover with filling, continuing in this way until the 9th/10th layer.

Just before baking, cut the characteristic diamond pattern into the top layer of *baklavás*.

Once the pastry has soaked up all the syrup, the *baklavás* is ready for serving.

ΣΠΟΡΑΔΕΣ

Above: preparations for the Easter celebrations in the church at Skópelos.
Background: view from Glossa across to Skiáthos.

SPORADES

Plums

Easter rituals

Sacrificial lambs

Time to eat

Time to bake

Almonds á la Sporades

The five main islands comprising the Sporades archipelago are some of Greece's lesser known islands. The northern Sporades seem like continuations of the Pílion peninsula which have broken away into the Aegean Sea. Euboea is the second largest island in Greece and and extends like a long protective barrier along the coast of central Greece and Attica. Its close proximity to the mainland lent it strategic importance in classical times, and in the 6th and 7th centuries B.C., it played a decisive role during Greek colonialization in the Mediterranean and the Black Sea. From 1204 onward, the Sporades islands of Skiáthos, Skópelos, Alónnisos, and Skyros found themselves ruled by an Italian noble family, while Euboea was under the control of the Venetians until the 15th century when they all became part of the Ottoman Empire.

The differences between the islands are reflected in their architecture. Whereas the buildings on Skiáthos, Skópelos, and Euboea are typical of those on the mainland, the architectural style on Alónnisos and Skyros is reminiscent of that found in the Cyclades. The colorful Skyriot marble has long been a coveted building material and attracted the attention of classical historian and geographer, Strabo (ca. 64/63 B.C. to A.D. 23). Skyros is also famous, however, for its goats and sheep, with more than 50,000 animals still kept on the island. During Carnival time, the island becomes a meeting place for many mainland Greeks who want to experience one of the country's most traditional festivals. Skópelos today is predominantly an island of pine forests and olive trees, but was once famous for its plum trees, the fruits of which were dried in special ovens and distilled into a brandy popular throughout Greece. Skiáthos, the smallest of the Sporades islands, is a wooded island, devoted mainly to olive groves as well as the all-important Aleppo pines grown for their resin used in retsina. In 1992, Greece's first marine national park was created around Alónnisos, its 850 square miles (2,200 sq km) making it the largest of its kind in the Mediterranean region. It is centered around the small uninhabited island of Pipéri, one of the few remaining refuges of monk seals. The park is also home to around 3000 species of fish and 82 varieties of birds. Even in this age of tourism, Euboea has managed to retain an almost untouched originality and is a paradise for honey bees.

This elderly plum grower is one of the last on Skópelos. As far as he is concerned, the best plums in Greece come, as they have always done, not from across the sea, but from "his" island alone.

Left: The majority of the tart purple Skópelos plums end up in drying ovens.
Right: The yellow *Avgáto* plum is still one of the island's most important fruits.

The sour yellow *Avgáto* plum is small and round.

Arsan is a large, sweet plum, which is good fresh or dried.

Xinó is a firm variety of tart-tasting plum.

Loukoumatia is soft and tastes very sweet.

PLUMS

The little Sporades island of Skópelos was once renowned for its wine, the reputed aphrodisiac qualities of which were extolled by the classical comic dramatist Aristophanes and even Casanova. It was exported in amphorae as far as the Black Sea coasts. It was the phylloxera catastrophe at the end of the 19th century that destroyed this most blessed of the island's resources by wiping out all the vinestock. However, Skópelos still had a second culinary string to its bow. Apart from the pine trees and olive trees that cover the island, it is also home to a large number of plum trees, as well as chestnut and walnut trees. Only a small proportion of the island's annual crop of plums is sold fresh at Greek markets. The bulk of this purple harvest is earmarked for two other long-established specialties, namely prunes and plum brandy, both of which are produced using traditional methods. Nowadays, the number of producers willing to preserve this island tradition is falling drastically.

One of the few is 60-year-old farmer Yannis. He grew up with plum trees planted by his grandfather. And although they are old and gnarled by now, they still bear fruit. After being picked, the plums are washed, dried, and spread out evenly on grids. These are then placed on shelves and dried at a constant temperature. All over the island, you will see characteristic little buildings next to houses. These contain the charcoal-fired drying ovens in drying chambers where the plums are processed. John has also learned that the plums have to be "massaged" occasionally so that they shrink evenly during the drying process. The island's plum brandy also deserves a mention.

The old charcoal-fired drying ovens are still in use on the island of Skópelos.

The plums remain in the drying chamber until they are dried and flat.

Despite their wrinkled appearance, the flesh inside remains soft and sweet.

Each plum is individually "massaged" so that it dries evenly on all sides and retains its shape.

KHTAPÓDI ME DAMÁSKINA
Octopus with plums

1 octopus, about 4 lbs/2 kg in weight
1 scant cup/200 ml white wine
1 scant cup/200 ml Greek extra virgin olive oil
1 scant cup/200 ml vinegar
24 plums
2 bay leaves
4 large potatoes, peeled and cut into strips
  (or 3 quinces may be substituted)
Salt
Freshly ground black pepper

Preheat the oven to 350 °F (180 °C). Separate the tentacles from the body and place in a casserole dish. Arrange the plums and bay leaves around the tentacles. Pour in the wine, vinegar, and oil, season with salt and pepper and cover the dish tightly with foil. Cook for about 2 hours in a preheated oven (the sauce will turn to jelly). Add the potatoes for the last hour of cooking time. Serve hot with freshly baked white bread.

MOSKHÁRI ME DAMÁSKINA
Veal with prunes

2 lbs/1 kg veal from the shoulder
1 scant cup/200 ml Greek extra virgin olive oil
3 onions, finely diced
1 scant cup/200 ml dry white wine
2 bay leaves
½ tsp ground cinnamon
½ tsp sugar
1 lb/500 g prunes
Salt
Freshly ground black pepper

Divide the meat into portions. Heat the olive oil in a saucepan and brown the meat on all sides. Add the onions and sauté quickly, adding the white wine before they begin to turn brown. Add the bay leaves, cinnamon and sugar, and season with salt and pepper. Pour in enough water to cover all the ingredients. Bring to a boil, then reduce the temperature and simmer over a low heat until the meat is almost cooked. Line the base of a saucepan with the plums and place the meat and stock on top. Simmer over a moderate heat for 15 minutes. Serve hot with rice.

EASTER RITUALS

The first full moon of spring heralds the high point of the church year in the Greek Orthodox calendar. Devout Christians have been fasting for 40 days, in other words going without meat, cheese and eggs. Even the less devout respect the fasting rules during "Holy Week," the week before Easter Sunday.

It is difficult to say precisely why there is a special magic about the Greek Easter festival. It is true that spring festivals have been held at this time of year since pagan times to reawaken the spirits of nature. Even now, witnessing a Greek spring can be an almost reverential experience and there can scarcely be anyone who does not succumb to its magic. In the week before Easter, this season of rebirth, people congregate on a daily basis to celebrate with growing anticipation the resurrection of Christ. During this, the most important festival in the Orthodox Church calendar, any cultural, ethnic, religious, or even culinary differences between the mainland and the Greek islands are forgotten. However, this final week in the run-up to Easter is a demanding time for the faithful. Each day, there is a church service lasting several hours, in which the Stations of the Cross are visited and the Gospels preached. At home, it is full steam ahead with spring-cleaning and preparing food for the coming festival. None of the important Easter specialties must be left out: candies, plaited bread rolls, fresh eggs, and drinks must be bought or carefully prepared. New clothes must be bought for the children.

On the Wednesday before Easter, the church candleholders are sprinkled not as they usually are with sand, but with flour. After the service, the women bake this into a loaf of bread and have it blessed in church. Maundy Thursday's preparations focus on dyeing the eggs and the evening mass is very taxing even for the most devout of souls. All the Gospels are read in a service, which seems to go on forever. During Thursday night, everyone goes into deep mourning. The church icons are covered with dark cloths and the mighty church bells fall silent until Easter Sunday. The *Epitaphios*, the symbolic representation of Christ's tomb, which has held pride of place in the church, is garlanded with flowers. On Good Friday evening, it is ceremoniously carried through the village in a magnificent candlelit procession, followed by the priest and the entire congregation.

Finally, Easter Saturday arrives and everyone is occupied with last-minute food preparations as there will be no time left later in the evening. Everyone proceeds to church with their Easter candles and red-dyed hard-cooked eggs – red to symbolize the blood of Christ. Prayers and singing continue all through the evening vigil until midnight when the priest announces the words of deliverance: "Christ is risen." The bells ring out, people embrace each other, exchange greetings, and bang their red eggs together – whoever's egg lasts longest without cracking will have good luck the following year – before hurrying home for *mayirítsa*, fresh Easter soup, which is already steaming in anticipation. Lent is over for another year.

Above and background: on Good Friday evening, the symbolic tomb of Christ is carried through the streets.

The Easter Sunday service lasts several hours and is something of an endurance test for the congregation.

The *Epitaphios*, a model representing Christ's tomb, contains offerings and fresh flowers.

The task of decorating the church begins during Lent. During Holy Week in the run-up to Easter Sunday, Christ's symbolic tomb stands in pride of place in the church.

The 40 days of Lent end with colored and decorated red eggs being knocked together: whoever's egg remains intact the longest will have good luck in the following year.

SACRIFICIAL LAMBS

The lamb, more often than not the male of the species, the young ram, has played an important role as a creature of sacrifice since classical times in the worship of Aphrodite, Zeus and, in particular, Hermes. It was slaughtered and sacrificed on special feast days on the altar to the deity in question. While parts of the animal, usually the most prized, such as the neck, went up in smoke on the sacrificial altar on their way to the deity, what was left was cooked over an open fire and eaten by those performing the ritual. In this respect, Greek mythology appears more progressive than the Old Testament: The

Greeks, after all, had already put their days of human sacrifice behind them by the time Abraham came to the place indicated by Jehovah, where he was supposed to sacrifice his own son Isaac – whereupon the latter said: "My father! And he replied: Here am I, my son! And

Isaac said: Behold the fire and the wood. But where is the lamb for a burnt offering?" (Gen. 22:7). Although God is merciful and accepts a young ram instead of an archaic human sacrifice, the Old Testament is nevertheless describing an incident from deep in the past.

In another story, Moses, who is to lead the people of Israel out of Egypt, has prepared lamb for the Passover meal in accordance with the Lord's instructions: "Your lamb shall be without blemish, a male of the first year: ye shall take it out from the sheep, or from the goats" (Ex. 12:5). This meal pressages the Last Supper. Byzantine paintings of the Last Supper depict roast lamb less commonly than fish, but still often enough for it to symbolize a firm belief in Christ's divinity.

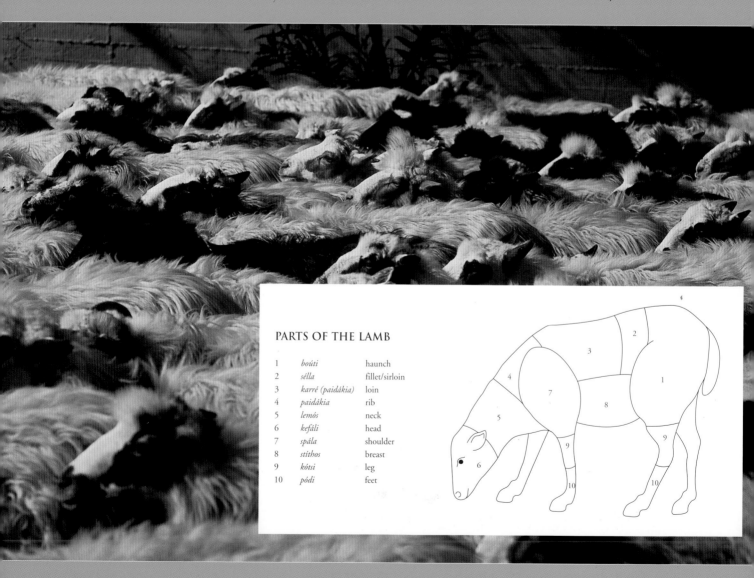

PARTS OF THE LAMB

1	*boúti*	haunch
2	*sélla*	fillet/sirloin
3	*karré (paidákia)*	loin
4	*paidákia*	rib
5	*lemós*	neck
6	*kefáli*	head
7	*spála*	shoulder
8	*stíthos*	breast
9	*kótsi*	leg
10	*pódi*	feet

SPIT-ROAST LAMB OR KID

The lamb or kid (in this case the latter) is prepared whole. Either one is too big for a normal household garden barbecue. An early start must be made, therefore, on digging out a shallow hole and filling it with charcoal, then getting the charcoal glowing well.

The kid must be skinned, gutted, and thoroughly cleaned, then rubbed with salt and pepper inside and out before cooking. The lean meat should be brushed frequently with oil during roasting. You will find that every barbecue expert swears by his own special recipe. Though opinions may differ as to the virtues of oregano, thyme, and sage, lemon juice always gets the thumbs-up.

The kid is skewered onto the spit along the length of its spine. An important factor in the cooking is the speed at which the spit rotates. The meat must cook evenly and the outside must be crisp while the inside remains juicy. This requires quite a lot of experience. It is best to have the spit rotate more quickly at the start to make sure that the meat cooks evenly, but to slow it down toward the end so that the outside becomes crisp.

The whole cooking process can take up to seven hours, although the outer layers will be done after about two hours and can be sliced off and served. All you need now are lots of good friends, plenty of wine, and fine weather.

While the kid itself should only cook very slowly, the variety meats need a much stronger heat. They are placed on a metal grill directly above the charcoal.

The variety meats are removed by hand, sometimes by several hands.

Heart, kidneys, stomach, liver, and, lastly, the intestine are prepared separately.

The variety meats will be ready first and can be served as appetizers.

The spit is skewered through the head and the chest. The front legs are secured against the body.

Once the chest cavity has been seasoned and brushed with olive oil, the slit in the stomach can be sewn up.

To prevent the meat from getting too crisp too quickly, it is frequently brushed with lemon and olive oil.

189

More people than you might expect observe the fasting period and after 40 days of abstinence during Lent it is time to enjoy a lavish meal again.

KOKORÉTSI
Grilled tripe roll

1 whole sheep's intestine
1 lb/500 g lamb's liver
1 lb/500 g lamb's lung
½ lb/250 g lamb's spleen
Mutton fat
Oregano
Juice of 2 lemons
½ bunch flat-leaved parsley, finely chopped
Salt
Freshly ground black pepper

Wash the intestine carefully, then turn it inside out and wash the other side.

Clean the variety meats and cut into medium-sized pieces. Rub a generous amount of salt, pepper and oregano into the intestine and meats. Spear alternate pieces of meat onto the spit, inserting a piece of mutton fat after every third piece. Wrap the whole thing tightly in intestine, tying regular knots as you go and pulling tightly to keep everything together. Rub in some more salt, pepper, and oregano and leave upright for a few hours to allow it to drain. Suspend over a charcoal fire and cook. The spit should rotate quickly at the start of cooking, then more slowly later on until it is cooked through. Remove the *kokorétsi* from the spit and cut into bite-sized pieces. Arrange on a plate, pour a generous amount of lemon juice over them and sprinkle with fresh parsley.

TIME TO EAT

Enjoying meals together is an important part of Greek life. They would do so every day if it were possible, but everyday commitments, particularly in the big cities, mean that there obviously has to be a compromise. On special occasions, however, there is no getting away from it: the whole family, if not the entire village, sits down around the table. This is true of private celebrations, such as weddings, baptisms or funerals, and is likewise the case on "official" religious holidays. The communal meal takes on special meaning, however, when it has been preceded by a long period of fasting and privation, as in the run-up to Easter. Not only is the occasion of having a meal together cause for celebration, but also the very fact of being able to eat normally again is reason to celebrate in itself. The tables groan under the weight of food and the talking and eating go on for hours. The holiday atmosphere is so tangible that many Greeks have no compunction at all in enjoying it without needing the pretext of a religious occasion.

ARNÁKI ME SPARÁNGIA
Lamb with asparagus

2 lbs/1 kg neck of lamb
1 scant cup/200 ml Greek extra virgin olive oil
1 large onion, finely diced
2 lbs/1 kg asparagus
Juice of 1 lemon
2–4 tbsp flour, mixed with a little water
½ bunch flat-leaved parsley
Salt
Freshly ground black pepper

Wash the meat and pat it dry, then divide it into portions. Heat the olive oil in a saucepan, sauté the onions until transparent, and brown the meat on all sides. Pour in enough water to cover the meat. Reduce the heat and leave the meat to simmer.

Meanwhile, wash and trim the asparagus. Bring some salted water to a boil, add the asparagus and simmer for about 15 minutes. Pour off the water and leave to drain.

Once the meat is tender, remove the saucepan from the heat, stir in the lemon juice and thicken the sauce with the flour-and-water mixture. Season to taste with salt and pepper. Arrange the asparagus on a plate with the lamb and sauce over it. Sprinkle with parsley and serve hot.

EASTER EGGS

Various explanations exist as to why Greek Easter eggs are always colored red: some people say that the red is a symbol of the blood shed in the Holy Land on Good Friday, others say that it reflects joy at Christ's resurrection. Then again, some people claim that long ago a sceptical woman scoffed that she would not believe in the Resurrection until the eggs she was holding in her hands turned red in front of her eyes – which did indeed happen. In other words, their red color should be seen as an admonishment to have faith.

You need a light touch for the traditional egg-bashing ritual, as well as a good bit of luck – not to mention eggs from well fed hens. Only someone with an egg whose shell remains intact is in line for any good luck. This custom, which is said to stem from the 13th century, has been preserved as a bit of Easter fun. Hence, you will find that everyone in church on Easter Saturday evening will have a red egg in his pocket. The eggs may not be eaten during Lent. They are only brought out, therefore, after the priest has ceremoniously opened the Easter celebrations with the words "Christ is risen" whereupon everyone wishes each other a happy Easter and starts banging their eggs together.

No Greek Easter table would be complete without the obligatory bowl of red eggs.

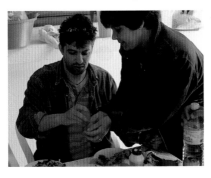

For the egg-banging ritual, one person holds his egg still, while the other knocks his own egg against it.

If the shell gets dented, there is nothing to do but to peel your egg and eat it without further ado.

MAYIRÍTSA
Greek Easter soup

Greek Easter soup, *mayirítsa*, is eaten in the early hours of Sunday morning following the midnight Easter service. It is too late for a celebratory feast like Easter lamb, but a good time for making use of what is left over after the lamb has been butchered and gutted. Serving easily digestible soup is also a good way of accustoming the stomach to more substantial food after weeks of going without meat.

1 lb/500 g lamb's liver
½ lb/250 g onions, sliced into rings
½ bunch dill, finely chopped
1¼ cups/250 g rice
2 eggs
Juice of 2 lemons
1 tbsp butter
Salt
Freshly ground black pepper

Wash the liver thoroughly and place in a saucepan filled with salted water. Boil the liver over a high heat until it is half cooked. Remove it from the liquid and cut up into small pieces. Strain the stock through a strainer into a large saucepan. Add the onions and dill and bring the liquid to a boil. Stir in first the rice, then the liver. Melt the tablespoon of butter in the soup and continue to simmer until the rice and liver are cooked, then remove the pan from the heat. Lightly beat eggs in a small bowl and add the lemon juice, stirring continuously. Spoon a few tablespoons of soup into the egg mixture and continue beating until the egg and lemon sauce is frothy. Pour this briskly into the hot soup, making sure that it does not boil or else the eggs will curdle. Season the soup with salt and pepper. Serve hot with freshly baked white bread.

This is the basic recipe for *mayirítsa*. Sometimes other variety meats, such as the spleen, kidneys, or even the intestine, may be added to the soup. Some regional variations may also contain spinach. Each family swears by its own recipe, which is passed down from generation to generation.

TIME TO BAKE

Tsouréki are traditional Greek Easter bread rolls (also known as *lambrópsomo*, Easter Sunday bread). They are regarded as a symbol of fertility and blessing. In some parts of Greece, the women still decorate their *tsouréki* with flower and leaf motifs or other symbols of spring. Almonds or dried fruit are also popular additions, not to mention red eggs. The wholesome ingredients of Easter bread are a clear signal that Lent is over.

Tsourékia vary from region to region: almond hares from Lagoudáki, elaborate wreaths from Kouloura on Crete or a simple plaited roll decorated with a red egg.

TSOURÉKI
Greek Easter bread

10 cakes/150 g yeast (if using active dry yeast follow manufacturer's instructions)
13 cups/1.5 kg all-purpose flour
1 pinch of salt
2 oz/50 g cinnamon sticks
1 tsp mastic, powdered (available in Greek and Turkish stores)
8 eggs
1¾ cups/400 g sugar
1 generous cup/250 ml milk
1½ cups/300 g butter
1 egg yolk
1 hard-cooked egg, dyed red
Sesame seeds or flaked almonds, according to preference

Dissolve the yeast in a little lukewarm milk. Add 5 tablespoons of flour, stir well and leave to stand in a warm place for one hour. Meanwhile, melt the butter, heat the milk and leave them both to cool. Place the cinnamon sticks in a small saucepan, adding enough water to cover them, then bring to a boil and simmer for 10 minutes. Pour off the liquid and set it aside. Sift the remaining flour into a bowl, then add the mastic and the risen yeast. Pour in the melted butter, milk, and cinnamon water. Beat the eggs and sugar together until frothy and add to the other ingredients. Mix together thoroughly. Knead the dough until it is completely smooth, then cover and leave to rise in a warm place for about two hours.

Preheat the oven to 350 °F (180 °C). Once the dough has doubled in size, punch it down and knead again thoroughly. Roll out the dough into three long sausage shapes and plait them into a large bun. Place the dough onto a well greased baking sheet and brush with egg yolk. Press the red egg into the middle of the plait, sprinkle a few flaked almonds over the top and bake in a preheated oven for about 35–45 minutes until the bread is golden brown.

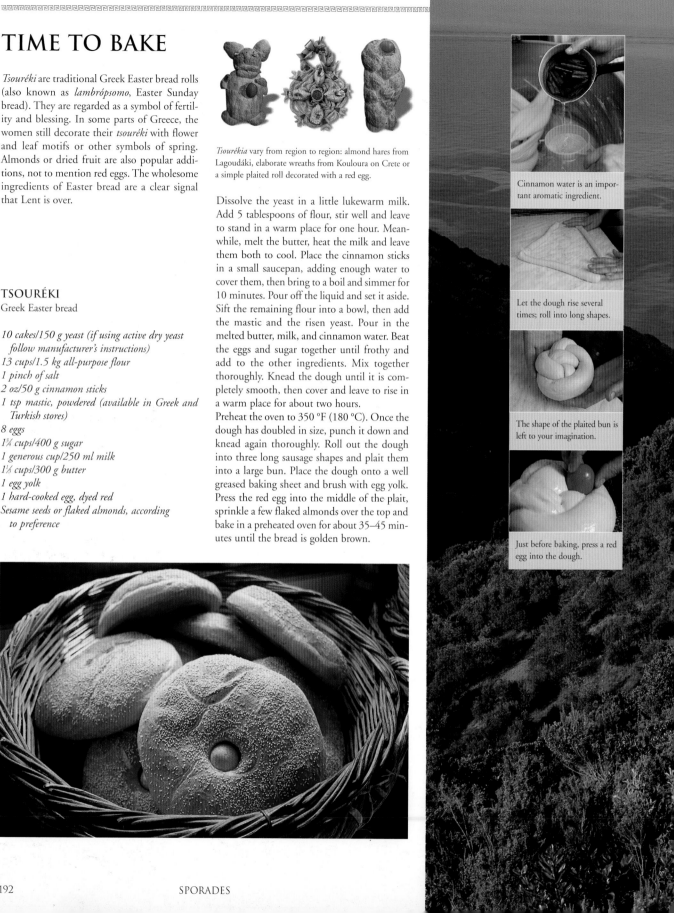

Cinnamon water is an important aromatic ingredient.

Let the dough rise several times; roll into long shapes.

The shape of the plaited bun is left to your imagination.

Just before baking, press a red egg into the dough.

KOULOURÁKIA ME KANÉLA
Cinnamon rings with currants

4 cups/500 g all-purpose flour
2 tsp baking powder
1½ tsp ground cinnamon
¼ tsp ground cloves
¼ tsp grated nutmeg
⅞ cup/200 g sugar
1 generous cup/250 ml Greek extra virgin
  olive oil
1 tbsp brandy
3 tbsp + 1 tsp/50 ml mineral water
3 tbsp + 1 tsp/50 ml orange juice
1 tsp orange zest
Currants for decoration

Preheat the oven to 350 °F (180 °C). Sift the flour and baking powder into a bowl. Mix in the cinnamon, cloves and nutmeg. Using the high setting on an electric blender, mix together the sugar, olive oil, brandy, mineral water, orange juice, and orange zest. Add this sugar mixture to the flour in the bowl and knead all the ingredients together to form a smooth dough. Taking a lump of dough at a time, roll it into thumb-thick sausages of pastry, about 4 inches (10 cm) long. Press the ends together firmly to make rings and decorate each one with two currants.
Spread out the rings on a greased baking sheet and bake for 20 minutes in a preheated oven.

STAFIDÓPSOMO
Raisin bread

1 generous cup/250 ml milk
A generous ½ cup/125 g butter
⅝ cup/125 g sugar
2 tsp lemon zest
1 tsp salt
½ tsp baking soda
2⅓ cakes/45 g yeast
13 cups/1.5 kg all-purpose flour
9 cups/500 g raisins
1 egg yolk, lightly beaten with a little water

Bring the milk to a boil, then remove it from the heat. Add the butter, sugar, lemon zest, salt, and baking soda and stir until dissolved. Mix the yeast with a generous cup/250 ml warm water and a little flour. Sift the remaining flour into a bowl and make a well in the center. Pour in the yeast mixture, add the milk mixture, and knead all the ingredients into an elastic dough. Place the dough in a greased bowl, brush a little melted butter over it, cover and leave to rise until it has tripled in size. Preheat the oven to 400 °F (200 °C).
Knead the dough briefly and shape into a ball. Press two fingers into the middle to make a well. Keep pulling until a hole, the breadth of two hands, appears in the middle, forming a ring. Place on a greased baking sheet, brush with egg yolk, and bake in a preheated oven for 50–60 minutes.

AMIGDALOTÁ
Marzipan cookies

2 scant cups/200 g ground almonds
⅞ cup/200 g sugar
3 egg whites
Seeds from 1 vanilla pod
About 20 almond halves

Preheat the oven to 350 °F (180 °C). Mix the ground almonds and sugar together in a bowl. Lightly beat the egg whites and mix in the vanilla seeds. Stirring constantly, add the egg whites very gradually to the almond mixture a little at a time. The resulting mixture should be fairly firm and stiff. Spoon the mixture into a pastry bag with a star-shaped tip and pipe about 20 small mounds of mixture onto a greased baking sheet. Decorate each one with half an almond and bake in a preheated oven until the peaks are golden brown. These cookies will keep for quite a long time in an airtight container.

It is customary in some regions to give each guest at a wedding or baptism a marzipan flower rosette, a symbol of purity and femininity. It used to be the women's task to make these and they would gather prior to the celebration to turn pounds of almonds, sugar, and oil of roses into marzipan which would later be molded into rosettes.

ALMONDS Á LA SPORADES

Above: inside the green case of unripe almonds (left), the white kernel is still soft (center). Once ripe, the flesh becomes dry and the hardened kernel (right) protects the seed, which is the actual almond.

In the same way that the chestnut tree spread from Asia Minor to Thessaly and thence to the Sporades Islands, the almond tree (*Prunus dulcis*) likewise found its way to these small, rocky islands where it quickly put down roots thanks to its ability to survive on very little water. Prior to the commercial cultivation of the almond tree, consumption of the seeds of the wild variety, which contain prussic acid, may well have caused unfortunate side-effects. Since about 500 B.C., however, sweet almonds, *amygdale*, have been a familiar ingredient in desserts, combined with eggs and walnuts, for instance.

Almonds, like pistachios, are classified as stone fruits. The part used in baking or in candies is the white inner seed, with its brown hull removed, and is found inside the stone enclosed by the green fleshy fruit case. The Sporades Islands, despite their limited agricultural possibilities, have developed almond cultivation to a level not seen on any other group of Greek islands. On Skópelos alone, which is also famous for its plums, 16.5 US tons (15 tonnes) of almonds are harvested each year.

The women of the Sporades make an almond cream from peeled almonds by grating them while still warm and mixing them quickly with sugar and water. This cream is served by the spoonful. Grated white almonds, lots of superfine sugar, lightly beaten egg white and flower essence are the ingredients which go to make *khamaliá*, a marzipan-type delicacy, which is usually served at weddings and on name days. The mixture is shaped into an appropriate form for the occasion, baked in the oven and finally dusted with confectioners' sugar. *Roxédes* is prepared in a similar way to *khamaliá*, but using coarse sugar instead and not baked, which means it does not keep as well. Almond milk, *amigdalozoúmi*, is a popular drink during Lent and at funerals. This is made by simmering peeled, ground almonds in boiling water and then straining the liquid through a cloth.

KOURABIÉDES
Almond cookies

1½ cups/200 g whole almonds, peeled
2 cups/ 450 g soft butter
⅞ cup/200 g sugar
3 egg yolks
4 tbsp brandy
Seeds from 1 vanilla pod
8½ cups/900 g all-purpose flour
2 tsp baking powder
4 tbsp rose water
Confectioners' sugar

Preheat the oven to 375 °F (190 °C). Lay the almonds on a baking sheet and roast in the oven, before chopping them up finely. Cream the butter and sugar together in a bowl, then add the egg yolks, brandy, and vanilla seeds in that order. Sift the flour and baking powder into the bowl, add the almonds and mix together well. Sprinkle your work surface with flour and tip the mixture out onto it, kneading it into a smooth dough. Roll this out until it is just under ½ inch/1 cm thick. Using the rim of a glass, cut out small semicircles and arrange them on greased baking sheets. Bake in a preheated oven for about 20 minutes. Leave to cool on a cooling rack, sprinkle with rose water and dust with confectioners' sugar.

Above and background: Countless almonds are cracked open to make the almond specialties.

Kroasanak – almond puff pastry

Roxédes – uncooked marzipan rosettes

Khamaliá – marzipan for a wedding

Glikó migsala – almond spread

Kritsinia – sesame and almond sticks

Uliria kakao – almond cookies

Khamaliá – marzipan cookies

Paximádia – almond rusks

Sabless – almond shortbread *sablés*

Amigdalosoúmi – almond milk

KARIDÓPITA
Almond and walnut cake

½ cup + 1 tbsp/125 g butter
1 generous cup/250 g sugar
5 eggs
2 cups/250 g almonds, finely chopped
2 cups/250 g walnuts, finely chopped
1 tsp ground cinnamon
1 tsp ground cloves
1 tsp baking soda
2 tbsp brandy
3½ cups/350 g all-purpose flour
3 tsp baking powder
12 oz/350 g rusks, grated
1 generous cup/250 ml milk

For the syrup;
3 ⅓ cups/750 g sugar
2 cups/500 ml water
1 tsp lemon juice

Preheat the oven to 400 °F (200 °C). Beat the butter, sugar, and eggs together in a bowl until frothy. Mix the nuts with the cinammon and cloves. Dissolve the baking soda in brandy and pour it into the nut mixture. Sift the flour and baking powder into the bowl with the butter mixture, adding the nuts, rusks, and milk. Mix all the ingredients together to form a smooth batter. Press this into a greased and floured baking pan and place in the oven. After five minutes, reduce the heat to about 300 °F (150 °C) and bake the cake for around one hour. Remove from the oven and leave to cool. To make the syrup, heat the water in a saucepan and dissolve the sugar. Bring to a boil several times, then add the lemon juice. Pour the syrup over the cake and wait until it has been absorbed before cutting it into generous slices and arranging it on a plate. The cake can then be dusted with confectioners' sugar, depending on individual taste.

ΧΑΛΚΙΔΙΚΗ

Above: statue of the philosopher Aristotle in Stágira.
Background: Símonos Pétras Monastery on Mt Athos.

CHALKIDIKÍ

Natural honey

Fasting

Fishing

Boat-building

Preserving fish

Fish with everything

The Garden of Mary

In the refectory

A holy vintner

Athos wine from Tsantalis

Mountain cherries

Squid and octopus

Chalkidiki extends out into the Aegean, resembling an outstretched hand with three splayed fingers. The peninsula, which is 56 miles (90 kilometers) across, is one of the most delightful regions of northern Greece and foreign settlers have gravitated here from the days of the ancient Greeks right up to more recent times. This splintered peninsula, which extends southeast of Thessaloniki, has a surprisingly varied landscape, with numerous beaches lapped by crystal-clear water along its coastline. Kassándra, the westernmost finger, with its landscape of low, undulating hills, is separated from the mainland by a canal, built between 1935 and 1937 in the same place that one existed in classical times. Sithoniá, the middle finger, is scenically more attractive by comparison. The rugged Ítamos mountains, which run the length of the peninsula and rise up to 2450 feet (753 meters), are thickly forested and fall away sharply to the sea in some places. Its rocky, fissured coastline, punctuated with numerous little bays, is quite different from the gentler coastline of Kassándra. Athos, the easternmost finger, is dominated by cone-shaped Mount Athos, which rises to a height of 6690 feet (2039 meters). The wild, virtually untamed natural beauty of the region has not only fascinated people since classical times, but has also prevented any systematic settlement. Toward the end of the 4th century B.C. the Greek architect Deinocrates had plans to turn the whole mountain, which on a clear day is visible from as far away as the Pílion, into a huge likeness of Alexander. Centuries later, this inhospitable peninsula seemed the perfect refuge for hermits, enabling them to withdraw into complete seclusion. The first monks settled on Athos in the year 843 and it quickly became a center of Eastern Christianity. Today, it is an autonomous monastic republic.

The Chalkidiki peninsula derives its name from settlers originating from Chalkis on the island of Euboea, who arrived here in the 8th century B.C. to grow grain and mine for natural resources, such as chromium, manganese, lead, and gold. When the region was conquered in 348 B.C. by King Philip II, Chalkidiki became part of Macedonia. It is hardly surprising, therefore, that its cuisine bears strong similarities to that found in Macedonia, perhaps with greater emphasis being placed on fresh fish. Nowadays, the region's most important agricultural products are honey, olives, and of course, the famous Athos wine.

Chalkidiki is one of Greece's main honey-producing regions. You will come across beehives almost everywhere you go. Thanks to the abundance of flowers, there is ample nourishment for all the bees.

NATURAL HONEY

The job of an apiarist or beekeeper is a very highly regarded profession in Greece. A beekeeper will keep on average 300 to 500 hives and these will produce around 55,000 pounds (25,000 kilograms) of honey per year. Chalkidiki is one of the country's main honey-producing regions. Beekeepers come here from all over Greece, drawn by the unspoiled, hilly countryside with its wealth of flowers and abundance of pine trees, spruces, and lime trees, all guarantees of consistency in aroma and high-quality honey. Honey production is geared to the following flowering periods: from March to May, meadow flowers; early June, lime blossom; mid-August, chestnut blossom (helps stop the honey from solidifying); the rest of the summer, spruce blossom (spruce resin makes the honey darker and stronger in taste). The heather in bloom at the beginning of September provides the final aromatic ingredient and the bees close up their honeycombs ready for hibernation. The honey is now ready for harvest. Gently stunning the bees with smoke from burning spruce needles, the beekeeper carefully removes this precious sweet product.

THEO ANGELOPOULOS: "THE BEEKEEPER"

One of the most famous films by Greek director Theo Angelopoulos is the sensitive story of the final days of a beekeeper, who travels down from the north of the country moving his beehives farther and farther south as he chases the summer, at the same time saying goodbye in his own way to all the things that have been important to him during his lifetime. Marcello Mastroianni, one of the last great stars of European film, delivers a unique portrayal of the solitary Greek beekeeper. It was no coincidence that Angelopoulos chose to tell the story of a beekeeper. There is a long tradition of beekeeping in Greece. The continual moving of hives from one region to another, as one finishes flowering and another begins to bloom, is meant as a metaphor for the way that each day represents an end to individual stages of life.

When the spring flowers are in bloom on the Chalkidiki peninsula, the bees are well catered for.

Even the beekeeper prefers to stun the bees a little before attempting to touch the honeycombs.

Above: the beekeeper samples the honey straight from the honeycomb. Background: The beekeeper and his worker bees.

Spruce honey

Regional honey

Natural honey with honeycomb

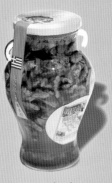

Honey with walnuts

FASTING

Daily meals take on special significance during the periods of fasting that precede the major festivals in the Greek Orthodox Church. Any dishes containing meat or dairy products are forbidden, as are all egg-based dishes. The sole permitted treat during fasting is the afternoon *kourabiés*, a sweet delicacy made from almonds, flour, and a large quantity of powdered sugar. Only the very simplest of dishes make an appearance on the lunch table, such as *domatósoupa me zimarikó*, a simple tomato soup with noodles, or plain fish dishes.

The most assiduous fasters will even forego their precious Greek olive oil. And that is quite a sacrifice in this region known for its fine-tasting Chalkidiki variety olives and olive oil, which is locally manufactured (as it is everywhere else in Greece) in Ouranoúpolis, the last freely accessible town before the monastic republic of Athos.

When a road was built to Ouranoúpolis in the 1960s, it brought many artists to the town. With its old fortified tower and close proximity to the Athos monasteries, the place held a special attraction for them, one that is still shared to this day by many travelers to Greece. The example of hermetic existence on Athos has not only been a magnet for visitors from all over the world, but has also influenced the lifestyle of all those living in close proximity to the surrounding area.

DOMATÓSOUPA ME ZIMARIKÓ
Tomato soup with noodles

4 large tomatoes, peeled, seeded, cored, and diced
2 small onions, finely diced
1 stick of cinnamon
1 lb/500 g fine soup noodles
A little flat-leaved parsley, freshly chopped
Salt
Freshly ground black pepper

Heat 4 cups/1 liter water in a saucepan and cook the diced tomato. Add the onions and cinnamon, and season with salt and pepper. Simmer over a medium heat for 20 minutes, then add the soup noodles and cook until soft. Remove the cinnamon stick and serve the soup in bowls, sprinkled with a little parsley. Serve hot with freshly baked white bread.

NISTÍSIMA
Lenten cakes

1½ cakes/20 g yeast (if using active dry yeast, follow manufacturer's instructions)
9 cups/1 kg flour
1 pinch salt
¼ cup/50 g sugar
⅓ cup/50 g cornstarch
1¼ cups/300 ml olive oil
⅔ cup/150 ml white wine
A little aniseed, finely ground

Dissolve the yeast in a little warm water. Sift the flour and salt into a bowl and make a well in the center. Pour the yeast mixture into this and mix with a little flour. Add all the remaining ingredients and work into a dough with the help of 1 cup/250 ml of water, more or less. Leave the dough to rise in a warm place for 3–4 hours. Heat the oven to 400 °F (200 °C). Shape the dough into thin rolls, the length of a finger. Taking three rolls at a time, place them side by side and braid them (leaving both ends open at the top and bottom). Brush a baking sheet with olive oil, spread the braids out on this and bake for 30 minutes in the preheated oven. Store in an airtight container. The cakes may be dipped in wine before eating.

METHISMÉNA
Cookies with retsina and Turkish delight
Makes about 60 cookies

9 cups/1 kg flour
5 level teaspoons of baking powder
1⅔ cups/400 ml sunflower oil
1 scant cup/200 ml retsina or other white wine
20 pieces of Turkish delight (from Greek and Turkish delicatessens or specialist candy stores)
30 walnuts, halved
Confectioner's sugar

Preheat the oven to 430 °F (220 °C). Sift the flour and baking powder into a bowl, add the oil and retsina and work into a smooth, soft pastry. Tip the pastry out onto a floured work surface and roll out to a thickness of ⅕ inch/5 mm. Using an upturned glass, cut out circles. Place one third of a piece of Turkish delight and half a walnut on each round and fold the pastry circle in half to make a pocket, pressing the edges down firmly. Place the pastry pockets on a baking sheet lined with baking parchment and bake in a preheated oven until they begin to turn color. Remove from the oven and leave to cool. Sprinkle with confectioner's sugar and store in an airtight container.

LITOURYÁ
Consecrated bread

1½ cakes/20 g yeast (if using active dry yeast, follow manufacturer's instructions)
6½ cups/750 g flour
1 tsp salt
Olive oil

Dissolve the yeast in a little lukewarm water. Sift the flour and salt into a bowl and make a well in the middle. Pour the yeast into this well and knead the mixture into a firm dough, adding 1–1¼ cups/200–300 ml water. Cover and leave to rise for 3–4 hours in a warm place. Preheat the oven to 430 °F (220 °C).
Brush a high-sided circular baking pan (about 8–10 inches/20–25 cm in diameter) with olive oil and place the dough in it. Using a bread stamp, make the mark of a cross in the center and, with a cocktail stick, make 8 small holes around the mark so that the dough will rise evenly. Bake in a preheated oven for one hour until the dough begins to turn color.

ATHOS OLIVES: TSAKISTÉS

Athos olives are prepared according to a special procedure using olives of the *vólos* variety. The first thing to remember about this process is that the green olives must not be picked until after September 14, the Greek "Festival of the Cross." Once they have been picked, they are usually split open straight away using a heavy stone, then stored in a container filled with water, which should be renewed on a daily basis. After about 12 days, all the bitter juices will have soaked out of the olives. They can then be drained, dried and placed in salt. You can reckon on two handfuls of salt to 6 pounds (3 kilograms of olives), adding a little oil and oregano seasoning. *Tsakistés*, olives which have been "split open" in this way, will keep for months in the refrigerator and can be served as an accompaniment to the daily glass of ouzo.

Litouryá, bread decorated with the stamp of a cross, is blessed during mass. One part of it is consecrated, while the rest is divided among the congregation after the service. It is eaten on an empty stomach.

FISHING

Most of the Chalkidiki fishermen know one another. There are no longer very many of them left, taking their boats out every day and sailing up and down the coast hoping for a good catch. Times have become hard for the 200 or so fishermen who still live along the coasts of Chalkidikí's three fingers, despite the fact that the fish stocks in this area are more abundant than in the rest of the Aegean. The sight of them brings to mind Ernest Hemingway's *The Old Man and the Sea*. The work is too onerous and insecure for the youngsters and the few remaining older fishermen are only able to survive thanks to the fact that the restaurants and hotels in the Chalkidikí tourist region are willing to pay good money for fresh fish. The Greeks themselves have long regarded fish as a luxury food and only those who live right by the sea are able to take their pick of the bream, sole, perch, red mullet, or even John Dory that are available when the boats come in.

Kakaviá, Greek fish soup, is one of the main traditional dishes in this part of Greece and you will find it on lunch tables all along the coast after a good catch has been landed. *Kakaviá* is made from various fish, large and small, which are passed through a sieve after being cooked. Sometimes, small shellfish are also added to the soup.

Tsipoúra – gilthead sea bream

Lithíri – red bream

Skiláki – cat shark

Sargós – white sea bream

Mourmoúra – mormyr (sea bass)

Sinagrída – snapper

Barboúni – red mullet

Gópa – sardine

Fangrí – sea bream

Loútsos – barracuda (pickerel)

Gofári – bluefish

Marída – whitebait

Skoumbrí – Atlantic mackerel

Koutsomoúra – red ocean mullet

Khristópsaro – John Dory

Toúrna – sea pike

Grivádi – carp

Kokkáli – blue runner

BOAT-BUILDING

In the eastern part of Chalkidiki, a few miles from the top end of the Athos peninsula, are the famous Ierissós boatyards where the wooden fishing vessels, *kaíkia*, are built. These boats have become popular with enthusiasts all over the world who want to fulfill their lifelong dream of owning their own boat. The boat-yards get orders not just from local fishermen, for whom a *kaíki* of their own means economic independence, but from people all over Europe who provide a great deal of business for the Ierissós boat-building yards. If you visit one of these yards, you can see the structure of a *kaíki* taking shape. The boat-builders use a particular wood for their *kaíki*: it has to be pine wood from the Kholomóndas mountains in central Chalkidiki. A single straight plank called the *karína* is used for the keel beam. Attached to this and tilted upward at a slight angle is the

SOOTHING OINTMENT

The fishermen of Chalkidiki use a very special homemade remedy for healing any injuries to the hands and feet incurred during their work. *Keralifi* (wax ointment) can be used to treat all cuts and grazes. It is marvelous for injuries caused by sea urchins in particular.

Keralifi:
1 crystal of mastic
1½ tbsp olive oil
1 piece of beeswax, heated
Herbs, according to preference

Heat the crystal of mastic in 1½ tbsp olive oil and add a small piece of beeswax, stirring constantly until the wax has melted. Add any herbs, such as sage, oregano, or thyme and allow to cool. The ointment keeps for years and should be applied thinly to a wound several times a day.

bow beam, the *podóstamo tis plóris,* and another for the stern, the *podóstamo tis prímnis.* Then, the curved ribs are fixed to the keel beam at intervals of 8 inches (20 centimeters) and gradually the shape of the boat begins to emerge. Once the ribs are in place, the open ends are held in position by an elegantly curving length of wood. The rest of the hull can then be covered with planks.

Before the boat can be varnished or named, the wood has to be impregnated with a substance that will protect the wood against salt water. In its first year, the boat is lifted out of the water during the winter. The paint is burned off again and a second coat of protective proofing is applied. After this, the *kaíki* will not need to go into dry-dock again for about three years. For the boat-builders, saying goodbye to a boat is rather a poignant moment. During the six weeks it takes to build the 32-foot (10-meter) long vessel, they tend to grow rather fond of it.

The boat-builders' yard is right on the beach at Ierissós. The finished fishing boats, the *kaíkia,* are easy to launch from here. The boats are all still made entirely by hand. It takes three to four men about six weeks to build a large boat.

After weeks of work, the boat is almost finished: The last planks are being fitted.

The products are constantly monitored in the modern smoking chambers.

It is the bottled fish products that sell best in Greece.

Pure oil still constitutes one of the best preserving methods.

Modern machines and conveyor belts guarantee consistency in the daily output of processed canned fish. Although this means fewer jobs in the fish processing industry as a whole, the old-established factories still provide long-term jobs in some of Greece's economically poorer regions.

PRESERVING FISH

Using salt to preserve fish is one of the oldest known methods of food conservation in the world. In Greece, *gáros*, the fish sauce of mythical fame (see page 54), involved successful experiments with fish, salt, and sun. An important commercial industry has developed in northern Greece, through its long history of fish-processing, with up to 2205 US tons (2000 tonnes) of canned fish being produced annually and exported all over the world. Even though most of the processing in these factories is now automated, they still provide a good deal of employment in the region. The canned fish produced here enjoys a good reputation and has received awards, such as the "Quality Assurance Certificate," on several occasions. They produce a wide range of products, including anchovies, sardines, and mackerel in brine, both whole and filleted. Smoked mackerel and herrings are also available, as well as marinated fish fillets and fish roe. Various types of packaging have been test-marketed over the past few years, as well as different formats, and now include plastic containers in addition to cans and glass jars.

Catching a sea perch, or ocean perch, a *rofós*, is always cause for great excitement. This fish with its monstrous mouth is among the finest delicacies in all Chalkidiki.

FISH WITH EVERYTHING

KAKAVIÁ
Greek fish soup
(Illustration top left)

2 lbs/1 kg fish fillets, skinned, from a selection of
  Mediterranean fish
½ cup/125 ml olive oil
2 onions, sliced into rings
2 carrots, sliced
2 sticks of celery, thinly sliced
3 tomatoes, peeled and sliced
1 garlic clove, crushed
½ bunch flat-leaved parsley, finely chopped
1 bay leaf
Juice of 1 lemon
Salt
Freshly ground black pepper

Heat the olive oil in a saucepan and sauté the onions, carrots and celery. Add the tomatoes and a little water. Cover and cook for 30 minutes. Add the fish, garlic, parsley, and bay leaf. Add enough water to cover the ingredients, season with salt and pepper, and cook gently for 10 minutes until the vegetables and fish are cooked through (stir carefully to avoid breaking up the fillets of fish). Remove the fish from the pan and arrange on plates. Add the lemon juice to the soup and season with salt and pepper. Pour this over the fish fillets. Serve with freshly baked white bread.
Tip: try and use at least 3–4 different varieties of fish and shellfish. The vegetables may vary according to the season.

KOLIÍ ME RÍGANI
Mackerel with oregano
(Illustration bottom left)

4 mackerel
4 garlic cloves, finely sliced
½ cup/125 ml Greek extra virgin olive oil
¼ tsp dried oregano
Juice of 1 lemon
Salt
Freshly ground black pepper

Gut and clean the mackerel, wash thoroughly, rub with salt and leave to stand for one hour. Preheat the oven to 350 °F (180 °C). Lay the mackerel on a shallow baking pan, scatter the garlic slices over them and pour over the olive oil. Sprinkle the oregano over the fish and pour over the lemon juice. Season with salt and pepper, pour a little water into the pan, and cook the mackerel in a preheated oven for about one hour. Serve with baked potatoes and freshly baked white bread.

PSÁRI SKHÁRAS
Grilled fish
(Illustration top right)

2 lbs/1 kg Mediterranean fish (e.g. red mullet,
  dentix, silver bream)
1 scant cup/200 ml Greek extra virgin olive oil
Juice of 2 lemons
½ bunch flat-leaved parsley, finely chopped
¼ tsp dried oregano
Salt
Freshly ground black pepper

Descale the fish, then gut and clean them, removing the backbone and other bones. Mix the olive oil with the lemon juice, salt and pepper and brush the fish with this mixture. Cook on both sides over a charcoal grill. Arrange the fish on a plate. Stir the parsley and oregano into the oil and lemon sauce and pour this over the fish. Serve with freshly baked white bread and a green salad.

PSÁRI VRASTÓ
Boiled fish
(Illustration bottom right)

2 lbs/1 kg fish fillet, skinned (ideally
  Mediterranean fish, otherwise Atlantic)
Juice of 2 lemons
2 carrots, sliced
2 large potatoes, peeled and diced
1 zucchini, sliced
2 onions, sliced into rings
2 stalks of celery, thinly sliced
1 generous cup/250 ml pureed tomatoes
4 tbsp/50 ml olive oil
Salt
Freshly ground black pepper

Cut the fish fillets into large chunks. Season with salt and pepper, pour over half the lemon juice and marinate for one hour. Place all the vegetables except for the tomatoes in a saucepan, cover with water, and cook. Halfway through the cooking, add the tomatoes and fish and cook for another 20 minutes, testing frequently to make sure that the fish and vegetables are not overcooking. Skim off any scum that forms on the surface. The liquid in the pan should be fairly thick. Stir in the remaining lemon juice and olive oil. Serve hot with freshly baked white bread.

THE GARDEN OF MARY

Agios Oros, the holy mountain of the Orthodox world, is a place of peace and reflection, geared totally to a monastic way of life. In actual fact, it is ruled over by a woman, even though it is now only accessible to men. The Holy Mother of God is supposed to have interrupted her journey to rest here. Since then, the Holy Mount Athos has been known as the "Garden of the Virgin Mary." The wild, rocky finger of land is dominated by the majestic summit of the 6690 feet (2039 meter) high Mount Athos. It is usually wreathed in cloud, intensifying the mystical atmosphere of the Athos monasteries, some of which are a thousand years old. This autonomous monastic state is the oldest religious community still in existence in the world and therefore an important center for all Orthodox Christians. It is believed that the first monks arrived here in the 7th century, although Mount Athos does not officially figure in history as a monastic community until the 10th century, when two monks named Athanasios the Athonite and Pávlos Xeropotaminos built the first monasteries here in A.D. 963. The 12th century brought other nationalities of Orthodox monks, such as Georgians, Serbs, and Russians. The monks on Athos cultivate everything they need to survive themselves. However, most of the peninsula is wild and uncultivated and home to herbs and plants, that have long since died out elsewhere. It is no coincidence that the only village and so-called "capital" of Athos is called Karyés after the hazelnut bushes that grow in such profusion along the donkey tracks and paths linking the monasteries. The unusual diversity of flora (over 1000 different species) is due to the favorable climatic conditions as well as the absence of any large animals. Only small animals survive in the impenetrable thickets near the mountain summit. Butterflies and birds provide the finishing touch to this earthly paradise. In the heyday of the monastic republic, the main monasteries could each accommodate several thousand monks, but they are now inhabited by just a couple of dozen brothers. In addition, there are other smaller monastic communities including *skítes*, small monastic settlements, small farms called *kéllia*, often home to two or even just one monk, and lastly, remote hermits' retreats, *erimitíria*. The larger monasteries have valuable libraries and collections of icons, which are documented *inter alia* in the renowned *Painter's Manual of Mount Athos*. The churches are full of sumptuous paintings and the architecture of the monasteries on Mount Athos, some of which have fortified walls facing the sea, is an amazing sight. Athos is a real cultural treasure and is receiving financial support from UNESCO to prevent it falling into further decline.

OURANÓPOLIS

Ouranópolis is the last town before you enter the monastic republic of Athos. If the schoolchildren there are requested to draw a boat, you will usually find that they have created a colored pencil drawing of a little boat with black figures on board. These drawings of black-clad men are an indication of what the children perceive to be the most prominent feature in their immediate surroundings. There are more monks in Ouranópolis than anywhere else in the world. This is no coincidence, for Ouranópolis (which means "Heavenly City" in English) represents the last bastion of all that is worldly. About 550 yards (500 meters) south of the town is a wall topped with barbed wire, behind which lies the Holy Mount Athos, the autonomous monastic republic. Every day, boats ply in and out of Daphne, the small harbor of Ouranópolis, forming the only link between Daphne and the rest of the world. Ouranópolis only came into being in the 1920s. Up until then, the old tower on the breakwater was a symbol of the monastic state, visible only from the sea. It was used as a watchtower to guard against strangers or robbers entering the Athos area unseen. It was not until 1922, when large numbers of Greeks fled from Asia Minor, that the monks finally acceded to requests by the Greek government and released the land to accommodate refugees. This changed the borders of Athos and gave rise to the 800-strong community, which now not only represents the extremity of the secular world, but also is a reminder of times of great social change. The people felt a debt of gratitude to the monks. Many of them were able to continue their trade as fishermen in Ouranópolis since the waters around Athos are among the richest fishing areas in Greece today. Others put their skills as craftsmen to good use on Mount Athos, doing carpentry work for the monks or helping to renovate buildings in the monasteries.

HOLY MOUNT ATHOS

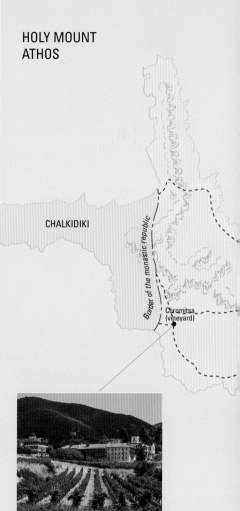

CHALKIDIKI

Border of the monastic republic

Chromitsa (vineyard)

The Chromitsa vineyard is run by a vintner named Tsantalis. Its special position has earned his Athos wine a worldwide reputation.

The Xenofóndos monastery, dedicated to St. Georgios, was first mentioned in 1033. Its library is world-famous.

0   9 miles/ 15 km

 N

+ monastery

------- footpath

All the main shops and offices in this monastic republic are in Karyés. For visitors, this is the starting point for walks on Athos.

The monks still cultivate their gardens themselves. Vegetables are the main crop, as well as a lot of wine and a little fruit as well.

Every monastery has its own spring, providing clear mountain water for all pilgrims to Athos.

Milopotámou is the peninsula's most successful vineyard. Vines have been cultivated here since the monastic republic was founded around A.D. 1000.

The monks' meagre daily fare often consists of no more than a bowl of lentil soup, which is eaten with a wooden spoon.

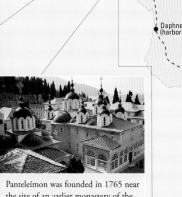

Panteleímon was founded in 1765 near the site of an earlier monastery of the same name. The basilica is situated in the inner courtyard.

The monks engage in traditional icon painting as handed down for generations from the master to his pupils, producing timeless holy pictures.

The monastery is built securely on a cliff. On clear days, the view from here is quite breathtaking.

The only monks to leave Athos are the ones transacting business. They catch the ferry from Daphne to Ouranópolis and continue by bus from there.

Esfigménou

ndári

Zografou

Kastamonítou

Dohiaríou

Xenofóndos

Karyés

Koutloumousíou

Ivíron

Milopotámou
(vineyard)

Panteleímon

Filotheou

Karakaloù

Xiropotámou

Daphne
(harbor)

Great Lavra

Simópetra

Highest point
6626 ft/2039 m.

Dionisíou

St. Paul's

IN THE REFECTORY

If monks occasionally encounter more lavish dishes than usual on their plates, this can only mean one thing: if it is not Easter, the most important celebration in the Greek Orthodox calendar, then it must be the name day of one of the saints connected with the monastery. These festivals begin with special religious rituals. Valuable relics, such as those at the Pantokrátor monastery, are brought out, or else an all-night vigil of prayers and singing is held. Afterward, some monasteries will include fish in the meal as a special treat in honor of the occasion. The fish will more than likely have been freshly caught just off the quay.

MEALTIMES

Monastery cuisine means meat-free cuisine. Meat is never eaten in these monastic communities. Fish may be served on important holidays, either boiled, grilled, in soup, or in lemon sauce. The everyday menu, however, includes vegetables of every kind, and beans, all prepared with olive oil. During periods of fasting, the fare consists of cooked pulses, vegetables, pastry dishes, and rice, but no olive oil. The monks maintain that the secret of good food is slow cooking over a low heat, unless you are cooking fish, which can stand a bit more heat. Monks who live in small communities outside the monasteries are also permitted to eat poultry or game.

Originally, there were two main directions of monastic life on Athos. Some monasteries practiced an idiorrhythmic lifestyle, whereby each monk retains his own property. This gave rise to a distinction between poor and rich monks, some of whom even employed servants. The others were

INCENSE

Olibanum, also known as frankincense, is the gum resin obtained from various Arabian and African trees (genus *Boswellia*) of the bursera family. The resin is dried and ground, then mixed with other resins and scented oils from gardenias, roses, or jasmine. When burned in special incense containers, the mixture exudes a characteristic balsamic, heavy aroma. It was already used widely in ancient Greece in the 7th century B.C. in cults and rituals.

cenobitic monasteries, where the monks lived according to a common set of rules, embracing poverty, celibacy, and obedience. Since 1990, all the monasteries on Athos are of the latter school. The monks take their daily meals together. These form part and parcel of the religious services since they consider that praying and eating belong together. Depending on the monastery, the evening meal may be attended by any visiting pilgrims. The evening mass is followed by a meal in the refectory (*trápeza*), which is often second only to the church itself in the sumptuousness of its décor. The fare will consist of a simple vegetarian meal, accompanied by water. During the meal, one of the monks reads from the Holy Bible, while the remainder observe silence. Then the abbot will signal the end of the meal and the monks will process back to the monastery church for the continuation of the religious services.

The monks do all their own cooking. Vegetables, and less frequently fish, are cooked slowly over an open fire in a real wood-fired oven.

The monks set off early in the morning to collect fresh wild herbs and vegetables for the monastery kitchen, some of which are unique to the Athos peninsula.

The refectory table at the Ivíron monastery is only ceremoniously laid on important church festival days.

ROFÓS AKHNISTÓS
Steamed sea perch

2 lbs/1 kg sea perch, oven-ready, cut into steaks
   about ½ inch/2 cm thick
Coarse-grained salt
2 large onions, sliced into rings
6 garlic cloves
1 scant cup/200 ml Greek extra virgin olive oil
½ bunch parsley, finely chopped
Juice of 2 lemons
Peppercorns
Oregano
Salt

Sprinkle the fish steaks with coarse-grained salt and leave to stand in a bowl for three hours. Place the fish in a steaming basket. The fish should lie just above the liquid. Bring the water, onions, garlic and olive oil to a boil and simmer for one hour, then add half the parsley, lemon juice, pepper and oregano to the stock, sprinkling the remainder over the fish steaks. Insert the steaming basket over the stock and steam for 15 minutes until the fish is flaky. Arrange on a plate, pour over a little stock and parsley.

AGRIOGOÚROUNO ME MELITZÁNES
Wild boar with eggplants

2 lbs/1 kg wild boar meat from the haunch
½ cup/100 g butter
2 onions, sliced thinly into rings
3–4 tomatoes, peeled and diced
1 lb/500 g small eggplants
Greek extra virgin olive oil
½ bunch flat-leaved parsley, finely chopped
Salt
Freshly ground black pepper

Cut the meat into medium-sized pieces. Melt the butter in a saucepan and sauté the onions until transparent. Add the meat and brown on all sides. Add the tomatoes and a little water, seasoning with salt and pepper. Leave to simmer over a very low heat for about 1½–2 hours until the meat is almost done. Keep adding boiling water to the saucepan from time to time. Meanwhile, wash the eggplants and cut off the stalk ends. Heat olive oil in a skillet and sauté the whole eggplants. Add these to the meat and cook for a further 5 minutes. Arrange on a serving dish and sprinkle with parsley. Serve hot with freshly baked white bread.

PRÁSINI OMELÉTA
Green omelet

⅔ lb/300 g fresh leaf spinach
4 tbsp/50 g butter
1½ cups/150 g hard goat cheese, grated
4–6 eggs
Salt
Freshly ground black pepper

Wash the spinach, remove the stems, and blanch the leaves for a few minutes in boiling water, then drain thoroughly. Melt half the butter in a saucepan, add the spinach, and sauté gently while stirring. Season with salt and pepper and stir in the goat cheese. Remove the pan from the heat. Melt the remaining butter in a skillet, lightly beat the eggs and season with salt and pepper. Pour a portion at a time into the skillet and allow to set. Place the omelets on plates, divide the spinach filling accordingly and spread it over one half of each omelet, then fold over the other half. Serve hot with freshly baked white bread.

A HOLY VINTNER

In view of their self-sufficiency, it goes without saying that the monks of Athos cultivate their own wine, particularly as they need an enormous quantity of sacramental wine for the evening liturgy. The wine of the Athos peninsula is a fair wine indeed. The winegrowing area is situated on the eastern side, more or less halfway along the finger protruding out into the sea. The climatic conditions are good for winegrowing: frequent brief showers of rain, humidity from the sea, and strong sun on the southeastern slopes provide excellent conditions for the vines to flourish. The Limnio and Agiorgitiko grape varieties are best suited to the dry soil of these hot and windy areas. The wines also carry the label "ecologically harmless" as there is no industry on Athos, no vehicle traffic, and as far as pesticides go, it is as if they never existed. The soil has been treated well for 1000 years; there have been no opportunities to do otherwise. Ten years ago, Pater Epiphanios took matters into his own hands by reactivating the traditional vineyard of Milopotámos. This is a *skítes*, a small monastic village, that belongs to the Megísti Lávra monastery. Milopotámos, founded in 963 B.C. by Athanasios the Athonite, one of the first monks to settle on Athos, is an important place on Holy Mount Athos. According to historical sources, vines have been systematically cultivated in Milopotámos since that time with an estimated production of 59–78 US tons (60–80 tonnes) of wine per year! The outbreak of phylloxera from America after World War II put an abrupt end to wine cultivation on Mount Athos until 1990, when Pater Epiphanios took matters in hand. Born into a family of winegrowers, he requested permission to start developing the old vineyards again. In 1992, he planted Merlot, Limnio, Muscat of Alexandria, and Rhoditis vines over an area of about 12 acres (5 hectares). Today, the organic wine business is thriving and annual wine production is back to 39–44 US tons (40–45 tonnes), some of which is exported to the United States.

Above: Pater Epiphanios' vineyards lie to the south of the Ivíron monastery on the east coast of Athos.

Below left: the Athos label should not prevent you from trying the red and white Milopotámos wines.

Below right: since Pater Epiphanios began exporting his wine, some labels are now available worldwide.

RECOMMENDATIONS FOR WINEMAKING

The monks of the Ivíron monastery who are in charge of the winemaking just follow a few basic rules. They know that:

- The grapes do not ripen before August 6, the festival of St. Sotíris, when a mass is said for the wine and the vineyards are blessed.
- All the grapes are picked during the harvest.
- They should only be harvested in dry weather.
- Pressed grapes must be left to ferment longer in cool weather than in warm for the same result to be achieved.
- Dry red wines must be kept for up to 40 days in the vat before being transferred into barrels.
- Sweet red wine is only drunk at Holy Communion.
- Wine should only be stored in places where there are no other predominant smells.

Preparing *petimézi* is time consuming: the freshly pressed must is simmered for several hours over a low gas flame...

It is filtered several times to remove any debris from the pressing...

...until the resulting syrup is clear and thick. It is used as the basis for all kinds of desserts.

PETIMÉZI

The skills acquired by the Athos monks in producing wine and all its by-products naturally spread beyond the boundaries of this holy province. The manufacture of *petimézi*, for instance, has become one of the specialties of the Chalkidiki region. *Petimézi* is boiled grape must syrup. It keeps for a long time and is the basic ingredient of many different desserts. It has a sweet-and-sour flavor and is regarded as a delicacy to be eaten with sweet fruit.

Petimézi is made by boiling the freshly pressed grape must (pomegranates or morello cherries also lend themselves to this process), while at the same time adding sugar, until the liquid has evaporated sufficiently for the gelatin from the grapes to thicken the juice without caramelizing it. In the past, this process was sometimes accelerated by boiling a linen bag containing ash and red, clayey soil along with the grape juice, but nowadays the same effect can be achieved by adding pectin or commercially bought gelatin.

SÍKA MOUSTOMÉNA
Figs in grape must

12 fresh figs
3 cups/750 ml grape must

Peel the figs, halve them and place them in the sun to dry. Then pour hot water over the figs and leave them to drain. Place them in a saucepan, add the grape must and cook.

DOMAINE CARRAS

Early in the 1960s, shipping magnate John Carras discovered Sithoniá, the middle of the three Chalkidiki peninsulas. He went on to build hotels and golf courses in a hitherto undiscovered and stunningly beautiful spot. He also built a winery and planted over 1100 acres (450 hectares) of land with vines. Tests carried out by winegrowing experts on various sections of the land indicated that although the yields from the slatey soil would not be all that huge, the resulting wine would be of particularly good quality. The Domaine Carras red wines, in particular, made from Limnio, Cabernet Sauvignon, Syrah, and Cinsault grape varieties, have found international acclaim. His white wines are made from white grape varieties, such as Athiri, Assyrtiko, Malagousia, Rhoditis, and Sauvignan Blanc. Almost 80 percent of the vines are traditional Greek varieties and only 20 percent are international grape varieties. When John Carras died in 1989, the business was taken over by one of his two sons.

In 1994, the winery was completely redesigned and modernized at great financial cost. This further augmented the quality of the wine. Meanwhile, though, this vast winegrowing business has become the property of the bank and its future is uncertain.

ATHOS WINE FROM TSANTALIS

The Athos region is used for wine cultivation not just by the monks, but also by an independent winegrower. In Ágios Pávlos, on Chalkidiki's western coast, are the headquarters of the Tsantalis winery and distillery. The firm has now been in the family for three generations and is currently owned by Evangelos Tsantalis, who also owns wineries in Náoussa and Rapsani. The vineyards belonging to this firm now extend beyond the Athos region and are scattered all over Greece. Meanwhile, the local ones are relatively small. The family vineyards cover an area of over 540 acres (220 hectares) and include Athos, Ágios Pávlos (Chalkidiki), Maronia (Thrace), and Náoussa (Macedonia). They are further supplied by grape growers in Rapsani, Thessaloniki, Samos, Limnos, Crete, and the Peloponnese. In this way, Tsantalis manages to produce 4,752,000 U.S. gallons (18,000,000 liters) of wine each year. In order to cope with such a huge quantity, the Tsantalis cellars have a storage capacity of 5,280,000 U.S. gallons (20 million liters) of controlled tank space as well as 2000 wooden casks with a capacity of 74 U.S. gallons (300 liters) each. Tsantalis is Greece's biggest exporter with over 3,170,000 gallons (12,000,000 liters) – in other words, two-thirds of his overall production – going for export. One of his main clients is Germany: Tsantalis provides 40 percent of the Greek wine there, dominating the market. German gastronomy benefits from the fact that Tsantalis offers a broad cross-section of Greek wines from every level of quality and price. He has upheld tradition and respected the family philosophy of concentrating on Greek grape varieties. For the red wines, he uses the classic Agiorgitiko grape, characteristic of the Neméa region, and the Xinomavro variety from Náoussa, processing them by fermentation in revolving steel tanks. They are acknowledged as red wines of international class. Stavroto and Krassato are also used, as well as Mavrodaphne for liqueur wine. The white wines are produced by the cold process from Rhoditis, Assyrtiko, Athiri and Vilana, while retsina is made from the smooth Savatiano, and Moscato is used for liqueur wine.

For Agiorgitiko, Tsantalis uses grapes from the monastic republic.

This velvety red wine made from Syrah grapes goes well with game.

Tsantalis also produces this excellent Chardonnay from international grape varieties.

Tsantalis is one of the few vintners allowed to use grapes from the Athos vineyards for his wines.

Tradition is important to Tsantalis and he favors the classic varieties of grape from Macedonia.

Athiri grapes produce a dry, smooth, and very aromatic white wine.

The yellowish-green Sauvignon goes well with fish and seafood.

The grapes for local Ampelonas wine come from Ágios Pávlos.

his Cava Tsantalis is a special 1979 vintage, illustrating e suitability of this combination of Xinomavro and abernet Sauvignon grapes for storage.

Grapes are still picked by hand at the Tsantalis vineyard. The head of the establishment makes it his business to check his wines very carefully before they are bottled.

Tsantalis, too, knows the value of the versatile, aromatic Merlot grape.

Rapsani red wine, matured in an oak cask, has improved in quality.

A classic wine from Macedonia: a pleasant red Xinomavro.

alent of about $1.25-1.50. It is not uncommon, as this example demonstrates, to find that the cherry grower is also a baker or, as in the case of some of the others, a Christmas tree grower. Despite the low income that cherries produce, the cherry growers of Taxiárchis are proud of the quality of their fruit, even if they only pick the cherries for their own use. The cherry season has always been the time for the women to make homemade *kerási glikó* or press and bottle the fruit's delicious juice. The Taxiárchis cherries and their by-products have become a secret to be shared during the Chalkidiki summer, and anyone who is offered a bowl of fresh Taxiárchis cherries can count him or herself very lucky indeed.

Above: the pear tree in the Taxiárchis bakery has become the village emblem.

Adjacent page: Taxiárchis is well worth a visit when the cherries begin to ripen.

MOUNTAIN CHERRIES

The village of Taxiárchis, situated at an altitude of 2067 feet (630 meters) in the Kholomóndas mountains in the heart of Chalkidiki, is surrounded by dense deciduous forest, which glows with wonderful browns and reds in the autumn. There is very little traditional agriculture in this thinly populated region and the majority of villagers make a living from cultivating and selling Christmas trees.

There is, however, a small, plucky group of residents, including the Taxiárchis baker, who have discovered a fondness for fruit trees, in particular cherry and pear trees. He has a tree growing right in the middle of his bakery. It goes up through the ceiling and emerges on the terrace above. And when the fruit is ripe, it sometimes happens that a customer, either a local resident or someone passing through, who is waiting to be served in the store below and enjoying the aroma of freshly baked bread, will suddenly end up with a pear as well. But this is only half the story. If you ask people on the Chalkidiki coast at the end of June where their cherries have come from, they will say: From Taxiárchis! For the baker not only bakes bread beneath the branches of a pear tree, but since 1984 has been the proud co-owner, along with four other farmers, of about 6000 cherry trees. With a crop of 44 pounds (20 kg) per tree per year, the total yield from these cherry trees is not yet sufficient for the farmers to be able to support themselves from the cherry harvest – two pounds (1 kg) of cherries brings the equiv-

KERASÓSOUPA
Sweet cherry soup

1 lb/500 g cherries
1 generous cup/250 g sugar
1 bottle dry white wine
Juice of 2 lemons
2 cups/500 ml heavy cream or whipping cream
2 tbsp cherry liqueur
Ground cinnamon

Pit the cherries and place in a saucepan with the sugar and white wine. Cook for 5 minutes over a medium heat. Allow the cherries to cool a little, then purée in a blender and add the lemon juice. Leave to cool for a little while before mixing in the cream, then the cherry liqueur. Add sugar to taste. The cherry soup can either be served hot or placed in the refrigerator to chill. Serve on plates that have been sprinkled with cinnamon.

In the countryside, children invent their own games each season, as their mothers and grandmothers did before them. During the cherry season, freshly picked cherries make pretty earrings for little Greek girls.

The ripe cherries are packed in flat crates and sent straight to local markets.

Sour cherry syrup, *vissinada,* is one of the most popular fruit juices in Greece.

The fisherman cuts off the boat's engine in the shallows and scans the clear water for squid and octopus. If he spots one, a single practiced thrust is usually enough to augment his catch.

SQUID AND OCTOPUS

Squid and octopus are both mollusks of the cephalopod family (*Cephalopoda*). They owe their name to the fact that their tentacles grow directly out of their head. In classical times, they were not only a popular and common source of food, but were also one of the best studied creatures in classical zoology. Their ability to change color as a means of camouflage was a source of great fascination. An octopus with curling tentacles was a subject frequently depicted in ancient Greek art and inspired writers like Athenaios to praise its "wonderful curls." Cephalopods have an ink sac from which they can eject a dark ink-like liquid to "screen" themselves from predators.

The cuttlefish (*Sepia officinalis*) is the most common type of cephalopod found in the Mediterranean. Its body measures up to 10 inches (25 centimeters) in length and is dark in color, making it almost invisible on the seabed. Its "ink" used to be extracted for use as a dyestuff to produce the color sepia. Generally speaking, no great distinction is made between cuttlefish and squid.

Whereas cuttlefish and squid each have ten tentacles, the octopus has only eight. The common octopus (*Octopus vulgaris*) and its relatives occur in such large numbers in the Mediterranean, particularly in Greek waters, that it is of much more importance, commercially speaking, than cuttlefish or squid. Its popularity in ancient Greece is evident from the frequency with which it was depicted on classical Greek vases. The average size of octopus sold at market, including tentacles, is 18 inches to 3 feet (50–100 centimeters) in length, but the common octopus can grow up to three times that length. Each tentacle has a double row of suckers. At the center of these tentacles is a mouth opening, with a jaw resembling a parrot's beak. The preparation of octopus and squid in Mediterranean cuisine has changed little since classical times. Whichever method you choose, be it grilled, fried, stuffed, or braised in red wine, the pearly white meat is always a delicacy. A dish incorporating octopus or squid is a welcome mealtime treat at any time of the year, especially since it can be enjoyed even during Lent. The reason for this apparently is that although it is difficult to know which category mollusks fall into, one thing is for certain: they are not mammals.

Squid – *Loligo vulgaris*

Octopus – *Octopus vulgaris*

Cuttlefish – *Sepia officinalis*

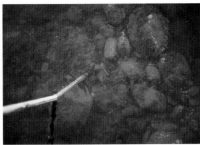

The fisherman jabs his long harpoon against the rocks in deep water to disturb the octopus.

Once he has speared an octopus, he lifts it carefully out of the water.

The fisherman must spear the octopus in the center of its body to prevent it escaping.

If an octopus gets caught in his net, it is very difficult to disentangle it without damaging the net.

The hard work begins after it is caught. The octopus first has to be thoroughly cleaned.

Rubbing the octopus against the stones in a circular motion draws out white foam from the creature's body.

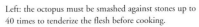

Above: octopuses are easy to cut. The length and size of the pieces depends on the individual recipe.

Left: the octopus must be smashed against stones up to 40 times to tenderize the flesh before cooking.

Right: the octopus is hung outside to dry inside fly-proof wire-mesh boxes.

EIGHT OR TEN ARMS ON THE TABLE

KHTAPODÁKI PSITÓ
Grilled octopus
(Illustration top row, left)

1 oven-ready octopus
Juice of 1 lemon
Olive oil
Oregano
1 lemon, quartered
Salt

Cut the octopus into large pieces, rub with salt and cook over a charcoal grill. Arrange the pieces on a plate and pour lemon juice and a little olive oil over them. Sprinkle with oregano and garnish with the lemon segments. Serve with other appetizers and a glass of ouzo.

Tip: the secret of this recipe is to use octopus that has been dried in the fresh air before cooking. The sight of octopuses hanging up to dry is a common sight in Greek villages. It should be left to hang in the sun for a whole day. Before this, it should have been banged on rocky ground up to forty times and kneaded occasionally in between. When you buy octopus outside Greece, it will usually have been tenderized by machine. Even if you cannot find an air-dried octopus, it will still taste delicious cooked over a charcoal grill.

KALAMARÁKIA TIGANITÁ
Deep fried squid
(Illustration middle row, left)

2 lbs/1 kg small squid
Oil for frying
Flour
1 lemon, quartered
Salt

Gut and clean the squid by peeling off the outer skin under running water, detaching the head and tentacles from the body section, taking care not to split the ink sac, and removing the transparent quill. Very small squid can be fried whole; larger ones should be cut into rings. Heat the oil in a skillet or deep-fat fryer. Mix the flour and salt together and toss the squid in the flour. Drop the squid straight into the hot oil and fry on all sides until golden brown. Arrange on a plate and garnish with the lemon pieces.

KHTAPÓDI ME FASOLÁKIA
Octopus with green beans
(Illustration top row, right)

1 lb/500 g green beans
1 onion, finely diced
3 garlic cloves, finely sliced
2 tomatoes, peeled and diced
1 bunch flat-leaved parsley, finely chopped
1 zucchini, diced
1 chile pepper, finely chopped
1 lb/500 g oven-ready octopus
Salt

Wash and top-and-tail the beans, then cut in half down the center. Place in a saucepan of salted water that covers the beans, and cook over a medium heat. Stir in the onions, garlic, tomatoes, chile pepper, and parsley, adding more boiling water if necessary. Add the zucchini to one side of the saucepan, cover and cook until everything is half cooked. Meanwhile, cut the octopus into pieces and put in a saucepan with a little water. Cover and cook over a medium heat until it too is half cooked. Then add the octopus in its liquid to the beans and cook until the liquid has been absorbed. Serve hot with freshly baked white bread.

KHTAPÓDI ME MAKARONÁKI KOFTÓ
Octopus with noodles
(Illustration bottom row, left)
Serves 4–6

2 lb/1 kg oven-ready octopus
1 generous cup/250 ml Greek extra virgin olive oil
1 large onion, finely diced
2 cups/500 ml tomatoes, puréed
1 scant cup/200 ml dry red wine
1 lb/500 g noodles
Salt
Freshly ground black pepper

Wash the octopus and cut it into pieces. Place in a saucepan with a little water and cook over a medium heat until the water has evaporated. Add the olive oil and onions and fry until the onions are transparent. Stir in the puréed tomatoes, bring to a boil, and add the red wine. Season with salt and pepper. When the octopus is nearly cooked, add a little water and the noodles. Lower the temperature and cook until the noodles have absorbed the liquid but are still *al dente*. Serve hot with freshly baked white bread.

KALAMARÁKIA ME RÍZI KE PIPERIÁ
Squid with rice and bell peppers
(Illustration center row, right)
Serves 4–6

2 lbs/1 kg squid
1 scant cup/200 ml Greek extra virgin olive oil
2 large onions, finely diced
2 red bell peppers, finely diced
2½ cups/500 g rice
1 tbsp flat-leaved parsley, finely chopped
Salt and freshly milled black pepper

Gut and clean the squid, peeling off the outer skin under running water. Detach the head and tentacles from the body, making sure that the ink sac does not split, and remove the transparent quill. Wash the body thoroughly and cut into large pieces.

Heat the olive oil in a saucepan and sauté the onions until transparent. Add the squid and peppers and sauté for another 5 minutes. Pour in 4 cups/1 liter of water and season with salt and pepper. Add the rice and parsley and cook over a medium heat for about 20 minutes. Serve hot with freshly baked white bread.

SOUPIÉS ME SPANÁKI KE FRÉSKA MIRODIKÁ

Cuttlefish with spinach and fresh herbs
(Illustration bottom row, right)

2 lbs/1 kg fresh cuttlefish
1 scant cup/200 ml Greek extra virgin olive oil
5 small onions, sliced into rings
1 bunch dill
Fennel
2 lbs/1 kg fresh spinach
⅔ cup/150 ml dry white wine
Salt and freshly ground black pepper

Gut and clean the cuttlefish, cutting off the head with the tentacles, extracting the insides and carefully removing the ink sac. Dilute the ink in a little warm water and set aside. Heat the olive oil in a saucepan and sauté the onions, dill and fennel. Cut the cuttlefish into rings, add to the onions and herbs, and sauté lightly. Season with salt and pepper and pour in a little water. Add some of the ink and simmer over a low heat for one hour. Wash the spinach, chop it up finely and add to the saucepan. Pour in a scant cup/200 ml of water and a little more ink and simmer for a further 40 minutes. Pour in the white wine and season. Serve hot with freshly baked white bread.

Above: Thessaloniki's flower market is in the heart of the bazaar district.
Background: Thessaloniki's waterfront promenade with the White Tower.

THESSALONIKI

Coffee and cakes

Coffee and conversation

At the kouloúri stall

In the marketplace

More than just tavernas

Sephardic neighbors

Thermal baths

The kafeníon

In the perípteron

Sesame and khalvás

Pastéli

Shopping for herbs and spices

Thessaloniki is the liveliest city in Greece. Thanks to its unique situation on the major trade and traffic routes linking East and West, as well as Greece and central Europe, it has grown into an important economic center, while the melting pot of different nationalities within its walls has turned it into one of the most culturally fascinating cities in all of Greece. The city was named in 315 B.C. by the Macedonian general Kassandros after his wife Thessalonike, a daughter of Philip II. It first began to flourish when it became the capital city of the Roman province of Macedonia, situated as it was on the Via Egnatia, the trade route to Byzantium. In A.D. 50 and again in A.D. 59, St. Paul visited the city and founded a church here. After the division of the Roman Empire in A.D. 395, Thessaloniki became the second most important city in the Byzantine Empire. It was not until the year 1430 that it became part of the Ottoman Empire. Since a large portion of the Greek population had either fled or been killed, the sultan began by resettling Turks here. Then, when the Sephardic Jews in Spain were persecuted and driven out of their country, he permitted about 20,000 of them to settle in Thessaloniki. This large Jewish community encountered another even older community of Jews, which had lived in Thessaloniki since the days of St. Paul, but the two groups did not integrate. This strong Jewish presence was to become a major influence on the city's cultural and economic development right up until recent times. By the time Thessaloniki became Greek again in 1912, there were over 60,000 Jews, nearly 46,000 Muslims, and 40,000 Greeks as well as Armenians and West Europeans living in the city. After centuries of leaving their mark on entire districts of Thessaloniki, a devastating fire resulted in many thousands of Jewish people emigrating to Israel in 1917. In the wake of the Asia Minor catastrophe and the population exchanges of 1922/23, 100,000 Greeks resettled in the city marking the start of a "Greekification" process. Even so, at the time of the German invasion in 1941, there were still 56,000 Jews living in Thessaloniki. Only 10,000 of these survived the Holocaust and only 2,000 of those survivors came back to the city. Today, hardly a trace of its rich Jewish past remains, but thanks to the influence of so many nationalities on the city's history, Thessaloniki has evolved into a dynamic international metropolis.

Thessaloniki's mile-long waterfront promenade is lined with restaurants, cafés, pubs and bars, offering something for everyone, be it simply a coffee or lemonade at the White Tower, or a several-course meal with a view of the sea.

COFFEE AND CAKES

It is more than just a pleasant way of whiling away the time, it is a social ritual of cult proportions: whether you are in town or in the country, drinking coffee and eating cake are an integral part of the social code of conduct in Thessaloniki. Any inadvertent breach of this can still give offense, even today. In short, the abiding rule is that if you want to do business with someone, you must offer them coffee. If you want to gain their confidence, then offer them cake as well. Even more importantly, it is a mark of hospitality. Consequently, wherever you go, you will find everyone offering you coffee and cake no matter what time of the day it is. It is also imperative that the cake is very sweet and the coffee very strong. Even a perfectly "ordinary" afternoon tea table may hold a lavish selection of cakes and include some culinary sensation or other, since everything is always put out at the same time.

BREAKFAST

If there is one thing in Thessaloniki that has remained unchanged since antiquity, it is breakfast. To this day, it remains a diffident harbinger of lunch. Breakfast is not a meal which is paid a great deal of attention in Greece, and in the city, there is even less time to enjoy a fulsome meal. Greek breakfast is designed around the climate. People are still feeling the effects of the previous evening's gastronomic forays and the rising temperatures of the day leave little room for breakfast fancies. Nevertheless, a cup of coffee is not complete without some sweet confectionery. As you pass by the bakeries in the morning, you may well choose something to eat from the abundant selection on offer, such as small fruit pastries or turnovers, sweet puff pastries or sesame rings. If you fancy something a bit more substantial, you might opt for a cheese pasty. Cafés and restaurants, which cater to the tastes of summer visitors, may serve traditional Greek dishes for breakfast such as yogurt with honey and walnuts, a plate of sheep's cheese, *khalvás*, olives, or tomatoes and white bread.

Above: the days when the coffeehouse was out of bounds to women are long since over.
Background: the cake display at Thessaloniki's oldest patisserie must be seen to be believed.

Tarta lemóni me kommátia mílu – lemon and apple tart

Tarta me krema vissino – cream slice with morello cherries

Trigona – this consists of a syrup-soaked pastry generously filled with vanilla cream

Saraglakia – delicate puff pastry filled with nuts

COFFEE AND CONVERSATION

Since the real business of eating does not begin for the Greeks until midday, it is only coffee that gets city dwellers, in particular, through the first hours of the day. This first cup of mocha coffee is both a reminder and a foretaste of an afternoon ritual. *Vále bríki*, which means something like "get the coffee pot boiling" is one of the most important phrases to be heard during the course of a Greek day. Not only does it signal coffee-time, but can also be an out-right invitation for a cozy chat over coffee or even a coffee *klatsch* to gossip about the various goings-on in the neighborhood. These get togethers over coffee have a special social significance in Greece as a means of contact and exchanging news. Anyone who does not participate or observe the rules will find it difficult to make friends in the community. The hostess serves the coffee on a tray with some sweet confectionery and a glass of chilled water. Her guests wish her success and happiness before sampling the sweet confectionery, then quenching their thirst with the water and only then

These brass coffee pots allow the heat to be distributed slowly and evenly as the coffee is brought to a boil.

Ground coffee and sugar are spooned into the pot according to personal taste.

Using just enough water to fill a coffee cup, pour it onto the coffee and sugar and bring to a boil

The coffee is ready when the froth has risen right up to the brim.

Pour the mocha coffee slowly and carefully into the cup, leaving as much of the grounds as possible in the pot.

reaching for the coffee. There are rules governing coffee-drinking too: Unlike espresso, mocha coffee is not downed in one go, but sipped deliberately slowly in order to leave the gritty sediment at the bottom of the cup.

These private coffee sessions can include mixed company with men present as well as women. Sometimes, it is just a women's get together. If only men, it is unlikely that they would make the coffee themselves, preferring to have it served to them in the *kafeníon*. Coffee-making is regarded as women's work. There are numerous ways of preparing it and sometimes it does not turn out successfully. There is a saying that you can't hide anything from the mocha, and the maker's mood is reflected in the resulting brew. There are basically three different ways of preparing mocha coffee: *skétos* (bitter), *métrios* (medium-sweet), and *glikós* (sweet). To make one cup of mocha coffee, you need one tea-spoonful of very finely ground coffee beans. Add sugar to taste, then a cup of water, and slowly bring it all to a boil in a special little long-handled pot, before carefully pouring the coffee into the cup. In days gone by, it was placed in glowing embers to heat up. The coffee sediment must then be given time to settle at the bottom of the cup, a period of waiting which can be filled with cookies and sweet confectionery.

In the 18th century, it was customary for young men, seeking a girl's hand in marriage, to be served a cup of mocha coffee by her family. This was not simply a symbol of the host's hospitality. If the coffee were sweet, the suitor had every reason to be pleased; if it were bitter, the young man would rise politely, say thank you for the conversation and never be seen again.

Φίλτρου
ΣΑΝΤΟΣ
3400

Φίλτρου
ΓΟΥΑΤΕΜΑΛΑΣ
3400

Φίλτρου
ΚΟΣΤΑ ΡΙΚΑ
3300

Φίλτρου
ΑΜΕΡΙΚΗΣ
3300

Φίλτρου
ΓΕΡΜΑΝΙΚΟΣ
3200

Φίλτρου
ΚΟΛΟΜΒΙΑΣ
3500

Φίλτρου
ΧΩΡΙΣ ΚΑΦΕΪΝΗ
3600

Above: coffee varieties from all over the world are weighed and freshly milled for you at the coffee store.

KAFÉS FRAPÉ

1 tsp soluble coffee
1 tsp sugar
1 spoonful of fresh cream or canned milk
Ice cubes

Place the coffee, sugar and ¼ glass of cold water in a shaker and shake vigorously until all the liquid has turned to foam. The firmer the consistency of the foam, the better the *kafés frapé* will be.

Pour the mixture into a tall tumbler, add a few ice-cubes and top up with cold water. Add a dash of fresh cream or canned milk and stir with a straw. Since coffee preferences vary, when you order a *kafés frapé*, currently mocha's biggest rival, you will be asked how you like it to be made.

YOUR DESTINY IN THE COFFEE CUP

The secret signs in the cup resemble a filigree pattern when the warm mocha sediment is slowly swirled around the inside of a coffee cup. The rest of the grounds are tipped out abruptly and the cup placed upside down on a plate. Then comes the moment everyone has been waiting for. The *kafetzoú*, the woman who can read coffee grounds, turns the cup around, looking deeply into its depths. After carefully studying the signs, she may say: "I see a bird, a road, up on the mountain lurks danger, there's a person in the valley with a name beginning with K. You seem sad but I see two rings in the distance, perhaps for a wedding." You have to believe in the *kafetzoú*, otherwise her prophecies will not come true.

Aristoteles Square is too young to remember those times. He just stands his money bowl and a price tag on top of the pile of sesame rings, which is already considerably depleted, and goes off for a short break. He knows he can do so with an easy mind, as his clients will be scrupulous in paying for their sesame rings even during his absence. A stolen *koulóuria* just wouldn't taste anywhere near as good.

Shape the dough into thin rolls, keeping them uniform in thickness and length.

AT THE KOULOÚRI STALL

The stall selling sesame rings in Thessaloniki's Aristoteles Square is nothing out of the ordinary. It is just an ordinary *koulóuri* stall of the kind you might find all over town, indeed, in towns all over Greece. The *koulóuri* is more than just a sesame ring, however. The *koulourás* (the sesame ring seller) believes that it is what unites the Greek people, and he should know. When he sets up his stall early in the morning and piles up a mountain of freshly baked, crisp, warm sesame rings, it is not long before he is literally besieged by passers-by who cannot resist this particular temptation. Since nobody wants to miss the morning *koulóuri*, all social barriers are swept aside for a brief moment, bringing together people from all different walks of life, who might otherwise never have met, or, under any other circumstances, might never have wanted to meet. You will find *koulóuria* all over Greece, but the people of Thessaloniki, naturally enough, firmly believe that theirs are the best. Some of the customers buying their sesame rings at the stall can remember the post-war period when food was not so plentiful. In those days, the aroma of fresh, warm *koulóuria* in the early evening was enough to make people think of better days, almost like scenting a breath of promise in the air. Children used to wear their *koulóuri* on their arm like a precious bracelet until they eventually had to break it in order to eat it. The *koulourás* in

KOULOÚRIA
Sesame rings

1 cake/15 g fresh yeast, or 1½ tsp dried yeast
8½ cups/1 kg flour
2 tsp salt
½ cup/100 g sugar
4 tbsp/50 ml sunflower oil
1¾ cups/300 g sesame seeds

Dissolve half the yeast in a scant cup/250 ml warm water and mix in 2–3 tablespoons of flour. Leave the rising yeast to stand for 24 hours. Next day, mix the remaining yeast with another cup/250 ml warm water, add 2–3 tablespoons of flour and leave to stand for about 15 minutes. Sift three-quarters of the flour into a bowl along with the salt, then make a well in the center. Pour the sugar, oil and the two lots of rising yeast into this and knead slowly until the mixture forms a dough. Cover the bowl with a cloth and leave to prove in a warm place until it has doubled in size. Then knock it back and knead for another 5 minutes. Pull off small lumps of dough and roll them into thin sausage shapes, about 14 inches/35 cm in length. Dip these in water and roll them in sesame seeds before pressing the two ends firmly together into a ring. Preheat the oven to 430 °F (220 °C), lay the sesame rings on a greased baking sheet and bake for 15 mins until golden on the outside and soft inside. Sesame rings are delicious warm as well as cold.

Dipping the pastry rolls in water helps the sesame seeds stick to the dough.

Roll the damp pastry rolls in sesame seeds until they are completely covered.

Close up the ends to make rings and place on a well-greased baking sheet.

The sesame rings are out on the street as soon as they are baked. Sometimes they are still warm and smell appetizingly of toasted sesame seeds.

IN THE MARKETPLACE

It is early morning and still pleasantly cool when the first trucks arrive. Here and there, you can hear the telltale clattering of aluminum doors being noisily raised. There is no doubt about it, Thessaloniki market is preparing for another hectic working day. Someone, somewhere, is throwing a bucket of water onto the concrete and brushing away the remains of the previous day's garbage. By now, you can hear the clanking of crates being stacked on top of each other and the first morning greetings being exchanged along with good wishes for the day. One more puff of cigarette, thinks Apostolos, before it is time to set the stall out at the edge of the road. It does not take him long: setting out the boxes in the right order is a job he can do in his sleep. And he is only just in time, for the first customers are beginning to appear among the stalls. The trick is to attract their attention by extolling the goods in a loud voice. Apostolos is bound to be hoarse again this evening when he goes home, but that is just part of his job. Apostolos is a fish-seller in the Modiano market hall, named after the architect who designed it. It is situated at the heart of the market area, which has been the hub of all trade in Thessaloniki since time immemorial. The Modiano market offers all you could wish for in the way of fruit and vegetables, meat, fish, cheese, and sausages. It offers an inexhaustible range of goods, not just from local suppliers, but from all over Greece. Prices and places of origin are displayed on boards.

Above: after a spell of shopping, you can recharge your batteries by enjoying a fortifying snack in one of the popular market tavernas.
Right: whether you want a whole sheep or a few strands of saffron, you will find what you are looking for in the market hall.

THE BARGAINING GAME

"Come on, step forward! You'll only find the best here! Take it home with you! Look what I've got for you today! Just for you, mind! Go on, pick what you want!" You will hear many different voices calling out from all sides, the stallholders all trying to attract the customers' attention with virtually the same promises. And that takes some doing given the fact that the Greek housewives, who are the ones they need to impress, have a reputation for not being easily taken in. They will only buy quality goods, regardless of how convincingly a stallholder might advertise his products. Yet somehow, by the end of the day, the stalls still seem to end up empty and you might well wonder how this happens.

The strategy employed by Greek tradesmen is as simple as it is successful: They see a customer, but address her as a woman. The purchase might revolve around nothing more than a pound of tomatoes, but they will playfully, yet unmistakably pay court to her. This ritual follows a strict procedure. After calling out the goods, shouting out the price per kilo or the price of the item in question, there will be a more personal invitation for "her" to come and look and not pass by without stopping. Then, stepping up their efforts, they beg "her" to turn back, stop for just a moment, touch, try, see for herself how fresh everything is for "her".

Once the stallholder and customer have established eye contact, the bargaining enters its second phase. The would-be purchaser feigns disinterest verging on indignation. No, no, it is all much too expensive! "Please, I beg you, that cannot be. Look how fresh it all is. You won't find fresher anywhere." The mistress of the house still refuses to bite. "Alright then, just for you I'll make an exception and drop the price. When you look at me like that, I can deny you nothing. You can have it cheaper. How about taking a couple of pounds then? There you are, then – will there be anything else?" By the end of the transaction, both sides have got what they wanted, each emerging with a sense of achievement – and that is something that did not cost a cent!

Eyes to the front! Greek stallholders take great pains to display their goods to their best advantage and orderliness is half the battle.

The selection of fresh fish available may not be as great as it was 10 years ago, but it is still an impressive array.

Pulses are an important ingredient in far too many recipes for a choice of a mere four or five to be sufficient.

The most colorful stalls are naturally those selling fruit and vegetables. Here you will find produce both from local growers and from all over Greece.

MORE THAN JUST TAVERNAS

Hardly any other country has developed as many different types of restaurants as Greece. Some serve nothing but fish dishes, others only have meat on the menu. Some specialize in one single dish. The same thing applies to drinks. If you want to sample the full extent of the individuality and diversity of Greek cuisine, the best advice is to take your courage in your hands and embark on a culinary voyage of delightful discovery.

Above right: the *mezedopolío* specializing in appetizers is packed at lunchtime. The tables groan under a variety of appetizers, which are shared by the diners.

Below right: the *estiatório* is the classic Greek restaurant where you can choose from a variety of main courses. All the top restaurants also offer musical entertainment in the evenings.

Below, far right: the atmosphere in the taverna is more casual. These offer a straightforward menu and include many grilled meat dishes.

VÓLTA

In the old days, going for a walk in Greece was not something that you did purely for pleasure. Going "*vólta*", as it was called, was governed by a fixed set of rules, particularly in rural areas. Here, the weekend *vólta* provided the sole opportunity for women and girls to escape from the confines of their domestic environment, to keep an eye out for eligible young men, or simply show off their new clothes. The young men, too, would try to look their best in order to please their girls. Only the older men would prefer to sit in their favorite *kafeníon*. Going *vólta* was really too much trouble, and it usually took a great deal of pleading before they would consent to accompany the rest of the family on such an outing. People only went promenading along the main street of the village or town, sauntering up and down several times, meeting the same people again and again, glancing at those strolling along the other side of the street out of the corner of their eye, or perhaps even flashing a brief smile at someone. The *vólta* is no longer so important in the towns, but it is still practiced nevertheless, especially at weekends, when you will see people strolling up and down the promenade in Thessaloniki in the balmy evenings, enjoying the tolerable hours of the day. Some go over to each other, smiling, happy to meet up again at last, whereas others deliberately avoid each other. One thing they will all do, however, sooner or later, is stop at the stalls along the way to buy bags full of nuts, *spória* or *kouloúria*.

AN ELEGANT EVENING OUT

It is quite legitimate to regard Thessaloniki as a bridge between East and West, but the city has become far more than just that. It is true that the ruins are a legacy of the Romans and evidence of the city's distinguished past, while the Byzantine churches reflect its strongly Orthodox character. It owes some of its bazaar culture to the East and its reputation as a center of learning to the centuries of Jewish presence. But more than this, present-day Thessaloniki is now the most modern city in Greece and can confidently compete with distant Athens.

If you want an evening out, you will find you are much better off in Thessaloniki than in Athens, even if the latter has made up some ground over the past few years. Nowhere else in Greece will you find so many gastronomic opportunities to choose from as you will in Thessaloniki, or such a colorful kaleidoscope of different cafés, restaurants, bars, pubs, and clubs. These range from long-established and cozy, to sheer elegance or chic and cool. If you are looking for something really special, however, you should leave the city with its fascinating, yet perhaps bewildering choice of culinary delights below you and ascend to the heights of pure luxury. In the Porfyra restaurant of the Macedonia Palace Hotel, you will find chef de cuisine Sotiris Evangelou in charge of one of the most creative restaurants in the city. You could do no better than place yourself in his hands if you want to really enjoy yourself in an elegant, sophisticated atmosphere with a breathtaking view over the sea. The special meal might begin with a slice of salmon, first sautéd, then baked in a honey and sesame seed coating and served with a mango and avocado sauce. The beef consommé to follow is Asian-inspired, flavored with a hint of tea, and accompanied by transparent vegetable wantans. Goat cheese, coated in egg and breadcrumbs and fried, served on a bed of green leaf salad, dressed with a blackberry and tarragon vinaigrette, paves the way for the highlight: beef fillet au gratin topped with a ginger crust and served with a morel wine sauce. Dessert could be a hot-and-cold surprise consisting of white and dark chocolate.

237

SEPHARDIC NEIGHBORS

While Greece was still under Ottoman rule, there was a Jewish community living in Thessaloniki, that bore the proud title of "City and Mother in Israel." This is an honorary title granted since biblical times to the largest and the most pious and erudite Jewish communities living in diaspora. The number of synagogues and centers of learning, not to mention secular Jewish cultural institutions such as theaters and music schools, was enormous. Only in such a cultural and religious diversity could a Jewish community flourish which, right up until the early 20th century, constituted at least half, if not more than half, of the city's population. Its influence ran deep and could be felt right into the 1920s, when it was still customary for all traffic to stop running from Friday evening to Saturday evening and for trade and work in the harbor to cease. Thessaloniki was a Jewish town and its way of life was determined not only by the Jewish clerics, but also by the Western-orientated Jewish merchants, industrialists, and self-assured Jewish workers and employees in the big tobacco manufacturing industries, for example. Jewish merchants also played a prominent role in the food sector. One of Greece's biggest cookie and candy firms was run by the Allatini family, whose name is the only one that has remained a household name in Greece since the Holocaust put a violent end to Jewish history in Thessaloniki. It is one of the few Mediterranean cities that has a living memory of a strong Jewish culture.

MARONKHINOS
Passover marzipan
(Illustration left)

1¾ cups/200 g ground almonds
1¾ cups/200 g confectioner's sugar
½ tsp almond essence
Whole almonds, skinned

Mix the ground almonds and confectioner's sugar together in a bowl. Add water, a spoonful at a time, and stir constantly until the mixture forms a stiff paste. Add the almond essence and knead the paste on a board for about 5 minutes. Pull off small lumps of paste and roll into little balls, making a small dent in the center. Place one whole almond in each dent. Toss the *maronkhinos* in confectioner's sugar and leave to stand for one day. The marzipan will keep longer if stored in an airtight container.

THE OLDEST BOOKSTORE IN THESSALONIKI

When Isaac Molho opened a bookstore in Thessaloniki in 1888, the same year that the railway line from Thessaloniki to Belgrade and Vienna was opened, he had a vision. He wanted to introduce Western European culture to his city, which had already felt the influence of centuries of various cultures existing alongside one another, and which could pride itself on cultural diversity and a tolerant way of life. From that time on, French, Spanish and English literature became available in a region where the individual population groups usually spoke only their own language and frequently clung to traditional ways. During its 100 years of history, the bookstore suffered two major setbacks. One was in 1917, when a catastrophic fire destroyed within three days nearly 10,000 buildings in the lower part of town, including most of the Jewish districts and the bookstore. After the fire, it had to be completely rebuilt. During the Second World War, not only was the Molhos family forced to sell the bookstore to the German occupiers for five Lire, but also most members of the family never returned from the concentration camps. Only two of the children managed to escape to the island of Skópelos. After the war, Solomon Molho once again stood in front of his father's store, determined to resurrect its fortunes, which, after a lot of hard work, he eventually succeeded in doing. Today, the Molho bookstore is once again a quiet oasis of intellectual life amid the busy *Tsimiskí*, the city's busiest shopping street. The walls of Thessaloniki's oldest bookstore represent a great treasure in themselves for they bear testimony to the many years of Jewish history and culture in Thessaloniki.

PESHE EN SÁLTSA
Fish fillets in walnut sauce
(Illustration top)

1½ cups/180 g matzo meal
6 carp or sole fillets
2 eggs, lightly beaten
Olive oil
Vinegar
1½ cups/150 g chopped walnuts
Salt and freshly ground black pepper

Mix half the matzo meal with salt and pepper. Dip the fish fillets in egg and coat with matzo meal. Sauté the fillets in olive oil until golden brown, then remove them from the skillet and set aside. Heat the oil, vinegar, and water and stir in the remaining matzo meal. Cook the mixture for about 10–15 minutes until the sauce thickens slightly. Place the fish fillets in the sauce and cook for another 15 minutes. Arrange the fillets on a plate to serve, pour the sauce over them and sprinkle with walnuts.

RODANKHAS DE KALAVASSA AMARILLA
Pumpkin tarts
(Illustration right)

For the pastry:
½ cup/125 ml Greek extra virgin olive oil
½ cup/125 g water
About 4 cups/500 g wheat flour
Salt

For the filling:
½ lb/250 g pumpkin flesh, diced
½ cup/125 ml water
1 generous cup/250 g sugar
1 cup/100 g ground walnuts
1 tsp ground cinnamon
Olive oil

Pastry: Bring the water and oil to a boil, remove from the heat, and work in the flour until you have a stiff dough. Season with salt and knead on a floured surface for about 10 minutes. Divide the pastry into 2–3 portions, cover and leave to stand. Then, roll the pastry out thinly and cut out circles 6 inches/15 cm in diameter. Preheat the oven to 350 °F (180 °C).
Filling: Cook the pumpkin flesh in the water. Add a little more water and mash the pumpkin with a fork. Stir in the sugar, walnuts, cinnamon, and a little olive oil and simmer slowly for a short while.
Line small tartlet pans with the pastry rounds, place some filling in the center and sprinkle with walnuts. Bake for 30 minutes in the preheated oven. Serve warm.

THERMAL BATHS

Present-day Thessaloniki is a vibrant city with wide boulevards, large squares, and modern stores. Its most famous landmark, the White Tower, was originally part of the Byzantine city wall. Those with a passion for religious architecture can wander through the city's churches, stopping off now and then in a taverna to sample the excellent Macedonian cuisine, or to refresh themselves in an ice cream parlor. There are several natural hot springs around the city, whose healing properties are greatly appreciated by visitors suffering from rheumatism, arthritis, and sciatica.

Thermal baths must have been a popular concept even in ancient Thessaloniki. Archaeologists excavating around the site of the ancient marketplace in Thessaloniki found the remains of ancient, presumably Roman, baths.

Public baths played an important role in daily life even prior to Roman times, during the Greco-Hellenistic culture. The steam baths, or sweat baths, were thought to have a similar effect to today's sauna. Glowing charcoal or stones heated over a fire were sprinkled with water, filling the enclosed room with hot air. Ritual bathing sessions were also held in which different herbs and sometimes hemp were added. One of the oldest Greek hot air baths dating from the beginning of the 5th century B.C. was discovered during excavation work on Cyprus in the Vouni palace grounds.

The best evidence of the basic layout of ancient thermal baths dates from Roman times. Not

Two women washing and brushing their hair by a large washstand, while a third one joins them, carefully folding up her clothes.

only did they include changing rooms, cold baths, hot baths, and steam or sweat baths, but also eateries, bars, libraries, parks, and ball game courts. Thanks to their growing popularity among well-heeled citizens and rulers, more and more public baths were built, outdoing each other in size and in the lavishness of their mosaic decorations. Baths were part of public life. Not only did they take care of personal hygiene needs, but they were also the place where decisions were made, where business was transacted, where you could eat and drink. Apart from certain bathing times set aside for women, the baths were mainly reserved for men, who came to the baths to find pleasures of a particular sort.

Four women bathing under showers in a bathhouse. The water is being sprayed from jets shaped like animal heads. The bathers have draped their garments over a pipe between the showers.

Several bathhouses dating from Thessaloniki's Turkish past, known as "hamams," have been successfully converted into atmospheric restaurants and interesting exhibition rooms.

PÁPIA STO FOÚRNO ME FOUNDOÚKIA
Roast duck with hazelnuts

1 oven-ready duck, weighing about 3 lbs/1.5 kg
2 cups/250 g hazelnuts
6 sprigs fresh mint, finely chopped
½ bunch flat-leaved parsley, finely chopped
6 sprigs basil, finely chopped
6 dried figs, finely chopped
Seeds of 1 pomegranate
4 juniper berries, crushed
1 tsp peppercorns, crushed
Saffron strands
1 generous cup/250 ml red wine
4 tbsp olive oil
2 tbsp red wine vinegar
⅔ cup/150 ml fish sauce (from an oriental delicatessen)

Rub the duck inside and out with salt and pepper, place in a roasting pan, and pierce the breast and legs in several places. Heat the oven to 350 °F (180 °C). Bake the hazelnuts for about 10 minutes in the oven, taking care not to burn them, then raise the temperature to 400 °F (200 °C). Crush the nuts finely with a pestle and mortar.
Place all the ingredients, except for the duck and hazelnuts, in a saucepan and slowly bring to a boil. Simmer for 20 minutes before straining the liquid into a bowl. Stir in the crushed hazelnuts and pour the sauce over the duck. Roast it for about 1½ hours, basting frequently with the sauce and making sure that the skin remains coated with the crushed nuts. The liquid will form a crust over the duck. Serve at once.

A scene from Greek society that has remained unchanged for decades: men directing operations from a table at a *kafeníon*.

TÁVLI

Távli is the favorite game of Greek men in the *kafeníon*. The Greek word *távli*, or *tavla* in Turkish, is derived from the Latin word *tabula*, meaning board. The game is played on a board divided into two sections, each marked out with 12 narrow wedges or points, in other words 24 wedges in all. Each player has 15 counters. Even though the moves are determined by a throw of the dice, *távli* is certainly no game of chance, but a game of strategy based on skill, intuition and a good deal of psychology. Three main versions are played in Greece, but even more variations exist, each with different rules. *Pórtes* (doors) is played more or less according to the familiar rules of backgammon. The second version is called *plakotó* (from the Greek for *plakóno*, meaning "to cover up"). The third version is known as *févga* ("run!" or

"quick, get away"). In all three games, the idea is to be the first one to get his counters from the starting position to the winning post. *Pórtes* is the most complicated game to set up, with the counters arranged in groups of two, three and five over the board. Your opponent's counters can be knocked out of the game and cannot be reintroduced except by a throw of the dice. In *plakotó*, the game begins with all the counters in play from the starting position. Counters standing on their own can be immobilized. In the case of *févga*, the counters start off diagonally opposite each other and the players play counter-clockwise in the same direction, chasing each other round the board. The different versions can be played separately, or one after the other, with the players collecting points as they go along.

KOMBOLÓI

The *kombolói*, or string of beads, a familiar sight in the hands of many Greek men, originally came from the Orient. The Turks introduced it to Greece via India and Persia. If it is a Muslim who is running the beads through his fingers, then it is a type of rosary for counting prayers. The 33 beads must each be touched one after the other until each has been touched three times in praise of Allah and his 99 names. Once it arrived in Greece, it became a form of plaything, always with an uneven number of beads. The word *kombolói* incorporates the word *kómbos*, meaning "knot." The fascination and magic derived from these "knots" running through your fingers must come from the thoughts conjured up from playing with these beads. During the course of a man's life, his *kombolói* becomes a sort of talisman and there are old men who fall into a deep depression if they lose their personal *kombolói* that has been their companion for decades.

The *kombolói* is certainly more than just a means of passing time. One is almost tempted to say that it reflects a way of life. There is the sound of the beads clicking together, the feel of the smooth beads between your fingers, the hours that slip away while playing with the beads, inducing an almost trance-like state. There is one important, yet very basic lesson to be learned from playing with the *kombolói* beads, and that is that the circular string of beads symbolizes the belief that everything returns, nothing really ends: in other words, the belief in infinity.

THE KAFENÍON

The *kafeníon*, the men's coffeehouse, is an altogether Greek institution. You used to see them everywhere, in the main square of every village, in every part of town and at every major city crossroads. Although they may have lost some of their importance in modern times, they still exist in the more rural areas, in small towns and on the islands. This is where the men meet up to talk about the harvest, complain about a bad crop, or grumble about the failure of Brussels' agricultural policy. Family tragedies and personal crises are discussed alongside politics. Anything and everything can be a potential topic of conversation. They argue, discuss, shout, and make jokes. Anyone preferring quiet and contemplation can let his thoughts wander in rhythm with the *kombolói* beads running through his fingers. They sit over a cup of mocha coffee, a glass of water, or even a glass of wine or ouzo. There is no food available here, except perhaps for a bowl of peanuts to accompany the ouzo. Hours can slip by in this way before the men have finally seen, talked, played, and drunk enough. Happy and content, they leave this exclusively male world in the knowledge that the *kafeníon* will still be waiting for them in the same place tomorrow.

The *kafeníon* is likely to be fairly sparsely furnished with simple chairs and tables, yet there is something enduring and timeless about it which has remained unchanged despite the great social changes within Greece. The classic *kafeníon* has managed to maintain its role in Greek life in the face of the dynamic developments of the modern age. While cafés in the big towns have moved on to become meeting-places for young people of both sexes, everything here has stayed pleasantly the same. Women do not feel they are missing out on anything in this male domain and they uphold it as part of the traditional role allocation. Women have their own get togethers, for instance at the former village washhouse or over coffee on a neighbor's terrace.

The most important place in the world for an old Greek man is his regular seat in his favorite *kafeníon*. Just to sit there quietly, joining in the conversation and hearing the backgammon counters clicking in the background, is enough to make any day a good one.

IN THE PERÍPTERON

If there is one person in Greece who has found his heart's content, it is surely the man in the *perípteron*. Whether situated on the loud, hectic main road or in a sleepy suburb, all is still right with the world in a *perípteron*. *Períptera* are the smallest supermarkets imaginable: They consist of a hut with a roof, measuring one square yard inside, providing just enough room for one chair and stuffed to the ceiling with goods. There are just a few crates stacked on the floor waiting to be unpacked. No town or village would be complete without this institution, and Thessaloniki is no exception. *Períptera* are sights just as worthy of seeing as the White Tower and the old district of Ladádika. And the man in the *perípteron* also merits a second glance. Hidden behind all the small items which somehow improve life for a brief moment, he sits there quietly selling candies, drinks, ice creams, savory snacks, toys for the little ones and beads for the grown-ups, batteries, cigarettes, newspapers, tissues…Now and again, he raises his head and looks out of the single window, but only for a moment. There is too much going on out there that he would rather not know about. He is content if he can put his hand out occasionally to take some money from passing customers. In the countryside, where the days are more unhurried and life in a *perípteron* more relaxed, the range of goods seems inexhaustible. They include napkins, knives, scissors, toilet articles and, somehow, as if by magic, you always seem to find the very thing you forgot to buy elsewhere. And if one of the neighbors is not at home, the mailman will leave the letters in the *perípteron*,

Above: the man in the *perípteron* requires patience, placidity, even some degree of serenity – and, above all, a well-padded behind!

knowing that they will be safely taken care of by the people there.

"If you are in a spot, we are happy to help," old Barba Yóryis used to say. This small, slightly stooped man was known throughout the district. Children thought he was the richest man in the world, for he seemed to have everything a child could want. If he was in a good mood, he would give the children candies when they stood wide-eyed but penniless before his *perípteron*. This happened often and was another reason for his popularity. Some people went to him to find out the latest news, as he handed this out for free. However inconspicuous Barba Yóryis appeared, he was a mine of knowledge about everything that went on in the district and the hub of a lot of information. His four walls were privy to many secrets, never to be revealed. Barba Yóryis did not have to go out into the world. His customers brought the world to him in his *perípteron*.

Left: few things are more endearing than the sight of a child, eyes shining, outside a *perípteron*.

Right: the *perípteron* is an integral part of the Greek street scene.

The *perípteron* has started stocking souvenirs in tourist areas, such as these popular sponges.

Whether in the outlying suburbs or the city center, you will find *periptera* everywhere. Sometimes, the ones that are more unprepossessing may, on closer inspection, turn out to be all the more interesting for their lack of touristy goods.

Whether situated at a major intersection or in a remote suburb, each *peripteron* employs an individual selling strategy based on one common principle: they stock everything that the man in the *peripteron* thinks is necessary.

A *peripteron* can supply individual advice or a private chat. Despite the fact that supermarkets are sprouting up like mushrooms, people would not want to be without their *peripteron* and the odds and ends sold there.

The seeds of the sesame plant (*Sesamum indicum*) spill out of the ripe seed pod once it has popped open.

Professor Gertsis is conducting a research trial near Thessaloniki with the aim of reintroducing sesame to Greece.

SESAME

The sesame plant (*Sesamum indicum*) is a very old cultivated plant, which originated in countries bordering on the Indian Ocean. A one-year-old plant, growing up to 6 feet (2 meters) in height, bears white or dark red flowers, resembling foxgloves. The plant ovaries produce numerous seed pods, measuring up to one inch (2–3 centimeters) in length. When they are ripe, they pop open at the tip – hence the expression "open sesame" – and release the small, flat, oval seeds. The main varieties grown today, however, have been cultivated to produce seed pods that do not pop, so that they can be harvested with combine harvesters and mechanically cleaned afterward. Sesame is used in Greece for the popular sesame rings, the *kouloúria*. Because of its high essential linoleic acid content, the sesame seed oil derived from pressing the seeds is valued as a nutritional source. The solid cake remaining after the pressing is so rich in protein that it is milled into a nourishing and delicious flour.

From the research laboratory of the Dimitris Perrotis College of Agricultural Studies in Thessaloniki, where Professor Gertsis is trying to reintroduce the cultivation of sesame in Greece on an ecologically sound footing, since imported products are generally too highly polluted (from left to right): Metaxades (Greek sesame variety), imported sesame seeds from the Sudan, Greek sesame seeds from Thrace, imported sesame seeds from India.

KHALVÁS

By the time people in the palace of the ancient Mycaeneans finally developed interest in "*sa-sa-ma*" – writing tablets listing deliveries of supplies also give an abbreviated form of the word as "*sa*" – (sesame) in 1500 B.C., the sesame plant had already been in use in East Africa and India for about 500 years. The plant had been deliberately cultivated there and the nutritious, aromatic sesame seeds were highly prized. Around 600 B.C., the Greeks discovered that sesame seeds were perfect for flavoring bread: "Seven couches and as many tables, crowned with poppy seed, linseed and sesame seed bread, and for the girls, buckets of a sweet dessert…this a sweet mixture of honey and linseed," enthuses Athenaeus in his book *Deipnosophistae* ("The Banquet of the Learned" or "The Gastronomers"), proving unequivocally that not only sesame seed bread, but also tasty combinations of plant seeds and honey, for instance, were extremely popular at the time. The list of household goods belonging to a rich Athenian whose possessions were to be auctioned included sesame seeds, alongside such mundane items as olive oil, lentils, and grain. And the poet Antiphanes from the 4th century B.C. also lists sesame seeds along with caraway, marjoram, and thyme in his list of spices.

But it was to be centuries before Greece eventually produced the most delicious and healthiest sweet confectionery of all: *khalvás*, halva. In northern Greece, *khalvás* is served for breakfast on account of its nutritional value, as well as for dessert along with a glass of wine. *Khalvás* consists of 50 percent milled and toasted sesame seeds (*takhíni*) and a warmed mixture of sugar and glucose. It is now possible to replace the sugar content with honey or fructose so that even diabetics may enjoy *khalvás*. The sesame paste is mixed with sugar or honey until it forms a solid mass. This is left to cool and harden. Before it sets completely, the paste is put into different-sized molds. *Khalvás* sets at 59 °F (15 °C). Cocoa, peanuts, pistachios, almonds, or candied fruit, as well as oil of roses may be added to produce a variety of flavors. Its appearance can also be varied by molding it into various shapes or coating it with chocolate. *Khalvás* is particularly popular with Greeks during Lent since it is thankfully not prohibited. Because of its high content of fat, calcium, iron, phosphorus, proteins, and vitamins A and C, it is a long-lasting and nutritious source of energy and is also believed to rejuvenate the cells of the body.

Only whole almonds are used for *khalvás me amigdala*, *khalvás* with almonds.

A more recent *khalvás* variation with a chocolate coating. Top: This old *khalvás* box is a collector's item.

Khalvás with cocoa produces an interesting veining effect running through the mixture.

Khalvás bars come in all flavors, including fruit, nuts, cocoa, honey or sugar.

Right: fresh fruit according to season and some small pieces of *khalvás* are all it takes to rustle up an interesting dessert, good enough to tempt everyone's palate.

PASTÉLI

In every *perípteron* in Greece, you will find a candy bar which is reminiscent of the natural food movement prevalent in the 1980s. *Pastéli*, however, is one of the cornerstones of Greek confectionery. The classic *pastéli* consists simply of sesame seeds baked with honey, and is therefore indigenous to the sesame-growing area around Thessaloniki, but almond, filbert and peanut *pastéli* have also become increasingly popular and are manufactured nationwide. This is not surprising in a country that produces such an abundance of nuts. Almonds grow in rocky regions, filberts and walnuts in agricultural areas and peanuts come from Cyprus.

There are still a a good many *pastéli* bakeries in this, the home region of *pastéli*. The aroma emanating from the bakeries can easily make you believe that *pastéli* may well have something to do with the legendary nectar and ambrosia that found their way here from nearby Olympus.

PASTÉLI
Sesame bars

4 cups/500 g sesame seeds
8 level tbsp/250 g honey
1 generous cup/250 g sugar

Preheat the oven to 345 °F (175 °C). Spread the sesame seeds out on a baking sheet and roast in the oven until golden brown. Heat the honey and sugar in a saucepan over a medium heat until the mixture caramelizes. Using a sugar thermometer, make sure that the temperature of the mixture does not exceed 470 °F (250 °C). Remove the saucepan from the heat and stir in the toasted sesame seeds. Grease a marble slab (or any other cool, smooth surface) with sunflower oil and tip the mixture onto it. Roll out thinly using a greased rolling pin. Cut small bars from the mixture and place on a wire tray to cool. Wrap the bars individually in plastic wrap. *Pastéli* will keep for a long time in a tightly closed container.

The sesame seeds or peanuts need to be evenly toasted for *pastéli*.

Boil the honey and sugar until it forms a compact mass. The firmer the mass, the quicker the *pastéli* will set.

Tip the mixture of sugar and sesame seeds (or peanuts) out onto a flat surface.

Use a rolling pin to spread the mixture into a thin layer, a process which requires a great deal of skill.

PASTÉLI FROM LEFKÁDA

The Ionian island of Lefkáda's version of *pastéli* has a substantial layer of sesame seeds, whole peanuts, and honey and is thicker than the *pastéli* generally found throughout Greece.

TAKHÍNI

Takhíni (tahini) is an oil-based paste made from roasted sesame seeds, finely ground in a stone mill. It does not usually contain preservatives and is sold in glass jars.

It is widely used in Greek cuisine, for instance, as a salad dressing, mixed with lemon juice, garlic, soy sauce, avocado, and herbs. *Takhíni* can also be used as the basis for sauces in numerous Greek dishes, such as the popular Greek *takhíni* soup.

TAKHINÓSOUPA
Vegetable soup with tahini
Serves 4–6

For the soup:
2 carrots, finely diced
1 eggplant, peeled and diced
Some white cabbage

2 green bell peppers
¼ celeriac, finely diced
2 stalks of celery leaves
3 potatoes, finely diced
1 leek, thinly sliced into rings
3 zucchini, finely diced
1 bunch dill, finely chopped
1 bunch flat-leaved parsley, finely chopped
1 lb/500 g soup noodles
Juice of 1 lemon
2 tbsp corn or potato starch
Salt
Freshly ground black pepper

For the sauce:
1 cup/125 g sesame seeds
½ cup/125 ml lemon juice
2 garlic cloves
Freshly ground black pepper

Mix all the sauce ingredients together in a blender with about 1 cup/200–250 ml water until the mixture forms a smooth, homogenous creamy paste. Heat some water in a saucepan and add the prepared soup vegetables a few at a time. Stir in the dill and parsley and season with salt and pepper. Just before the vegetables are cooked, add the soup noodles to the saucepan.

Mix 3 heaped tablespoons *takhíni* sauce with a dash of lemon juice and a little water and beat with a whisk until frothy. Remove the soup from the stovetop and carefully stir in the *takhíni* sauce. The soup can be thickened, if desired, with a little corn or potato starch.

Fennel

Cumin

Aniseed

Cinnamon

Bay leaves

Cardamom

Juniper berries

Wild roses

Cloves

Peppercorns

Medlar leaves

Eucalyptus

Wormwood

Hyssop

SHOPPING FOR HERBS AND SPICES

People have been using herbs and spices since cooking began. Initially, they would have only had access to the wild herbs found growing locally, but eventually, as trade began to develop, exotic, foreign spices began to appear in kitchens. Some herbs made an appearance in conjunction with various rituals, magic ceremonies or cult practices. And it was not long before herbs and spices found their way into medicine. Medical and botanical writings dating from classical times are full of descriptions relating to the curative effects of herbs. Theophrastus the Greek made a study of medicinal plants and herbs as did the Roman physician, Galen, who is regarded as the father of pharmacy. Shopping for herbs and spices for the kitchen in a well-stocked spice shop or at the market, therefore, is almost like embarking on a botanical or medicinal voyage of discovery. People in Greece are very knowledgeable about the effects of herbs and have a great deal of respect for herbal remedies. The best and rarest herbs in Europe still grow in Greece's Pílion mountains and are still used by Greek doctors. Natural healing is an important branch of medicine in Greece and there is a correspondingly large variety of herbs available at market. And if there is no large market in the immediate vicinity, the old folk still go out and collect their secret herbs themselves.

SPICES USED IN GREEK CUISINE

Greek cuisine places more store on the quality and freshness of its ingredients than on polished sophistication. Fresh herbs such as dill, garlic, thyme, mint, lavender, or oregano are extremely important, but so, too, is an unusual ingredient called mastic. Meat dishes are sometimes seasoned with spices such as cinnamon and cloves, that you might have thought more likely to be found in sweet dishes.

Greek people are not fans of experimentation with spices. Salt, pepper, lemons, and olive oil constitute the basic seasonings. Anything more than this would be regarded as an acquired taste for the Greek palate. And although Greeks apparently love chaos – order always reigns in the kitchen. Any dishes that they have not been familiar with since childhood are simply ignored. A foreign dish is only sampled with the utmost caution.

That is why so few spices are used, as you must be able to taste what is in the dish in front of you. If the food is sweet, then it is really sweet, and if it is salty, then it is very salty.

There is, of course, a place for garlic in Greek kitchens, an ingredient which should always be tasted. The same is true of onions and strong chiles. They alone are permitted the privilege of being allowed to burn the tongue. No other hot spices have any place in Greek cuisine. And the one thing that you must never be without is olive oil. From salad to dessert, Greeks love their olive oil and enjoy it in large quantities.

Spices and teas are sold in small quantities so that they get used up quickly. Pre-packaged products are still something of an innovation in Greece. If you want quality, you will continue to have your fragrant cooking seasonings carefully weighed and packed in a paper bag.

ΜΑΚΕΔΟΝΙΑ

Above: work has been in progress since 1914 on excavating the ruins of ancient Philippi, 10 miles (16 km) northwest of Kavala. Background: Mount Olympus overlooks the fertile plains.

MACEDONIA

When a big wave of immigration flooded into the Greek peninsula at the beginning of the "dark centuries" around 1200 B.C., the Macedonians came pouring down from the north. Historical and archaeological traces of their society, dating from about 700 B.C. onward, can be found in the area of modern Macedonia. In contrast to the *poleis*, the autonomous, independent Greek communities ruled by an aristocratic elite, Macedonian society was based on an aristocracy of horsemen, led by a king, who in turn were surrounded by a small group of loyal and committed followers. There were evidently very few points of contact between the Greeks and the Macedonians, as the latter do not appear in the myths. Not even Heracles, whose exploits took him all over the Mediterranean area, went to Macedonia. For the Greeks, the land beyond Mount Olympus, the home of the gods, was barbarian country and to be ignored. Only with the increase in military strength under Philip II (382–336 B.C.) did Macedonia become not just a part of Hellas, but also the center of a huge Hellenic empire.

Though there were ancient cities such as Philippi, Pella, and Vergina, Macedonia was on the whole a thinly populated, agricultural region and the settlements were comparatively small. At first the king had no center of power; he traveled around the country in state, to show himself everywhere and make his presence felt. After the fall of the Hellenic Empire, the Romans were the first to make Macedonia into an important province again, and with the building of the Via Egnatia to Byzantium, they laid the foundations which made the region economically attractive. Being so close to Byzantium, Macedonia became the target of early Christian missionary activity. On his second missionary journey, St. Paul the Apostle founded the first Christian community on European soil at Philippi in A.D. 49. But its proximity to Istanbul also resulted in the region enduring a long period of Ottoman rule. It was not until 1913 that a part of the once great province of Macedonia become Greek again; another part of the province was given to former Yugoslavia and now constitutes the independent nation of Macedonia.

The fertile lowland plain stretches across almost the whole of northern Greece and is still largely agricultural. Almost all the crops that are important for the international market thrive here.

MACEDONIAN FRUIT BOWL

The whole of Macedonia is more or less an enormous fruit bowl, because this is the garden of Greece. People who are used to going to the store to buy fruit that has traveled a long distance, or buying it prepacked in the supermarket, can scarcely imagine what it means to live on the Plain of Imathias, where you only need to go as far as the nearest orchard in order to choose exactly what you fancy. The selection is so great that especially on the hottest days of the year, the abundance of sun-ripened fruits is almost irresistible. Freshly picked, naturally ripened fruit has had the chance to develop its own flavor fully. It emits an intense perfume, which has had no need of assistance from chemistry or artificial ripening. All the natural vitamins and nutrients are retained. Strawberries, figs, kiwis, peaches, or grapes – it is all as healthy as we have every right to expect. For the people who live here, it goes without saying that there should be fruit on the table at the end of a meal. It does not need any preparation to enhance it, it is simply peeled immediately before eating, but there is scarcely anything more delicious.

KRÁNA

Circe fed them to the companions of Odysseus, after she had turned them into swine, because in Homer's day *k17rána*, the fruits of the Cornelian cherry (*Cornus mas*) were considered to be food fit for pigs. If you bite into them at the wrong time, they taste as sour as quinces – if you want to eat them raw, you must wait until they are fully ripe. In Macedonia they are much appreciated as *kra43na-glikó*, that is, preserved in syrup or in very strong alcohol.

THE NAME OF THE PEACH

Macedonia is the classic area of Greece for growing peaches (*Prunus persica*), which turn the springtime plains into a sea of white blossoms. The farming cooperative of Meliki, located 35 miles (55 kilometers) to the west of Thessaloniki and close to the ancient city of Vergina, grows up to 20 different varieties of peach on more than 1000 acres (4 million square meters) of land. During the whole of their growing period, peaches are very susceptible to changes in the weather. The hail and cold in spring can not only destroy their blossoms, but also damage the young fruits, so that every year several tons of slightly damaged peaches end up in juice production, rather than fresh and spotless on the market.

But even if the weather conditions were ideal and no damage or disease occurred, the crop would still only be moderate in size, because the farmers have a part to play too. In winter they must fertilize the soil with manure and

Carefully packed in boxes, tons of fresh peaches leave the cooperatives of Macedonia to be sold on international markets.

prune the branches, then thin out the peaches in spring. This involves picking up to 30 percent of the fruits that are just beginning to develop, so that those remaining are vigorous enough to reach the requisite size. Picking them off early also protects the branches from breaking because of the weight. This carefully directed operation enables the farmers of Meliki on the Macedonian Plain to produce up to 22,000 US tons (20,000 tonnes) of peaches, plus 11,000 US tons (10,000 tonnes) of nectarines, despite all the vagaries of the weather and the annual plagues of pests. Macedonian peaches are sent to European, Asian, and American markets in the form of fresh or frozen fruit, canned peaches in syrup, or freshly squeezed juice.

The peaches exported to the East are more or less going home, as the fruit arrived in Europe from China via Persia thousands of years ago. This is why the ancient Greek writers, who had some difficulties with naming and distinguishing round, juicy, yellow or red-cheeked fruit originating in the near or far East, often spoke of the peach as the "Persian apple." The *kítro*, citron, probably had first claim on this name (see page 360), which at times led to mistakes and caused confusion, but it established itself with most of the ancient authors and later turned into *persike*.

Peaches were probably introduced into Greece as early as the 3rd century B.C., but the Romans were the first to grow them on a regular basis.

The Latin description of a particular peach variety as *duracinus*, hard centered, later came into Greek as *dorakinon*, which then

became *rodákinon* in modern Greek. So the Greeks have still not given their favorite "apple" a proper name that originates in their language.

RODÁKINA SE KRASÍ
Peaches in red wine

8 ripe peaches, peeled, halved and stoned
A scant ½ cup/100 g sugar
1 tsp cinnamon
3 cups/750 ml medium dry red wine
1 cup/250 ml whipping cream

Put the peaches, sugar, cinnamon and wine in a pan and boil briefly over a high heat. Reduce the temperature and allow the fruit to steep for about another 10 minutes. Remove the peaches, and put two halves on each plate. Boil the juice again, until it forms a thick syrup. Divide the syrup over the peaches and put the plates in a cool place. Whip the cream until firm peaks form, and give each portion a topping of cream. Serve cold.

KOMPÓSTA RODAKINO
Peach compote

2 lbs/1 kg peaches
1–1½ cups/250–350 g sugar

Peel and halve the peaches and remove the stones. Cut the flesh in quarters or smaller pieces according to preference. Half fill as many canning or preserving jars as required with water, and divide the sugar among them. Then put in the pieces of peach and top up the jars with water. Briefly dip the lids in hot water and seal the jars so they are airtight. Half fill a large pan with water, stand the jars in it, and boil for about 1 hour. The peach compote will keep for months. In Greece it is a particular favorite to serve as dessert in winter.

No one can say whether the first nectarine was a mutant peach or a cross between a peach and a plum, but it does not affect their popularity.

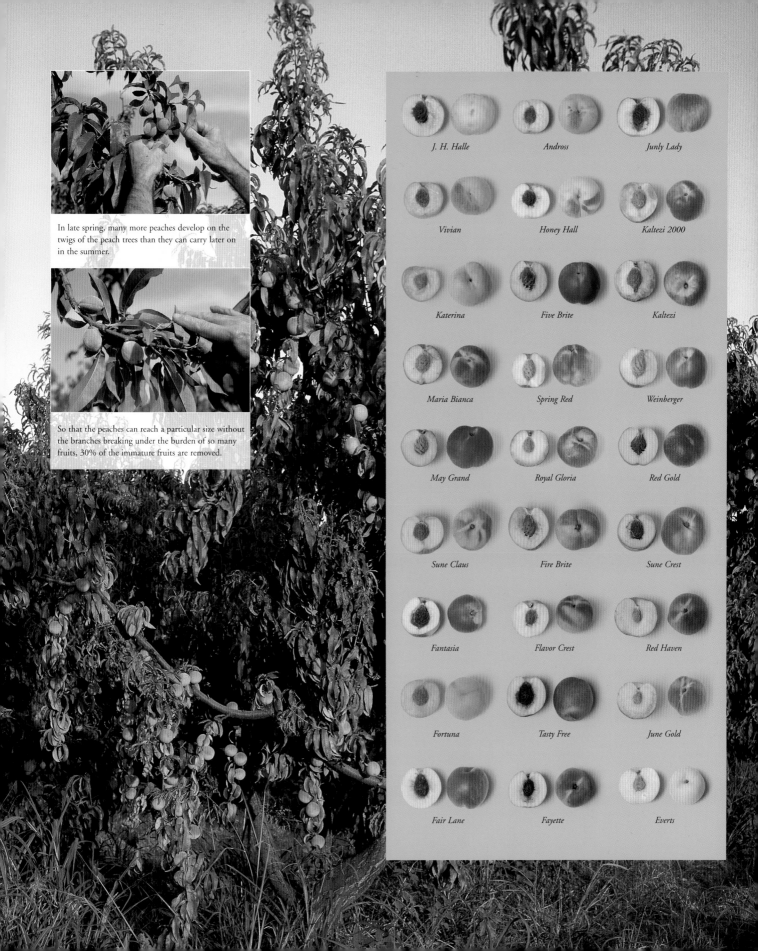

In late spring, many more peaches develop on the twigs of the peach trees than they can carry later on in the summer.

So that the peaches can reach a particular size without the branches breaking under the burden of so many fruits, 30% of the immature fruits are removed.

J. H. Halle

Andross

Junly Lady

Vivian

Honey Hall

Kaltezi 2000

Katerina

Five Brite

Kaltezi

Maria Bianca

Spring Red

Weinberger

May Grand

Royal Gloria

Red Gold

Sune Claus

Fire Brite

Sune Crest

Fantasia

Flavor Crest

Red Haven

Fortuna

Tasty Free

June Gold

Fair Lane

Fayette

Everts

It is officially frowned on, but no one can resist a secret nibble while baking or cooking.

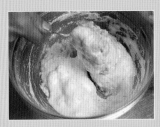

Beat the egg whites and some of the sugar until firm peaks form.

Mix the egg yolks with the remaining sugar, butter, and orange juice.

Mix the egg yolk mixture into the flour, baking powder, semolina and orange juice.

Carefully fold in the egg whites with a spoon, so they do not collapse.

REVANÍ AND LOUKOUMÁDES

Revaní is one of the classic Greek syrup cakes, though its homogenous texture seems to contradict this, as the name "syrup cake" is more often associated with the flakier *baklavás*. The sugar-syrup glaze moistens the relatively solid *revaní* and the distinctive orange flavor makes it seem fresher, despite the high sugar content. Of course the syrup does not make it any lighter, so *gliko* addicts have to keep their cravings under strict control. The important thing for *revaní* is the same as for other syrup cakes: it is better to serve it in wintertime, when the days are getting shorter and the winter festivities are beginning.

The name of this syrup cake comes from the Turkish, but the Greeks kept it even after the departure of the Turks. The Jews of Thessaloniki also incorporated this cake into their annual calendar of sweet things. All prefer to have it served the same way: chilled and with a portion of cream or vanilla ice cream. They also agree that *revaní* tastes best if you leave it to stand for 24 hours. If eating a piece of semolina cake starts you thinking, you just might feel a little sad that such similar tastes on the part of others in the past have had so little effect on mutual understanding.

Another traditional Greek cake is *loukoumádes*, little balls of yeast dough fried in hot olive oil. In summer they are sold on the beaches at Greek resorts.

Left: the syrup cake *revaní* is actually a kind of semolina pudding, but that does not make it any less delicious.
Right: *loukoumádes*, mocha and water belong together.

REVANÍ
Syrup cake

For the dough:
4½ cups/500 g all-purpose flour
3½ tsp baking powder
½ tsp salt
1 cup/250 ml orange juice
1½ cups/250 g fine semolina
6 eggs
⅔ cup/150 g sugar
1⅓ cups/300 g soft butter
Rind of 1 unwaxed orange, grated
1 cup/100 g almonds, finely chopped

For the syrup:
2⅚ cups/650 g sugar; 2 cups/500 ml water
2 tbsp brandy

Sift the flour, baking powder, and salt into a bowl. Stir alternate spoonfuls of orange juice and semolina into the mixture to form a smooth paste.

Preheat the oven to 350 °F (180 °C). Separate the eggs and beat the whites with half the sugar until firm peaks form. Whisk the yolks to a foam with the remaining sugar, butter and grated orange rind, then work into the semolina dough. Carefully fold in the beaten egg whites, so that they do not collapse. Grease a baking pan, distribute the dough evenly in it, and sprinkle with chopped almonds. Bake on the middle shelf of the preheated oven for about 40 minutes, until the top of the cake is golden brown. Remove from the oven and allow to cool slightly.

To make the syrup, dissolve the sugar in 2 cups/500 ml hot water and bring to a boil. Add the brandy, and pour the syrup, little by little, over the cake while still hot. After about 30 minutes, pour off all the syrup that has not been absorbed, allow the *revaní* to cool completely and cut into not too large portions.

LOUKOUMÁDES
Honey doughnuts

1¾ cakes/30 g fresh yeast
9 cups/1 kg flour
1 tsp sugar
Oil for frying
Honey
Cinnamon

In a bowl, knead a generous 2 cups/250 g flour with the yeast, sugar and a little water into a smooth dough. If using active dry yeast, follow the manufacturer's instructions. Cover the bowl with a cloth and allow to rest in a warm place until the dough has doubled in volume. Work in the remaining flour, adding water as needed to form a workable dough. Cover the bowl and allow the dough to rise again, this time for about 1½ hours, until no bubbles form on the surface. Heat plenty of oil in a deep-fry pan. Using a spoon, scoop out little balls of dough and drop gently into the boiling oil. Fry the dough balls until they are crisp and golden brown, then remove the *loukoumádes* from the oil with a ladle and drain on towels. Finally, arrange the doughnuts on a serving dish, pour over plenty of honey, and sprinkle with cinnamon.

WHERE THE GODS GAZE DOWN

Zeus, ruler of the world of the ancient gods, deliberately chose to have his throne on Mount Olympus, because nowhere else in Greece offers such an exciting view of a fertile plain as you have from one of the ten peaks of Olympus. Here the gods were certainly set apart, but not left completely in peace. Many temples, great and small, were built on the slopes of Olympus, as if the mortals wanted to share the gods' far-sightedness. To the north of the massif, which is about 280 miles (450 kilometers) wide and 25 miles (40 kilometers) in length, stretch the fertile plains of western Macedonia. If you had the wide-ranging view of the gods, you could watch the farmers going about their daily labors every day on this, the second biggest plain in Greece. Vegetables, grains, fruit, and wine are grown here and sometimes harvested in abundance. Things are no different for Greek farmers than for other farmers in the European Union. What with worrying about good harvests, hoping that the subsidies from Brussels will not dry up, and endeavoring to make sure that the agricultural produce meets the European Union guidelines on size and appearance, they sometimes produce too much. But that is in the lap of the gods!

ZEUS, THE FATHER OF THE GODS

Occasionally, when his many amorous affairs would allow it, Zeus actually had time to rule the world. It was, after all, his important task to maintain the fruitfulness of the earth. However, he did not want to make life too easy for mortals, as can be seen from the story of Prometheus, who strove to improve man's lot and was cruelly punished for it. Yet this highly complex father of the gods, whose image is surely not only composed of Greek conceptions of gods, continued to help mortals. He was the cloudless azure sky, without which no harvest could be successful, but he was also the thunderstorm (his name means illu-minating), through which he launched his thunder-bolts, which could destroy everything again. He was the almighty ruler of both gods and humans, and gave the right advice in disputes – so it was advis-able to be on good terms with Zeus.

In every small town there are weekly markets, in which the local farmers participate. And even the most insignificant provincial markets are distinguished by the high quality of their goods.

A PROBING LOOK AT THE SOIL

Here at the foot of Mount Olympus, under the stern gaze of Zeus, the father of the gods, people have learned from their experiences. If you sacrificed enough to the gods, you could expect help and support from them, because then they could be sure of receiving the next sacrifice. When the old gods were driven out of the rational world, and yet life did not necessarily get any easier, the farmers found themselves new gods to whom they annually sacrifice a piece of the earth. "And the white-coated scientists read the signs with scientists' probing, testing minds." All over the agricultural areas of Macedonia, famous institutes have set up offices where the farmers can have their soil tested. This gives them information about the pH factor (acidity) of their soil, the nature and quantity of the minerals it contains, which crops it is best suited for, and also what is lacking in their soil and must be added to it to guarantee maximum yields. Farmers can also come here for expert advice if the leaves wither early or worms attack the fruit. Then they do not have to rely on capricious gods for favors, but can fall back on tried and tested and, increasingly, ecologically sustainable resources.

No one here objects if the customer wants to subject the goods to close scrutiny. Why should they? Every trader is convinced their goods are absolutely perfect.

What might look like a weed to many, the Greeks turn into a delicacy. Wild plants such as dandelions and wild mustard are as tasty as they are good for you. Eating weeds is the best way of getting rid of them.

FRESH AND CRISP

Very few midday or evening meals are served in Greece without an appropriate salad. There are two very important things to note: Greek salads are always freshly prepared immediately before the meal, so they do not lose their vitamins, and they are always eaten at the same time as the main course. They usually reach the table in the biggest bowl in the house, and everyone is allowed to stick their own fork in and pick out their favorite items. In Greece it is considered miserly and inhospitable if people only eat what is on their own plate, as the food on a Greek table is there for everyone. Moreover, communal eating from one bowl is an important symbol of the family community. This applies to all appetizers and salads. The most famous of Greek salads is the country-style or farmer's salad, which did not, of course, get its name because it was only eaten by farmers. It had more to do with the fact that, in the old days, it was only on country farms that the tomatoes, cucumbers, peppers, onions, olives, and sheep's cheese that went into it were really fresh. On farms, the ingredients were available in sufficient quantities at the appropriate time of year, so this salad could be eaten every day. Now this Greek salad is one of the most frequently imitated salads in the world.

KHÓRTA

When Greeks talk about *khórta,* they actually mean grass or hay. But when they order *khórta* salad in a restaurant, they expect something else. In Greece the term *khórta* also covers a number of wild herbs, which can be picked in the meadows or by the roadside and used in salads, after a brief blanching. They have an unusually spicy taste, contain a lot of bitter substances, and greatly enrich the already copious selection of salads. Immediately after the first rains of winter, the first *khórta* sprout from the earth and are a sought-after appetizer or addition to a main course right through until spring. The species vary from region to region, but there are also different names for the same species. The term *khórta* includes dandelions, stinging nettles, wild radish, sorrel, ribwort, and other wild plants. What is more, the law of private property does not apply to *khórta.* Anybody is allowed to gather the herbs in the fields.

KHORIÁTIKI SALÁTA
Country-style salad

2–3 tomatoes, diced
1 cucumber, diced
1 onion, cut in rings
2 pale green peppers, cut in rings
Black olives
8oz/200 g sheep's cheese
Capers and eggs, as desired
Greek extra virgin olive oil
Vinegar

Oregano
Salt
Freshly ground black pepper

Put the prepared vegetables in a bowl, pour over vinegar, season with salt and pepper, and mix well. Garnish the vegetables with the black olives, sheep's cheese, and possibly also capers and eggs. Be sure to pour over plenty of olive oil. Finally sprinkle with the oregano. Serve with white bread that has been freshly baked.

THE SALAD BAR

Along with appetizers (*mezédes*) and to some extent identical with them, salads have a central position in the Greek diet. As a result, they are omnipresent, and because they are combined in so many different ways, there seem to be many more kinds of salad than there are vegetables. Indeed, the list appears to be endless. However, in the test of everyday life, certain favorites emerge, chosen by a random jury consisting of school-children, those who eat appetizers, and office workers spoiled by eating in canteens.

1 *Domatosaláta* and *Khoriátiki saláta:* as you would expect, tomato salad and country-style salads head the fictional popularity poll.
2 *Khórta:* various combinations of wild plants as salads come as a surprise only to those who are not Greek.
3 *Maroúli:* as a rule, lettuce leaves are not roughly torn apart but finely shredded.
4 *Lakhanosaláta* or *politiki:* cabbage salad, either just with grated carrot, or with a colorful mixture of chiles, celery, and other things.
5 *Pantzária:* boiled beets with garlic, onion, apple, or sheep's cheese has a good position in the middle of the field.
6 *Salátes me lakhaniká:* every other imaginable kind of vegetable salad.
7 *Yígantes, makromátika,* etc: salads made from various boiled, dried beans, either just one variety or mixed.
8 *Revíthia me krémidi:* boiled chickpeas, or garbanzo beans, combined with red onions.
9 *Róka* or *pikralída:* arugola (rocket) and dandelion, used raw in a salad, and thus clearly distinguished from *khórta.*
10 *Patatosaláta:* potato salad with olive oil instead of mayonnaise must also be on the list.
11 *Rossiki saláta:* Russian salad, the "foreigner" on the Greek salad bar.
12 *Karóto saláta:* grated carrot, highly spiced in a great variety of ways.
13 *Saláta apó kókkino lákhano:* shredded red cabbage, marinated more or less dry with salt, is at the bottom of this list, but of course it cannot really be in last place, as in the salad bar, every single one is delicious.

Saláta apó kókkino lákhano
Like white cabbage, red cabbage must be shredded very finely, but unlike white cabbage salad, it must be prepared in advance, so the salt can penetrate thoroughly. A little lemon juice tops it off.

Karóto saláta
Grated carrots are also dressed only with olive oil, lemon juice, and salt, but because of their sugar content, you need to be generous with the herbs and spices. A little dill cannot do any harm.

Róka
Olive oil, salt, and lemon juice also predominate in arugola (rocket) salad, but the picture is enhanced by mixing in pieces of tomato or halved sweet cherry tomatoes.

Maroúli
Lettuce, which is finely shredded rather than roughly torn apart, is a good example of the ideology behind Greek salads. Olive oil, lemon juice, and salt seem uninventive as a dressing, but they bring out the flavor of the lettuce.

Lakhanosaláta
White cabbage is first thoroughly washed, then finely shredded and mixed with lemon juice, salt, and olive oil. A little flat-leaved parsley adds visual accents.

Zokhós
Zokhós are a kind of wild herbs, which are in a class of their own in Greece. They can be used alone, or mixed with others according to season and region. They should always be blanched before being eaten.

Glistrida

The fleshy, aromatic leaves of purslane should be thoroughly washed and dressed with salt, lemon, and olive oil. A little thinly sliced, fresh tomato makes a very good addition.

Yigandes

Using salt, a little pepper, onions, thyme according to taste, and wine vinegar to give a slightly sharp flavor, you can prepare a substantial salad from different varieties of boiled beans. In summer this salad is best served chilled.

LEMON OR VINEGAR?

Since ancient times, many learned people have argued about lemons, especially about their name. Several centuries elapsed as it changed from "apple of the Medes" to *kitrion*, and finally to *lemóni* in the Byzantine period. The fact that in general no distinction was made between the different citrus fruits may have added to the confusion. For a long time, writers had little to say about their origins and how they had spread, except that lemons were not grown in Greece until quite late. In contrast, they gave clear information about vinegar, especially wine vinegar. After all, this flavoring was developed very early in conjunction with wine. Both lemon and vinegar have become indispensable in Greek cuisine, but the following should be noted: Because of their high vitamin C content and refreshing character, lemons can liven up any salad. With rare exceptions, they are used with everything that comes fresh to the table. They make certain that leafy salads, in particular, still look fresh and taste good, even on hot days. By contrast, vinegar can be found in most Greek soup pots. Ancient tradition has it that wine vinegar diluted with water, *phoúska*, was a substitute for wine for poorer people.

Khoriátiki saláta

Salt, pepper, lemon juice, and sometimes a little basil, but always freshly cut onion rings and plenty of olive oil, make this simplified version of the country-style salad into one of the most popular of all Greek salads.

Pantzária

Beets for use in salads are cooked until tender and, while still lukewarm, flavored with thin slices of garlic, pieces of apple, and crumbled sheep's cheese. It is fine for the taste of olive oil to be noticeable.

Politiki

Concealed in the basic mixture of finely grated carrot and finely shredded white cabbage are finely chopped red chiles and sometimes also grated celery. Because of the strong flavors, it is better to use vinegar than lemon juice to go with the olive oil.

SAFFRON

Around the middle of October every year, the violet glow of hundreds of thousands of flowering *Crocus sativus*, a member of the iris family, spreads over the countryside around Kossini, 95 miles (150 kilometers) west of Thessaloniki. But some 1500 families from 37 villages to the south of Kossini have little leisure to admire the picturesque sight of the blossoming crocuses, as the members of the Kosáni saffron cooperative are gearing up for the harvest. Everything is still done by hand, just as it was a thousand years ago. To obtain just 2 pounds of saffron, some 160,000 crocus flowers have to be picked and the stigmas carefully removed and dried on the same day.

The five-or six-petaled crocus flowers contain three long red stigmas and three yellow stamens. However, the highly-prized saffron can only be obtained from the tips of the three red stigmas. The red stigmas are quickly and carefully dried in special ovens, so that they retain their aroma and the essential oils they contain. During this process, they lose about another 80 percent of their fresh weight. Not until the following day are they put into containers or bags to be sold on.

Saffron has been grown in Greece on a regular basis since the 17th century. Kosáni saffron is particularly sought after for its intense flavor. There are another 20 varieties of wild saffron on the Cyclades and Crete, all differing in color, size, and appearance. Here it is mainly the local women who know about saffron and sometimes pick small amounts for their own use. Cultivated saffron exhausts the soil. The bulbs multiply underground and release poisons into the soil that interfere with their own growth, so a saffron field needs to lie fallow on average every nine years, so the soil can recover. Saffron, which was originally native to the Near East, has for centuries been highly valued as a

Above: The red filaments are sold in small bags or decorative jars.

Below right: Saffron harvesting requires years of experience. Not everyone is skillful enough to harvest the flowers without damaging the stigmas.

spice by oriental and Mediterranean nations and it also played an important role as a dyestuff. Greek mythology tells us that Crocus was a friend of the god Hermes. When the two friends were fighting one day for fun, Hermes wounded his friend in the head. Three drops of blood fell from the wound on to a flower, and were transformed into three red filaments. Since then, any plant with three filaments has been called crocus. Saffron is mentioned frequently in Homer. Frescoes in Crete show saffron as tribute paid to the Phoenicians. The famous fresco of Thira (Santorini) shows women picking saffron, their work being just as labor intensive as it is today.

The Arabs later brought saffron to Western Europe via Spain and gave it its present name *az-zafaran*, meaning yellow.

Using carefully calculated wind power, the farmers separate the petals from the saffron filaments.

When you throw the flowers up into the air, the dried petals blow away, while the filaments fall down onto the sheet below.

The precise quantity of the precious spice for each packet is weighed out in milligrams, using very sensitive scales.

The saffron crocus has very short stems. It is picked as soon as it sprouts from the soil.

Persian rulers used saffron to dye their robes; for Phoenician, Greek, and Roman ladies it was a cosmetic. It has been used as an aphrodisiac and as an antithrombosis preparation, and many women use saffron successfully to regulate their menstrual cycle and benefit from its beneficial effects during pregnancy. Nowadays it is chiefly recognized as a spice in Asian, Indian and Mediterranean cookery. The carotinoids and essential oils in particular give risotto its distinctive taste. False saffron, such as the stigmas of other crocus flowers or the ligulate flowers of marigolds or saffron thistles, also produce the same intense color. Faking saffron was no mere peccadillo – the penalties were draconian. The perpetrators risked being burned, buried alive, or blinded. It should perhaps not go unmentioned that five to ten grams of saffron are enough to cause severe poisoning, with fatal consequences.

KRÉMA ME KRÓKO
Saffron cream

4 tbsp golden raisins
3 cups/750 ml milk
1 cup/250 ml light cream
A generous ½ cup/130 g sugar
8 tsp flour
A tiny pinch/¼ g saffron
1 vanilla bean
Caramelized almonds for garnishing

Soak the golden raisins in hot water. Put the milk in a pan on the stovetop and mix in the remaining ingredients a little at a time. Heat everything until the cream begins to thicken, stirring continuously. Remove the pan from the heat, and divide the cream into individual dishes. Garnish with the caramelized almonds.

VOÚTIRO ME KRÓKO
Saffron butter

1⅓ cups/300 g butter
2 leeks
20 threads of saffron
½ tsp salt

Take the butter out of the refrigerator and allow to soften. Remove the tough outsides of the leeks and cut the tender insides into thin rings. Melt 1 tablespoon butter in a pan, and sauté the leeks. They should be tender, but they should not start to brown.
Add the salt and saffron, remove from the heat and allow to cool. Reduce to a very fine purée in a blender and mix with the remaining butter. Saffron butter should be stored in the refrigerator for about 4–5 hours before it is ready to be served.

KROKÓSKORDO
Saffron garlic

4 cloves garlic
15 threads of saffron

Preheat the oven to 350 °F (180 °C). Peel the garlic and lay it with the saffron on a piece of greased kitchen foil. Fold the foil into a parcel and bake in the preheated oven until the garlic has become quite tender. Finally crush the garlic to form a cream.
Stored in a tightly closed jar in the refrigerator, saffron garlic will keep for a comparatively long time. It can be used to improve sauces or served on bread as an appetizer.

BÁMIES LADERÉS
Okra in oil

1 lb/500 g small, fresh okra
½ cup/125 ml vinegar
½ cup/125 ml Greek extra virgin olive oil
2 medium onions, finely chopped
1 lb/500 g tomatoes, peeled and diced
1 tsp sugar
Salt
Freshly ground black pepper

Wash the okra, cut off the stalks and the tops, and drain. Put in a bowl, add salt, pour over the vinegar, and allow to steep for about 30 minutes. Heat the olive oil in a pan and sauté the onions. Drain the okra, add to the pan, and fry, stirring continuously. Then stir in the tomatoes and sugar, and season with salt and pepper. Cook for about 45 minutes over a low heat. This vegetable can be eaten hot or cold, served with freshly baked white bread. Okra is also a perfect accompaniment to roast and grilled meat.

Above: okra as long, narrow, and pointed as these have been picked too late and are no longer really fit to eat. They taste best when they are no more than 2 inches (5 cm) long.

Opposite, top: okra is a member of the mallow family. It has pretty yellow flowers and upright seedpods.

OKRA

Okra (*Abelmoschus esculentus*), in Greek *bámia*, is a member of the mallow family, and is considered exotic even in Macedonia, as its original home was probably East Africa. Wild forms are to be found in Asia. Okra is an annual plant, growing up to 8 feet (2.5 meters) tall, which produces delicate yellow, mallow-like flowers and, hidden inconspicuously under the leaves, chile-like, polygonal seed capsules or pods with longitudinal ribs. They taste a bit rough on the tongue, a sensation caused by the fine down on their surface. Nevertheless, these okra pods are excellent with braised and especially roast meat. You can always pick out the taste of okra, because of its distinctive flavor, which is difficult to define. It is actually almost neutral, yet slightly sour and piquant to slightly sharp, and somewhat reminiscent of beans or green gooseberries.

The plants grow equally well on various kinds of soil, as long as the ground is not too dry or sandy. They produce an average yield of 1750–3300 pounds per 10,000 square feet (800–1500 kilograms per 1000 square meters). Okra needs a lot of heat to develop; only then will it grow and thrive without interference. Okra is harvested in September, when the nighttime temperature does not fall below 60 °F (15 °C). The plants flower on into October,

Right: picking okra rapidly becomes a tiresome job, because of the continual bending.

and continue to produce small fruit. Harvesting is particularly tiring, because okra is picked when quite small. The fruits are best when they are 1 inch or, at most, 2 inches (3–5 centimeters) long. They should not be any bigger because, as the size increases, they also get harder. Okra that is frozen for export is the exception to this rule, as the consistency will have changed when it thaws. The three Greek varieties of okra, *piléas, livadiás,* and *korinthías,* are by far among the most expensive vegetables on the market.

During cooking, okra can exude a milky secretion, which also occurs in canning, and has caused people to have certain reservations about this delicious vegetable. However, the problem can be prevented by the following procedure: First cut off the stalk, if it is still attached, without injuring the pod. Then with a small, sharp knife, cut the conical base of the stalk to the shape of a pencil point, and at the same time remove the thin brown ring immediately under it, without injuring the fruit. The down can be removed, if you so desire, by carefully rubbing the pod with a fine brush, preferably under running water. This is not necessary with young okra. Now dry the okra well with a towel, or leave it spread out until dry. Then put the pods in a bowl and pour over them water that has been soured with vinegar or lemon juice. Gently stir them with your hand, so that the liquid covers all the pods. They should remain like this for about 30 minutes, then they are ready for use.

BRIÁM
Stewed vegetables with okra

1 lb/500 g small, fresh okra
½ cup/125 ml vinegar
1 lb/500 g potatoes, peeled and sliced
1 zucchini, sliced
1 eggplant, sliced
2 bell peppers (yellow and red) cut in strips
3–4 tomatoes, peeled and diced
2 onions, roughly chopped
1 tsp fresh mint, finely chopped
1 cup/250 ml Greek extra virgin olive oil
Salt
Freshly ground black pepper

Wash the okra, remove the stalks, and drain. Marinate for 30 minutes in a bowl with salt and vinegar. Preheat the oven to a temperature of 350 °F (180 °C). Mix the potatoes with the remaining vegetables. Drain the okra, and add to the vegetables. Mix in the mint, olive oil, salt and pepper, and pour into an ovenproof dish. Pour water over the vegetables and cook in the preheated oven for about 90 minutes.

TOMATOES

Though the tomato (*Lycopersicon lycopersicum*) is now so widespread, the Greeks were quite late in discovering it for use in their cuisine. The original tropical plant from the Peruvian and Ecuadorian Andes was already being cultivated by the Aztecs in Mexico. Columbus brought it back to Europe from his second journey to America, but until about 1820, it was still thought of as a purely decorative plant. Since then, the tomato has developed into one of the most important vegetables all over the world, and is grown principally in Europe and America. With its versatility, delicate flavor, and bright red color, the tomato has long been established in Greece too. There is good reason for the country-style salad to be considered the king of Greek salads. The soil of Macedonia seems to have been created especially for tomatoes. It contains a lot of nutrients, especially calcium and potassium. The roots of the plants can spread unhindered in the soft soil. The Greek tomato industry is in third place in world production after the American and Italian tomato industries. Up to 3.3 million US tons (3 million tonnes) of tomatoes are made into paste, sauce, or juice, or peeled and canned.

As the tomato plant has very few natural enemies, it copes very well without chemical assistance, and still grows rapidly. The planting of early tomato seedlings begins from mid April, when the ground is already quite warm. Tomatoes are the classic summer vegetable, in almost daily use in the kitchen of every Macedonian household, either in salad or in stews with other vegetables. So the production of *sáltsa*, Greek tomato sauce, is traditionally connected with Macedonia, just as much as the actual cultivation of tomatoes.

Many Greeks plant a few extra bushes in the small gardens around their own houses, and wait for the annual red crop.

To increase the yield of tomatoes for their own use, many country farmers put up small greenhouses in their front gardens. These could also be simple tunnels covered with plastic. This means the young plants can be planted out in the fields earlier.

The traditional Greek *sáltsa* starts like any other tomato sauce, with peeling the tomatoes. To do this you immerse them in hot water for a few minutes.

Then the skin can easily be removed, at least while the tomatoes are still hot. Then the tomatoes are cut up, and the seeds are carefully removed.

Bring the tomatoes to a boil in 2 cups/500 ml water, and season well with salt and pepper. Simmer until the sauce has attained the desired thickness and consistency.

The preserving jars are topped up with a ⅜-inch (1 cm) thick layer of olive oil, so that the *sáltsa* will keep for a long time.

FLÓRINES

Flórines is the Greek name for the long red pimentos that were named after the little town of Flórina in west Macedonia, where they used to be grown in great numbers. Nowadays they can be found in every farmer's private garden. *Flórines* are very suitable for grilling, because of their delicate skins. They are also marinated in oil and vinegar and served as a little appetizer with ouzo.

SÁLTSA
Tomato sauce

4–4½ lbs/2 kg tomatoes
Salt
Freshly ground black pepper
Greek extra virgin olive oil

Wash the tomatoes and place briefly in boiling water. Peel off the skins, cut the tomatoes in half, and remove the core and seeds. Boil the remaining tomato flesh in about 2 cups/500 ml water over a medium heat, stirring continuously. Season with salt and pepper and simmer until the water has evaporated and the sauce has become quite thick.
Divide the sauce into sterilized canning or preserving jars, filling them only ⅘ full. Fill up the remaining fifth of the jars with olive oil, and seal the jars so they are airtight. *Sáltsa* will keep in the refrigerator for several months. It is indispensable in Greek cookery for adding to sauces and vegetables, but it can also be spread on slices of white bread and baked in the oven to make a versatile side dish.

YEMISTÁ

Yemistá simply means "filled." It refers not only to tomatoes or peppers, but also to any other vegetables that can be given a spicy filling. They are served fresh from the oven, and also cold from the refrigerator. *Yemistá* is a popular summer dish, prepared from different ingredients in the various regions. Rice is the most important of these, and meat or other vegetables are favorite ingredients.

DOMÁTES YEMISTÉS
Stuffed tomatoes

8–10 large or beefsteak tomatoes
1 cup/250 ml Greek extra virgin olive oil
½ lb onions, finely chopped
1¼ cups/250 g rice
4 sprigs fresh mint, finely chopped
A little tomato juice
Salt
Freshly ground black pepper

Wash the tomatoes, cut a slice off the top to form a lid, and set aside. Scoop out the insides of the tomatoes with a spoon and purée the flesh. In a pan, heat a scant ½ cup/100 ml olive oil and sauté the onions. Stir in the rice, season with salt and pepper, fry briefly, and add the puréed tomato flesh. Bring briefly to a boil, then remove the pan from the heat and allow the rice to swell a little. Stir in the mint, and two-thirds fill the tomatoes with the mixture. Preheat the oven to 350 °F (180 °C). Place the tomatoes in an ovenproof dish, season with salt and pepper, pour over olive oil, a little tomato juice, and 1 cup/250 ml water. Place the lids on the filled tomatoes, and bake in the pre-

To stuff beefsteak tomatoes, cut off the tops and scoop out the contents.

Carefully spoon the prepared filling into the hollowed out tomatoes.

Replace the lids on the tomatoes and drizzle with some olive oil.

heated oven for about 1 hour. Then remove the lids and bake for a further 10 minutes, to brown the filling. Remove the tomatoes from the oven, replace the lids, and serve while still hot. Serve with freshly baked white bread.
Tip: As a variation, the filling can also be made with raisins and nuts.

RICE IN GREECE

Alexander the Great's armies first encountered rice (*oryza*) when they reached the Indus River in the 4th century B.C., in the course of their Asian campaigns. Rice had long since been naturalized in the area, but though it was eaten in Greece, and later also in Rome, it was very expensive because it had to be transported so far; thus it was not widely used and was restricted to medicinal purposes. In the centuries that followed, rice spread from India as far as Syria, but was not cultivated in either Greece or the Roman Empire. It did not reach southern Europe until it was brought in by the Arabs via Spain in the 8th century.

Rice (*Oryza sativa*) is still not grown in economically significant quantities in Greece. Only in the fertile delta of the river Axios near Thessaloniki have relatively small areas close to the water recently been turned into rice fields. The annual harvest here is about 165,000 US tons (150,000 tonnes). Rice is an annual paniculate grass, which germinates only 20 days after sowing at a temperature of 59–62 °F (15–17 °C) and takes 130–150 days from then until harvest. It grows in flooded fields and requires a minimum temperature of 53 °F (12 °C). By the time it matures, it has produced a panicle up to 20 inches (50 cm) long, which bears small ears with grains enclosed in husks, which still contain 25–27 percent moisture. To enable the grains of rice to be separated from the husks, the ears must be dried after harvesting.

Although Greek cuisine has a clear preference for potatoes, rice has become established as an accompaniment to certain dishes of boiled fish and grilled chicken. It also proved to be an adequate meal in monastery kitchens, especially during Lent. Rice is prepared in two different ways, either *spirotó*, that is grainy, or *piláfi* (Turkish *pilav*), meaning boiled until soft in fat or butter.

EGGPLANT

Not very long ago, it was considered an exotic vegetable in much of Europe. By contrast, in India, where it originated, and in China, eggplant (*Solanum melongena*) has been one of the favorite vegetables for thousands of years and has a firm place in many national dishes. The Arabs brought it to Europe in the 13th century, and until recently it was only cultivated in the very warm and sunny areas around the Mediterranean. It has been grown in Italy since about 1550, a little later in the neighboring countries. The plant, related to tomatoes and nightshades, grows up to 6 feet (2 meters) high and, thanks to modern methods including greenhouses, has found its way as far north as the Netherlands. Although the dark purple variety is the commonest in Europe, there are a large number of variations in shape, size, and color. Colors range from white through yellow and purple to black; there are long and thin, pear-shaped, and large or small globular varieties. The aubergine was given the name eggplant because of the shape of the original fruit, which was white and about the size of a hen's egg. Eggplant has a firm skin and whitish, spongy flesh.

The so-called *langadá* variety is the typical eggplant of Greece. It is smaller than many other varieties, and has a slender pear-shaped fruit. As soon as the plant reaches a height of about 20 inches (50 centimeters), fruits begin to form, and as it grows, it can bear up to 50 of them if it has enough sun and plenty of water. It may not look like it, but the fruit contains up to 92 percent water, which it gives back to the plant if necessary, so eggplant quickly become dry, unsightly, and virtually unsalable.

The traders then have to fall back on imports from northern Europe, which do not, however, find much favor in Greece, as the local eggplant can beat any imports in the matter of taste and flavor. Typical national eggplant dishes like moussaka and *papoutzákia* only taste right if you use the *langadá* eggplant. Apart from these dishes, which are known all over Greece, you can use sliced eggplant fried in oil in many different ways as side dishes, though the flesh can absorb huge quantities of oil.

When it has ripened to its own special color, the eggplant can be used directly in cooking. The same applies to eggplant as to all other kinds of vegetable: it tastes best when fresh.

EGGPLANT DISHES

MOUSAKÁS
Moussaka
(Illustrated below)

3 large eggplants
1 lb/500 g potatoes
Greek extra virgin olive oil
1 large onion, finely chopped
1 lb/500 g ground lamb or beef
1 lb/500 g tomatoes, peeled and diced
1 cup/250 ml dry white wine
¼ tsp sugar
½ tsp ground cinnamon
1 bunch flat-leaved parsley, finely chopped

For the béchamel sauce:
4 tbsp/60 g butter
½ cup/60 g all-purpose flour
3 cups/750 ml milk
1 egg yolk
½ tsp sugar
Freshly grated nutmeg
2 tsp lemon juice
Breadcrumbs
Grated graviéra cheese for topping
Salt and freshly ground black pepper

Wash the eggplants. Remove the base of the stalk and cut lengthways in ⅜ inch/1 cm slices. Place the slices in a bowl, cover with water, sprinkle with salt, and leave to draw for 20 minutes. Meantime, peel the potatoes, cut into similar ⅜ inch/1 cm slices, and add salt. Drain the eggplants and pat dry. Heat the olive oil in a pan and brown the eggplant on both sides over a high heat (you will have to keep adding oil). Remove the slices from the pan and place on paper towels to drain. Put fresh olive oil in the pan, and fry and drain the potato slices in the same way. Sauté the onions until transparent, add the ground meat and brown over a high heat. Stir in the tomatoes, white wine, sugar, cinnamon, and parsley, reduce the temperature, and simmer for 10 minutes. Melt the butter in a pan, stir in the flour, and cook for a minute or two. Slowly pour in the milk, stirring continuously. When the mixture thickens, remove the pan from the heat, stir in the egg yolk, and season the sauce with sugar, nutmeg, lemon, salt, and pepper. Stir in 2 tbsp of the grated *graviéra*, and allow to cool.
Preheat the oven to 350 °F (180 °C). Cover the base of a large ovenproof dish first with a layer of potato slices, then half the ground meat mixture. Next come the eggplant slices, then the remaining ground meat. Pour over the béchamel sauce, smooth over the top, and sprinkle with breadcrumbs, cheese, and if desired, with cinnamon. Cook in the preheated oven for about 45–60 minutes, until the top is golden brown. Allow the finished dish to cool a little before cutting into large portions for serving. Serve with freshly baked white bread.

PAPOUTSÁKIA
Stuffed eggplant (Little slippers)
(Illustration opposite above)

4 medium eggplants
Olive oil for frying
2 onions, finely chopped
10 oz/300 g ground beef or lamb
1 tbsp tomato purée
2–3 beefsteak tomatoes, peeled and diced
1 bunch flat-leaved parsley, finely chopped
2 tbsp breadcrumbs
1½ cups/100 g kefalotíri, grated
3 tbsp/40 g butter
2 tbsp flour
2 cups/500 ml milk
2 tsp lemon juice
Freshly grated nutmeg
1 egg, beaten
Salt and freshly ground black pepper

Wash the eggplants and remove the base of the stalks. Heat olive oil in a pan and brown the eggplants on all sides over a high heat. Allow to cool, and cut off one third lengthways. Scoop out the flesh from the remainder with a spoon, leaving a ⅜-inch (1 cm) thick edge, finely chop the flesh, and set aside.
Preheat the oven to 375 °F (225 °C). For the filling, heat some olive oil and fry the onions and ground meat. Add the eggplant flesh, tomato purée, and diced tomatoes and simmer gently for about 5 minutes. Stir in the parsley, breadcrumbs, and half the cheese. Place the eggplant halves on a greased baking sheet, and fill with the ground meat mixture. Melt the butter in a pan and stir in the flour. Stir in the milk, and allow to thicken slowly. Simmer for about 5 minutes, and season with lemon juice, nutmeg, salt and pepper. Allow the sauce to cool, and stir in the egg and the remaining cheese. Pour over the filled eggplants and bake in the preheated oven for about 50 minutes. Serve hot, with freshly baked white bread.

MELITZÁNES YAKHNÍ

Eggplants in tomato sauce
(No illustration)

2 large eggplants
1 cup/250 ml Greek extra virgin olive oil
2–3 onions, finely chopped
5–6 cloves garlic, thinly sliced
4–5 tomatoes, peeled and diced
1 tbsp sugar
½ tsp dried oregano
1¾ cups/200 g sheep's cheese, crumbled
Salt
Freshly ground black pepper

Wash the eggplants, remove the base of the stalks, and cut in thin slices. Heat the olive oil in a pan and brown the slices well. Then pour the oil and eggplants into a casserole and add the onions, garlic, tomatoes, sugar, and oregano. Add a little water, salt and pepper, and cook for about 20–25 minutes over a medium heat. The dish is ready as soon as the eggplant is tender and the sauce has thickened. Arrange on plates, and scatter over the crumbled sheep's cheese. Serve hot.

MELITZÁNES TIGANITÉS

Fried eggplant slices
(Illustration below left)

2 large eggplants, sliced
Juice of 1 lemon
2 eggs
Flour (for coating)
Greek extra virgin olive oil
Salt
Freshly ground black pepper

Wash the eggplants, remove the base of the stalks, and cut them lengthways in thin slices. Drizzle over the lemon juice. Beat the eggs in a deep plate. In a second plate, mix the flour, salt, and pepper. Dip the eggplant slices first in egg, then in flour. Heat the olive oil in a pan, place the eggplant slices in it and fry until golden brown. Despite the coating, the eggplant will absorb the oil, so you will have to keep adding more. This dish can be served hot with salad or cold with *tzatzíki*. Serve with freshly baked white bread.
Melitzánes tiganités are frequently served as an appetizer with a glass of ouzo.

STUFFED GRAPE LEAVES

The appetizer *dolmadákia*, or dolmades, is without question one of the best known dishes in Greek cuisine. Stuffed grape leaves, also known as vine leaves, are very versatile, and the recipes for the filling so varied, that the imagination knows no bounds, and it is easy to choose a filling to suit the courses that are to follow. Freshly prepared *dolmadákia* become a special experience when you cut into them and the filling of rice, raisins, and nuts is still steaming, wafting the scents of the herbs and spices over you like a breath of the Orient. Preserved in olive oil, *dolmadákia* can be made to keep for quite a long time, and it is worth using them all up, because they are delicious cold as well, when all the flavors of the filling and the grape leaf have intermingled.

The herbs are chopped and mixed with all the other ingredients for the filling, then left to steep for a short time.

This helps the filling to stick together so it does not fall to pieces when placed on the grape leaf.

When rolling up the leaf, it is important to fold in all the "fingers" of the leaf as you go along.

The filling is now firmly encased and the grape leaf is rolled up tightly from the broad end toward the tip.

HOMEMADE WINE

As well as the big traditional wine companies and the newer, more innovative growers who want to bring Greek wine up to par with international standards, there are still many farmers in Greece who make their own wine every year exclusively for their own use. Their production methods often appear quite primitive, as if little has changed since ancient times. A farmer may have an old barrel, in which he himself treads the grapes harvested from vines growing up the side of his house or in a little field nearby, or he may send the crop to the local cooperative, which will then return the pressed must to him. The wine he makes from it will certainly not be as pure as the estate bottled or branded *vins ordinaires* of the region, but the result will certainly be a strong, full-bodied wine.

There is a long tradition of vine-covered roofs in agricultural areas like Macedonia, where awnings and fixed canopies have never been usual. Tall, fast-growing vines twining around the walls of houses or simple pergolas are useful in more ways than one. They offer perfect natural protection from the sun, keeping the house cool in summer, and the grapes that ripen in the autumn provide a welcome annual incentive to make homemade wine. And what is more, the residue from the pressing is excellent for distilling in your own cellar to make tsípouro, the Greek marc brandy.

DOLMADÁKIA
Stuffed grape leaves

2 cups/400 g rice
Juice of 2 lemons
Greek extra virgin olive oil
1 bunch scallions, finely chopped
2 bunches dill, finely chopped
½ bunch flat-leaved parsley, finely chopped
1½ lbs/750 g grape leaves preserved in oil or brine
Salt and freshly ground black pepper

Wash the rice and put in a pan, add lemon juice, a little olive oil, onions, dill, and parsley (set aside the stalks of the dill and parsley), season with salt and pepper, mix thoroughly, and leave to stand for 2–3 hours. Boil some water in a pan, and soak the leaves, then thoroughly rinse to remove much of the salty flavor of the brine. Gently pat the leaves dry with paper towels. Set aside any damaged leaves. Lay the soft undamaged leaves smooth side down on the work surface. Place a small amount of rice at the stalk end of the leaf and fold the stalk over it, so that the rice is partly covered. Then roll the leaf one more turn firmly over the rice, so that it is completely surrounded by the leaf. Fold the sides of the leaf into the middle and continue rolling toward the end. Spread the dill and parsley stalks over the base of a pan, and cover with some of the rejected leaves. Tightly pack the filled grape leaves on top, arranged in concentric circles. Sprinkle with salt and pepper, pour over 3¼ cups/800 ml water and some olive oil, and cover with more of the rejected leaves. Use 4 or 5 plates to press the *dolmadákia*, to prevent them from coming open during cooking. Cook over a medium heat until all the water has been absorbed and the rice is soft. Serve hot or cold.

When each of the *dolmadákia* is fully rolled up, the grape leaf and its filling have become a firm little parcel.

Then the *dolmadákia* are tightly packed into a deep pan, with the open ends of the leaves underneath.

Press the *dolmadákia* down with plates, and pour over the exact amount of water and the olive oil.

After cooking, the water has been absorbed, and the olive oil forms a shiny film on the *dolmadákia*.

Left: The woman playing the double pipe (or aulos) on this red-figured krater (wine bowl) clearly shows that the wealthier hosts of drunken symposia also organized a suitable program of entertainment.

WINEGROWING COUNTRY

Though knowledge of winegrowing and wine-making came to Greece via Minoan Crete from Egypt and the Near East, the Greeks believed wine (*oinos*) was the discovery and gift of the god Dionysus, in whose honor orgiastic wine festivals were held. Poets, philosophers and artists not only sang the praises of wine, they also wrote treatises on winegrowing areas, the diseases of grapes, and the building of wine-making troughs, as well as descriptions of wines of specific quality and origin – and, of course, even in those days, wine imitations. Homer tells us that winegrowing was widespread through-out Greece and specifically mentions several

places as being especially rich in grapes, so we know there were estates in Attica with 75 acres (30 hectares) of land given over to grapes. In the 4th century, Theophrastus already recognized the connection between the variety of grape, the composition of the soil, and the climatic conditions of each region. Taking cuttings and layering were recommended as a way of increas-ing the numbers of plants. Fork-shaped vine supports were considered usual and in many places the vines were allowed to grow up trees, but that made harvesting more difficult. Pros-trate or bushy varieties, which did not need any support, were common. The grapes were usu-ally pressed close to the vineyards, as people used their feet to trample the grapes in baskets standing in quite large troughs. Spindle presses did not come in until Roman times. Fermenta-tion took place in large barrels, so-called *pithoi*, after which the wine was drawn off into amphorae. The wine was not usually filtered, so a strainer was an essential piece of equipment at a symposium. Altering the taste by adding ingredients such as resin was not only the result of chance, it was often quite deliberate.

Even from the economic point of view, the growing of wine, which was labor-intensive compared with grains, was important. Many of the city-states stamped their coins with wine motifs, and potteries making amphorae for transporting wine flourished. The wine amphorae found all over the Mediterranean area, whose origins can be seen from their seals, bear witness to a busy trade in Greek wine.

ON HANDLING WINE

"The Cyclops took the wine and drank it up. And the delicious drink gave him such exquisite pleasure that he asked me for another bowlful. 'Give me more, please, and tell me your name, here and now – I would like to make you a gift that will please you. We Cyclopes have wine of our own made from the grapes that our rich soil and rains from Zeus pro-duce. But this vintage of yours is a drop of the real nectar and ambrosia.'

So said the Cyclops, and I handed him another bowlful of the sparkling wine. Three times I filled it for him; and three times the fool drained the bowl to the dregs. At last, when the wine had fuddled his wits, I addressed him with soothing words.

'Cyclops,' I said, 'you ask me my name. I'll tell it to you; and in return give me the gift you promised me. My name is Nobody. That is what I am called by my mother and father and by all my friends.'

The Cyclops answered me from his cruel heart. 'Of all his company I will eat nobody last, and the rest before him. That shall be your gift.'

He had hardly spoken before he toppled over and fell face upwards on the floor, where he lay with his great neck twisted to one side, and all-compelling sleep overpowered him." (Homer: Odyssey IX, 353-574. E.V. Rieu's translation for Penguin, revised by D.C.H. Rieu, 1991)

DIONYSUS, THE GOD OF WINE

Even in ancient times, opinions differed over the birth of Dionysus, the god of wine and vegetation, also known to the Greeks as Bacchus. He was probably the son of Zeus and Semele, daughter of the King of Thebes. When she died as a result of jealous Hera's cunning plot, Zeus took the unborn Dionysus from her womb and sewed him into his thigh. When it was time for him to be born, Zeus pulled out the child. Thus Dionysus became known as the twice-born god. To protect him from Hera, he trans-formed him into a kid (or a fawn), and entrusted him to the care of Her-mes, who had the boy brought up by

nymphs on the mythical mountain of Nysa. As the Maenads, these nymphs later became part of his perma-nent retinue. One day, when his nursemaids had lost sight of him, Dionysus was carried off by pirates, who thought he was the son of rich parents. During the crossing from Ithaca to Naxos, his bonds suddenly fell away, tendrils of ivy and vines twined around the oars and sails, and the ship could no longer sail. The sailors realized that he was a powerful god, and jumped into the sea in fear, where they were all changed into dolphins.

Men thanked Dionysus for the gift of the vine by ritual acts, which offered a welcome pretext for ecstatic and orgiastic rites, and at the same time honored him as a god and the guaran-tor of the annual rebirth of vegetation.

On smaller Greek estates, grapes are still pressed in simple presses, scarcely changed from the ancient lever presses.

The principle has remained unchanged since wine was first made. Under mechanical pressure, the juice separates from the solid parts of the grape and flows out at the bottom.

After successfully modernizing their businesses, many growers exhibit the old winemaking equipment. In Macedonia too, wine-makers endeavor to provide interesting destinations for the flourishing wine tour trade since people rarely go home without a couple of bottles after visiting the cellars, tasting the wine, and getting to know the grower personally.

MACEDONIAN WINEMAKERS

Nineteen winemakers in the tradition-conscious winegrowing area of Macedonia have founded the "Association of Macedonian Winegrowers." They are committed to cultivating and tending the classic regional grapes, such as Xinomavro. To promote cultural tourism, they have also created wine routes, along which Greek and foreign wine connoisseurs can stop to visit the cellars, taste the latest vintages on site, and get to know the Macedonian countryside. In this region there are a number of very interesting estates which are worth visiting.

Gerovassiliou Chardonnay: with its well-balanced nature, it goes well with seafood and with strong soft cheese.

Gerovassiliou Fumé: this cuvée of Sauvignon Blanc and Malagousia is the ideal type of perfectly matured white wine.

Gerovassiliou: this red wine – like all wines from this estate – is classified as a *vin ordinaire* from Epanomi and matures well.

Gerovassiliou: the white wine made from Assyrtiko and Malagousia tastes young and fresh, with hints of paprika and basil.

Merlot Xinomavro Boutari: this dry, opulent red wine is matured for one year in oak barrels and six months in the bottle.

Moschofilero Boutari: a very light, 11% vol., dry white wine, to accompany fish and seafood appetizers.

Xinomavro Boutari: the grapes for this attractive, dry, 12% vol. red wine come from Naoussa.

Chardonnay: Boutari grows the grapes for this *vin ordinaire* on Crete. It is good with lobster and shrimp.

Goumenissa: named after the area, this dry, red wine made from Xinomavro and Negoska has good structure.

Agiorgitiko Boutari: a quality-tested wine from the Neméa estate, with a convincingly rich aroma.

Sauvignon Blanc: this dry *vin ordinaire* of Cretan grapes from near Iráklion goes well with vegetable dishes and cheese.

Nikteri: Boutari has an estate on Santorini, where the grapes for this dry white wine are harvested in the cool of the night.

Merlot: a dark, red *vin ordinaire*, with a flavor of woodland berries and nuts – an ideal accompaniment for meat dishes.

Assyrtiko Boutari: like the Nikteri this fruity and full-bodied 13% vol. dry white wine also originates on Santorini.

Roditis-Xinomavro: a well-balanced, fresh, and lively wine, which provides a good accompaniment to both meat and fish dishes.

The Gerovassiliou estate is internationally known. It aims to develop French wine culture and is trying to elevate its *vins ordinaires* to the same high level. Constantin Lazaridi created a very modern estate in 1992, with the aim of producing wine of international class in the Drama region. His labels, designed by a resident artist, are typical of this approach. The special thing about the Markovitis estate is that it produces high quality, individualistic wines using organic methods. Yannis Boutaris makes high quality red wine in deliberately small quantities, while his family has a presence nationally and abroad under its label John Boutari & Son, with their headquarters in Macedonia and branches all over Greece.

Grande Reserve Naoussa: Boutari's quality-tested wine of Xinomavro grapes from the area of Naoussa has a scent of dried fruit.

Cava Boutari: a table wine that acquires a rich bouquet and delicate vanilla flavor after two years maturing in oak.

Visanto Boutari: a sweet wine made from Assyrtiko and Aidani grapes – best served as an aperitive or dessert wine.

Amethystos: Lazaridi produces a light red hybrid between the native Limnio and Cabernet Sauvignon and Merlot.

Amethystos: the taste of this white cuvée is reminiscent of peaches and exotic fruits against a flowery background.

Amethystos: the rosé variety of the series is made purely from Cabernet Sauvignon and has a fruity taste of berries.

Château Julia Chardonnay: Lazaridi from the Adriani area makes this fruity white wine. At 50 °F (10 °C) it goes well with fish.

Cava Amethystos: a long-lasting *vin ordinaire*, matured in oak barrels, with a spicy taste and a delicate scent of raspberries.

Kir-Yanni Merlot: the estate of Yannis Boutaris makes Merlot grapes from the Imathia region into a good *vin ordinaire*.

Kir-Yanni Syrah: this pleasantly dry, purplish red wine is also marketed as a *vin ordinaire* and is available in small quantities.

Kir-Yanni Yianakohori: this wine made from Merlot and Xinomavro tastes particularly good with spicy meat and barbecued foods.

Kir-Yanni Ramnista: from the Naoussa area, Yannis Boutaris produces this wine which has a rich and balanced nature.

Château Pegasus: the Markovitis estate produces the organically grown Pegasus range without using artificial fertilizers.

Château Pegasus: this 13% vol. white Chardonnay is recommended as an accompaniment to white meat and fish dishes.

Château Pegasus: this strong, promising red wine made from Xinomavro grapes comes from the designated Naoussa area.

The red Cava Boutari is made from the Xinomavro grape. It was one of the first wines of this kind on the Greek market. Its good storing qualities and individuality will be demonstrated by the 1985 vintage.

INVITATION FROM A WINE-GROWER

In the temperature-controlled wine cellar, surrounded by oak barrels, all senses are alert to check the "nose" and body of the wine and assess its value.

John Boutari & Son is an important Greek wine company with a long tradition behind it. It was founded by Yannis Boutari back in 1879, and the bottling of his first branded Greek wine marked an important stage in the history of Greek wine and the development of the Greek wine market. Boutari's red Naoussa was the first wine to be sold nationwide. In 1906 he founded the company's first estate in Naoussa. This estate, close to the historic town of Stenimachos, is the firm's present headquarters. New customers and connoisseurs have been drawn there since 1993, by guided tours of the production areas and cellars as well as illustrated lectures and wine tasting. John Boutari & Son has now become a wine empire; the fourth generation is now working there, and it is managed by Constantine Boutari. Around 1.2 million cases of wine are produced each year, and exports are flourishing worldwide. A second estate has been started in Goumenissa, and there are branches in Crete (the Fantaxometocho estate) and on the island of Santorini in the Cyclades (the Megalochori estate), where successful experiments are being carried out with the main local grape varieties.

Boutari produces successful top quality wines. His classic wines guarantee his success. Still numbered among these is the company's first branded wine mentioned above – Naoussa Boutari, which is made from Xinomavro, the predominant grape in the Naoussa region. The dry red wine matures for one year in oak, has a deep red color and, after further storing, acquires a rich bouquet composed of cinnamon and woody scents. It has a well-balanced body with good structure and a mild tannin flavor as it fades. Other Boutari classics that can be stored are Grande Reserve Naoussa, Goumenissa Boutari, and Cava Boutari. The storing and handling of the old, quality vintages of these classic wines demands long years of experience and suitable conditions. Boutari has the treasures stored separately in a specially designed cellar on the Naoussa estate, at an even temperature of 57–61 °F (14–16 °C) and 75% humidity. Boutari's new wines, such as Moscofilero Boutari, Assyrtiko Boutari, Agiorgitiko Boutari, and Xinomavro Boutari present a modern face and demonstrate the competitiveness of Greek wines on the international wine market. In addition, the company is also experimenting successfully with the proven international grape varieties, such as Cabernet Sauvignon, Merlot, and Chardonnay. Boutari was the first grower in Greece and the fourth in Europe to introduce a quality assurance system. Since 1993 Boutari has also conquered the beer market. His latest creation is a beer with the resounding name of "Mythos."

THE SYMPOSIUM

In ancient times, an invitation to dinner, *deipnon*, was often followed by the symposium, a drinking session for men, from which wives and children were excluded. It took place in a room specifically intended for the purpose furnished with couches, *klinés*, each of which could accommodate some three people, who took part in the festivities reclining. Originally a symposium was much more than just a jolly drinking session, it was a sort of ritual celebration, and it has never quite lost that character. So every symposium began with the ceremonial offering of wine to individual gods, the celebratory song, *paean*, and the formulaic toasts. Then a chairman, the symposiarch, would be chosen by lot, and he decided the rules for the rest of the evening. For instance, he decreed the proportions in which the wine and water should be mixed or the size of the drinking vessels. He called on the company or individuals to drink, and made the participants "dip into the pot." A true symposium provided a program of entertainment. Poems and songs were performed, stories and anecdotes, riddles and probably also jokes were told. Many famous poets composed verses for these occasions. Schools of philosophy used the symposium format for their learned discussions, and the famous dialogues of Plato and Xenophon made certain that there was a corresponding literary genre. Female flute players and dancers and *hetairae* (courtesans) were hired for the evening, which might well end in the orgiastic scenes sometimes depicted in Greek vase painting, especially on drinking vessels. If the symposium became very boisterous, it ended up in *komos*, wild drunkenness. Modern-day symposia are much less riotous. In the restaurant on the Boutari estate, they respect the ancient tradition and serve food along with the best wine in the house. In this case, however, civilized enjoyment replaces the more rough-and-ready customs of antiquity.

From left to right: Moscofilero Boutari is a dry wine, that has already won international competitions and is one of the firm's most important wines. The dark red Xinomavro Boutari has a full aroma and stores well. The younger Cava Boutari has a fruity taste of red berries and a hint of bitter almonds. The red Naoussa Boutari is the firm's classic: it is the wine that began its history and still achieves outstanding quality today.

Left: Virginia tobacco grown in Macedonia can reach a height of up to about 6 feet (2 meters).

BLUE HAZE

Why do the Greeks smoke so much and with such pleasure? The writer Lawrence Durrell discovered the answer during his travels in Greece in the mid-20th century. Not for religious reasons or for ritual purposes – no, the Greeks measure distances and times in cigarette lengths. In his writings he recalled that if you asked a farmer how far it was to a particular village, nine times out of ten he would tell you the distance in cigarettes. You might think smoking was the Greeks' third favorite pastime after eating and drinking. And that would come as no surprise, since the Greek cigarette industry can sell these luxury goods, which soon vanish in a blue haze, 50 percent cheaper than any other cigarette producers in the world. The reason for this is mainly because the tobacco is grown locally. The fact that many American tobacco companies obtain part of their raw materials from Greece and later sell the finished product abroad for a great deal of money does not seem to disturb anybody. It seems likely that many Greeks, who swear by American cigarettes, are not even aware that they are actually smoking the same Greek tobacco that they could buy more cheaply as a local product – though it should be added that the tobacco used for Greek cigarettes is lighter and usually unscented. The tobacco farmers are happy with this development, as it means they can make the best deals with the brown "Macedonian gold." With annual sales abroad of up to 90 thousand tons, Greek tobacco has become an important economic factor.

The tobacco plant (*Nicotiana tabacum*) is an annual plant growing up to about 6 feet (2 meters) high, with alternate broad lanceolate leaves and pink or white flowers. The nicotine is built up in the root and transported to the leaves where it is stored. The plant was originally a native of northwest Argentina and Bolivia. When the Spanish set foot on American soil, one of the things that amazed them was the cigar-smoking Indians. Tobacco reached Europe around 1560 aboard Spanish ships, and dispersed rapidly when they reached their home ports.

Tobacco is an annual, so it must be planted out fresh each year. Now it has almost become a comfortable job, as you can be carried slowly along the furrows while you sit in the seat and put in the plants.

BASMÁS TOBACCO

In the area around the small Thracian town of Komotini they grow the Basmás tobacco plant, which was imported from Turkey. This variety arrived in Thrace with the Greeks from Asia Minor around 1923, and since then has represented an important source of income for the region.

SMOKING IN GREECE

Of the varieties of tobacco grown in Greece, some are grown chiefly for export, namely *Basmás, Katerini, Kabakulak, Verginia,* and *Burley.* The varieties *Samiótika, black Thessalierin,* and *black Elassóras* are grown purely for home consumption. Smoking finds its highest expression not so much in the act itself as in the extravagant design of the cigarette packets. But the "corporate design" does not always match the contents, and many a feminine package has been the undoing of a young man.

It looks like soap, but is medium strength and has no filter: *Santé.* Right, smokes for gourmets: *Karelia Verginia* from Virginia tobacco.

From *Basmás* or *Verginia* tobacco: the taste of *Asso* tends toward that of the major American brands. *Old Navy* uses added perfume to achieve its British image.

Karelia and *Assos I* from Papstratos are all-purpose cigarettes, from non-filter to ultralight in *malako* (softpack) or *Skíró paleto* (box); they are for everyday smoking.

In the second rank for quantity, but not for quality, are *Twenty-two* and *Saga.*
Below: many brands are still sold in unusually luxurious packaging.

Tobacco prefers sandy soil, plenty of heat (77–95 °F, 25–35 °C), and ample rain in the growing season, conditions which are normal in Macedonia. Whole tobacco villages have now grown up there, and the farmers make a very good living, primarily from tobacco growing, as almost no other agricultural product brings in so much profit. This means the hard work in the fields, which begins with the sowing from mid February and ends in winter with the removal of the tobacco roots, is well worthwhile.

In the meantime, everybody has their hands full, as tobacco growing is labor-intensive. The farmers talk of a 50-day rhythm: the seed takes 50 days to grow into a plant; the first leaves are picked 50 days after the tobacco seedlings are planted out in the fields, and the entire tobacco harvest lasts 50 days. The leaves of any individual plant will be picked four times, working from the bottom up, at intervals determined by their maturity. "Four hands," the Greek farmers call it, and they look forward to the last hand, as those are the best and most aromatic tobacco leaves. The leaves in each "hand" must be stored, dried, and pressed separately because they are very different from each other in scent and taste. Drying takes 10 to 15 days. In the old days, the tobacco farming family gathered in the yard to bundle the leaves, string them together, and hang them to dry in the barn. Nowadays, this job is done on the spot by machines.

Another of the tobacco farmer's jobs is compressing the tobacco into bales or barrels, which can take up to two months, and serves to ferment the tobacco, building up the desired brown coloring matters and aromatic substances. After the harvest, all the tobacco roots must be carefully removed from the soil and the ground left unplowed so that no shoots or fungi develop which might harm the young plants the following year.

It has been established that a tobacco farming family invests around 2000 to 4000 hours per year in tobacco growing. The next stage is selling on to the dealers, who appraise the goods and set the price. Prices are high but unstable and, with tobacco as with any other sale, it is not just the quality of the goods that is crucial, but also the seller's bargaining skill. There are also subsidies from the European Union, which the farmer receives for each kilogram of tobacco. Today, up to 4 percent of all the world's cigarettes contain tobacco grown in Greece, as this is considered particularly aromatic.

While still green, the tobacco leaves are individually sewn together before being hung to dry in a special drying room.

From a distance, the lofty tobacco barns look like abandoned huts. Only when you get close do you see the slowly drying tobacco leaves.

When the tobacco is completely dry, it is compressed into bales to ferment. Then the leaves are sorted according to color and quality.

FISH FOR
ST. PAUL

When the Apostle Paul, on his second missionary journey in A.D. 49, landed at the east Macedonian port of Neapolis, modern-day Kavala, he did not know what was awaiting him. After his first journey to Cyprus and Asia Minor, he had grown into the role of leader within the group of Jesus' apostles, and had made this second journey independently. He had surrounded himself with a large crowd of helpers, set off for Europe, and landed here on the coast of Macedonia, intending to proceed from here to Philippi. There, together with some Jews from the city, he founded the first Christian community in Europe. His task as a missionary was dangerous, and there was still doubt as to whether he would succeed. But one thing was quite certain: he would not go hungry here. The coast of eastern Macedonia was rich in fish, and there was a large selection of fresh fish available. Today Kavala, which was an important center for the tobacco trade in the 19th century, is one of the major harbors for east Macedonian fishermen to land their catch. Every day they sail out as far as the islands of Samothrace and Thassos and almost to the Turkish coast to cast their nets. Of all the fish they land, fresh sole are the most prized, and in A.D. 49 they may have been served to St. Paul in the same way as they are to many foreigners arriving in the area today.

Below: the harbor of Kavala is one of the places where east Macedonian fishermen land their catch.

Above: in the hinterland of Kavala is the ancient city of Philippi, founded in 355 B.C. by Philip II, father of Alexander the Great. Here St. Paul established the first Christian community on European soil in A.D. 49 during his second missionary journey.
Background: the shipyard at Kavala harbor, with a view of the aqueduct dating from 1550.

GLÓSSA STO FOÚRNO
Baked sole

2 sole, filleted
1 tbsp Greek extra virgin olive oil
2 tbsp fish sauce (from an Asian delicatessen)
⅔ cup/150 ml sweet white wine
2 scallions, thinly sliced
1 tbsp coriander leaves, chopped
1 tbsp lovage, chopped
    (celery leaves can be used as a substitute)
1 tsp fresh oregano, chopped
2 eggs, beaten
Black peppercorns

Preheat the oven to 350 °F (180 °C). Place the sole fillets in an ovenproof dish and pour the oil, fish sauce, and wine over them. Sprinkle over the scallions and chopped coriander, and bake in the preheated oven for about 15 minutes. Remove from the oven, put the fillets in a warm place, strain the stock and set aside. In a mortar, grind the pepper, and crush the lovage, oregano, and the cooked vegetables from the stock. Stir this mixture into the stock, and mix in the eggs. Cover the fish with this sauce, and return to the oven until the sauce thickens. Sprinkle with freshly ground black pepper and serve hot.

Tip: This dish is an adaptation of an old recipe, and with a little imagination, you can picture St. Paul eating something similar on his missionary journey. It is probably a good idea to use the Asian fish sauce mentioned in the ingredients as a replacement for the ancient Greek garos, the legendary salty sauce made from small fish and fish remains that have fermented for weeks in the sun.

289

MACEDONIAN FISH SPECIALTIES

MIDOPÍLAFO
Mussels with rice

2 lbs/1 kg fresh mussels
1 scant cup/200 ml Greek extra virgin olive oil
1 large onion, finely chopped
1 scant cup/200 ml dry white wine
3 tomatoes, peeled and diced small
2¼ cups/450 g rice
1 tbsp flat-leaved parsley, finely chopped
1 tbsp dill, finely chopped
Salt and freshly ground black pepper

Wash the mussels, scrub them thoroughly, and discard any that are already open. Heat the olive oil in a pan and sauté the onions. Add the mussels and a little water and bring to a boil. Discard the mussels that do not open. Pour in the white wine, add the tomatoes, and season with salt and pepper. Pour in enough water so the mussels are well covered, and simmer for about 15 minutes. Then add the rice, and cook until tender and the stock has been absorbed (add hot water if necessary). Arrange on a serving dish and garnish with parsley and dill.

XIFÍAS MARINÁTOS
Marinated swordfish

4 swordfish steaks
Juice of one lemon
Grated rind of 1 unwaxed lemon
⅔ cup/150 ml Greek extra virgin olive oil
1 bunch flat-leaved parsley, finely chopped
8 bay leaves
2 sprigs fresh thyme
Salt
Freshly ground black pepper

Salt and pepper the swordfish steaks. In a bowl, combine the lemon juice, grated lemon rind, 4 tbsp olive oil, and parsley. Brush the steaks with the marinade, place 1 bay leaf on each, stack them one on top of the other, and marinate in the refrigerator for 1 hour.
Heat 4 tbsp of olive oil in a pan, add the remaining bay leaves, and lay the swordfish steaks on them. Fry the fish for about 5 minutes on each side, until cooked through. Pour over the marinade, add salt and pepper to taste, and remove the pan from the heat. Arrange the fish on a serving plate and garnish with fresh thyme. Serve hot with freshly baked white bread. As a side dish, you can also serve fresh country-style salad or *skordaliá* (see recipe page 343).

Midopílafo – Mussels with rice

Xifías marinátos
Marinated swordfish

PSÁRI STO FOÚRNO ME RÍGANI
Fish fillet with oregano

4–6 large fillets of dorado or whole sea bass
2¼ lbs/1 kg potatoes
1 cup/250 ml Greek extra virgin olive oil
Juice of 2 lemons
3 sprigs fresh oregano, chopped
Salt
Freshly ground black pepper

Preheat the oven to 350 °F (180 °C). Brush the inside of an ovenproof dish with oil, place the fish in it, and sprinkle with salt and pepper. Peel the potatoes, slice them thinly, season with salt and pepper, and spread the slices over the fish. Pour over the olive oil, lemon juice, and 1¼ cups/300 ml water, and sprinkle with oregano. Cook in the preheated oven for about 45 minutes. Serve hot with green salad and freshly baked white bread.

GLÓSSA YEMISTÍ
Stuffed sole fillets

A scant ½ cup/100 g butter
3 cloves garlic, crushed
1 large onion, finely chopped
1 green pepper, diced very small
10 oz/300 g peeled shrimp, finely chopped
2 cups/100 g fresh breadcrumbs
½ bunch flat-leaved parsley, finely chopped
8 fillets of sole
1¼ cups/300 ml fish stock
3 eggs, beaten
Juice of 1 lemon
Salt
Freshly ground black pepper

Heat half the butter in a pan and sauté the garlic, onion, and pepper. Add the shrimp, breadcrumbs, and parsley, and season with salt and pepper. Bring briefly to a boil, stirring continuously, then remove from the heat and allow to cool.
Preheat the oven to 350 °F (180 °C). Salt and pepper the fillets of sole. Divide the shrimp mixture over the fillets, then roll them up and place in a greased ovenproof dish. Melt the remaining butter and pour it over the fish rolls. Cook for about 30 minutes in the preheated oven. Heat the fish stock in a pan. Mix the beaten eggs with lemon juice, slowly stir into the fish stock, return to the heat, but do not bring to a boil. Arrange the stuffed fish fillets on a warm plate. Pour over the egg and lemon juice sauce, and garnish with a little chopped parsley. Serve hot.

Psári sto foúrno me rígani
Fish fillets with oregano

Situated by the lake that shares its name, the little town of Kastoriá is an important regional economic center because of its fur industry. The lake is full of fish and there are cultural and historical sights to visit.

LAKE FISH

The city of Kastoriá is situated 2035 feet (620 meters) above sea level, on a rocky peninsula stretching far out into the lake of the same name, which is richly populated with fish. The fact that people greatly valued this richness as far back as Neolithic times is proved by the excavated remains of a village built out over the lake on piles. Nothing worth mentioning remains of the ancient town of Keletron. A new city was founded there in the 6th century. Because of the lake's abundant fish population and the beavers, which were the basis of the fur industry that has had such a profound effect on the history of the town, Kastoriá quickly became prosperous. More than 70 churches – some adorned with magnificent frescoes – and the splendid villas of the fur traders bear witness to this.

In the nutrient-rich waters of the lake are eels, carp, trout, and tench. The abundant supply of fish is also enjoyed by more than 140 different species of birds, which make a brief stop here. Even pelicans venture into "fur town." In the little lakeside tavernas of the picturesque town, you can eat fish fresh from the lake every day.

A particular specialty of these tavernas is *Kastorianí psarósoupa*. This "Kastoria-style fish soup" is made from fish heads and vegetables. The fish is baked with tomatoes, paprika, garlic, oil, and spices and served with bread and a sauce of fish stock, nuts, and garlic.

LAKE PRÉSPA

Today, the Lakes of Préspa are one of the most beautiful and remote of Greece's national parks. They lie in a wide, high valley 2790 feet (850 meters) above sea level. The borders of Greece, Albania, and Macedonia run through Great Préspa Lake. Little Préspa Lake belongs almost entirely to Greece. On account of their rich fauna and flora the Greek parts of the lakes have been declared a nature reserve, providing an important habitat for 40 different species of mammals, including bears and wild cats. Of the world's remaining 1000 pairs of Dalmatian pelicans, 150 have their breeding grounds here, the last in Europe, along with cormorants, herons, and storks.

PÉSTROFA LEMONÁTI
Stuffed lemon trout

1 onion, quartered
1 bunch herbs and vegetables for soup,
   finely chopped
1 lb/500 g mussels, cleaned
1 lb/500 g peeled shrimp, roughly chopped
3 tbsp lemon juice
¼ cup/50 g butter
1 tbsp finely chopped flat-leaved parsley
2 tbsp fresh breadcrumbs
⅓ cup/50 g black olives, roughly chopped
1 tbsp tarragon, finely chopped
6 tbsp Greek extra virgin olive oil
4 fresh trout
2 lemons, sliced
Salt
Freshly ground black pepper

Bring the onion, herbs, and soup vegetables to a boil in about 1¼ cups/300 ml salted water. Discard any mussels that are already open, then add the remainder to the vegetables and cook for 5 minutes. Remove from the heat, take the mussels out of their shells – discarding any which have not opened – drain, and roughly chop them. Put them in a bowl, add the shrimp, pour over the lemon juice and marinate for 1 hour. Heat the butter in a pan, pour in the mussel and shrimp mixture, add parsley, salt, and pepper, and fry everything well. Remove from the heat and allow to cool.

Preheat the oven to 420 °F (220 °C). In a bowl, mix the breadcrumbs, olives and tarragon, add the mussel and shrimp mixture and 2 tbsp olive oil, and stir thoroughly. Clean and gut the trout, wash thoroughly, and pat dry. Season inside and out with salt and pepper, and fill the cavity with the prepared mixture. Brush 4 large pieces of kitchen foil with 1 tbsp olive oil each, and wrap each trout individually. Cook for 20 minutes in the preheated oven. Remove the trout from the foil, arrange on plates and garnish with slices of lemon. Serve with freshly baked white bread.

THE FUR TRADE

The fur trade first flourished in Kastoriá in the 17th century. At that time, the profitable beaver trade attracted many furriers to the lake of Kastoriá to take advantage of the high prices beaver skins were fetching on the European fur exchanges. Products made from beaver skin are still sold all over the world, though there are hardly any beavers left in "beaver town" whose skins could be taken to market. The 3000 furriers' workshops, silently carrying on the industry in cellars and backyards, now get their pelts from northern Europe, Canada, and Russia. So the experts still think of Kastoriá as the biggest furrier's workshop in Europe. However, the picturesque town with its quaint wooden houses is still waiting to be discovered. The splendid, partly restored, manor houses from Ottoman times bear witness to the town's former prosperity, and the 40 or so of the 70 Byzantine churches that are well-maintained certainly justify a stay in Kastoriá.

WOLVES

Wolves are a protected species in Greece. But, as almost everywhere else in the world, modern civilization has forced them into the last retreats of the inaccessible forests, far from the towns. Only in very remote mountain villages in northern Greece can you still sometimes hear them howling in the dusk of evening. Their numbers are currently estimated at only a few hundred.
The Greek writer Siranna Satelli had good reason to call her best-selling novel *And They Return Again by Wolf Light*. "Wolf light" in Greek means the evening dusk.

ANASTENÁRIA

Anastenária, one of the most unusual festivals in Greece, is celebrated annually in Macedonia on May 21. The name probably comes from *anastenázo* and means "to sigh." There is indeed a lot of sighing at this festival, as it comes to a climax with a spectacle that is well worth seeing: the dance on glowing embers! It all began in the middle of the 13th century, when a village church in a remote area of Thrace fell victim to an arson attack. This threatened to destroy the icons of St. Constantine, the first Christian emperor, and his mother Helena, which were kept there. But suddenly the inhabitants heard a great moan coming from the church. "The icons are calling for us to help," they thought. A few intrepid volunteers stormed into the burning church and saved the icons, without suffering any burns themselves. The less courageous, who had waited outside, thought a miracle had happened. So every year on May 21, the feast day of Constantine and Helena, their spirits are called upon once more to work new miracles at the fire-walking. However, fewer villages in Macedonia are holding this festival, and it is threatening to vanish completely into oblivion.

The first preparations begin the previous evening. They decorate a calf, and there is music and dancing. Each of the initiates dances alone, carrying an icon above his head, with only the lyre, bagpipes and tambourine to give the dancers the beat. Then the next morning it begins in earnest. After church, people gather in the village square. The calf is slaughtered, and a sigh of relief goes through the crowd of onlookers. Women can be heard shrieking. The rest of the day is spent in eating, drinking, and dancing, and the first fires are lit. At first the pyre blazes brightly; sparks fly in the wind; the air is filled with the smell of burning wood. Late in the afternoon, when only a red glow remains, the fire-walkers begin their daring leaps. Wide-eyed children cannot believe what they see, and doctors cannot explain why the fire-walkers do not get burns on their feet. But gradually the fire dies down, the background murmur falls silent, and many an Orthodox priest is relieved that the whole thing has passed off smoothly again this year.

Before the great run over the glowing embers, the masters of ceremonies gather in a room and pray in front of the icons of St. Constantine and St. Helena.

The initiate runners, men and women, kiss the icons, under whose protection they will later be placed. Only their faith saves them from blisters on the soles of their feet.

HEPHAESTUS GOD OF FIRE

When Hera gave birth to Hephaestus and discovered that he was lame, she reluctantly threw him down from heaven into the sea. There Thetis, the goddess of the sea, took care of him and hid him in a cave, unnoticed by Hera or the other gods. But Hephaestus had not gotten over his mother's unnatural behavior and, being a skillful and talented artist, he later presented her with a beautiful golden throne. When Hera seated herself upon it, she could not get up from it again. The gods begged Hephaestus to forgive his mother and set her free and, when he hesitated, only Dionysus succeeded in taking advantage of his credulity to get him drunk and bring him to Olympus, where he then set Hera free.

According to Homer, however, it was Zeus who cast Hephaestus out of Olympus onto the island of Lemnos for coming to Hera's aid when Zeus wanted to punish her, because she had opposed him. Hephaestus, lamed by the fall, set up his forge there and became not just a simple blacksmith but a gifted artist, whose skillful hands created marvelous inventions which became the stuff of legend. He made palaces for the gods, Zeus's scepter, and Achilles' famous suit of armor. It was also Hephaestus who released Athena from Zeus's head with a blow from an ax and later crafted the aegis – a shield decorated with the head of Medusa – for her. Commanded by Zeus, he also chained Prometheus to the rocks.

On Lemnos or on Sicily, Hephaestus' work was always connected with the subterranean fire, the earth's volcanic activity, which he harnessed. But he is also the lame, crippled, or dwarfish smith of folk tales who, with his helpers, the Cyclopes, created ingenious devices in his forge. Along with Prometheus, he was worshiped as the creator and protector of crafts and craftsmen.

In the meantime, the men of the village prepare the wooden pyre for *anastenária*. They subject every single treetrunk to expert examination.

The blazing fire is surveyed from a distance. Even the runners do not approach until it has burned down, and the glowing embers begin to flicker in the darkness.

Background: the *Anastenária* initiates run barefoot over the glowing embers, without injuring the soles of their feet. This act demands not only deep faith, but also a good measure of courage.

After the ceremony is over, the tired but contented spectators return to the village to the sound of drums, and gather in a taverna.

In the center stand the fire-walkers, some of whom may be women (see background picture), whose ash-blackened feet are one of the evening's great attractions.

After their great exertions, there is a communal meal for all those who took part in the *anastenária*, which livens up the weary spirits and can last into the early hours of the morning.

ΘΡΑΚΗ

Around 190 B.C. the *Nike of Samothrace*, goddess of victory, stood on the bow of a stone ship on one of the island's mysterious temples. She was a gift of thanks given by the people of Rhodes on the occasion of a victorious sea battle.

THRACE

Historians like to speak of "areas of ethnic fluctuation," when describing areas where people of different customs and faiths have come together with a greater or lesser degree of tolerance. By this they mean regions like Thrace, which historically included more than just the strip of Greek coast bounded in the north by the high Rhodope mountain range. Ancient Thrace covered a large area of southern Europe, including modern-day Bulgaria and parts of Turkey. Xerxes passed through here in 480 B.C. The Roman Via Egnatia ran from the Adriatic Sea to Byzantium, through the province of Thrace. Byzantine monks came this way en route to the monastic republic of Mount Athos. In the Middle Ages, people built mighty fortresses and castles here to protect themselves from the invading Slavic Bulgars, but the area remained open to Ottoman-Turkish and Serbian influence. The collapse of the Ottoman Empire (Thrace did not become a part of the Greek state until 1913) and the Asia Minor catastrophe of 1922 were followed by expulsions, resulting in a large-scale exchange of populations in 1923.

Today, Thrace is the easternmost province of Greece, with a large Muslim minority living side by side with the Greek Orthodox majority, where Christians and Muslims have come to an arrangement with one another for everyday life. Most of the children have grown up bilingual, but they attend their own schools. Religious festivals are celebrated in mutual harmony and with respect for the beliefs of others. The busiest shopping streets in the cities of Xánthi and Kommotini offer a taste of the atmosphere of oriental bazaars, an impression heightened by the minarets of the many mosques. In the villages of the Pomaks, Bulgarian-speaking Muslims, everyday country life seems to follow a more leisurely rhythm. Since ancient times, Thrace has always been known for its grains. Newer industries of greater economic importance for Greece are tobacco, sugar, cotton, paper, and embroidery. As a transit area for many peoples, the region has had the opportunity to become familiar with a multitude of culinary curiosities and integrated them into the local cuisine which, though varied, is now also well-established. As foods are equally well known by both their Greek and Turkish names, the mixture seems to be stable.

In this agricultural region of northeastern Greece, many farmers still work their fields in very simple conditions, but their hard work is directly connected to their daily food. "From hand to mouth" does not have to be a negative concept.

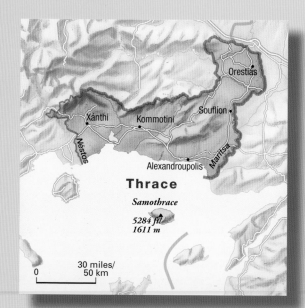

Orestiás

Xánthi   Kommotini   Souflion

Néstos

Alexandroupolis   Maritsa

Thrace

Samothrace

5284 ft
1611 m

0   30 miles/
      50 km

THE TURKISH INHERITANCE

It almost seems as though tolerance enters the human system through the stomach. There is virtually nothing the Greeks argue so vehemently about as their historical relationship with the Turks. But although they tried to destroy everything that was even a distant reminder of the occupation after the liberation, the centuries of Ottoman domination have left clear traces in the Greek way of life, not least in Greek cuisine.

The merging of Greek and Turkish cultures occurred on many levels. In the Middle Ages, the Turkish rulers not only brought their customs and traditions with them from the Orient, they also brought their cooking practices, which they blended with those of the Greeks into a harmonious taste. It is still possible to identify a number of dishes which clearly bear the marks of Turkish influence in their names as well as in their methods of preparation.

A quick glance into Greek kitchens will soon convince even the most hardened doubter. With some dishes, the naturalized Turkish name is proof enough of culinary intervention by the foreign culture. For others, the way they are made betrays the fact that they are equally at home in both cultures (see box on following page).

The Greeks regard the nutritious meeting of Greek and Turkish recipes as clear evidence of common tastes, and see it as a good basis for living together in peace.

The overlap begins early in the morning. Some say *tsai* for tea, others drink *çay*. Some drink Greek and others Turkish mocha, which on closer inspection turn out to be identical. *Khalvas*, the sweet sesame-seed cake, is not only pronounced the same in both cultures, they both equally enjoy eating it. At midday, similar appetizers appear on Greek and Turkish tables. There are also obvious parallels in the way fish and meat are prepared. Anything that can be broiled or grilled is highly esteemed, and Greek *yíros* are just as spicy as Turkish *döner* kebabs. When it comes to *kadéfi*, the dessert they have in common, the last mutual resentment fades into the background, at least while the taste still lingers on the tongue. This mutual culinary understanding is particularly strong in western Thrace, where members of the biggest Turkish minority in Greece live side by side with their Greek neighbors, notwithstanding the way politicians on both sides continually exploit the situation of the people of this region for their own ends, in the everyday game of power politics.

Close to the mosques, whose slender minarets are visible from far away, and the Orthodox churches, which are more plentiful here than anywhere else in Greece, the Turkish and Greek traders in the shopping districts sell their wares next door to one another, while the women peer into each other's cooking pots. And despite all the social prejudices that can be clearly sensed in the rest of Greece, people here have long since thrown their common problems into one pot, and have come to a friendly agreement on matters concerning taste.

From slender, long-necked brass pots with elegantly curved spouts the tea flows into the glasses in a thin stream.

Even objects that could be taken on a journey were made out of brass, with great attention to detail and design.

Intricately patterned brass trays may often have a decorative rather than a practical function.

Even simple kitchen utensils like salt and pepper shakers were made of brass.

ORIENTAL RUGS

Making hand-woven woolen rugs is still one of the most important traditional crafts in Thrace. In ancient times these rugs, originally made by nomads, were highly prized as wall hangings or covers for couches and chairs, and they have been used as a floor covering since the time of Alexander the Great. More recently, Greek weavers brought the necessary skills and patterns with them from Turkey to Greece at the time of the resettlement. They combined the oriental patterns with Greek ornamentation, and successfully marketed them all over Greece. As in ancient times, these rugs were not only intended for the floor; they adorned the walls of a house as often as they were used as throw-over bedspreads. A quick look inside a Thracian farmhouse clearly shows that things have remained the same right up to the present day. On the

great looms, which could once be found in every Greek household, they also wove woolen cushion covers, bags, and other useful articles.

Oriental woven rugs, also known as *kelims*, found their way into farming households in Greece, especially in Thrace. Today they are mainly made in Thrace, Macedonia, and Epirus. There are still workshops in Thrace where rugs are made according to ancient traditional patterns. In the agricultural areas, where the Turkish minority live, weaving is an important activity, just as it was a hundred years ago, and is considered to be women's work. The wooden looms are still made by hand in the traditional way, and the warp beam is strung by hand, an operation requiring much hard and patient work.

GRAECO-TURKISH MENU

baklavás	*baklava*	puff pastry with nuts in syrup
bouréki	*börek*	pastry
khalvás	*helva*	sweet made of sesame or semolina
yíros	*döner*	lamb or pork kebab
imam baildi	*imam bayıldı*	stuffed eggplant
yakhní	*yahnı*	vegetables sautéed with tomatoes, sometimes with meat, a kind of stew
yaoúrti	*yogurt*	yogurt
kaimáki	*kaymak*	the froth that forms when making mocha
kadéfi	*kadayif*	nut rolls
keftés	*köfte*	small meat balls
moka	*kahve*	mocha
dolmádes	*dolma*	(leaf) stuffed grape leaves
piláfi	*pilav*	soft rice cooked in fat or butter
sarailí	*saray tatlısı*	rolled puff pastry in syrup
tzatzíki	*cacık*	yogurt with cucumber and garlic
tsaí	*çay*	tea

KOTÓSOUPA AVGOLÉMONO
Chicken soup with egg and lemon sauce

*1 chicken weighing just
over 2¼ lbs/1 kg, oven
   ready
1 onion, peeled and
   halved
1 carrot, peeled and
   halved
1 stick celery, halved
1 bay leaf
1¼ cups/250 g rice
2 eggs
Juice of 1 lemon
Finely chopped flat-leaved parsley to taste
Salt
Freshly ground black pepper*

In a pan, cover the chicken with water and bring
to a boil. Add the onion, carrot, celery, and bay
leaf, and season with salt and pepper. Skim off
the scum that forms on the surface. Reduce the
temperature and simmer the chicken for about
1 hour, until the flesh falls away from the bones.
Drain the chicken, save the stock, and set aside.
Cut the chicken meat in pieces and add it to the
stock, together with the rice, and simmer the
soup over a medium heat for about 20 minutes,
until the rice is tender (add more boiling water
if necessary). Remove the soup from the heat,
and add salt and pepper to taste. Beat the eggs,
and add the lemon juice and a little stock, stirring continuously. Allow the chicken soup to
cool slightly and stir in the lemon sauce.
Ladle the soup into deep plates, sprinkle with
parsley, and serve with freshly baked white bread.

CHICKENS WITH A HISTORY

Compared with hundreds and thousands of their kind throughout the world, Greek chickens still lead a relatively free and unrestricted life – so free that when you are driving through the countryside, you see chickens everywhere, running across the fields and meadows and even the roads. But the relationship of Greek farming families to their chickens is not over-sentimental in character. There is no doubt that they love their birds even more after they have wrung their necks. Chicken is made into a variety of dishes. It has always been recognized as a good roast meal for a celebration, but is increasingly thought of in terms of everyday food. Chickens are not fussy eaters. They prefer wheat or corn, and they enjoy leftover scraps. The farmers recycle the chicken manure as a valuable fertilizer in their orchards and vegetable plots.

Though large-scale chicken farming is now quite widespread in Greece, you can still buy free-range chickens from small retailers in the cities or bigger country towns. In the country, you can get the occasional chicken from your next-door neighbor, if you do not have a little family of chickens on your own piece of land. And in Greece killing a chicken in the kitchen is as much an everyday matter as cooking.

The people of the ancient Mediterranean area first encountered the domestic chicken around 600 B.C., by which time it was already being farmed. It probably came to Greece from China via Central Asia, where farming began around 1400 B.C. That is probably why some literary sources also call it the "Persian bird" or the "Persian waker." As long ago as the 6th century B.C., images of people offering each other animals as presents or love tokens appear on both black-figured and red-figured vases and bowls, probably as a part of courtship. Besides game birds, hares, and also small deer, you sometimes see hens or roosters with magnificent plumage. While the gift of a hen was on the whole offered to a woman, when it was men or boys whose favor was being courted, the aggressive nature of the rooster would come to the fore. Cock fighting was probably already known from Asia Minor, and roosters were no doubt also valued as guards and for their early morning calls.

Chickens did not play a leading role in ancient Greece as providers of meat and eggs. At the start of the classical era, in the 5th century B.C., it was quail that were considered more useful creatures to keep on farms. They laid a lot of eggs, they were edible, and very tasty into the bargain. Chicken farming did not come to have any serious importance until later in Roman times.

KOTÓPOULO PSITÓ
Roast chicken

1 chicken weighing about 3¼ lbs/1.5 kg,
  oven ready
Juice of 2 lemons
1 tbsp mustard
2 lbs/1 kg small potatoes, peeled
3 sprigs fresh thyme, finely chopped
1 scant cup/200 ml Greek extra virgin olive oil
Salt
Freshly ground black pepper

Preheat the oven to 350 °F (180 °C). Rub the chicken inside and out with the juice of 1 lemon. Season with salt and pepper, place in an oven-proof dish, and brush the skin with mustard. Arrange the potatoes around the chicken and sprinkle with salt, pepper, and thyme.

Mix the juice of the second lemon with the olive oil, and pour over the chicken. Add some water and roast in the preheated oven for about 1½ hours, turning the bird occasionally, so that it is crisp and brown on both sides.

In the country, people are not squeamish in their dealings with poultry. Use the right grip, and even the angriest rooster will hold still.

SECRET GRANARY

If Thessaly is the acknowledged granary of Greece, then Thrace is the secret one. Even connoisseurs of Greece are largely ignorant of the fact that large areas of land here are used for growing all the common grains, so-called soft or seed wheat, as well as hard or spring wheat, and also rye, barley, and oats.

The cultivation of grains, that is grasses with seeds that represent an important food for people, is the basis of all farming. It is not just in the earliest written evidence of the Greek world that grains are recognized as the start of any kind of civilization. But if there are few detailed descriptions of the way grains were used and prepared in ancient times, the reason must lie precisely in the fact that something as generally well known as grains did not seem to require detailed discussion.

It is certain that the primitive grain varieties of emmer (*zeiai, olyra,* and einkorn (*tiphe*), which were later developed into the wheat we know today, reached Greece from the Near East, probably from Syria, where some forms of civilization were already in existence around 7000 B.C. As the climatic conditions were not always suitable for wheat growing, barley (*krithe*) was often preferred, and was probably found in Greece before wheat. Finds made in caves inhabited before 7000 B.C. provide evidence that wild forms were at least being gathered. Barley grew better in Greece and probably continued to be the basic food for quite some time.

The use of grains in cooking quickly became established in ancient times. While Homer offers no clear evidence of how grains were prepared, Hesiod seems to have been very impressed with wheat meal and barley porridge. According to him, *ametiskos,* a kind of milk cake, was served as an accompaniment to game and poultry. In the 5th–4th centuries B.C., wheat bread and barley cakes were already part of the diet. Oats (*bromos*) do not seem to have been very popular, as they were used mainly for cattle food. *Pyros,* a kind of grain related to emmer – sometimes also described as a hard wheat – which had spread into eastern Europe in the early historic period, reached Greece via southern Russia.

Today, most kinds of hard wheat in Greece are made into cattle food, whereas the soft wheats are used to make bread and sweet cakes.

In a few towns in the Evros Valley in eastern Thrace inhabited by the Pomaks (an ethnic group of Slavonic, Bulgarian-speaking Muslims) traditions and farming methods reminiscent of centuries long past have been maintained. The fields are still plowed using a hand plow and a team of oxen; corn is sown, reaped, threshed, and ground by hand, and made into bread to be used in dishes that are almost unknown, even in Greece. Pomaks make up some 20 percent of the population of the villages lying at the foot of the Rhodope Mountains, and they are almost self-sufficient.

In the villages of the Pomaks, a Bulgarian-speaking Muslim ethnic group, the hours seem to pass at a more leisurely pace.

Rye (*Secale cereale*) is mainly used for cattle food in Greece.

Oats (*Avena sativa*) are made into oat flakes and oatmeal or used to feed horses.

One of the oldest cultivated plants in Europe is barley (*Hordeum vulgare*).

Durum wheat (*Triticum durum*) is used for making semolina and pasta.

Soft wheat (*Triticum aestivum*) is used for making almost all kinds of bread.

DEMETER

In Greek mythology, Demeter is an ancient, possibly pre-Greek, mother goddess. As goddess of the earth, of fruitfulness, of growth, and especially of crops, she was not so much interested in the "Olympian society" but instead wandered the earth, taking care that the seeds flourished. As a result, she was greatly venerated, especially by women. Her daughter Persephone was once abducted by Hades, god of the underworld. When Demeter learned that her daughter was no longer living in the light of the sun, she withdrew from the earth, so no more seeds sprouted. Zeus, concerned at the lack of sacrificial offerings, succeeded in making a bargain with Hades, which allowed Perse-phone to leave the underworld for two thirds of the year to dwell on Mount Olympus. So Persphone's annual release from and return to the underworld have become a metaphor for the annual growth and death of the seeds and plants on the earth.

KISKÉKI
Pork with wheat

¼ cup/50 g shortening
2 lbs/1 kg lean pork, roughly diced
2–3 red chiles, seeded and finely chopped
1 cup/200 g wheat grains
¼ cup/50 g butter
2 onions, finely chopped
Salt
Freshly ground black pepper
1 tsp ground cumin
1 scant cup/200 g Greek yogurt

Melt the shortening in a pan and brown the meat all over. Pour over sufficient water so the meat is well covered. Add the chiles, season with salt and pepper, cover, and cook over a low heat for about 2 hours. Put the wheat in a pan with plenty of water, add salt, and bring to a boil. Reduce the temperature, cover, and boil for 1½ hours until the wheat is soft. Add more boiling water if necessary.
Melt the butter in a pan and sauté the onions. Cut the cooked meat into smaller pieces and mix in a bowl with the onions and the drained wheat. Add salt and pepper to taste, and then sprinkle with the ground cumin. Serve with

small bowls of Greek yogurt, which can also be spooned onto the plates and stirred in with the wheat, if preferred.

KOTÓPOULO ME PLIGOÚRI
Chicken with wheat

1. The previous day, boil 2½ cups/500g wheat grains in 2 cups/500ml water until the liquid is absorbed. Allow to dry overnight and break up the next day.

2. Brown 8 pieces of chicken all over in olive oil with an onion, then season with paprika, oregano, salt, and pepper and cook until almost tender.

3. Pour over 6 cups/1½ liters boiling water and add the wheat meal. Simmer until the water has boiled away and the wheat has doubled in volume. Remove from the heat, allow to stand for a short time, and serve hot.

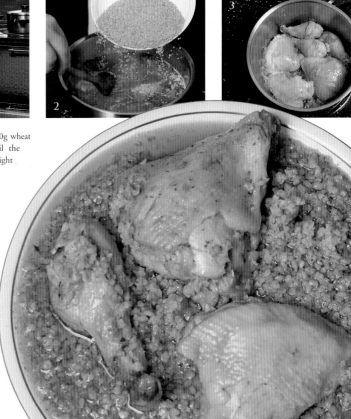

DAILY BREAD

One food is an indispensable part of any Greek meal: bread. You have it with appetizers, between meals, with salads, potatoes, noodles, meat and fish dishes. During a meal people take great care that the bread basket is never empty. In Greece, using a piece of bread to dunk in the sauce or wipe your plate is understood as paying a compliment to a good and successful meal, and the Greeks prefer freshly baked bread for this purpose. Until the 1980s, light, white wheat bread was the favorite, and no other kind was eaten in many areas of Greece. Dark rye bread or even black bread has only recently appeared in Greece, where it is sold in health food stores.

Greeks have the highest level of bread consumption in Europe. They bake special bread for many important festivals, and give it appropriate names. They still use mainly wheat flour. Barley meal is used almost exclusively for making *paximádia* (dry bread or zwieback). Known in Byzantium as barley cracker and probably named after Paxamos, one of the later kings of ancient times, *paximádion* spread outward from Byzantium, like so many other luxury goods. The same word, the Greek *paximádia*, lies behind the Arabic *bashmat* or *baqsimat*, the Turkish *beksemad*, the Serbo-Croat *peksimet*, the Rumanian *pesmet*, or the Venetian *pasimata*.

Athenaeus, in his *Deipnosophistae* (109, b, c) has his character Pontianus describe a classification of bread by ingredients which he has read in *Plant Life* by the Alexandrian writer, Tryphon. "If I remember rightly," says Pontianus, "raised bread, unleavened bread, bread made with fine flour, with groats, with unbolted meal [...], bread made from rye, of spelt, and of millet. Tryphon says the groat-bread is made of rice-wheat, for it cannot be made of barley." Pontianus then goes on to mention other types, this time classified by how they are prepared. For instance there is oven-bread, which, he says, is referred to by a character in Timocles' play *The Sham Robbers*: "Seeing that a dough-pan fresh from the fire was lying there, I ate some of the oven-bread piping-hot." Then there is brazier-bread, mentioned by Antidotos in *The Chorus-Leader*. "He took some hot brazier-bread – why not? – and folding it over he dipped it into the sweet wine." (Gulick Loeb's translation, 1928)

THE OVEN NEXT TO THE HOUSE

In the agricultural areas of Thrace, people still have their own ovens, rather than using the baker's. Bread ovens can be as much as 6 feet 6½ feet (2 meters) high, and ideally have a base of 6 feet × 5½ feet (1.8 × 1.7 meters). The oven builder first builds a brick and cement base about 2½ feet (80 centimeters) high, which he fills with stones and earth. Then he stands on the base and builds up the oven from the inside. He leaves an opening on one side, through which he can climb out when the oven is finished, and through which the bread will later be pushed in. The oven is cleaned inside and out, and sometimes the outside is covered with colored tiles. As a rule, the building of a simple oven is completed in four days. The oven is fired by kindling a huge wood fire inside and, as soon as it has died down, the ashes and embers are cleared out, and the bread is baked in the heated chamber.

Below: Greek white bread is a pure wheat bread, and is eaten with all dishes.

HESTIA

Hestia was the eldest daughter of Cronos and Rhea, the parents of the gods, and was chosen to be the protectress of hearth and home, and of the fire which burned there. Later the goddess, called Vesta by the Romans, was elevated to goddess of the family and the house, and so she represents the basic idea of justice and protection in the home. She is the one who has all household activities and the entire household under her protection, offers people a place of calm around the home fire, and sees to it that there is plenty of food on the table. The Roman Vesta was so beloved that she was even appointed the mother of the city of Rome, projecting the cult of hearth and home onto the whole city. They did not erect magnificent shrines to her like those built for and dedicated to other gods, as the hearths in the houses were her

temples. Although Poseidon and the handsome Apollo both sought her hand, she remained a virgin all her life as a goddess. Her priestesses too, known as Vestal Virgins in Rome, vowed to renounce marriage in her honor.

PSOMÍ
Bread

2⅓ cups/400 g wheat flour
1½ cakes/20 g fresh yeast
2 tsp sugar
2 tsp salt
1 tbsp olive oil

Sift the flour into a bowl and prepare the starter yeast: ½ cup/150 ml lukewarm water, sugar, salt, and some of the flour. Cover the bowl with a cloth and allow the starter to rise for 15 minutes. Knead the remaining flour into the starter dough, cover, and let rise for 20 minutes. Work in a further ½ cup/150 ml warm water, then turn the dough out onto a floured work surface and knead for 10 minutes. Work in the olive oil, replace the dough in the bowl, cover, and allow to rise until it has doubled in volume. Preheat the oven to 350 °F (180 °C). Knead the dough briefly one more time and bake, either in a greased baking pan (20–30 minutes), or shaped into loaves on a baking sheet lined with baking parchment (8–10 minutes). The bread should be crisp on the outside and soft and white inside.

The globular portions of kneaded dough are left to rise for a time, then formed into the required shape, which often varies with the region.

The longish pieces of dough are placed in baking pans, so they keep their shape during baking, and they all look alike when they come out of the oven.

The freshly baked bread is placed in big baskets according to type, and these stand on the bakery floor, where everyone can reach them. The customers themselves can dip into the baskets and choose the right bread for the day.

Litouryá is a loaf baked at home and brought to the church, where it is blessed during the liturgy. Before baking, a big round stamp …

… is pressed into the dough. A Byzantine cross is carved into the stamp, with letters standing for *Yisús Christós Niká* (Jesus Christ is victorious). After the liturgy…

… and the blessing, the bread is broken by the priest and offered with wine for Communion. The bread and wine become the living body and blood of Christ.

SPECIAL OCCASION BREAD

January 1: *Vasilópsomo*

Carnival: *lagána, litouryá* (bread that has been blessed; see illustration left)

Eight days before Easter: for the feast of St. Lazarus, *lázari*, small, filled, sugar-glazed pastries are distributed to the children on Amorgós.

At the beginning of Lent: *kyria sarakosti* ("woman 40") are baked, a bread shaped something like a woman with six legs which symbolizes the six weeks of fasting before Easter.

Easter Sunday: *lambrópsomo fanourópsomo* – a cake honoring St. Fanourios, who helps to find lost articles.

Beginning of June: on Sifnos, for the feast of the Holy Spirit, there is a loaf in the shape of a dove.

Christmas: *christópsomo*. At Christmas, there are also *lalangia* from Mani, strips of fried dough with honey and nuts. They are supposed to drive away evil spirits.

New Year: *vasilópita* is a sweet nut cake with a coin in the dough. In Epirus *vasilópita* is salty and filled with meat.

Weddings: in Annoia on Crete the women bake a special wreath of bread, garnished with roses, lemon flowers, pomegranate seeds, and grapes, and decorate it with snake and bird motifs. It is said to bring good fortune.

Eptásimo ("seven times kneaded"): A bread from Chalkidiki and Crete. There they have small dry rings made from barley meal which are not easy to prepare. That is because you must not tell anyone when you are baking them, otherwise a curse will come

upon them and the dough will not rise. No-one believes it but, strangely enough, this dough is usually made at night, when most people are fast asleep.

Psomomakárona (bread macaroni from Rhodes): dry bread, boiled with broth and sprinkled with goat's milk cheese.

Krasópita: bread dipped in wine, eaten with a meal.

Poutinga (from the Ionian Islands): this is a bread pudding made with sweet wine.

Zoúpa (soup) from Cephalonia: a dish made with bread that the ancient Greeks ate for breakfast. Nowadays, during the olive harvest, the farmers eat a toasted, dark rye bread, moistened with hot red wine and with olive oil poured over it.

Christópsomo

Vasilópita

Litouryá

Elliniko

Agiorítiko

Eptásimo

Vasilópsomo

Prosími

Lagána

Khoriatiko

Kyria sarakosti

Lázari

Cretan wedding bread

CORN

In country areas, corn bread still offers an alternative to the usual wheat bread. Sometimes corn meal is mixed with wheat flour when baking bread. You can easily tell if a loaf contains any corn by the delicate yellow color of the crumbs. A well-known specialty from northern Greece is *bobóta*, a savory cake of cornmeal, cheese, and eggs, which is first boiled and then baked. It exists in a number of variations; for example, after boiling, the paste may be mixed with sheep's cheese and a little dill. Other variable ingredients are spinach, wild herbs, and *trakhanás*. Bakers use whatever is in season. Sweet *bobóta* can have raisins or chopped pumpkin flesh mixed in during cooking, according to taste.

The first corn, or maize, was brought back to Europe by the Spanish conquistadors after the discovery of America. The details of how corn (*Zea mays*) then arrived in Greece are now impossible to trace. It was cultivated in Mexico as long ago as 3000 B.C. Although the approximately 6 feet (2 meter) tall plant is considered one of the world's most important agricultural crops, in Greece it is still treated as a poor relation compared with other kinds of vegetables. There is a distinction between forage maize and

Above: in many places, freshly picked corn is still laid out in the farmyards to dry, just as it was in this old photograph.

sweet corn, which has only been grown here since about the middle of the 19th century. Thracian farmers sow both kinds at the end of April and beginning of May, in rows 2½ feet (80 centimeters) apart. Because corn thrives particularly well in temperate, not-too-dry regions, the western side of Thrace, which is close to the sea, offers better growing conditions than many other parts of Greece, especially as corn makes the most intensive demands on the soil of all grain crops. The majority of land is still reserved for forage maize for cattle feed, but more and more farmers are growing sweet corn, as it is now highly valued in Greece as a healthy snack between meals. You can buy charcoal-roasted corn from street stalls, just like chestnuts, especially in the cities, and hold it in your hand while you munch the kernels off the cob. The scent of roasting corn travels a long way, and if you follow your nose, it will take you straight to a corn vendor. Another important use for corn is in the manufacture of cooking oil. The kernels that accumulate during the production of cornmeal and corn starch are pressed after soaking to obtain the corn oil, which is valued as a health food. It provides a good alternative to the widely used olive oil.

BOBÓTA GLIKIÁ
Sweet corn cakes

6 cups/1 kg cornmeal
2 tsp baking powder
1 tsp ground cinnamon
Sugar or honey
½ cup + 2 tbsp/150 g butter
Sesame seeds
Salt

Preheat the oven to 375 °F (190 °C). Heat about 8 cups of water in a pan. Combine the corn meal and baking powder and stir into the boiling water. Add a pinch of salt, a little cinnamon, and sugar or honey to taste, and cook until a fluid paste is formed. Add the butter and simmer for a few minutes, stirring continuously. Remove from the heat and allow to cool a little. Pour the mixture into a greased, deep baking pan. Sprinkle with sesame seeds and bake for about 30 minutes in the preheated oven until golden brown. Remove from the oven, allow to cool a little, cut into large portions and serve while still warm.
If desired, raisins or finely chopped pumpkin flesh can be added to the mixture.

A corn cob is only ripe when the leaves of its outer husk are almost withered and can easily be pulled off.

This old corn mill gives a vivid impression of how hard it was to process corn without modern machinery.

All the major oil companies in Greece now produce nutritious corn oil as an alternative to their high quality olive oil. Corn oil can be recognized by its bright yellow color. Its flavor is easily distinguishable from other vegetable oils, mainly by its much sweeter taste.

TRAKHANÁS

Trakhanás is the oldest recorded Greek soup. This dish of coarsely ground wheat and goat's milk was already known in ancient Greece. Today *trakhanás* is known as wheat and sour milk soup, but it is rarely found on the menu, because it is thought of as poor people's food. Its basic constituent keeps for a long time and, eaten as a fortifying soup in winter, it can work miracles. Nowadays you can only get *trakhanás* in the country areas of Thrace and Epirus, whereas in Cyprus it is virtually considered a national dish. *Trakhanás* was originally made from leftover milk, because that was a way of conserving it. However, in these days of European overproduction, that is no longer of concern. If you want to make your own sour milk, mix one cup (250ml) of milk in a pan with a pinch each of salt and powdered rennin, and leave it for three days. Then stir the milk and set aside again. On the fourth day, you add another cup (250ml) of milk, on the fifth day, two cups (500ml), and on the sixth a little more, depending on how sour the milk has become. When the sour milk is ready, it is mixed with coarsely ground wheat in a proportion of two to one and boiled over a very low heat, while stirring continuously, until a paste is formed that is firm enough to cut with a knife. This is divided into evenly sized pieces, which are then dried in the sun for four or five days. If kept in airtight containers, they will keep for a long time, and can be boiled up to make soup all during the year. If you prefer, you can also crumble the pieces. In many parts of Greece, yogurt is used for *trakhanás* instead of sour milk.

TRAKHANÁS
Wheat and sour milk soup

6 oz/150 g trakhanás
1 large onion, finely chopped
½ lb/200 g tomatoes, peeled and puréed
A generous ½ cup/130 g butter
4 cups/1 liter meat stock
½ tsp dried thyme
1 bunch flat-leaved parsley, chopped
1½ cups/100 g kefalotíri cheese, grated
Salt
Freshly ground black pepper

Heat the butter in a pan and sauté the onion. Mix in the tomatoes and simmer briefly. Pour over the meat stock, add the thyme, and bring to a boil. Slowly pour in the *trakhanás*, stirring continuously. Cover and simmer over a low heat for about 20 minutes, until the soup becomes creamy, stirring occasionally. Add parsley, salt, and pepper, ladle into plates and sprinkle with grated cheese.

KÓLIVA

8½ cups/1 kg wheat grains
Breadcrumbs
Raisins
Chopped walnuts
Grated almonds
Grated hazelnuts
Sesame seeds
Sugar
Pomegranate seeds
Cinnamon
Confectioner's sugar
Salt
Whole almonds and walnuts for garnishing

Wash the wheat, cover with water, add a little salt, and boil for 10 minutes. Cover the pan and let it stand in a warm place overnight for the wheat to swell.

Next day, drain the wheat thoroughly and transfer it to a bowl. Add sufficient breadcrumbs to absorb the remaining moisture from the wheat. Mix in the remaining ingredients. The proportions of the individual ingredients are variable and can be adjusted according to taste. Transfer the *kóliva* to a decorative bowl, distribute evenly, press down, and sprinkle with confectioner's sugar. Finally, decorate the top with whole almonds, walnuts, or raisins.

KÓLIVA – IN MEMORY OF THE DEAD

Kóliva is a death ritual, which, like many other traditional customs, has pagan origins. On the commemoration day, the friends and relatives of the deceased gather at the grave, and an Orthodox priest is present to guarantee the blessing of the Church. A big tray of *kóliva*, a mixture of soaked wheat grains, raisins, nuts, pomegranate seeds, cinnamon, and sugar, is brought by the relatives and distributed to those present at the end of the religious ceremony. This ritual is reminiscent of ancient funeral feasts, such as the *anthesteria*, at which men tried to put the dead and Hermes, who guided them, in a merciful mood by setting out barrels full of the cooked fruits of the earth. Nowadays, the swelling grain symbolizes the body, which is laid in the earth so that it can rise again on the Day of Judgment.

SWEET SEMOLINA

One of the Greeks' favorite desserts is pan-fried semolina *khalvás*. It is made from wheat semolina, cinnamon, sugar, and nuts, and tastes particularly good when still warm. From here to the syrup-soaked semolina cake *revaní* (see page 261) is only a small step, consisting basically of the addition of eggs.

KHALVÁS ME SIMIGDÁLI
Semolina halva

3⅓ cups/750 g sugar
1 cup/250 ml oil
1½ cups/250 g fine semolina
1½ cups/250 g coarse semolina
Ground cinnamon

Put the sugar in a pan, add 4 cups/1 liter water and bring to a boil, stirring continuously, to make a syrup. In a second pan, heat the oil very hot and add both kinds of semolina. Stir continuously until the semolina is evenly browned. Now pour the syrup over the semolina. Add cinnamon to taste and simmer, stirring continuously, until the mixture has thickened (*khalvás* should come away easily from the pan). Transfer the mixture to a bowl and allow to cool. Then turn it onto a plate and sprinkle with a little cinnamon. The basic recipe can be augmented with chopped nuts to add more texture if desired.

TRADITIONAL EMBROIDERY

Traditional Thracian embroidery can be divided into two basic categories according to use. In one there are household textiles, such as tablecloths, napkins, cushions, runners for the tops of kitchen cabinets, and bed linen; in the other is embroidery forming part of women's costumes. Most embroidery is done with silk or cotton on linen. The yarns are colored red, green, blue, yellow, and black using natural dyes. The motifs used in these embroideries are texts and geometrical patterns. The amazing skill of the women really becomes apparent when you look at the back of the work, which presents exactly the same picture as the front.

SUNFLOWER POWER

In Greece, sunflowers grow mainly in the eastern part of Thrace. There are some 25,000 acres (10,000 hectares) of *Helianthus annuus*, one of the most attractive plants in this thinly populated area of Greece and, unlike other, less spectacular crops, it is a real experience to see them at flowering time. The harvest takes place every year at the beginning of July. Those farmers who only grow small amounts of sunflowers sometimes still gather the seeds by hand, whereas on large areas of cultivation, they have converted to the use of agricultural machinery. Sunflowers are annual, fast-growing plants that can reach as much as 16 feet (5 meters) in height, with hairy stems and equally rough-haired oval or heart-shaped leaves, which can grow to a length of up to 16 inches (40 centimeters). In early summer they produce daisy-like flower heads up to 1 foot (30 centimeters) in diameter, composed of tiny yellow ligulate petals and brown to purple tubiflorae. The seeds (in botanical terms: achene) ripening inside them contain 50 percent oil and about 27 percent protein and lecithin, and are a very valuable source of edible oil. Sunflowers are grown for commercial use particularly in southeast Europe, France, China, North America, and Argentina. Three large sunflower oil companies have set up business in Thrace in the last few years, so the seeds are processed on site immediately after the harvest. The seeds are made into sunflower oil and margarine, but they can also be cleaned and packed, hulled or unhulled, for both the local and the international market. The unhulled seeds are roasted and salted rather like peanuts so that they will keep longer. Although this means they lose some of their taste, it gives them a delicate, spicy flavor. Hulled seeds can be stored for up to a year, and like walnuts and almonds, they have many uses.

SPÓRIA

Along with white pumpkin seeds, *spória*, sunflower seeds, are a favorite snack in Greece. They are sold in the streets in little bags and eaten walking along or in a free moment. Most Greeks are very skilled at opening the seed cases. There are said to be Graecophiles, who have made tireless efforts to acquire this culinary skill before giving up in despair, because you either learn the art of cracking *spória* as a child or not at all. In theory it sounds easier than it actually is. You put the sunflower seed between your front teeth, pointed end forward, and bite carefully to open it up. If the husk is half open, you skillfully remove the kernel with your tongue. That's all there is to it!

Spória, sunflower seeds, are sold in the streets of Greece in little bags and nibbled immediately while walking along or in a spare moment.

SUNFLOWER OIL

High quality sunflower oil is produced by cold pressing sunflower seeds. It is a pale yellow, pleasant smelling oil with a high fat content, and is considered to be one of the most biologically valuable oils. It contains saturated fatty acids of palmitic, stearic, and oleic acid, and unsaturated fatty acids of linolenic and oleic acid. Sunflower oil is used in Greece as an alternative to olive oil, especially in salads and in cooking vegetable stews, but should not be heated too long. Sunflower oil also provides the raw material for the production of margarine and spreads.

PASTOURMÁS

Pastourmás is made from beef from the back of the animal. The meat is separated from the bone and the attached fat completely removed. The meat is then marinated in brine for two to three days, after which it is removed from the brine, wrapped in cloths, and dried thoroughly. The meat must be left for 24 hours, pressed down by a thick piece of wood. Meanwhile, a spreadable paste is made out of garlic, black and red pepper, a little flour, and fenugreek. This is spread evenly and relatively thickly over the meat, covering it completely. The meat must be stored in a cool place in this dry marinade for at least three weeks, so that it takes in as much of the flavor of the herbs and spices as possible. After that it is ready for use.

Pastourmás is cut in wafer thin slices and served as an appetizer with wine or ouzo. Cypriots know *pastourmás* as a kind of sausage, seasoned with hot pepper and fennel, which can be served as a spicy accompaniment to any kind of appetizer.

Pastourmás was evidently not known to Homer, though he writes in detail about Thrace and the horse breeders there, whose white horses were held in very high esteem and considered valuable gifts, not only by the Thracians. Homer could not have been familiar with smoked beef either, as it was brought to Thrace more recently by Greeks from Asia Minor.

The boundaries of Thrace were redrawn in July 1923 under the Treaty of Lausanne, and a large-scale exchange of populations between Greece and Turkey was agreed upon. Over one million Greeks had to leave their homes in Asia Minor, and in return 500,000 Turks left northern Greece – 380,000 Turks and 50,000 Bulgars emigrated from Thrace alone. This forced resettlement not only gave rise to a merging of ancestral ways of life, but also resulted in changes in the agriculture and traditional cuisine of Thrace. For instance, the newcomers of Greek ancestry arriving from Turkey not only drained the low-lying, wetland areas near the coast in order to grow the famous Turkish tobacco, they also brought with them their accustomed specialty dishes, such as *pastourmás*.

EASTERN CHRISTMAS

In Greece, Orthodox Christians celebrate Christmas by going to church and with festive food. But there are no special duties or lavish family reunions, even if the obligatory giving of Christmas presents has gradually found its way to Greece, as it has all over the world.

In some parts of Thrace, special Christmas games have developed. For instance, on December 24, thirteen young men (*rougat-sádes*) walk through the town singing, twelve of them dressed as disciples, the thirteenth as Christ himself. By way of thanks the young men receive a financial reward, as they are all just about to be called up for military service. On the other hand, *kálanta*, Christmas carols, no different from those of Western Europe, are sung all over Greece. Children go into shops and houses and wish the owners a year full of blessings, and in return they too are given money and candies. On December 25, the only day when all the family gets together, the *galopoúla*, stuffed turkey, is roasted in ovens everywhere, and for dessert there are Greek Christmas cookies, *melomakárona* (honey macaroons).

The most important winter festival in Greece is the New Year, beginning on New Year's Eve with the New Year cake *vasilópita*. The first festival on the Greek calendar is marked by honoring St. Vasilios (Santa Claus), who comes down to earth on that day. *Vasilópita* can be made as a Madeira sponge or a puff pastry cake with nuts, or in a savory version with meat, and a coin is hidden in the cake after baking. The

cake is cut on New Year's Eve, with all the family present. The pieces are distributed in a pre-determined order: the first is for Christ, the second for Mary, the third for St. Vasilios, the fourth for the house, the fifth for the head of the family, the sixth for the mother, then one for each of the children. A piece is also cut for each absent member of the family. Whoever finds the coin can look forward to special success in the coming year.

VASILÓPITA
New Year Cake
(Illustration facing page, top)

8½ cups/1 kg wheat flour
2 tbsp baking powder
1 tsp salt
1 cup + 2 tbsp/250 g butter, at room temperature
2¼ cups/500 g sugar
4 eggs
1¼–1½ cups/300–350 ml milk
Rind of 1 unwaxed lemon, grated
Confectioner's sugar

Sift the flour, baking powder, and salt into a bowl. Cream together the softened butter and sugar, and beat the eggs into the mixture one at a time. Gradually stir in the milk and the flour. Mix to a smooth dough, and flavor with grated lemon rind. Preheat the oven to 350 °F (180 °C). Line a 12-inch diameter (30 centimeter) baking pan with baking parchment, put in the dough, smooth it over, and bake in the preheated oven for 40 minutes, until the cake begins to brown. Turn out the cake, allow it to cool, and dust with confectioner's sugar. Finally hide a coin in it from underneath.

MELOMAKÁRONA
Christmas cookies
(Illustration facing page, bottom left)

For the dough:
18 cups/2 kg wheat flour
2 tsp baking powder
1 tsp baking soda
1 generous cup/250 g sugar
1⅔ cups/400 ml olive oil
⅔ cup/150 ml orange juice
3–4 tbsp/50 ml brandy

For the syrup:
1½ cups/500 g honey
2¼ cups/500 g sugar
2 cups/500 ml water

To decorate:
1½ cups/100 g chopped walnuts
Ground cinnamon

Preheat the oven to 350 °F (180 °C). Sift the flour, baking powder, and baking soda into a bowl, and repeat the process twice. In a second bowl, mix the sugar with the olive oil, orange juice, and brandy. Add the mixture to the flour, and work into a malleable dough. Line a baking sheet with parchment, shape the dough into small, elongated balls, and arrange on the baking sheet, gently pressing them flat. Bake in the preheated oven for about 30 minutes. Meanwhile, dissolve the honey and sugar in water and boil down for about 5 minutes. While the cookies are still warm, place them in a bowl and pour over the syrup. After 15 minutes, take out the cookies, arrange on a serving dish, and sprinkle with cinnamon and walnuts. (Makes about 40).

Left: a selection of modern Christmas decorations.
Right: a festively decorated Christmas table would not be complete if even one of these dishes were missing.

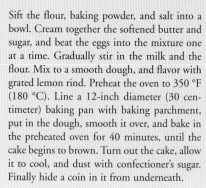

GALOPOÚLA
Stuffed turkey

1 turkey, about 11 lbs/5 kg in weight
1 large onion, finely chopped
½ lb/250 g ground beef
½ lb/250 g ground pork
2 tbsp/25 g cooked ham, chopped
1 tbsp fresh sage, finely chopped
1 scant cup/200 ml sweet white wine
½ cup/100 g fine noodles
1 cup/200 g rice
½ cup/80 g raisins
¾ cup/100 g pine nuts
1 medium apple, peeled, cored, and chopped
2 cups/300 g boiled or roasted chestnuts
1 scant cup/200 g butter
1 scant cup/200 ml mavrodaphne
   (red fortified wine)
Salt
Freshly ground black pepper

Remove the giblets from the turkey and set aside. Clip the tips of the wings and cut the neck off short. Wash the turkey and rub with salt and pepper. For the stuffing: cut the giblets in small pieces and fry in oil with the onion, ground meat, and ham. Boil the sage in water, add the white wine, and pour over the giblets. Add the noodles, rice, raisins, pine kernels, and apple, pour over the water and cook for 15 minutes. Finally stir in the chestnuts and season with salt and pepper. Preheat the oven to 350 °F (180 °C). Stuff the turkey with the mixture, place in a large roasting pan and cook in the preheated oven for 1½–2 hours. Melt the butter, mix with a little water, and baste the turkey with it every 30 minutes.
Place the roasted turkey on a large serving platter, stir the wine into the oven juices, bring to a boil, and pour over the turkey.

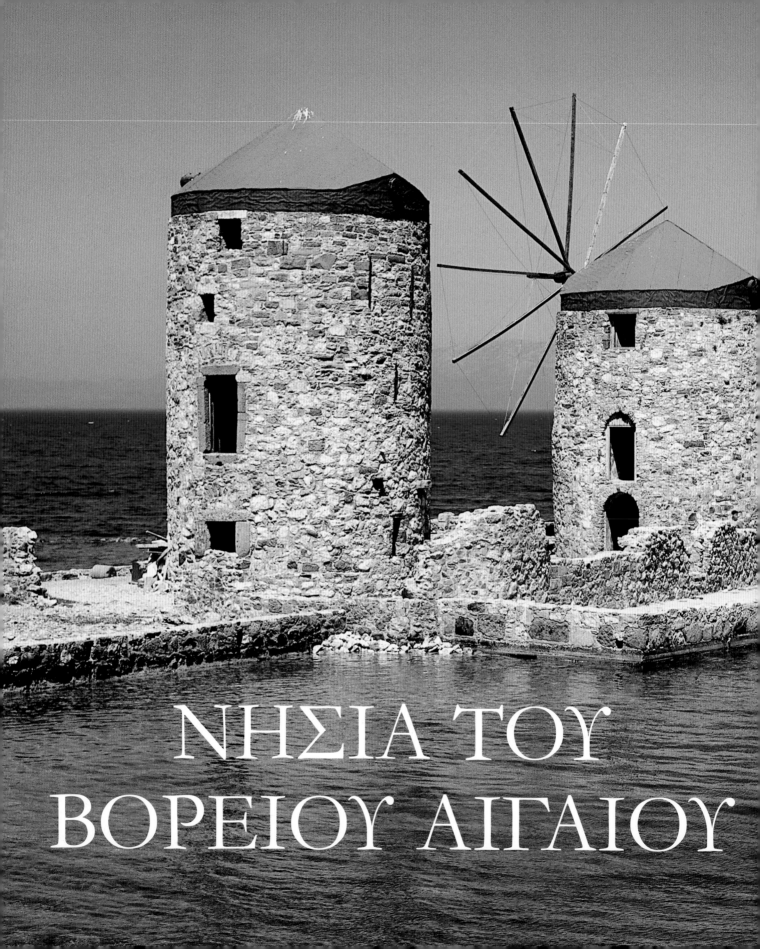

ΝΗΣΙΑ ΤΟΥ ΒΟΡΕΙΟΥ ΑΙΓΑΙΟΥ

Above: in Pyrgi and Chios, many houses are decorated with frescos in geometric patterns.
Background: old windmills in the city of Chios.

NORTH AEGEAN ISLANDS

Of crayfish and sardines

Wines of the North Aegean

Island variations

The heart of ouzo

Ouzo

Mastic

Goatkeeping

Filáki

Saint's day festivals

Five large and innumerable small islands at the eastern edge of the North Aegean Sea form the border between Greece and Asia Minor. If all of them except Samos are merely white dots on the map for most Western European holidaymakers, it probably is not just because of their position. It is also because of the very short summers and the infamous *meltémi*, the very strong, cold wind, which even in high summer can reach force nine here and bring shipping traffic to a standstill for days on end. This has meant that the North Aegean Islands have so far remained relatively untouched. There is also the fact that the islands – which do not constitute a single historic or cultural entity like the Cyclades, for instance – did not become a part of independent Greece until the 20th century. Lesbos, Chios, and Samos are geologically a part of the mainland of Asia Minor, which can be seen from there, and the main cities of Chios and Lesbos have an oriental atmosphere that you can almost taste. Over the centuries their cooks have created fascinating mixtures of Greek, Venetian, and Turkish elements, which are particularly appealing because each island's cuisine has a different individual emphasis distinguishing it from the others.

The islands that are farthest from one another, Limnos and Samos, have been famous for their wine since ancient times. One of the best-known vineyard sites in Greece is located on Samos and exports Samos Muscat, one of the best muscat wines, throughout the world. On the island of Limnos, the legendary home of Hephaeistos, god of fire and blacksmiths, they also sell an outstanding muscat, which is converted into both a dry and a fortified wine. On the island of Lesbos, which is covered with olive groves and pine forests, there is a sizeable olive-growing industry, and also one of the oldest centers in Greece for the production of ouzo. Since the early Middle Ages, Chios has had the greatest acreage of mastic trees in Europe. They now number two million, and their coveted golden resin is exported throughout the world. The biggest shipowning families in Greece also come from Chios and the small neighboring island of Inusses. They have now settled in America, and only visit their native islands on vacation. The image of the island of Ikaría is characterized by wild, romantic landscapes and chestnut forests.

When the fishermen speak of *astakós*, confusion is bound to follow, as the word means both lobster and crayfish in Greek. The connoisseur sees the distinction immediately: if it does not have claws, it is not a lobster.

ASTAKÓS SKHÁRAS
Grilled crayfish

2 crayfish
Juice of 1 lemon
1 lemon, quartered
Salt
Freshly ground black pepper

Divide the boiled crayfish lengthways, using a sharp knife. Season the meat with salt and pepper and place the halves, shell down, on the charcoal grill. Grill for about 20 minutes. Arrange on a serving plate, pour over the lemon juice and garnish with lemon quarters.

OF CRAYFISH...

The much sought-after European lobster (*Homarus gammarus*) is comparatively rare in Greece, even though it was widespread and popular in ancient times. Aristotle's zoological writings include detailed descriptions of its shape and color, and the places where it was caught. Nowadays it only occurs in a few places in the Mediterranean, and its actual habitat is known only to a few fishermen. There were said to be fishermen who took their knowledge with them to the grave, because they were afraid that otherwise the lobster would completely die out. Anyone ordering lobster in Greece today should not be surprised to be served crayfish instead, as in Greece the name *astakós* applies to both the common lobster and the crayfish. Gourmets are in total disagreement as to which has better tasting meat. If you ordered crayfish, you are highly likely to be served *Palinurus elephas*, the European crayfish or spiny lobster. It is easily recognizable by its brick-red color and the light patches on its sides and abdomen. These creatures, which in exceptional cases can grow up to 20 inches (50 centimeters) long, are on average 12 inches (30 centimeters) in length and require about 30 minutes cooking time. In contrast to lobsters, crayfish have to manage without the two powerful claws, which makes it easy to distinguish between the two. Unlike lobsters, they prefer comparatively warm waters.

ASTAKÓS MAYÁTIKOS
Crayfish with vegetables

1 crayfish, weighing about 2½ lbs/1.2 kg
1 scant cup/200 ml Greek extra virgin olive oil
5 scallions, cut in rings
1 lb/500 g tomatoes, peeled and diced
1 bunch dill, finely chopped
1 bunch flat-leaved parsley, finely chopped
1 lemon, sliced
Salt
Freshly ground black pepper

Put the crayfish head first into boiling salted water and boil for 20 minutes. Lift out the crayfish and reserve 1 scant cup/200 ml of the stock. Remove the meat from the shell and slice. Heat the olive oil in a pan and sauté the scallion rings. Add the tomatoes, dill, and parsley, stir thoroughly, and pour in the stock. Simmer for about 20 minutes over a medium heat, until the water has almost evaporated. Add salt and pepper to taste, lay the crayfish slices on the bed of vegetables, and simmer for a further 5 minutes. Arrange on a serving plate, garnish with lemon slices, and serve hot.

Despite the animal protectionists, crayfish, like all crab and lobster species, are still dropped head first, live, into boiling water.

AND SARDINES

The sardine (*Sardina pilchardus*) is definitely one Greek fish specialty that is quick and uncomplicated to prepare. It makes life easy for those not used to eating fish, as its bones are thin and delicate and can usually be chewed when small, so there is no need for troublesome filleting. Although the Greeks usually prefer their fish grilled, sardines are often fried in plenty of hot olive oil. After washing them carefully, you cut them open along the belly and carefully remove all the entrails. The sardines are then lightly salted, tossed in flour, then dropped straight into the hot olive oil and fried golden brown. With a glass of ouzo, the traditional Greek anise liqueur, they can become a highly promising appetizer. Sardines play an important role in the fish processing industry, because they can be marketed in a huge variety of ways: with or without skins, with or without bones, smoked, fried, preserved in oil, in sauce, or in brine. Sardines, which are among the most common fish, usually guarantee fishermen a secure income, because you can still always count on a rich haul of sardines – the current annual catch in the Mediterranean is 275,000 US tons (250,000 tonnes).

The simplest fish course in the world consists of freshly caught sardines, which are first carefully washed.

North Aegean cooks then toss their sardines in flour, so they get nice and crisp.

Finally, the sardines are fried in hot oil. That's all. Except for serving (see below).

GÁVROS STO FOÚRNO
Baked sardines

About 2 lbs/1 kg sardines
1 scant cup/200 ml Greek extra virgin olive oil
¾ cup/100 g black olives, pitted and
finely chopped
4 cloves garlic, thinly sliced
1 tsp dried oregano
Juice of 2 lemons
Salt
Freshly ground black pepper

Preheat the oven to 350 ºF (180 ºC). Remove the heads from the sardines, cut open the fish along the belly and remove the entrails and backbones. Wash thoroughly, press open a little and place in an ovenproof dish greased with olive oil. Season with salt and pepper, and sprinkle with black olives, garlic, and oregano. Pour the remaining olive oil and lemon juice over the fish and bake for 40–50 minutes in the preheated oven. Serve hot with fresh salad.

The white Moscato grape, which is native to Samos, is mostly made into aromatic fortified wines.

BAKED ONIONS

At grape harvest time on Samos, whole onions are served, which are put into the oven unpeeled. This gives them more flavor, and they are not peeled until after they have been baked.

Samos Vin Doux: a fine quality wine with just a touch of roses and chamomile.

Samos Anthemis: an aromatic fortified wine, which matures for up to five years in oak barrels.

Samos Nectar: a deliciously sweet "*vin naturellement doux*," matured in oak for two or three years.

Samos Grand Cru: a "*vin doux naturel*" with lively acidity, this is the company's top product.

Samena Golden: the first modern dry muscat white wine, this has a very refreshing acidity.

Samos Nectar: a deep golden "*vin naturellement doux*" that is made from sun-dried grapes.

Samos Grand Cru: "*vin doux naturel*" from the small-fruited variety "Muscat à petits grains."

Samos Vin Doux: a golden yellow, fruity fortified wine, with the scent of Muscat grapes.

WINES OF THE NORTH AEGEAN

Two of the most famous Greek wines have been produced on the North Aegean islands since antiquity. Limnos, the most northerly island, is the home of the Limnio grape, which has now conquered the mainland as well, and there produces full-bodied wines with distinctive acidity. This variety, which Aristotle called *lemnia*, is a rather rustic, unconventional variety, with spicy nuances of sage and bay. The island's *appellation controlée* wines are pressed from Moscato grapes. "Limnos Muscat" is an outstandingly delicate fortified wine, whereas very little of the dry version is exported. Almost all is drunk on the island.

Samos also has one of the best-known vineyard areas in Greece. The 3700 acre (1500 hectare) area of cultivation produces one of the best Muscat wines in the world. The vineyards, which are frequently terraced and often only two rows wide, reach an altitude of up to 2600 feet (800 meters) and produce grapes with very different degrees of maturity. The appellation "Samos Muscat" may only be pressed from the variety "Muscat blanc à petits grains" (Moscato Samou), which thrives in 98 percent of the cultivated area.

Several variations of "Samos Muscat" are sold. "Samos Doux" is a fortified or dessert wine, that is, a wine that has alcohol added before fermentation, while "Samos Vin Doux Naturel" is a naturally sweet wine, whose fermentation is halted by the addition of ethyl alcohol, so that the wine keeps part of its natural sugar and is guaranteed not to turn to vinegar. Some good white wines are also made on Samos from Muscatel grapes.

The wine cooperative Samos (EOSS), founded in 1934, which all winegrowers on Samos belong to, is probably the best organized cooperative in Greece and has the absolute monopoly for the appellation. Since then, a large French customer (La Martinique) has bought two thirds of their production each year; indeed, France was already a major purchaser under Louis XVI. In Germany there was great interest in sweet Greek wines some 40 years ago, as they were used as the basis for a medicinal syrup for the circulation. Even the Roman Catholic Church obtained its communion wine exclusively from Samos. Nowadays communion wine from Samos is only exported to Austria, Belgium, and Switzerland. Some is made into Metaxa and sold to local restaurateurs. Sweet Samos is best drunk as an aperitif or as an accompaniment to spicy cheeses, nuts, and fruit salad.

ISLAND VARIATIONS

Food on the North Aegean islands is as rich and varied as the islands themselves, but having it freshly prepared is always at the forefront. The inhabitants prefer simple vegetable dishes that do not take too long to cook, but though meals are quickly prepared, they are eaten slowly to make up for it. Preferring to invest the time they saved in the preparation in eating, the inhabitants leave themselves as much time as they possibly can. Depending on the time of year and what vegetables are available on the islands, they eat soups, vegetable stews, meat, and fish. Large quantities of meat are only brought in from elsewhere for foreigners in the tourist season. And the fishermen prefer to sell the dwindling supplies of fish to restaurants, because the catering trade is prepared to pay much higher prices. Fresh vegetable stews and light, carefully prepared rice dishes are part of the islanders' everyday culinary life, and are served hot, or even chilled on very hot days.

KOLOKITHOLOÚLOUDA YEMISTÁ
Stuffed zucchini flowers

12–16 zucchini flowers
A generous ⅖ cup/100 ml Greek extra virgin olive oil
2 onions, finely chopped
½ bunch flat-leaved parsley
1 bunch dill
1 cup/200 g rice
Salt and freshly ground black pepper

Briefly dip the zucchini flowers in water and pat dry with paper towels. Carefully open out the petals and remove the pistils. Heat the olive oil in a pan and sauté the onions. Add the parsley and dill, and pour over 2 cups/500 ml of water (or vegetable stock). As soon as the water boils, add the rice, but do not allow it to become completely soft. Season with salt and pepper. Fill the zucchini flowers with the mixture and carefully pull the tips of the petals together.
Place the zucchini flowers close together in a casserole, pour a little water over them, and place the dish over a medium heat until the rice is completely cooked. Serve hot or cold.

SOGÁNIA
Stuffed onions, Lesbos style
(Not illustrated)

4 large onions, peeled
1 scant cup/200 ml Greek extra virgin olive oil
1 lb/500 g ground beef
1 scant cup/200 ml dry red wine
2 tomatoes, peeled and diced
2–3 cloves garlic, finely chopped
2 bay leaves
Salt
Freshly ground black pepper

Preheat the oven to 350 ºF (180 ºC). Heat some water in a pan, boil the onions for a few minutes, remove, and allow to cool. Carefully remove the inside of the onions and chop finely. Place the hollowed onions in an earthenware dish brushed with olive oil. Heat the olive oil in a pan and brown the ground beef with the chopped onion. Pour over the red wine and add half the diced tomatoes, garlic, bay leaves, and a little water. Season with salt and pepper and cook until tender. Stuff the onions, and distribute any remaining filling around them. Drizzle with olive oil and sprinkle over the remainder of the diced tomatoes. Cook in the preheated oven until the onions are quite soft. Arrange the onions on plates, and pour over the juices if desired. Serve hot with freshly baked white bread.

PETALÍDES SAMIÓTIKES
Venus clams, Samos style
(Not illustrated)

About 2 lbs/1 kg small venus clams
1 scant cup/200 ml Greek extra virgin olive oil
2 onions, finely chopped
1 scant cup/200 ml dry red wine
4–5 tomatoes, peeled and diced
½ bunch parsley, finely chopped
Red wine vinegar
1 lb/500 g wide noodles
Salt
Freshly ground black pepper

Wash and clean the venus clams. Discard any that are damaged or do not react to pressure by closing. Heat the olive oil in a pan and sauté the onions. Add the clams and cook for 5 minutes over a medium heat until they open. Discard any that have not opened. Pour over the red wine, and add the tomatoes, parsley, and a shot of red wine vinegar. Season with salt and pepper and cook for 10 minutes. Meanwhile, heat some salted water in a pan and cook the noodles. Drain the noodles thoroughly and add to the clams. Arrange on plates and serve while hot.

BRIÁMI
Vegetable stew au gratin

1 lb/500 g zucchini, thinly sliced
1 lb/500 g potatoes, peeled and thinly sliced
1 lb/500 g eggplant, thinly sliced
1 lb/500 g tomatoes, peeled and diced
2 onions, cut in rings
1 green pepper, cut in strips
½ bunch flat-leaved parsley, finely chopped
½ tsp dried oregano
½ tsp dried thyme
1 cup/250 ml Greek extra virgin olive oil
1¼ cups/200 g sheep's cheese, crumbled
Salt
Freshly ground black pepper

Preheat the oven to 350 ºF (180 ºC). Place all of the prepared vegetables in an ovenproof dish and season with parsley, oregano, thyme, salt, and pepper. Mix the vegetables and herbs well, and pour the olive oil and 1 cup/250 ml water over them. Cook for about 1½ hours in the preheated oven, adding water if necessary. Shortly before the end of the cooking time, sprinkle with the sheep's cheese and place under the broiler. Serve hot with freshly baked white bread.

PIPERIÉS YEMISTÉS
Stuffed bell peppers

4 large bell peppers
1 cup/250 ml Greek extra virgin olive oil
1 large onion, finely chopped
3 sprigs parsley, finely chopped
½ bunch dill, finely chopped
3 sprigs mint, finely chopped
1 cup/200 g rice
1⅔ cups/400 ml tomato juice
1 tbsp tomato paste
Zwieback, grated
Salt
Freshly ground black pepper

Preheat the oven to 350 ºF (180 ºC). Wash the peppers, cut off a lid where the stem joins the fruit and set it aside, then remove the seeds. Heat half the olive oil in a pan and sauté the onions in it. Add the dill, parsley, mint and rice, stir thoroughly, and pour half the tomato juice and a little water over the rice. Stir in the tomato paste, season with salt and pepper, and partially cook the rice. Stuff the peppers with the rice mixture (remember, the rice will still swell a little), place on a baking sheet, and pour over a little water. Replace the lids on the peppers, pour over the remaining tomato juice and oil, and sprinkle with grated zwieback. Bake in the preheated oven until the rice and peppers are tender. This dish may be served hot or cold.

SPANAKÓRIZO
Rice with spinach

1 scant cup/200 ml Greek extra virgin olive oil
1 onion, finely chopped
A generous 2 lbs/1 kg spinach, washed and finely chopped
1 bunch dill, finely chopped
1¼ cups/250 g rice
Juice of 2 lemons
Salt
Freshly ground black pepper

Heat the olive oil in a pan and sauté the onions. Add the spinach, dill, and 2½ cups/600 ml of hot water and bring to a boil. Stir in the rice, and season with salt and pepper. Reduce the temperature and simmer over a low heat until the rice is cooked and all the water has been absorbed (adding boiling water if necessary). Pour over the lemon juice and stir. Serve hot.

THE HEART OF OUZO

Anise-flavored spirits have been widespread throughout the Mediterranean area probably ever since the days of Byzantine rule, and almost everywhere they enjoy the status of a national drink: raki in Turkey, sambuca in Italy, and pastis, especially in southern France, to name but a few. In this case, as with many herb-flavored spirits, the original idea behind it may have been to capture and preserve in alcohol the effectiveness of a valued medicinal herb, as anise (*Pimpinella anisum*) had already reached Greece from the Orient in ancient times by way of Egypt and Crete, and was equally valued as both a herb and a medicine.

If ouzo and tsípouro, which is also an anise-flavored Greek spirit (see pages 62–63), were originally distilled in small concerns and by Greek winegrowers trying to augment their meager incomes a little, production now takes place in large distilleries all over Greece. Ouzo production on the North Aegean island of Lesbos can be considered to exemplify the highest level of the distillers' art. Each company has its own production methods and uses its own carefully guarded recipes.

Ouzo is based on pure alcohol from various sources. It could, for instance, be a distillation of molasses produced during sugar manufacture. The alcohol is diluted with water, then the herbs are added. As well as the obligatory anise, these can also include fennel seeds, star aniseed, coriander, cardamom, and others. Here on Lesbos, a trace of mastic is also part of the recipe (see pages 332–333). This mixture is left to stand overnight, so the herbs can release their flavors into the mixture of water and alcohol. On the next day it is distilled several times in huge copper vats (distillation tanks). Copper provides the best conditions for distillation, as it guarantees an even temperature in the container, which is of absolutely crucial importance for the way the aroma develops in any distilled product. The first part of the distillation is called the forerun or head (Greek *kefáli*). The result will not be satisfactory, especially as at this stage the substances which give it its aroma and flavor have not yet been able to develop to the full and they will be collected for a second distillation, just as they will in the after run, or tail (Greek *ourá*). Isolating the middle run, the heart or *kardiá*, is the true art of the distiller, as both the forerun and afterrun already contain elements affecting the taste. The heart is also distilled a second time, and then finally adjusted to the correct grade of alcohol using distilled water.

THEÓFILOS

Theófilos Hatzimichalis, who was born on Lesbos around 1870, took a childhood interest in the work of his grandfather, an icon painter, who also tutored him in the various techniques of painting. His own artistic activity began in 1911/1912 with murals, with which he decorated villas in the Pílion region of Thessaly. Subsequently he painted mainly murals and facades or store signs in Vólos and the surrounding area or on Lesbos, where he returned in 1925. Later he also worked on wood, cardboard, and increasingly on cotton fabrics. He found the subjects of his highly inventive paintings in ancient mythology or in Homer, in the exotic world of the Orient, in the Greek war of independence and also in the Bible. His pictures, executed in bright, home-made, natural colors, portray an unconventional, naively colorful view of the world. The pictures are often provided with detailed explanatory commentaries. The Greek art dealer Tériade, who lived in Paris, greatly encouraged Theófilos and exhibited his paintings all over the world. The artist died in 1934 on Lesbos, where a museum is now dedicated solely to his work.

Ouzo bottles come in different sizes. Many are so small that their contents are only enough for two aperitifs, though in this case "Mini" is actually the brand name.

Above: The most important herbs for ouzo are anise, star aniseed, cardamom, corn, angelica, lime flowers, and coriander.

Right: In the distillery laboratory the finished ouzo is subjected to constant checks, to make sure the taste and quality remain consistent.

Copper guarantees that an even temperature is maintained in the containers during distillation.

The concentrated distillation is kept in modern stainless steel containers.

Samples taken during the production process are checked for their appearance and strength.

Bottles on the conveyor belt on their way to be packed have passed all the checks.

OUZO

Every region of Greece produces its own ouzo. The most famous comes from the North Aegean island of Lesbos, which has the oldest tradition of ouzo production. The crucial factors are the water quality, the origin of the herbs, and how much of each is added. The most common brands are the following (from left to right): Mini is an ouzo from the EPOM company and at 40 percent alcohol is one of the milder ouzos from Lesbos. Ouzo Mageia is a lower quality, more regionally distinctive ouzo from the mainland. Ouzo Plomariou is the most famous ouzo from Lesbos, and has unique corks. It has now been bought by Ouzo 12 and is also marketed abroad. Ouzo Apallarina is a local ouzo from the neighboring island of Chios, and provides no more competition for the Lesbos ouzo than does Ouzo Athenée. Ouzo Babatzim is a Macedonian ouzo of the highest quality, produced according to hygiene regulations, flavored with fresh herbs, and filtered during the three-part distillation. Ouzo Barbayanni is the first class Lesbos ouzo, a 45 percent spirit, which follows an old recipe. Ouzo 12 from Macedonia is the ouzo which is best known outside Greece. It is produced from alcohol that is bought in ready-made and an herbal essence, so Greeks describe it as ouzo from the chemistry lab.

On the subject of ouzo, we must also point out the small distilleries on the island of Samos.

Ouzo is so popular in Greece that each region has its own distilleries.

The surface of the mastic crystals is cleaned with a pointed knife.

The pieces of collected resin come in different shapes and sizes, and soon set hard.

MASTIC

Below the low, sclerophyllous evergreen growth of the maquis tree, the form of vegetation that is so characteristic of the Mediterranean area, there is a shrub which only occurs on the south of the island of Chios. This is the subspecies *Pistacia lentiscus* var. *chia*, the mastic bush. When its bark is damaged, it exudes a sweet smelling, white, transparent resin, already much prized in ancient times. It was particularly valued for its stickiness, which is preserved, indeed only really develops, when a lump of resin is chewed. So it was used very early on, mainly for oral hygiene. Dioskourides refers to it in his pharmacology as a cosmetic substance. Because of its scent it was used in perfumes and as incense for improving the air. The oil obtained from the resin was used to ward off colds, coughs, and sneezes.

In the Middle Ages, it was the Genoese in particular who carried on the trade in mastic throughout the Mediterranean area and helped the island to achieve relative prosperity. During the time of Ottoman rule on Chios, the Sultan permitted the inhabitants to continue the mastic trade virtually unhindered. However, instead of taxes he demanded an annual tribute of half the production of this valuable raw material, a large part of which ended up in the seraglio in Istanbul, the sultan's harem, where it was used as chewing gum. In addition, mastic soon found a use as a food additive. Though the mastic farmers of Chios were highly regarded throughout the Middle Ages in Greece, the few farmers left today must fight for survival. Even if growing conditions on

Above: the evergreen mastic bush *Pistacia lentscus* var. *chia* barely grows to 6 feet (2 m) in the maquis.

Left: the much-prized resin flows from the cuts.

Right: mastic-flavored candies (clockwise): *loukoumia*, below that *mastikha*, pure mastic, *pasteli*, *masticópita* (front), on top of these "mastic tears," and to the left of them, mint and caramel candies with mastic.

Chios are good for the shrub, and the resin is still used, it is under increasing pressure from synthetic resins, except for flavoring the ouzo produced on the island. The resin, which is traded in the form of a firm, granular material, is used among other things as an element in the formulation of adhesives, special cements and varnishes, and as an aromatic additive to incense, toothpaste, and chewing gum (Greek: *mastikha*). Mastic has an unusually intense taste and a fragrant, flowery aroma and is therefore used in various Greek and oriental sweets or confections such as *khalvás* and *loukoúmia*.

Mastic collecting begins in the middle of August, when up to eight cross-shaped cuts are made in the bark, so the resin can flow out and set. It takes about 15 days to dry before it can be collected. The grains of mastic are sifted to remove pollutants such as sand, then it is washed with cold water and soap, and laid out to dry. At the same time, the last particles of dirt are scratched off with a knife. Finally, it is sifted again, during which the individual lumps or "tears" of resin are sorted according to quality and size.

Above: where anise once provided the taste, sweet mastic is the predominant flavor in Chios Clear.

GOAT KEEPING

Katsika, the goat, is a versatile domestic animal kept in all parts of Greece. Even on the barren rocks of the Greek islands, goats can find enough grass and twigs in the most inhospitable places to thrive. Because they have such modest requirements, there are now more goats than sheep in the pastures of Greece. Round about the month of July, when the kids are thought to be the right age, the numbers in the herd are controlled, or to put it plainly, some of the young animals are slaughtered. On the islands, the animals first have to be found and rounded up in the mountain pastures where they have been more or less left to themselves for the whole summer, a job that takes many hours. When the majority of the herd is finally penned, the farmers make their selection from among the kids and take them back to the village. There, in the presence of the butcher, the kids are slaughtered. The goatherd cuts the animals' throats and lays them side by side on the ground so the blood can drain into a pit that was dug beforehand. Later the entrails will also go into it, after which it will be filled in. The animals are skinned, drawn, examined by the butcher and weighed. Money changes hands and everyone goes away contented. This is what happened on a July day in Ikaría.

Usually the weaker animals in the herd are killed. Their throats are cut and the blood flows into a specially prepared pit.

With practiced movements, skinning goes quickly. If you want to make a backpack from the hide (see p. 336) you must pull it off in the opposite direction.

The action is drawing to a close. It took place in the presence of the butcher, who checked the quality of the meat, paid for his goods, and will now process them.

FILÁKI

Ikaría is just a small inconspicuous island in the North Aegean Sea, which at best is remarkable for its slate-roofed houses of natural stone. It owes its name to the myth of the inventor and craftsman Daedalus and his son Icarus, who fell into the sea off the shores of this island. Since then it has lain in the sea like a lost bird. The only thing that makes it stand out among the Greek islands apart from its name is a tradition that is only carried on here and whose origins probably go back to ancient pastoral times: making the *filáki*, a goat-hair backpack. In the weeks before the Easter festival, when the lambs and goats for the feast are killed, the inhabitants of Ikaría process the ani-

ICARUS

In order to escape from the labyrinth he himself had designed, in which he and his son Icarus had been imprisoned by King Minos, the ingenious inventor Daedalus made wings out of feathers and wax. He advised Icarus not to fly too low, but not too high either, as the sun might melt the wax. Having taken to the air, Icarus forgot this advice and flew too near the sun. His wings lost their feathers, and he fell into the sea, just south of the island of Samos. Since then, the sea has been known as the Ikarian Sea, and the island on which his body was washed ashore as Ikaría.

Left: the most natural backpack in the world, made from a goatskin, keeps food fresh and is therefore suitable for lengthy stays in the mountains.

and ensures that the hairs cannot break or fall out later. After two days, the skin is taken out and hung up to dry, having been turned inside out again, so the hair is outside as it was to start with. The dried skin is thoroughly brushed and the two right legs and two left legs, front and back, are tied together in pairs. This makes a practical backpack, whose size is entirely dependent on the size of the animal. This so-called *filáki* backpack is suitable for shopping and short walks, and is easily carried on the back or over the shoulder.

Below: what was originally the neck of the goat is quite hard when finished, but it can be turned down and used as a lid.

mal hides in an unusual way. Instead of the skin of the slaughtered animal being pulled over the head, it is pulled toward the legs, so the goat's hooves remain attached to the skin. The skin is turned so the hair is inside. At the same time, it is stuffed so full of hay that the skin is stretched tight. Then salt and ashes are rubbed into the outside, which was originally the inside, to prevent the untreated skin from decaying and to keep vermin away. After that it spends several days drying in the sun. The goatskin sack is then placed in the sea and weighted with stones to keep it under water and prevent it from being washed away by the waves. The seawater makes the skin supple,

SAINT'S DAY FESTIVALS

As on many Greek islands, in almost every town on the North Aegean islands, each village church holds a festival once a year. This is held on the feast day of the patron saint to whom the church is dedicated. The festival usually starts on the evening of the previous day with a church service. Then the actual feast day begins with another solemn mass. On this day many towns also organize processions, large or small, solemn or profane. At the festival in the picturesque seaside town of Mólyvos in the north of the island of Lesbos, a bull decked with flowers is led through the streets, preceded by an icon and accompanied by a band. The inhabitants stand outside their houses and, as the procession passes, hand over their donations to the church or give the man leading the bull a refreshing and fortifying drink. The traditional feast-day soup, which is a must at every festival, is there to fortify everybody. The previous evening, the cauldron is set up in the open air, usually near the church. What goes into the soup depends on what time of year the patron saint has his or her feast day. If it falls during Lent, the soup must manage without meat, otherwise there is a free choice of meat. At any rate, it is not the bull in the procession.

Above: an icon of the Madonna is carried at the head of the procession with the (still young) bull to emphasize the religious nature of the festival.

Top left: while the band continues to play, the procession comes to a halt from time to time, giving the participants a chance to fortify themselves.

Top right: the cauldron containing the festival soup stands ready over a fire out in the open.

SAPPHO

In ancient Greece she was already considered the greatest of poetesses, but at the same time, the picture painted of Sappho's life and work has not been free from misinterpretation. Of good family, she lived in Mytilene on Lesbos around 600 B.C. Only fragments remain of her work, which was published in nine books in ancient times and included marriage songs as well as lyric verse, but, above all, descriptions of all shades and interactions of feelings in simple, graphic language. We learn that she worked within a circle of young women, whom she taught music and educated for their role in society, and for whom she felt great affection. In ancient times, the interpretation of the relationships within this circle was already speculative and defamatory, and says more about those who judged her than about the object of their examination.

ΚΥΚΛΑΔΕΣ

Above: Santorini has the most and also the best restaurants in the region.
Background: view toward Thíra, the island capital of Santorini.

THE CYCLADES

Skate wings

Against the wind

Fresh from the sea

Snails

Sausage and ham

Meat dishes

Mushrooms by thunder!

Pulses and vegetables

Nutritious island cuisine

Wines of the Cyclades

Kítro

Forces of nature

Of all the Greek islands, the Cyclades give the impression of being the most self-contained, not only in geographical, but also in cultural and historical terms. An independent cultural milieu developed here as long ago as the 3rd millennium B.C., and even now the products of what is known as Cycladic culture intrigue archaeologists and inspire visual artists. Around 2000 B.C. the Minoans extended their sphere of cultural and economic influence northward, but 500 years later, their important settlement on the island of Santorini was destroyed by a powerful volcanic eruption. Even in classical times, the Cyclades were popularly said to owe their name to the fact that the islands lay in a circle, or *kyklos*, around the island of Delos. However, this is easier to understand if viewed in contextual rather than geographical terms, thereby emphasizing the significance of Delos as the religious and political center of the Ionian Greeks in the first half of the 1st millennium B.C. Although the Cyclades lost their political status with the rise of Athens, they retained their rank in terms of trade and shipping in the Aegean, acting as an important link between Greece and Asia Minor. They offered valuable bases to crusaders and Venetian merchants, and provided hiding places to pirates. Under Ottoman rule, the Cyclades were able to retain their cultural and religious independence.

Although nowadays each of the islands has a character of its own, the name "Cyclades" is associated with the picture of square, whitewashed houses and small chapels, sometimes with blue domes, picturesquely perched within a barren, rocky landscape, and people talk of a typical Cycladic architecture. The islands' stony-rocky soil and lack of water prevent any comprehensive agricultural use. Only Santorini and Melos, with their volcanic subsoil, can support more productive farming. The main products grown here are pulses, wine, and tomatoes. The decline in fish stocks, due in no small way to competition from large fishing fleets, means that fishing, such an important economic factor in the past, can now barely support the usually small fishing concerns run by individual fishermen. In this situation, the rise in tourism, although it brings many problems in its wake, has led to some economic consolidation, with the increasing number of attractive restaurants creating greater demand as their cuisine becomes more sophisticated.

On the small, sparsely populated islands, the fisherman has long been a focal point of interest for tourists. The glorification of his occupational status cannot, however, conceal the hard working conditions.

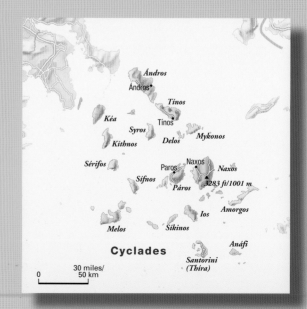

SKATE WINGS

The most famous species of ray caught fresh from the sea by Greek fishermen is the devil fish (*Mobula mobular*). It belongs to the ray family and can have a wingspan of anything up to 15 feet (5 meters). Of course, these are not really wings, but greatly enlarged pectoral fins. Like the shark, rays belong to the family of cartilaginous fish, in other words fish that have a cartilage "skeleton" instead of ordinary bones. The skate wings, which are by far the largest and fleshiest edible parts of the fish, consist of closely packed, translucent cartilage bones surrounded by long, narrow, firm, meaty strips of muscle. Rays prefer a diet of shellfish and crustaceans when they can find them, and perhaps that is what gives the ray its delicate, crab- or scallop-like flavor. Unlike the genuine ray, the devil ray, which lives in the deep waters around the Cyclades, especially along the volcanic coast of Santorini, is more often eaten as a local delicacy. You are therefore more likely to come across it in Cycladic cuisine, although fishermen rarely catch more than one at a time.

Thornback ray
(*Raja clavata*)

Cuckoo ray
(*Raja naevus*)

Undulate ray
(*Raja undulata*)

SALÁKHI KOKKINISTÓ
Skate in tomato sauce
(Illustration top left)

2 lbs/1 kg skate wings
1 scant cup/200 ml Greek extra virgin olive oil
2 onions, finely chopped
4 cloves of garlic, finely sliced
4 large beeefsteak tomatoes, skinned and puréed
1 tsp sugar
1 bunch flat-leaved parsley, finely chopped
Salt
Freshly ground black pepper

If the skate wings are large, remove the flesh from the cartilage skeleton and cut into pieces. Heat the olive oil in a deep skillet, soften the onions and garlic in it, and add the puréed tomatoes together with a little water. Season with salt, pepper, and sugar, and stir in the parsley. Now add the pieces of skate, lower the heat, and braise for about 45 minutes. Serve while still warm with freshly baked white bread.

Starry ray
(*Raja asterias*)

Speckled ray
(*Raja polystigma*)

Sandy ray
(*Raja circularis*)

SALÁKHI SALÁTA
Skate salad
(Illustration top right)

2 lbs/1 kg skate wings
A scant ½ cup/100 ml vinegar
2 onions, finely chopped
½ bunch flat-leaved parsley
1 scant cup/200 ml Greek extra virgin olive oil
Juice of 1 lemon
Salt
Freshly ground black pepper

Rub the wings in salt and some of the vinegar to remove the mucous layer. Boil sufficient water in a pan to cover the wings, add some salt and the remaining vinegar, and poach the skate wings for 10–20 minutes. Drain the fish, then remove the flesh from the cartilage skeleton, cutting it into bite-sized pieces if necessary. In a bowl, carefully combine the skate flesh with the onions, parsley, olive oil, and lemon juice. Season with salt and pepper and leave in a cool place until you are ready to serve.

SALÁKHI ME SKORDALIÁ
Skate with garlic sauce
(Illustration bottom)

4 small skate wings, each weighing about ¾ lb/350 g
All-purpose flour
1 scant cup/200 ml Greek extra virgin olive oil
4 tbsp/60 ml white wine vinegar
Salt and freshly ground black pepper

For the skordália:
1½ lbs/750 g stale white bread, crusts removed,
  and soaked in water
4 cloves of garlic
1 scant cup/200 ml Greek extra virgin olive oil
Juice of 1 lemon
Salt

Skin the skate wings and trim all around the edges. Sprinkle the wings with salt and coat in flour. Heat the olive oil in a skillet, and quickly brown the skate wings. Remove them from the skillet and transfer to a large plate. Deglaze the frying deposits with the vinegar, quickly bring it to a boil, then pour over the skate wings.
Squeeze the white bread well and purée together with the garlic cloves in a blender (at the lowest setting), then gradually add the olive oil and lemon juice in a thin stream. Season the *skordália* with salt and serve, in a separate bowl, with freshly baked white bread.

AGAINST THE WIND

The wind often blows right in the faces of the 2500-odd fishermen of the Cyclades. Their work has always been hard and bears little resemblance to the adventurous romance and freedom of the waves. In the past, fishermen rarely owned any land, and therefore did not enjoy much security, and the situation is not much different even now. The fisherman's income, and thus his ability to provide for his family, still depends on the fish stocks in the area in which he can fish. Since the islands have to feed a vastly increased population in the tourist season, and the Greek government still grants fishing permits to the modern fishing fleets from farther afield, the Cycladic fishermen feel they have been let down. The in-depth knowledge of the fishing grounds, handed down for generations from father to son, is increasingly worthless when just one of the large fishing boats with its small-mesh trailing net can inflict noticeable damage on the food chain and thus the entire ecosystem.

THE GREEK WINDS

Garbís	southwesterly wind
Grégos	northeasterly wind
Levántes	east wind
Maístros	northwesterly wind
Meltémi	northeasterly wind
Notiás	the south/southerly wind
Óstria	southerly wind
Ponéntes	west wind
Sirókos	southerly wind from the Sahara
Tramountána	north wind
Voriás	the north/north wind

The Boreas, now called *meltémi*, a northeasterly wind that blows with wild, often destructive force between sunrise and sunset, was king of the winds. It saved the Athenians from the invasion of the Persians by helping to destroy the Persian fleet at Salamis in 480 B.C.

Many tavernas and restaurants in the Cyclades serve mackerel, *skoumbría*. These fish may be very bony, but they nevertheless taste delicious.

Fagrí, the dentex fish, is one of the Aegean's best edible fish and you will have to pay a bit more money if you want to find it on your plate.

A real fisherman knows all possible ways of catching fish. He also knows precisely which method to apply to catch a particular fish in his fishing grounds. And anyone worth his salt in the trade is also sufficiently skilled at catching fish in shallow water using the old-fashioned harpoon to provide food for his own table.

POSEIDON GOD OF THE SEA

When Cronous, that cruel, child-eating father, was defeated by his children, they divided the universe up among themselves. Zeus got the heavens, Hades the underworld, and Poseidon the sea. The earth and Olympia, however, belonged to them all equally, and Zeus was king of all, thus guaranteeing constant arguments between them, and Poseidon became very pugnacious. He usually lived in his water palace on the north coast of the Peloponnese. He was married to Amphitrite, the daughter of Oceanus, who was brought to him by a dolphin. When he drove over the surface of the water in his horse-drawn chariot, with the marine inhabitants such as the Nereids and Tritons in his wake, the waves of the sea became calm. However, anyone who had incurred his displeasure would quickly feel the full force of his temper. In the name of Odysseus, Homer sang a song about it. With his trident, Poseidon churned up the sea or produced powerful earthquakes, from which the Cyclades have also always suffered.

In the last several years fish stocks in the Cyclades have declined dramatically, and as a result prices for sea-fresh Aegean fish have rocketed sky-high. It is precisely this shortage in relation to the tourists' purchasing power that at present still guarantees the fishermen a regular income, so that their laughter has not quite become a thing of the past. Yet, with increasing impatience, they are waiting for immediate measures to stabilize and regenerate fish stocks. If these do not materialize, it will one day be possible to experience one of the country's most traditional occupations, indeed one of the oldest occupations in the history of mankind, only by viewing artifacts in museums.

It is by no means a matter of chance that fishermen and fish frequently feature strongly in mythology and religion. Take the Bible, for example, with Jonah in the whale's stomach, the fisherman Simon Peter, the Greek word for fish, *ichthys*, being used as the acronym for the name of Christ (I–CH–TH–Y–S: Jesus Christ, Son of God, Redeemer), and the wonderful story of the loaves and fishes. These are just some of a whole range of examples, all of which demonstrate that anyone trying to teach an audience to appreciate a message of salvation by finding shared aspects of their everyday lives was well advised to use the image of the fisherman and his world. That way, he was sure to be understood.

SARDÉLA ME SÁLTSA LEMONIOÚ
Sardine fillets in lemon sauce

1 tbsp olive oil
2 lbs/1 kg sardines, ready prepared,
backbone removed
Juice of 2½ lemons (reserve the zest)
½ cup/125 ml sour cream
½ tsp dried oregano
2 green chiles, cut in rings
2 tomatoes, cut into small wedges
Salt
Freshly ground black pepper

Preheat the oven to 430 ºF (220 ºC). Arrange the sardine fillets in a baking dish brushed with olive oil, and season with salt and pepper. Combine the lemon juice with the sour cream and oregano. Season this sauce with salt and pepper, and pour over the sardines. Scatter the chiles, tomatoes, and half a lemon, finely sliced, over the sardines. Bake in a preheated oven for about 20–30 minutes. Serve while still warm with a green salad and freshly baked white bread.

MARÍDES TIGANITÉS
Fried *marídes* (picarel)

1 lb/500 g marídes (picarel)
1¼ cups/200 g all-purpose flour
Olive oil
2 lemons, cut into wedges
Salt

Remove the heads of the *marídes*. Scale, wash, and salt the fish, then coat in flour. Heat the olive oil in a skillet and fry the *marídes* until golden brown. Then transfer to a large plate, garnish with the lemon wedges, and serve hot. *Khórta* (wild herbs in an oil and vinegar dressing, see page 264) or beet salad, *pantzária*, (see page 267) go well with this dish. *Marídes* (*Spicara smaris*) are small picarel, and can be eaten bones and all, served both as an appetizer and as a main dish.

GET YOUR FINGERS DIRTY

If you really want to enjoy eating, and you see the act of putting food into your mouth as a haptic-sensual experience, and not just a remote, mechanical process, then fingers are always the best way of bringing both culinary delight and nourishment into harmony. It takes the combined presence of the senses of sight, touch, and taste to bring out all the aspects of the food.

GOÚNA
Cyclades mackerel

4 mackerel
1 tsp dried oregano
1 scant cup/200 ml
  Greek extra virgin olive oil
Juice of 1 lemon
Salt
Freshly ground black pepper

A day ahead of time, clean the mackerel and remove the heads and fins. Cut the fish lengthways, but not quite in two. Wash them, pat dry, and then place them, skin side up, on a large plate. Season with plenty of salt, a little oregano, and pepper, then cover with a thin cloth and leave in the sun for one day to dry. The next day, cook the mackerel on both sides on a charcoal grill. Combine the olive oil, lemon juice, salt, pepper, and oregano, and brush over the fish. As soon as they are cooked, transfer them to a plate and serve with the remaining oil and lemon sauce, freshly baked white bread, and a green salad.

FRESH FROM THE SEA

It comes as no surprise that the islands of the Aegean Sea have far and away the most fish recipes. Each island cuisine has developed its own particular preferences for this or that type of fish, depending on the fish that is most frequently caught on their respective coast. On the Cyclades, the broiled or baked fish can hold their own among all the other dishes on the menus. There is a pleasingly wide variety, and in many recipes the main ingredient can easily be replaced by another fish or beneficially supplemented by others with no ill effects on flavor. The imbalance between supply and demand in the tourist season in the past several years has led to tavernas and restaurants on the islands most visited by tourists frequently being forced to serve imported frozen fish (which must be described as such on the menus). The local fishermen, chefs, and restaurateurs are not happy about this, but correcting the errors of an insufficiently forward-looking fishing policy is a slow process.

SINAGRÍDA STO FOÚRNO
Baked porgy

2 porgy, ready prepared
Juice of 1 lemon
2 small sprigs of rosemary
A generous ½ cup/125 ml Greek extra virgin
* olive oil*
1 bunch scallions, cut in rings
3 tomatoes, skinned and puréed
1 bunch flat-leaved parsley, finely chopped
2 cloves of garlic, chopped
¼ lb/100 g black olives, sliced
1 scant cup/200 ml dry white wine
⅞ cup/100 g sheep's milk cheese, crumbled
Salt and freshly ground pepper

Preheat the oven to 400 ºF (200 ºC). Place the fish on an oiled baking sheet, add lemon juice, and salt and pepper. Soften the scallions in olive oil, add the tomatoes, parsley, garlic, and olives, and bring to a boil. Add the wine, salt and pepper, and simmer for 10 minutes. Pour the sauce over the fish and bake in the oven for 40 minutes. Scatter the sheep's milk cheese over the fish. Serve with white bread.

PSÁRI SPETSIÓTIKO
Spetses fish

2 lbs/1 kg Mediterranean fish (porgy, sea bass,
* snapper, or similar)*
Juice of 1 lemon
5 tomatoes
1 tbsp tomato paste
2 cloves of garlic, chopped
½ bunch flat-leaved parsley, finely chopped
1 scant cup/200 ml Greek extra virgin
* olive oil*
Crackers, crushed
Salt
Freshly ground black pepper

Preheat the oven to 350 ºF (180 ºC). Scale and clean the fish, then wash them well and fillet them. Brush a baking sheet with olive oil, place the fish fillets on top, sprinkle with the lemon juice, and season with salt and pepper. Skin and purée three tomatoes. Put the puréed tomato, tomato paste, garlic, parsley, olive oil, salt and pepper in a bowl and mix well. Pour the sauce over the fish fillets. Slice the remaining tomatoes and arrange over the fish. Sprinkle with the crushed crackers and bake in a preheated oven for about 40 minutes. Serve with a green salad and freshly baked white bread.

SNAILS

When excavating the Minoan town of Akrotíri on Santorini, archaeologists found snail shells and concluded that this mollusk must have featured in the menu even then. The Greeks, and later still the Romans, had no particular term to clearly distinguish these types of mollusk from others, such as mussels, calling them all crustaceans. However, a few types of snail were clearly described and, as the Roman physician Galen (A.D. 129–199) wrote in a treatise on the properties of foods, they were also eaten: "The Greeks, however, eat snails every day. Their flesh is firm, but they are extremely nourishing when cooked."

Even now, many centuries later, every village path and sidewalk, the front of every house, and every set of steps is still full of snails each autumn. Snails often appear after the first late-summer rain, and continue on into October. In low-lying places on soft, uncultivated land they are easy prey for birds, too. Because they are not commercially bred, they make only a brief appearance in Greek island cuisine, but always in an astounding variety of tasty dishes, served with rice or onion, or alternatively with pasta as an appetizer. Snails are thus an established part of autumn cuisine in the Cyclades.

Snails seldom come singly. If you see one, there are bound to be plenty more.

SALINGÁRIA ME DOMÁTA KE DENDROLÍVANO
Snails with tomatoes and rosemary

1 lb/500 g snails
4 sprigs of rosemary
A scant ½ cup/100 ml Greek extra virgin olive oil
5 onions, grated
1 lb/500 g tomatoes, skinned and chopped
A bunch flat-leaved parsley, finely chopped
Salt
Freshly ground black pepper

Remove the slime from the snails (see recipe below for "Snails with pasta"), place them in a pan with their shells, and add sufficient water to cover. Add two sprigs of rosemary and a little salt, and boil for 10 minutes. In a separate pan, heat the olive oil, quickly soften the onions in it, then add the tomatoes, parsley, and the remaining two sprigs of rosemary. Boil for 10 minutes and then add the snails with a little of their juice. Simmer until cooked, then transfer to a bowl. Serve with rice, freshly baked white bread, and a green salad.

SALINGÁRIA ME MAKARÓNIA
Snails with pasta

1 lb/500 g snails
A scant cup/200 ml Greek extra virgin olive oil
2 cloves of garlic, crushed
A bunch flat-leaved parsley, finely chopped
2 lbs/1 kg tomatoes, skinned and diced
½ tsp cinnamon
1 lb/500 g pasta
Salt
Freshly ground black pepper

The evening before, put the snails in a bowl, add water, and cover with a plate. The next day, wash them well, discarding any dead ones. Put the snails in a pan of boiling water and cook for 10 minutes. Remove from the pan and bore a hole in each shell using a pointed knife. Wash well once more and leave to drain.

Heat the olive oil in a pan, and fry the snails, garlic, and parsley. Add the diced tomatoes and season with the cinnamon, salt and pepper. Simmer over a low heat for 20 minutes. Bring salted water to a boil in a pan and cook the pasta. Drain the noodles, transfer to plates, arrange the snails on top, and serve warm.

THE DOVECOTES
OF TÍNOS

Evidence of dove breeding dates from as far back as the Ancient Egyptian Empire. In classical times, too, the very prolific and easily fattened birds, whose flesh was considered tasty and very healthy, were kept in tall, free-standing towers. Their religious significance – from the cult of the Phoenician Astarte through that of Aphrodite right up to the Christian symbol of the Holy Ghost – did nothing to alter this.

The Venetians, who ruled on Tínos from 1207 to 1715, and thus longer than on any other island in the Aegean, are said to have introduced intensive pigeon breeding. Construction of the first towers dates back to at least this time. Although they are also found on other islands in the Cyclades, there are more than a hundred examples of the attractively ornate constructions on Tínos, and they have become an architectural symbol of the island. You come across them unexpectedly on terraced fields in the countryside, mainly in the vicinity of the former Venetian fortress and island capital on Mount Exoboúrgo, in the heart of the island. Sadly, the tradition of building such dovecotes has died out, but they are an excellent example of a not only harmonious, but also visually attractive combination of functional and decorative architecture. The upper area of the sides of the rectangular towers that are sheltered from the wind contains entrance holes, concealed behind geometric patterns, for the doves to fly in through. The birds are thus relatively safe from their natural enemies such as snakes or birds of prey. The extremely varied patterns created with the affixed slate or clay tiles are based on the basic shape of the triangle and help give each tower its unique appearance.

SAUSAGE AND HAM

Many written sources handed down from classical times refer to the manufacture of sausage, *loukániko*. There was a brisk trade in the many different types of sausage. Even in those times sausage and sausage sellers were a source of amusement. Thus in Aristophanes' comedy *The Knights*, a sausage seller appears as the out-and-out antihero. Nobody knows whether it was the shape of the sausage that lent itself to caricature, or the character of the sausage seller, who was perhaps not trusted even then, (for the question of what can be used to fill a sausage casing is certainly not new), that ultimately led to many things to do with sausages being represented in classical times in mocking or crudely disparaging images. In late classical times it is reported that a saint called Simeon Salos expressly went to a marketplace with a garland of sausages so that he could tuck into them there in full public gaze, thereby attracting attention to himself and his message.

Generally speaking, sausages do not attain any great significance in Greece. Yet there are a few regions that are really famous for their specialty sausages: some of the most noteworthy are special sausages from Corinth, Lefkáda, Náousa, Réthimnon, Vólos, and Tríkala. And in the Cyclades you can discover small butcher's stores, hidden away down narrow alleyways, selling excellent homemade sausages. They are usually made from pure pork, and sometimes are simply seasoned with salt and pepper, but marinated in wine. On the Greek mainland you can find firm, spicy sausages that are generally sold as "country sausage." The Greeks do not have any main dishes using sausages. Sausages are usually cut up small and served as *mezés* or used in omelets in the same way as diced bacon.

As pork was the most important meat on the menu even in classical times, it made sense to make some of it storable. Athenaeus reports a ham being made storable by being cured. That is how pork is made into *apokhtí* even today.

LOUKÁNIKA
Sausages

Pig's intestine
1 generous cup/250 ml lemon juice
About 4½ lbs/2 kg pork
2 lbs/1 kg bacon
1 whole garlic, peeled and crushed
Thyme
Salt and freshly ground black pepper

Wash the intestine thoroughly inside and out, put it in a bowl, add the lemon juice together with 2 teaspoons salt, stir, and leave to soak for 30 minutes. Then wash the intestine thoroughly once again, place in a strainer, sprinkle with salt, and leave for 3 hours to extract the water. Put the meat and bacon through a meat grinder and transfer to a bowl. Add the garlic, thyme, salt, and pepper and knead thoroughly. Now fill the intestine with the desired amount of meat mixture, tie it to seal, and then repeat this process to make small sausages. Hang the sausages in a cool, well-ventilated room to dry.

APOKHTÍ

Unlike *pastourmás*, which is made from ox meat and beef in Thrace and Cyprus, *apokhtí* is made from pork fillet. The meat is first marinated for 24 hours in red wine vinegar. It is then coated with spices, including black pepper and cinnamon, which ultimately give *apokhtí* its distinctive flavor. Having been prepared in this way, the apokhtí is hung up to dry in a cool, well-ventilated place until it becomes hard.

MEAT DISHES

In the past, meat was always in short supply on the barren Greek islands, and certainly did not appear on the table every day. This was no great hardship, as the Aegean Sea was still very rich in fish. It was most likely sheep or goats that were slaughtered. Pork and beef were used even more exceptionally. Now, however, the regional island cuisine has changed. With wonderful regularity, the boats that bring the tourists now also bring the meat sellers from the major markets on the mainland, and for many families, boiled or roasted meat has become a feature of their everyday diet. This is particularly true of people from the older generation, who can remember it being quite different in their youth. This may be the reason for a surprisingly large number of interesting pork recipes, which are undoubtedly indigenous to the Cyclades, even though these islands are not one of Greece's traditional pork regions. A striking feature is the frequent use of animal fat, melted with or without herbs and preserved in ceramic containers. That way, the aromatic dripping is always ready to be used for cooking and frying.

KHIRINÓ BOÚTI STI LADÓKOLLA
Pork shank in foil

4 pork shanks, skin removed
4 cloves of garlic, quartered
1 scant cup/200 ml dry red wine
Olive oil
Salt
Freshly ground black pepper

Preheat the oven to 400 °F (200 °C). Wash the pork shanks, make incisions, and insert 1 quartered clove of garlic in each shank. Rub well with plenty of salt and pepper. Place a double sheet of baking parchment on four large pieces of aluminum foil. Place the pork shanks on top, brush with olive oil, and pour on the wine. Fold the baking parchment and foil over the shanks, seal to form a firm parcel, and bake in the oven for 1 hour. Turn the oven down to 350 °F (180 °C) and leave the meat to cook for a further 2 hours. To serve, remove the bones, slice the meat, and transfer to plates. Pour over a little of the cooking juices and serve while still warm with a green salad.

DOMATOKEFTÉDES SANTORÍNIS
Santorini tomato fritters
(Illustration right)

2 lbs/1 kg tomatoes
3 large onions, peeled
2 zucchini, stalk removed
4½ cups/500 g all-purpose flour
1 bunch mint, finely chopped
Olive oil for frying
Salt
Freshly ground black pepper

Dice the vegetables and purée in a blender. Season with salt and pepper, add the mint, and then combine with the flour. Heat the olive oil in a deep skillet. Add tablespoonfuls of the mixture, flatten them out with the back of the spoon, and fry until crispy. Serve while warm. Tomato fritters make a good snack and can also be served as an accompaniment to quick roasts.

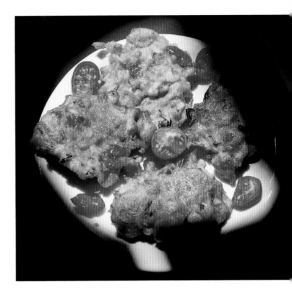

ARNÍ ME PATÁTES STO PÍLINO
Lamb with potatoes cooked in an earthenware pot

8–12 lamb cutlets (depending on size)
A generous ½ cup/125 ml Greek extra virgin oil
1 lb/500 g potatoes, peeled and sliced
2 large onions, coarsely chopped
2 carrots, sliced
4 bay leaves
Salt
Freshly ground black pepper

Preheat the oven to 350 °F (180 °C). Fry the lamb cutlets in olive oil, and season with salt and pepper. Brush four flameproof earthenware pots with some of the olive oil, arrange the carrots, onions, and potatoes in layers, seasoning each layer with salt and pepper, and place a bay leaf on the potatoes. Place the cutlets on top. Add ⅔ cup/150 ml water and 1 tablespoon oil to each pot, cover with aluminum foil, and leave to cook in a preheated oven for about 1 hour. Remove the foil and bake for a further 30 minutes until the potatoes are golden brown. Serve while still hot in the earthenware pots.

TSILADIÁ
Jellied pork with seasonal vegetables

About 4½ lbs/2 kg pig's trotters
1 scant cup/200 ml lemon juice
2 tbsp vinegar
1 tsp cinnamon
4 bay leaves
3 carrots, thinly sliced
3 scallions, thinly sliced
Salt
Freshly ground black pepper

Chop the pig's trotters into small pieces, place in a pan with plenty of water, and bring to a boil. Skim off any scum that forms on the surface, lower the heat, and simmer the stock until it has reduced by half. Drain, reserving the juice. Add the lemon juice, vinegar, bay leaves, cinnamon, salt and pepper to the juice and quickly bring to a boil. Fill deep plates with the thinly sliced carrots and scallions, pour the stock through a strainer into the plates, and leave to cool until the liquid sets. Serve with freshly baked white bread.

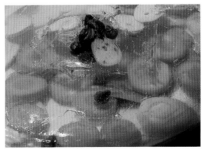

MUSHROOMS BY THUNDER!

Greece does not have many fungi, and the few species that do grow in the wild are naturally only there for a short time. They always sprout up from the ground in fallow fields and moist wooded areas when the winters are mild and damp, and therefore mostly frost-free. On Santorini you can even find some types of mushroom along the volcanic crater. Of course, they are not all edible; in-depth knowledge about this is more a matter of family tradition than something learned from a book. As with snails, mushrooms are rarely referred to by their proper names, all edible mushrooms being grouped together under the general terms of *moskhomaníti* and *glistríti* for the sake of simplicity.

It is known that mushrooms have been eaten in Greece since late classical times at least. Their sudden and inexplicable appearance after autumn rain was seen as one of nature's humors. Homer considered *myces* or *amanites* to be a sort of link between heaven and earth, and Plutarch was convinced that they were created by lightning. People knew the genuine mushroom as well as the truffle (*hydnon*), which they believed sprouted depending on the force and number of thunderclaps.

The local dried tomatoes are a specialty of Santorini cuisine. They are cut in half horizontally, and the rest is left to the sun. As the water evaporates, the flavors intensify, making it an ideal accompaniment to fish and meat dishes.

MANITÁRIA ME KREMMÍDI
Mushrooms with onion
(Illustration opposite, top left)

2 lbs/1 kg mushrooms
⅔ cup/150 ml Greek extra virgin olive oil
1 onion, finely chopped
3 cloves of garlic, crushed
1 lb/500 g tomatoes, skinned, seeded, and diced
3½ tbsp/50 ml red wine vinegar
5 sprigs flat-leaved parsley, finely chopped
½ tsp dried rosemary
2 cloves
1 bay leaf
1¾ lb/750 g small onions, peeled
1 tbsp butter
1 generous ½ cup/125 ml red wine
Salt
Freshly ground black pepper

Clean the mushrooms and remove the stalks. Cut the heads in half, fry in hot olive oil, then set aside. Add the finely chopped onions and garlic and cook until softened. Add the tomatoes, vinegar, parsley, rosemary, cloves, and bay leaf, season with salt and pepper, and simmer gently for 30 minutes.
Meanwhile, boil the small, whole onions in water for 10 minutes, pour off the water, leave to drain, and then sauté in butter. Pour in the red wine and then add to the tomato and mushroom mixture. Braise the vegetables for a further 20 minutes, then add the mushrooms and cook for 10 more minutes. Season to taste with salt and pepper and serve while still warm with freshly baked white bread.

MANITÁRIA SALÁTA
Cyclades mushroom salad
(Illustration opposite, bottom left)

Salad greens
½ lb/250 g small mushrooms, cleaned
   and thinly sliced
1 red bell pepper, cored and cut into thin strips
½ bunch flat-leaved parsley, finely chopped
5 tbsp Greek extra virgin olive oil
3 tbsp mild white wine vinegar
¼ lb/100 g kefalotíri cheese, crumbled
Salt

Put all the salad ingredients into a bowl and combine with the oil, vinegar, and a little salt. Scatter with the cheese and serve.
This salad has been adapted to suit the tastes of tourists who have certain expectations of Mediterranean cuisine. It was originally an Italian recipe that calls for arugola (rocket).

MANITARÓSOUPA
Mushroom soup
(Illustration opposite, top right)

2 lbs/1 kg mushrooms
1 tbsp/25 g butter
1 tbsp Greek extra virgin olive oil
1 large onion, finely chopped
1 clove of garlic, crushed
1 generous cup/250 ml chicken stock
½ tsp grated nutmeg
1⅓ cups/300 ml milk
1⅓ cups/300 ml whipping cream
1 bunch flat-leaved parsley, finely chopped
Salt
Freshly ground black pepper

Clean the mushrooms and remove the stalks. Set aside ¼ lb/100 g, leaving them whole, and finely chop the remaining mushrooms. Heat the butter and olive oil in a pan and soften the onion and garlic. Add the chopped mushrooms and sauté. Pour in the chicken stock, season with the nutmeg, salt, and pepper then cover and simmer for 10 minutes. Heat a little oil in a skillet and fry the whole mushrooms. Pour in the milk and add to the soup. Serve the soup in deep plates with a splash of cream, and garnish with parsley.

MANITÁRIA YEMISTÁ
Stuffed mushrooms
(Illustration opposite, bottom right)

4 large mushrooms
2 tbsp corn oil
1 large onion, finely chopped
6 oz/150 g ground lamb
1 tbsp breadcrumbs
A generous ⅓ cup/80 ml whipping cream
1 egg yolk
2 tbsp/25 g butter
1 scant cup/200 ml dry white wine
Salt
Freshly ground black pepper

Preheat the oven to 430 °F (220 °C). Clean the mushrooms, remove the stalks, and set aside. Heat the corn oil in a skillet, soften the onion in it, and remove from the heat. In a bowl, combine the ground lamb with the softened onion, breadcrumbs, cream, and egg yolk, and season with salt and pepper. Grease a baking dish with butter and add the mushrooms. Spread the filling evenly over the mushrooms and bake in a preheated oven for 30 minutes. Stuffed mushrooms are a popular appetizer.

Pulses are a staple food on all the inhabited Greek islands. Clockwise: lima beans, brown beans, lentils, black-eyed peas, fava, chickpeas (garbanzo beans); in the middle: yellow lentils.

PULSES AND VEGETABLES

Chickpeas (garbanzo beans) (*Cicer arietinum*), lentils (*Lens culinaris*), peas (*Pisum sativum*), and beans (*Phaseolus vulgaris*) all belong to the legume family (*Leguminosae*), most of which have whitish or purple flowers. The Mediterranean region is the main area in which they are grown in Europe. Pulses are regarded as a staple food throughout Greece, but the inhabitants of the Greek islands must have developed a special taste and hence suitable recipes for them, because on their arid fields, it was hard to grow anything else at the best of times, and quite impossible during periods of repression and poverty.

In some ways, not much has changed even today. On the Cyclades not only chickpeas (garbanzo beans), but also beans, fava, lentils, and peas are sown after the first rain showers, from October to December, and they are exposed to difficult climatic conditions. On the poor, rocky, and dry soil, the plants have to make do with nothing more than rainwater.

The volcanic rock on Santorini is able to store rainwater, releasing it to the plants as they need it. Thus, since classical times, even Greece's most notorious volcanic island has played a part in the history of cultivating pulses, especially the yellow lentils. For pulses to develop properly, it is important that they get sufficient water, particularly after flowering in spring, to prevent the setting pods from drying out. That is why people eagerly await the spring rains. If they do not come, or are only slight, the entire crop can be destroyed. There can never be a glut of pulses in Greece.

Chickpeas (garbanzo beans) are used as an ingredient in winter soup dishes. Combined with plenty of olive oil and fresh tomatoes, they make a hearty, nutritious meal that is enjoyed throughout Greece. On the islands, where opportunities for agriculture have always been limited, they have become very inventive when preparing the few staple foods available. That is why you can discover dishes on the islands that are not common on the mainland, such as chickpea puddings, vegetarian rissoles, and salads.

YELLOW LENTILS

Among the pulses, yellow lentils – forerunners of the modern cultivars were used as long ago as 10,000 B.C. in Syria – occupy a special place in Greece, because there is evidence that they were cultivated on Santorini as long ago as 2000 B.C. Soft, sandy soils rich in potassium, iron, and magnesium, and the short, heavy rainfall typical of the Cyclades provide perfect growing conditions. Yellow lentils have a sweeter flavor than other lentils and can make a simple lentil purée into a culinary delight. In the last several years, this has led to increased demand outstripping supply, so that yellow lentils have almost become a delicacy, available only from inland markets.

FÁVA SANTORÍNIS
Yellow lentil purée

1 scant cup/200 ml Greek extra virgin olive oil
1 onion, finely chopped
2½ cups/500 g dried yellow lentils
3 bay leaves
1 tsp capers
1 onion, cut into rings
10 cherry tomatoes
1 tsp dried oregano
Juice of 1 lemon
Salt
Freshly ground black pepper

Heat a scant ½ cup/100 ml olive oil in a pan and soften the finely chopped onion in it. Add 4 cups/1 liter water, bring to a boil, and add the lentils. Remove any scum as it appears. When the water has been fully absorbed, the lentils should have become mushy. Season with salt and pepper, and quickly process with a hand-held blender. Leave the purée in a cool place to set. Before serving, stir in lemon juice to taste and the remaining olive oil. Transfer to a large plate, garnish with the capers, onion rings, and cherry tomatoes, and sprinkle with the oregano. Serve cold.

FAVAKEFTÉDES ME KÁPARI YAKHNÍ
Lentil rissoles with caper and tomato sauce

1 generous cup/250 ml Greek extra virgin olive oil
1 large onion, finely chopped
2½ cups/500 g dried lentils
Salt and freshly ground black pepper

For the caper and tomato sauce:
½ cup/100 g dried capers
A scant ½ cup/100 ml Greek extra virgin olive oil
1 small onion, finely chopped
A scant ½ cup/100 ml red or white wine
½ lb/250 g tomatoes, skinned and finely diced
Salt and freshly ground pepper

For the lentil rissoles:
3½ tbsp/50 ml Greek extra virgin olive oil
3 onions, sliced into rings
1¼ cups/200 g sesame seeds
½ bunch flat-leaved parsley, very finely chopped
3 sprigs mint, finely chopped
Olive oil for frying

To cook the lentils, heat half the olive oil, soften the onion in it, and add 4 cups/1 liter water. Bring to a boil and add the lentils. Simmer until the lentils become mushy, removing any scum that may form. Stir in the remaining olive oil and set aside. For the sauce, soak the capers overnight to remove any bitterness, then pour off the water, rinse, and leave to drain. Heat the olive oil and soften the onions. Add the wine, followed by the tomatoes and capers. Season with salt and pepper and simmer until the sauce has thickened. Set aside and leave to cool. For the lentil rissoles, heat the olive oil and soften the onions. Add the mushy lentil mixture, sesame seeds, parsley, and mint, stir well, and quickly cook the mixture. Remove from the heat and leave in a cool place for several hours. Heat plenty of olive oil in a deep-fry pan, shape the mixture into small rissoles, and fry in the oil until crispy. Transfer the rissoles to a large plate and serve warm with the caper and tomato sauce.

REVITHOKEFTÉDES
Chickpea rissoles
(Not illustrated)

2¾ cups/500 g dried chickpeas (garbanzo beans)
1 onion, finely chopped
1 clove of garlic, crushed
3 sprigs flat-leaved parsley, finely chopped
1 sprig mint, finely chopped
1 tbsp tomato paste
1 tsp cinnamon
All-purpose flour
Olive oil for frying
Salt
Freshly ground black pepper

Soak the chickpeas overnight. The next day, wash them well and leave to drain. Pound them into a paste with a pestle and mortar and transfer to a bowl. Add the onion, garlic, parsley, and mint and combine thoroughly. Stir a little water into the tomato paste and add to the chickpea mixture, together with the cinnamon. Season with salt and pepper and knead into a dough, adding a little flour if it has become too moist. Heat the olive oil in a deep-fry pan. Shape the mixture into small, flat rissoles, and deep fry in the hot olive oil until golden brown. Chickpea rissoles are a delicacy that can be served either warm or cold with a fresh salad as an appetizer.

REVÍTHIA STO FOÚRNO
Baked chickpeas (Not illustrated)

6 scant cups/1 kg dried chickpeas
   (garbanzo beans)
2 onions, finely chopped
Juice of 1 lemon
1½ cups/350 ml Greek extra virgin olive oil
3–4 bay leaves
All-purpose flour
Salt
Freshly ground black pepper

Soak the chickpeas overnight. The next day, pour off the water, rinse, and leave to drain thoroughly. Put the chickpeas in an earthenware casserole dish with a tight-fitting lid and combine with the onions, lemon juice, and olive oil. Season with salt and pepper, and place the bay leaves on top. Combine the flour with a little water to make a thick paste. Place the lid on the casserole and seal all around with the flour-and-water paste. Place the casserole in the oven and leave to cook overnight at a very low temperature. Serve in the casserole dish garnished with a couple of lemon wedges.

SALÁTA ME ÁSPRI MELITZÁNA KAI ME KHTAPÓDI
White eggplant and octopus salad

1 small octopus, ready prepared
Olive oil
White wine vinegar
¼ tsp dried oregano
1 large white eggplant
1 beefsteak tomato, diced
1 small onion, finely chopped
½ bunch flat-leaved parsley, finely chopped
Parsley to garnish
Salt
Freshly ground black pepper

Put the octopus in a pan, add sufficient water just to cover it, and cook until soft. Then pour off the water, leave to drain, and transfer to a bowl. Add the olive oil, oregano, salt and pepper, and a little vinegar, and leave in the refrigerator for a few hours to marinate.
Preheat the oven to 400 ºF (200 ºC). Wash the eggplant, rub with oil, and place on a shelf in the oven. Bake until the eggplant is cooked. Cut away about a third of the eggplant so that it can be hollowed out and stuffed. Blend the eggplant flesh, then stir in the tomato, onion, parsley, salt and pepper, and a little oil. Take the octopus out of the marinade, cut it into small pieces, and combine with the eggplant mixture. Spoon the filling into the eggplant, drizzle with olive oil, and leave in a cool place. Garnish with parsley and serve as an appetizer.

NUTRITIOUS ISLAND CUISINE

The advantage of pulses is that they are easy to grow and store well, so that their high protein content is always available, whatever the season. Proteins form the basis of all vegetable, animal, and human cells, and every organism depends on a constant supply of them for its survival. For that reason, pulses are viewed as a blessing by some, and as the food of the poor by others, which they make do with until they can afford something better.

PRICKLY PEARS

Of the fruit-bearing cacti, the prickly pear (*Opuntia ficus-indica*) is one of the few that can be found in the fruit market. The plant originated from Mexico or Central America and was introduced to the Mediterranean region by Spanish sailors around 1600. There it quickly spread. Today it is indigenous to almost all the arid zones of the tropics and subtropics. If the conditions are right, it can grow into an impenetrable thicket, spreading like a weed, which is why it is even sometimes planted as a boundary between plots of land. The plant grows up to 13 feet (4 meters) tall and is made up of disk-shaped stem sections (*phylloclades*) up to 16 x 8 x ¾ inches (40 x 20 x 2 centimeters). These flattened sections are armed with prickles arranged in tufts on short shoots, and store water in dry periods. Yellow flowers that appear at their edges develop into the edible prickly pears, which grow to a length of 1½–4 inches (4–10 centimeters). The fruits, which are yellow, salmon pink, or red depending on how ripe they are, also have prickles. The flesh of the fruit is either light green, yellowish, or deep red. It is juicy with a jelly-like texture and contains small, hard seeds. The flavor is sweet and slightly acidic, reminiscent of pears. The fruit has a high vitamin C content, and also contains B-group vitamins, potassium, calcium, magnesium, and phosphorus. It is thought to reduce cholesterol levels.

FASOLÁKIA ME DOMÁTA
Beans in tomato sauce

2½ cups/500 g dried navy beans
1 scant cup/200 ml Greek extra virgin olive oil
3 onions, finely chopped
3 carrots, sliced
4 tomatoes, skinned and diced
½ bunch flat-leaved parsley, finely chopped
Salt
Freshly ground black pepper

Soak the beans overnight. The next day, rinse them well, put in a pan, cover with water, and bring to a boil. Lower the heat and cook the beans until they are soft. Meanwhile, heat the olive oil in a pan and soften the onions. Add the carrots, tomatoes, and parsley, season to taste with salt and pepper, cover the pan, and simmer for 30 minutes. Add the beans to the vegetables and stir. Serve either warm or cold with freshly baked white bread.

YÍGANDES PLAKÍ
Baked lima beans

2½ cups/500 g lima beans
1 onion, finely chopped
2 cloves of garlic, sliced
4 tomatoes, skinned and strained
⅔ cup/150 ml Greek extra virgin olive oil
1 bunch flat-leaved parsley, finely chopped
Salt
Freshly ground black pepper

Soak the beans overnight. The next day, rinse them well, put in a pan, add sufficient water to cover, then bring to a boil and cook for 5 minutes. Drain the beans, rinse, and return them to the pan. Add fresh water, bring to a boil, lower the heat, and simmer until they are soft.

Preheat the oven to 400 ºF (200 ºC). Pour off the water, leave the beans to drain, and transfer them to a flameproof dish. Add all the remaining ingredients, season with salt and pepper, and combine well. Add a little water and bake the beans in a preheated oven for about 1 hour. The beans should be very soft and have a mealy texture.

MAVROMÁTIKA ME SÉSKOULO
Black-eyed peas with beet greens
(Illustration opposite)

1 cup/200 g dried black-eyed peas
1 lb/450 g beet greens
2 tbsp lemon juice
Olive oil
Parsley, for garnishing
Salt
Freshly ground black pepper

Soak the peas overnight. The next day, drain them, rinse well, and leave to drain. Then put the peas in pan, cover with water, and bring to a boil. Lower the heat, simmer the peas for about 15 minutes, then drain, rinse, and return to the pan. Cover with fresh water, add salt, and simmer over a moderate heat for 30 minutes. Meanwhile, wash, trim, and shred the beet leaves. Stir into the peas shortly before the cooking time is up, and simmer together for about 5 minutes until the beans are soft and the beet leaves have wilted. Then pour off the water and leave to drain. Transfer the peas and beet leaves to a plate, season to taste with salt and pepper, and drizzle with lemon juice and olive oil. Sprinkle with parsley and serve while still warm with an accompaniment of freshly baked white bread.

YÍGANDES TIGANITÍ

Fried lima beans
(Illustration right)

2½ cups/500 g dried lima beans
1¾ cups/200 g all-purpose flour
2 eggs
2 tbsp milk
2 crackers, crumbled
Greek extra virgin olive oil
½ bunch flat-leaved parsley, finely chopped
Salt and freshly ground black pepper

Soak the beans overnight. The next day, drain and rinse them. Fill a pan with plenty of water, then add the beans, together with a little salt, and cook until soft. Pour off the water and drain the beans well. Sift the flour into a bowl and add salt and pepper. In a second bowl, beat the eggs and stir in the milk. Put the crumbled crackers in a third bowl. Heat plenty of olive oil in a deep-fry pan. Coat each bean first in the flour, then in the egg mixture, and finally in the biscuit crumbs. Then deep fry the beans in the hot oil. Transfer to a plate, sprinkle with parsley, and serve hot.

This recipe, which is usually served as an appetizer, will be sufficient to satisfy even the healthiest appetite.

WINES OF THE CYCLADES

Historians believe that the first vineyards in the Mediterranean region were on Crete. From there, the vine was taken by the Minoans to Santorini, classical Thera, which, along with Páros, is now the only significant wine-producing island in the Cyclades. Both islands are considered quality wine regions with their own *appellation*. Here, the Aegean wind, which is often really raw, forces the winegrowers to grow the vines very low. On Santorini they have developed a method that is as original as it is idiosyncratic. The vine is pulled down quite close to the ground, often even down into a shallow hollow, and forms a sort of basket to protect against the powerful gusts of wind. The cool wind of the Cyclades, the *meltémi*, which is strong even in summer, sometimes even prevents pests from becoming established. The soil on this volcanic island consists primarily of slate and limestone, and the vineyards can tolerate the parching sun by retaining the moisture that rises from the sea at night for a long time, releasing it gradually to the plants. The soil also absorbs the water from the few rainy days in the year, which generally fall between October and March/April, and as a result of the enormous capacity of the porous, volcanic rock to store water, it is released to the plants only gradually. The island's extremely distinctive microclimate favors the production of the best white wines of the Greek Assyrtiko grape variety.

The white wine from Santorini, which at one time had a very high alcohol content but is now produced in a predominantly "modern" way, displays a harmonious balance of fruit, alcohol, and acidity. A "*vin de paille*," a wine made from

Santorini's specialty wine is Vinsanto, a sweet liqueur wine, which the Russian Orthodox Church also used to believe was "holy."

ready-dried, raisin-like grape, called Liastos, is also produced here. Its name is derived from the old Greek word for the sun, *helios*. A special feature of the Nikteri white wine is that it is harvested at night (*níkhta* in Greek), because the cooler temperatures give the wine a special note. The sweet Vinsanto dessert wine, which was originally produced for church services, is also highly regarded. As part of its production process, the grapes are laid out to dry on terraces for ten days. The wine is then aged in oak casks for two years before it can be bottled.

On Páros, as on Santorini, which has a similar microclimate, most of the vineyards are stocked with the Mandelaria grape. This grape variety is highly regarded by many vermouth producers throughout the world. A dry red wine with rather bitter tannins is made from the Mandelaria grape with a special blend of grapes. By adding about half the quantity of white Monemvasia, which is named for the Peloponnese port of the same name and is called Malvasia in Spain and Italy, the deep red color of the Mandelaria grapes is made lighter.

KHALVADÓPITA

Khalvadópita is a dessert found throughout Greece. Sugar and almonds are combined to form a sticky, but very firm, mixture that is then pressed between thin wafers into sheets. It is similar to *toúrkiko méli* (Turkish honey), a kind of white nougat.

SIGALAS WINERY

Vinsanto: sweet liqueur wine that is made from organic grapes.

Santorini: dry white wine with fresh citrus notes.

HATZIDAKIS WINERY

Nikteri: dry white wine aged in old oak casks.

Santorini: dry white wine made with 90% Assyrtiko grapes.

ROUSSOS WINERY

Santorini: a wine which is dry, pale yellow, and fruity.

Nikteri: aged dry white wine made from Assyrtiko grapes.

BOUTARI WINERY

Vinsanto: well-aged and sweet liqueur wine.

Nikteri: dry cuvée white wine with very distinctive mineral notes.

GAIA WINERY

Thalassitis: dry, acidic, fresh white wine with a flowery nose.

Thalassitis: dry, cask-aged white wine that is top quality.

Grape-pickers have to stoop to pick the grapes lying just above the ground.

To protect the vines against the strong winds that regularly blow over the Cyclades in summer, they are pulled toward the ground to form a basket shape. This way, the leaves provide a certain amount of shelter for the grapes inside the "basket."

For some wines, the white wine grapes are laid out to dry in the midday sun.

As they dry, the grapes lose water, so that the sugars and flavors become more concentrated.

The fruits and leaves of the *kítro* tree can be processed: the former to make a sweet, the latter a liqueur.

You are unlikely to see a citron tree either laden with fruit on every branch or entirely bare, because it flowers throughout the year, and as a result there is always a branch or two with fruit on. The individual fruits look too large and heavy for the evergreen tree, which grows to a height of only 6 to 14 feet (2–4 meters).

KÍTRO

Kítro, as the citron (*Citrus medica*) is called in Greece, reached the Middle East from northeast India as early as the 7th century B.C., and around 300 B.C. it became the first citrus fruit in the Greek Mediterranean under Alexander the Great. In classical times it was often called the Persian or Median apple, and its intensely scented leaves are primarily used to deter moths and in the perfume industry.

Since 1915, *kítro* has been systematically cultivated on Naxos. The thorny evergreen tree, which grows to a height of between 6 and 12 feet (2–4 meters), has lilac flowers and sets fruit throughout the year. There are sweet and sour varieties, and their fruits vary greatly in size, color, and shape, but they all have an extremely thick rind, which accounts for about 60 percent of the fruit. On Naxos there is a family-run business that makes a *kítro* liqueur, which is known far beyond the island. The juice obtained from the leaves of the *kítro* tree is distilled by a special process. Single distillation produces the 35 percent liqueur *Kítro Náxou*, while *Kítro Náxou spezial* is the result of a double distillation process.

Above: this small distilling apparatus has now served its purpose and can be admired on Naxos as an exhibition piece. Greece's unique *kítro* liqueur is made only in a very small area here.

Left: these brightly colored bottles do not come from a perfumery. The liqueur they contain is simply colored and every bottle tastes the same.

KÍTRO-GLIKÓ

On Naxos, the thick rind of the *kítro* is boiled in syrup and made into *glikó* – a very good way of using citron.

Quality *kítro* liqueur is served in style in small, crystal liqueur glasses, decorated with a *kítro* leaf.

Above: large earthenware vessels, *pithária*, are used to store supplies of food. They can keep wheat, oil, water, wine, and many other things cool and fresh for a long time.
Background: the excavations at Akrotíri have been roofed over to protect them from the elements.

FORCES OF NATURE

People do not always get off so lightly when a natural disaster strikes, as it did around 1600 B.C. on Santorini. The inhabitants were forewarned, because the volcanic mountain, about 6600 feet (2000 meters) high, had already released minor ash eruptions across the island. These were also followed by earth tremors, causing walls to collapse. Although not that much was happening, people still recognized the imminent danger. The inhabitants left the island, returning shortly to repair the damage, perhaps even to rebuild. But events repeated themselves. This time powerful earth tremors gave warning of something much more threatening. Today, people still believe that the inhabitants were again able to leave their island uninjured. There were violent eruptions, with pumice ash and gas clouds being hurled up to 22.5 miles (36 kilometers) into the sky. An ash rain fell as far away as modern-day Turkey, leaving behind a layer of pumice three quarters of an inch (two centimeters) deep. The island itself was buried under a 53-foot (16 meter) deep layer of pumice and ash. Fissures formed at the crater's edge, through which seawater flowed into the volcano, coming into contact with the glowing magma and causing even more powerful eruptions. As a result of these explosive eruptions, first the volcanic plug was blown away, then the crater's unstable walls collapsed, leaving only the remains of the crater rim that form the islands now grouped around Santorini. This violent explosion with the subsequent implosion of the crater created a tidal wave, and there is proof that this led to floods on Crete. Whether Atlantis fell here, as has always been speculated, will remain a myth, however. Even later, the island, which was not occupied again until around 1200 B.C., did not enjoy a tranquil life. Minor eruptions created more and more active volcanic islands in the center of the crater-lake. In 1956 an earthquake shook the island, causing major damage. Knowledge of the major catastrophe and what was lost as a result is still relatively new. After initial finds in 1866, the archaeologist Spyridon Marinaos came upon a thick pumice layer during excavations on Crete, which he linked with the volcanic eruption on Santorini. Systematic excavations in the village of Akrotíri did not begin until 1967, when the remains of a 3600-year old town were brought to light. The links between the culture that existed here before the catastrophe and Crete, and the suppositions about its high degree of civilization and its high standard of living were quickly confirmed. The first settlements on Santorini as long ago as 3000 B.C. mark the beginning of the Cycladic civilization, and a new stage of civilization and cultural development is indicated by the increasing influence of Crete around 2000 B.C. This lasted until around 1600 B.C. There were three-story buildings, water pipes, and baths; people lived in a prosperity that they owed to the intensive agriculture, cattle farming, and fishing, but especially to trade. Since no palaces have been found, scholars assume that an autonomous community lived here, relatively independent of Crete, a community that administered itself, and in which social and economic differences were very slight.

View from the crater's edge over Néa Kaméni, the most recent lava island of the Santorini Archipelago, on which the volcano continues to emit sulfurous vapor.

A marble vessel with a conical neck from the early Cycladic period, around 3000–2500 B.C. It was used for liquids. Cords were threaded through the eyelets to make it easy to carry.

The marble cord eyelet beaker (right) is early Cycladic. The marble pyxis, a lidded vessel that also had eyelets so that it could be carried, is slightly later.

TEMPLE GATE AT NAXOS

Around 530 B.C. the tyrant Lygdamis started the construction of an impressive temple on the small island that used to be offshore from the harbor of Naxos. The fact that it was so close to the harbor and looked out toward Delos may mean that it was consecrated to Apollo. A thousand years later, a Christian basilica rose up from the ruins, and the Venetians in turn later plundered the site for its stone.

ΔΩΔΕΚΑΝΗΣΣΑ

Above: you can spend many a pleasant day and evening in the picture-book setting of harmonious architecture developed over time in Lindos.
Background: the entrance to the Mandráki harbor of the new section of Ródhos.

DODECANESE

Cool and refreshing

Pomegranates

The strawberry tree

Time for soup

Dodecanese fish

Yíros and döner kebabs

Capers

Aegean gold

The name "Dodecanese" is really rather misleading, because it literally means "twelve islands" (and originally described only those lying next to the Turkish coast), whereas there are actually 20 permanently populated islands. The way the islands are positioned on the southeastern edge of the Aegean, far from the Greek mainland, looks almost as if it had been planned.

Patmos, the biblical setting for the Revelation of St. John, Rhodes' citadel of the medieval Knights of St. John, Kos with its well-organized Turkish area, and the island of Kálimnos with its traditional sponge fishing all emphasize distinctive features of the overall picture of Greece. Anyone leafing through the history books is struck time and again by the varied past of this group of islands, particularly its main island, Rhodes. The Canaanites and Phoenicians, who inhabited the islands around 2000 B.C., were followed around 1700 B.C. by the Minoans of Crete. They, in turn, succumbed about 250 years later to Mycenaean Achaeans from the Peloponnese, who were finally ejected by the Dorians around 1150 B.C. Linked thereafter with the Persians, Greeks, Turks, Romans, and Ottomans depending on the political situation, the islands have withstood occupation, plundering, and changes in religion. From 1912, the Dodecanese belonged to Italy. From 1943–1945, they were occupied by Germany, and have been officially Greek only since December 31, 1947.

Today, the islands can offer culinary traditions dating back to the times of the Knights of St. John, although there is still a decidedly Italian influence on their way of life and eating habits. The custom of using various parts of the caper tree, for example, is definitely a legacy from the Italian period. Close relations with neighboring places on the Turkish coast have also given rise to a kebab culture, giving many travelers an early taste of oriental cuisine while they are still on Greek soil.

The Dodecanese, with the famous sun island of Rhodes, is also one of Greece's most important travel destinations because of its climate, which is rather moderate for the southeastern Mediterranean region. The islands are heavily dependent on tourism, which is why olives, potatoes, and tomatoes are increasingly cultivated on Rhodes and Kos, as well as grapevines, while other types of vegetables and fruit have to be imported.

On hot summer days, a glass of ice-cold water with a spoonful of creamy sweet *vanília* is a very special treat – a real taste of childhood for the Greeks.

COOL AND REFRESHING

Seventeenth-century travelogues occasionally sing the praises of a very innocuous drink made of water, sugar, and lemon juice, which also came in rose, lotus, or rhubarb flavors. Around the Mediterranean, chilled non-alcoholic, spring water-based cordials have been appreciated as a welcome sweet refreshment since the Roman Empire, but particularly so since Byzantine times. Alcoholic beverages, on the other hand, unless forbidden on religious grounds, were usually only taken after sunset, an admirable custom that is still respected in Greece today – or usually, at any rate. On hot summer days, an ice-cold fruity drink provides welcome relief at midday. The great variety of such drinks has no difficulty holding its own alongside the ubiquitous Coca-Cola. Topping the list of favorite summer drinks are *lemonáda* (lemon soft drink), *portokaláda* (orange soft drink), and *gazóza* (sweetened carbonated mineral water). These are closely followed by fruit juice cordials, produced in Greece itself because it grows such a huge variety of fruit, such as peach, apple, orange, grapefruit, cherry, pear, and banana juice. But the number one drink continues to be a cool glass of freshly squeezed fruit juice.

Soft drinks are served ice-cold, as only then will they refresh tired shoppers, hectic business people, and sun-starved vacationers.

Above: a spoonful of *vanília* in a glass of pure, ice-cold spring water is a double pleasure.

Below: *vanília* comes in many flavors, rose being one of the most popular.

VANÍLIA NOSTALGIA

To a certain extent, *vanília* is the first Greek soft drink, because even up to 20 years ago it was one of the most important refreshing beverages chosen by mixed groups in the tavernas. While the mocha was being served, they sipped a little syrup slowly from the spoon, then drank the slightly sweetened water, followed by the mocha.

BASIC RECIPE FOR VANÍLIA

2½ generous cups/600 g sugar
A generous ½ cup/125 ml water
2 tbsp lemon juice
1 tsp vanilla sugar

Heat the sugar and water until the sugar has dissolved and the syrup has thickened. Add the lemon juice, quickly bring the mixture to a boil, then remove from the heat. Leave to cool, and when tepid, stir in the vanilla sugar using a wooden spoon. It is important that you always stir in the same direction. *Vanília* is ready when the syrup has become thick and white. Transfer to a container with a tight-fitting lid and store in a cool place.

| Naturally cloudy lemon soft drink | Clear lemon soft drink | Orange soft drink | Cherry soft drink | Naturally cloudy lemon soft drink | Naturally cloudy lemon soft drink | Orange soft drink |

Peach-flavored mineral water, orangeade, lemon cola, cola drink (from left to right).

Although there is a great range of non-alcoholic beverages, the overall choice is still visible at a glance because, despite a wealth of branded goods from a few supraregional firms and the numerous products of regional companies, there is a limit to the flavors that can actually hold their own on the market.

SPARKLING WINE FROM RHODES

It is not one of the traditional refreshing beverages, nor is it non-alcoholic, yet no one can deny the reviving effect of a glass of foaming sparkling wine. The C.A.I.R. (Compagnie Agricole et Industrielle de Rhodes) cooperative winery, founded on the island of Rhodes in 1928, was for a long time the only place to go within Greece for the quality wine that is produced using the French champagne method. According to the *méthode champenoise*, the carbon dioxide required to create the sparkling effect is produced by means of a second fermentation in the bottle. To do this, the base wine, along with a "full dosage" of wine and sugar to promote fermentation, is transferred to new, pressure-resistant bottles and temporarily sealed with a crown cork. This full dosage starts the fermentation and comprises the necessary quantity of sugar (either dissolved in the wine or in the form of grape must) and cultured yeast. After about

nine months, this dosage, which has become sediment, is removed by placing the bottles tilting downward in a riddling rack. The bottlenecks are then dipped in a coolant to freeze the sediment. The crown cork is quickly removed and the vacuum shoots the frozen sediment out of the bottle, which is then topped up with a final dosage of sparkling wine and sealed with its permanent champagne cork. C.A.I.R. sells more than half a million bottles of its dry sparkling wine made from the white Athiri grape, and this trend is rising as more careful vinification using modern technology guarantees a sophisticated range of aromas. Today, as in antiquity, the vines are grown preferably on the island's northern slopes, where they are exposed to the fresher winds of the Aegean Sea.

Grenadine, the syrup flavored with pomegranate seeds, adds a dash of color to cocktails. Its specific gravity means that it sinks to the bottom in a Tequila Sunrise, thus conjuring up the whole spectrum of the colors of the sunrise in the glass.

If the pomegranate stays on the tree until fully ripe, you can see how the leathery skins of the fruits burst open and numerous seeds fall to the ground. And then you can understand not only the fertility symbolism that is attached to the pomegranate, but also the origins of its name (exploding apple).

POMEGRANATES

"Let us get up early to the vineyards; let us see if the vine flourish, whether the tender grape appear, and the pomegranates bud forth: there will I give thee my loves." When these lines from the Song of Solomon were written, the fruit of the pomegranate tree (*Punica granatum*), indigenous throughout Persia, was already an established symbol of love and fertility in Palestine, perhaps because of its wealth of seeds, each pomegranate having up to 150 seeds. The attempt to link the name of the island of Rhodes etymologically with the ancient Greek word *rhoa* for pomegranate tree and *rhoidion* for pomegranate is also based on archeological finds, providing evidence that the myrtle-like plant has existed in the region since the second millennium before Christ. As an ornamental plant, the shrub-like evergreen tree can grow to a height of over 15 feet (5 meters), a height it never attains in the wild or when cultivated commercially. It grows in tropical, subtropical, and warm moderate climates. From July to September, orange-red flowers similar to those of the rose species appear. In autumn, these mature into apple-sized fruits. The best fruits thrive in places with hot, dry summers followed by cool winters. Its main areas of cultivation are in Spain and Morocco. Today, there is not much pomegranate cultivation in Greece. In antiquity, the seeds were grated as a spice, while the juice from the seed coats was used as an acidifier long before citrus fruits were known. The leathery skin was used in tanning and dyeing. The flowers and seeds have traditionally been used for medicinal purposes, and also as an aphrodisiac. The latter, however, owes far more to the fact that the pomegranate was thought to be a symbol of fertility than to any demonstrable effect. The seeds and seed coats of the pomegranate are used today in the manufacture of grenadine, that heavy, red syrup that lends color and extra flavor to many cocktails.

POMEGRANATE DELIGHT

2 medium-sized ripe pomegranates
2 tbsp ground almonds
1 tbsp sesame seeds
1 tbsp chopped pumpkin seeds
1 tbsp chopped pine nuts
2 tbsp tsípouro (marc brandy)

Wash the pomegranates and cut them across into thin slices (reserving the juice), making it easier to remove the seeds from their chambers. Finely chop all the seeds and combine them with the sesame seeds, pumpkin seeds, pine nuts, and ground almonds. Stir in the tsípouro (one without aniseed flavoring if possible) to make the mixture easy to spread, adding a little pomegranate juice if necessary. This concoction, which is said to have an aphrodisiac effect, is served as a spread on nut or whole-wheat pastries. The pomegranate mixture should be stored in a cool place and kept for no more than a week.

THE STRAWBERRY TREE

You have to look carefully if you want to spot the strawberry tree (*Arbutus unedo*) in its wild form in among the chestnut oaks, olive trees, myrtles, and rock roses of the extensive, dense bush. The tree grows to 3 to 15 feet (1–5 meters) high in the dry scrub land, developed by nature in the Mediterranean region over a thousand years ago to adapt to the rocky soils made barren as a result of land clearance and the concomitant soil erosion. However, the strawberry tree is easier to spot from October to March, when at one and the same time it bears both lily-of-the-valley-sized clusters of flowers and round red fruits, which from a distance look like cherries, but bear a closer resemblance to lychees when viewed close up. This juxtaposition of flowers and fruits makes the plant an attractive ornamental shrub on deep soils in frost-free regions, especially as

the fruits are edible. There is evidence they were gathered as long ago as the Neolithic period, and even in the 2nd century A.D. the physician Galen, who was born in Pergamon and practiced in Rome, considered them to be a food worth picking. Not everyone agrees with him today. Although the soft, creamy, yellow flesh of the fruit, which is full of seeds, has a pleasant sweet-sour taste, it does not have much else to offer in terms of flavor, so that they are not often eaten fresh. In addition, a surfeit of under-ripe fruits can cause intoxication and nausea, a fact of which the *unedo* (I eat but one) of the botanical name perhaps gives due warning. While the fresh fruits perish quickly and thus do not export well, they are good for cooking or drying, which is why they are made into jellies and compotes, or feature in the ingredient list for bitters.

Left: the fruits of the Arbutus are more like strawberries in appearance than taste.
Below: strawberry trees, which grow to assume majestic proportions, are also popular ornamental garden plants.

PERSEPHONE – GODDESS OF CONTRADICTIONS

Persephone, wife of Hades and hence Queen of the Underworld, was also responsible for matters relating to fertility by virtue of being the daughter of Demeter, goddess of the earth and corn. With Zeus' consent, but against Demeter's wishes, Hades had abducted Persephone. In response, Demeter forced Zeus to secure the return of their daughter by inflicting famines, which she sent out across the earth. The father of the gods had to yield – as long as Persephone had not eaten anything in the Underworld. She had, however, eaten the pomegranate seeds offered to her by Hades, and was therefore forced to spend a third of the year in the Underworld, thus being able to spend only the remaining time with her mother. Since then, Persephone has watched over the seed sown in the earth and hence over the vegetation as it dies back and subsequently reappears. As a result, the fertility symbolism of the pomegranate that banished her acquires the additional aspect of rebirth.

TIME FOR SOUP

The national dish of the Greeks, whether they live on the mainland or on the islands, involves neither expensive meat nor extravagant fish recipes, for it is a simple but satisfying bean soup. The art of turning simplicity into a delicacy is passed on from mother to daughter, so that preparing *fasoláda* can be considered the ultimate test of a good cook. Soups in all their many varieties are generally very popular in Greece, particularly in winter, of course, but also at other times of year. Some recipes are associated with particular occasions. One such dish is *mayirítsa*, the classic Easter soup made from lamb's organ meat (see page 191). It is eaten to signify the end of the fasting period, the start of which may well have been marked 40 days earlier by serving *patsás*, calf's foot soup (see page 142), a specialty that is served throughout the year in Greek tavernas. *Kakaviá*, which people living on the coasts make from freshly caught fish, must be eaten as soon as it is made. In contrast, the flavors of soups made from chickpeas (garbanzo beans), lentils, meatballs, chicken, and many other Greek soups are usually even more intense and powerful on the second or even third day. Pulses are particularly common on the often barren Greek islands, because these extremely accommodating plants thrive well even under difficult climate conditions such as strong winds, arid, rocky soil, and the strong summer sunshine.

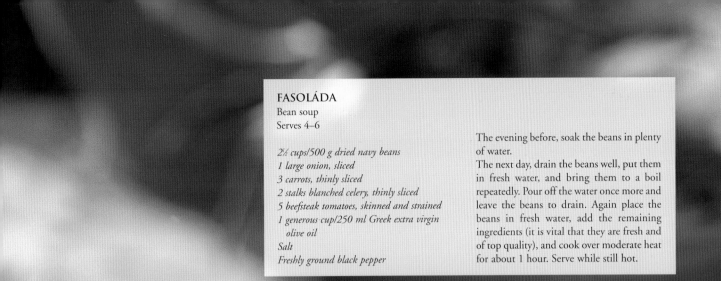

FASOLÁDA
Bean soup
Serves 4–6

2½ cups/500 g dried navy beans
1 large onion, sliced
3 carrots, thinly sliced
2 stalks blanched celery, thinly sliced
5 beefsteak tomatoes, skinned and strained
1 generous cup/250 ml Greek extra virgin
    olive oil
Salt
Freshly ground black pepper

The evening before, soak the beans in plenty of water.

The next day, drain the beans well, put them in fresh water, and bring them to a boil repeatedly. Pour off the water once more and leave the beans to drain. Again place the beans in fresh water, add the remaining ingredients (it is vital that they are fresh and of top quality), and cook over moderate heat for about 1 hour. Serve while still hot.

KREATÓSOUPA
Meat soup
(Illustration below)

A scant ½ cup/100 ml Greek extra virgin olive oil
2 lbs/1 kg beef, diced
1 large onion, sliced
2–3 stalks blanched celery, thinly sliced
2 carrots, thinly sliced
1 bunch flat-leaved parsley, finely chopped
3 beefsteak tomatoes, skinned and strained
1 cup/200 g rice
1 bay leaf
Juice of 1 lemon
Salt
Freshly ground black pepper

Heat the olive oil in a pan and quickly brown the meat all over. Then add the onion rings and fry until golden. Top up with water and bring to a boil, removing any scum that is produced. Lower the heat and leave the meat to simmer gently for about 1 hour. Then add the remaining ingredients, except for the lemon juice, and simmer until cooked. Finally, stir in the lemon juice and serve the finished soup steaming hot.

KHORTÓSOUPA
Vegetable soup

¼ cup/50 g butter
1 small onion, finely chopped
1 leek, finely sliced
4 beefsteak tomatoes, skinned and strained
4 cups/1 liter clear meat stock
2 carrots, finely diced
1 celery root, finely diced
Celery leaves, finely chopped
1 bell pepper, finely diced
1 zucchini, finely diced
2 potatoes, finely diced
½ cup/100 g rice
½ cup/100 g soup pasta
3 tbsp lemon juice
Salt
Freshly ground black pepper

Melt the butter in a pan. Add the onion and leek and soften. Add the strained tomatoes and pour in the meat stock. Add the prepared vegetables and the rice and leave the soup to simmer over a low heat until the ingredients are almost cooked. Stir in the soup pasta, bring the soup to a boil, then lower the heat. As soon as the pasta is soft, remove the soup from the heat and season with lemon juice, salt and pepper. This soup is usually left to cool slightly before being served with freshly baked white bread and garlic butter.

YOUVARLÁKIA
Soup with meatballs

1 lb/500 g ground beef
½ cup/100 g rice
1 medium onion, puréed
1 egg
A generous ½ cup/125 ml Greek extra virgin olive oil
Salt
Freshly ground black pepper
1 bunch flat-leaved parsley, chopped

For the egg and lemon sauce:
2 eggs
Juice of 2 lemons

In a bowl combine the ground beef, the uncooked rice, puréed onion, and the egg. Knead thoroughly and season with salt and pepper. Shape the mixture into small balls (rub your hands with a little oil first). Bring some water to a boil in a pan, add the olive oil, and slide in the meatballs one at a time. Leave the soup to simmer gently for about 30 minutes until the meat and rice are cooked. Prepare the egg and lemon sauce using the recipe on page 117, and stir into the soup. Season to taste with salt and pepper, sprinkle with chopped parsley, and serve hot with freshly baked white bread.

REVITHÓSOUPA
Chickpea (garbanzo bean) soup
(Illustration opposite)

3 cups/500 g dried chickpeas (garbanzo beans)
1 tsp baking soda
3 large onions
1 generous cup/250 ml Greek extra virgin olive oil
Juice of 1 lemon
Salt
Freshly ground black pepper

The evening before, soak the chickpeas (garbanzo beans) in plenty of hot water. The next day, drain the soaked chickpeas, add the bicarbonate of soda, mix well, leave for a short while to take effect, then rinse thoroughly. Put the chickpeas in fresh water, together with the onions, and bring to a boil, removing any scum that is produced. Lower the heat, cover, and leave the soup to simmer for about 2½ hours, adding more boiling water if necessary. Just before the chickpeas become soft, add the olive oil, and season the soup with salt and pepper. Return to a boil and drizzle with the lemon juice before serving.

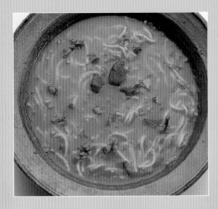

DOMATÓSOUPA
Tomato soup

*4 lbs/2 kg beefsteak tomatoes, skinned
and strained
4 cups/1 liter clear meat stock
1 cup/200 g small soup pasta
¼ cup/50 g butter
1 bunch flat-leaved parsley, coarsely chopped
Salt
Freshly ground black pepper*

Put the meat stock in a pan and stir in the strained tomatoes. Season with salt and pepper and cook the soup for about 20 minutes until it thickens. Add the soup pasta and boil in the soup until soft. Remove the pan from the heat and melt the butter in the hot soup. Pour the soup into bowls, sprinkle with the chopped parsley and a little freshly ground black pepper to taste. Serve while still hot with freshly baked white bread.

FAKÉS
Lentil soup

*2 cups/400 g dried brown lentils
1 medium onion, sliced
2 cloves of garlic, thinly sliced
5 beefsteak tomatoes, skinned and strained
⅔ cup/150 ml Greek extra virgin olive oil
1 bay leaf
Butter
Salt
Freshly ground black pepper*

The evening before, soak the lentils in plenty of water. The next day, drain the lentils, put them in a pan with the remaining ingredients, and cover with fresh water. Bring to a boil, lower the temperature, and leave the soup to simmer for 30–45 minutes. Serve hot! Melt a knob of butter in each plate (optional).
Tip: The flavors in this soup will develop even better if the soup is reheated.

KREMMIDÓSOUPA ME TIRÍ
Onion soup with cheese

*⅞ cup/200 g butter
4 medium onions, sliced
2 tbsp all-purpose flour
2 cups/500 ml clear meat stock
2 cups/500 ml milk
4 slices of white bread
2 cups/125 g coarsely grated kefalotíri cheese*

Melt half the butter in a pan and fry the onions until transparent. Add the flour, stirring constantly. Fry the roux until golden brown, then add the meat stock, stirring constantly, and season with salt and pepper. Leave to simmer over a moderate heat for about 5 minutes. Heat 2 cups/500 ml water. Quickly bring the milk to a boil in a pan. Combine the water and milk and stir into the soup. Leave to simmer over a moderate heat for a further 10 minutes. Meanwhile, dice the slices of white bread and fry in the remaining butter. Serve the hot soup in bowls, scatter with the croutons, and sprinkle with the grated cheese.
Alternative: Fry the slices of bread whole, place one in each bowl, sprinkle with cheese, and pour the hot soup over the bread.

DODECANESE FISH

It goes without saying that fish is a staple food on the Greek islands. The sparser the vegetation and as a result the more difficult it is to keep livestock, the more valuable seafood becomes as a substitute for meat. And here the Dodecanese are no different, even though the main islands of Rhodes and Kos are among the most fertile islands. Fish preparation here does not differ in any fundamental way from that on other islands, but not much action is required to make the most of freshly caught seafood. As was clearly the case 3000 years ago, fish and cuttlefish are still broiled, baked, and sometimes served in a light sauce. A "modern" note is added only by those ingredients that have arrived over time, such as tomatoes, spinach, potatoes, or rice, and the chefs in the island tavernas, especially on Rhodes and Kos, know full well how to make the most of them in terms of taste. Thus the gastronomy in the tourist centers is simultaneously enhanced and hindered by the annual influx of visitors, as their increasing demand for fresh fish threatens the fish stocks of the Aegean.

Soupiés me piláfi –
Cuttlefish with rice

Galéos tiganitós me skordaliá –
Smooth dogfish with garlic and potato purée

SOUPIÉS ME PILÁFI
Cuttlefish with rice

2 lbs/1 kg cuttlefish, ready prepared (reserve
the ink sac)
1 generous cup/250 ml Greek extra virgin olive oil
2 large onions, finely chopped
5 beefsteak tomatoes, skinned and strained
1¾ cups/350 g rice
Salt
Freshly ground black pepper

Put the ink sac in a bowl with a little water (note: the ink must be used within 24 hours). Cut the tentacles into pieces and the body into rings.

Heat the olive oil in a pan, soften the onions, and quickly fry the cuttlefish pieces. Add the strained tomatoes and season with salt and pepper. Cover with water and leave to simmer gently for about 1 hour. Add the ink and some boiling water, stir in the rice, and continue to cook over a low heat until it is soft and has absorbed most of the liquid. Serve while still hot!

GALÉOS TIGANITÓS ME SKORDALIÁ
Smooth dogfish with garlic and potato purée

4 large potatoes, boiled and puréed
6 cloves of garlic
1 generous cup/250 ml Greek extra virgin olive oil
Juice of 2 lemons
4 smooth dogfish steaks, each weighing ½ lb/250 g
All-purpose flour
Olive oil for frying
Salt
Freshly ground black pepper

Crush the garlic cloves and stir into the puréed potatoes, together with the olive oil and juice of one lemon. Season with salt and pepper and add a little water if necessary to achieve a creamy consistency. Place in the refrigerator. Drizzle the juice of the remaining lemon over the fish steaks and coat them in flour. Heat the olive oil in a skillet, add the fish steaks, and fry on both sides until golden brown. Serve with the garlic and potato purée.
Tip: The purée can also be freshly made and served while still warm.

SOUPIÉS ME SPANÁKI
Cuttlefish with spinach

2 lbs/1 kg cuttlefish, ready prepared
1 generous cup/250 ml Greek extra virgin olive oil
1 large onion, sliced
1 clove of garlic, finely chopped
3–4 tomatoes, skinned, seeded, and finely diced
2 lbs/1 kg spinach
1 bunch flat-leaved parsley, finely chopped
Salt
Freshly ground black pepper

Cut the cuttlefish tentacles into pieces and the body into rings. Heat the olive oil in a pan, soften the onion and garlic, and fry the cuttlefish. Stir in the diced tomatoes and season with salt and pepper. Cover with water and simmer gently for 1½ hours.
Wash, blanch, and finely chop the spinach. When the cuttlefish meat is tender, stir in the spinach and the chopped parsley. Quickly bring to a boil and serve while still hot, preferably with freshly baked white bread.

Soupiés me spanáki –
Cuttlefish with spinach

YÍROS AND DÖNER KEBABS

It cannot be a bad thing if international understanding comes about as a result of cooking or if borders start to disappear on plates. In Greek and Turkish cuisine there is a whole range of such culinary blends, their presence being explained to a great extent by the centuries of Ottoman rule over Greece. However, if you are just sitting with friends in a taverna on the village square in Platáni in the east of the Dodecanese island of Kos waiting for your döner kebab, such questions are not uppermost in your mind. And yet there are extremely obvious reminders, because in the small village of Platáni, the second largest Turkish Muslim community in Greece lives peacefully alongside Orthodox Christians – and the cuisine, which is firmly in Muslim hands, sometimes looks pleasantly familiar. Whether the kebabs turning on the spit are *yíros* or *döner* depends largely on the meat. While the fact that both words mean "something that turns in a circle" clearly focuses on one aspect of their preparation, religion governs the main ingredient. Whereas Orthodox Christians with a clear conscience prefer pork, the Muslim inhabitants follow Allah's prohibition and opt for lamb or mutton instead. Once

the religious prescriptions have been taken care of, the marinade for both the *yíros* and *döner* kebab meat is the same. The mixture of salt, pepper, oregano, ground cumin, and olive oil, which can be enhanced with chili powder, pepper, rosemary, thyme, and onions, gives the marinade its hot spiciness.

If we were now to return to the questions mentioned at the start of the section, we could perhaps conclude that, as far as broiling meat on a spit is concerned, neither cuisine has had to influence the other, this shared aspect probably being as old as the use of the fire itself. Broiling is a way of cooking meat, not restricted to any particular area, that requires no heavy, heat resistant vessels, and which was therefore used by hunters and soldiers in situations where every unnecessary expense had to be avoided. It therefore comes as no surprise when ethnologists consider plain grilled or fried meat simply as food for humans, whether in Greece or elsewhere. If nowadays *yíros* and *döner* kebabs are undisputedly, and equally unjustifiably, considered to be the embodiment of Greek or Turkish food in Western Europe, the reason behind it may to some extent lie in the provisions the first foreign workers brought with them for their journey.

Above: Greeks and Turks both take great pleasure in a meal shared with friends.

Opposite: it's not a matter of how they turn – it's the meat that decides whether they are *yíros* or *döner* kebabs.

The balance, rather than the number, of spices (oregano, salt, cumin, and chili) is what really matters.

Lean meat that is suitable for quick frying is cut into ⅜ inch (1 cm) thick slices.

The meat is marinated in a mixture of oil and spices for up to 24 hours.

Grilling over a barbecue adds a flavor that you just don't get when the meat is broiled.

The meat is cut into strips while still hot. Roasted meat can also give a convincing result.

Warm pita bread and the fresh taste of tzatzíki are the perfect accompaniments to this dish.

TAS KEBÁP
Lamb or veal casserole

2 lbs/1 kg lamb or veal
A generous ½ cup/125 g butter
1 lb/500 g onions, sliced
A generous ½ cup/125 ml dry white wine
5 beefsteak tomatoes, skinned, seeded, and
*   coarsely chopped*
1 bunch flat-leaved parsley, finely chopped
Salt
Freshly ground black pepper

Cut the meat into large cubes; melt the butter in a skillet, brown the meat in batches, and set aside. In the same skillet, fry the onion rings until golden brown. Transfer the contents of the skillet to a pan, together with the cubed meat. Add the tomatoes and bring to a boil. Season with salt and pepper, add the parsley, and simmer over a low heat for 30–60 minutes (depending on the meat used). If necessary, add sufficient water to produce a creamy sauce. *Tas kebáp* goes well with sautéd or puréed potatoes, or rice.

Much of the caper bush can be used in cooking: apart from the buds whcih are known as capers (top right), the gherkin-like fruits (bottom right) and in some regions even the firm, fleshy leaves (top left) are also preserved. Dried buds (bottom left) have a milder flavor.

One particular island specialty uses only the tender tips of the cane-like branches of the caper bush, which can grow up to 13 feet (4 m) long.

The thorns can sometimes simply be plucked off. Having been pre-treated in this way, the canes are soaked in hot water for a while, then carefully rinsed and finally thoroughly patted dry.

The branch tips are spread out in the sun with a little salt to dry and shrivel. Special plant enzymes release the characteristic mustard oil, while the salt draws out more moisture.

The caper branches are preserved by placing them in a glass container, which is then filled with wine vinegar. They make a spicy salad ingredient or an interesting appetizer.

CAPERS

They are white, soft, and extend a wealth of long, slender purple filaments gracefully toward the sun. But these filigree flowers must not be allowed to unfurl if you want to obtain the condiment ingredient whose distinctive flavor you may already have tasted countless times in salads or fish dishes. Capers are the preserved flower buds of the unassuming caper bush (*Capparis spinosa*), which still grows wild in the warm, rocky coastal regions around the Mediterranean Sea. When cultivated, it grows to a height of barely 3 feet (1 meter) and each plant produces an annual yield of up to 7 pounds (3 kilograms) for almost 50 years. They are still always harvested by hand, and it is a troublesome business, as the smallest buds are the best. After picking, the buds are left overnight to shrivel before being preserved either dry in salt, or salted in vinegar or, less commonly, oil. It is this short shriveling time that turns the flower bud into a spice, because an enzyme contained in the plant releases the mustard oil that is so critical for creating the flavor.

Capers are used in cooking less often in Greece than in other Mediterranean countries. Where they have been able to become established, as on Rhodes, for example, it is a legacy from the Venetians. Here they have not specialized in the buds or the small, gherkin-like fruits that are left to ripen on some plants, but on the tender upper part of the long branches. They are first washed and rinsed well to remove some of their bitterness, and are then salted and pickled in vinegar. They are used as a tasty salad ingredient or served as an appetizer.

If you go walking on Kos or Rhodes in June, your eye will perhaps be caught by the pretty white-pink blossoms on the thorny branches of an almost creeper-like bush with pale, round leaves growing between stones along the edge of the path. These have escaped being pickled in vinegar.

GAVROKEFTÉDES
Fried anchovy rissoles

2 lbs/1 kg anchovies, ready prepared
1 tbsp finely chopped capers
1 onion, finely chopped
5 cloves of garlic, crushed
2 eggs
5 slices of stale white bread, soaked
½ tsp dried oregano
2–3 sprigs flat-leaved parsley, finely chopped
All-purpose flour
Olive oil for frying
Salt
Freshly ground black pepper

Chop the anchovies, combine with the capers, onion, garlic, eggs, and bread, and season with the oregano, salt and pepper. Blend the mixture and leave to rest in a refrigerator for 2 hours. Shape the mixture into golf-ball sized balls, toss in flour, gently press flat, and sauté or deep fry in hot olive oil. Serve while still warm. Anchovy rissoles are often served as part of a selection of appetizers.

PATATOSALÁTA
Potato salad
Serves 4–6

2 lbs/1 kg potatoes, boiled and peeled
1 tbsp finely chopped capers
1 bunch flat-leaved parsley, finely chopped
1 large onion, finely chopped
Juice of 1 lemon
1 scant cup/200 ml Greek extra virgin olive oil
1 hard-cooked egg, sliced
1 tomato, sliced
Caper fruits
Salt
Freshly ground black pepper

Slice the potatoes while still warm, then combine carefully with the chopped capers, parsley, and onion, and season with the lemon juice, salt and pepper. Pour over the olive oil, garnish with the sliced egg, tomato, and the caper fruits. Serve warm.

HIPPOCRATES

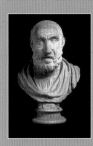

Not much is known about the famous Greek physician as a person. He was born on Kos in 460 B.C., the son of a physician, and died around 375 B.C. in Lárisa (Thessaly). The fame he attained even during his lifetime certainly contributed to the scantiness of information about him as a person: His reputation not only led to the creation of legends about him, but also led to medical successes being popularly associated with the name of the great man. This seemed reasonable, as subsequent generations knew that Hippocrates had traveled widely and had also taught. Moreover, due to the large number of medical treatises designated as "Hippocratic" – they were apparently collected in the 4th century B.C. but the earliest preserved copy dates from the 10th century – were in fact written by several authors, the name today stands less for the real person than for a fundamental medical stance. The distinguishing feature of the Hippocratic approach is the conscious attempt to concentrate on precise observation of the symptoms and of the patient in his environment when making a diagnosis, ignoring religious or supernatural explanations as causes of illness. His therapeutic methods aimed at creating the optimal conditions to let nature help itself. Hygiene, diet, and surgical measures were used, but only if they seemed helpful, and this did not preclude the patients from believing that they had greater chances of healing at the mercy of the gods.

With regard to surgical interventions, it is an interesting aspect in the context of the phenomenon of Hippocrates that precisely the treatise most closely associated with the name of the famous physician, the *Hippocratic Oath*, is also one of the most disputed. Among the things that the oath banned the physician from using in its original form are the use of the knife, administering contraception, and the induction of abortions. Thus the literal content of the oath stands in total contradiction to the writings in the *Corpus Hippocraticum*, which deals knowledgeably with precisely these subjects. It has therefore been supposed that the physicians around Hippocrates on Kos never took such an oath. The text, which in these points reflects a much older set of ideas, was perhaps only included in the *Corpus* subsequently and has been handed down with it ever since.

It is certain that Hippocrates never set foot in the famous Asclepion on Kos, which people have liked to think of as Hippocrates' center of activity, because it had not even been built in his time: the beginnings of the temple to Asclepius date from around 320 B.C. Over the centuries the site was gradually extended, until in the Roman period it was not unlike a busy health resort, complete with thermal bath.

The sponge divers return to the Bay of Kálimnos in autumn. The small harbor town still basks in its former glory as the center of Greek sponge fishing, although yields are falling.

Sponges can be sold at a profit only when they "look right." For this reason, most of them are washed and then bleached, and given a clean-cut look.

AEGEAN GOLD

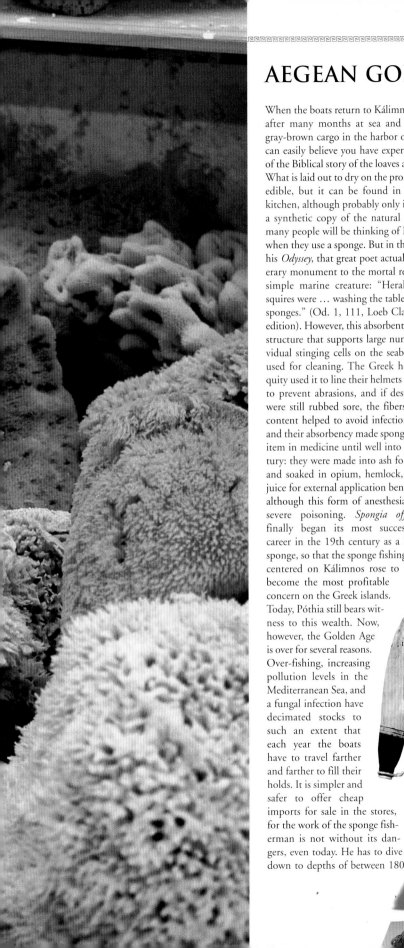

When the boats return to Kálimnos in autumn after many months at sea and unload their gray-brown cargo in the harbor of Póthia, you can easily believe you have experienced a little of the Biblical story of the loaves and the fishes. What is laid out to dry on the promenade is not edible, but it can be found in almost every kitchen, although probably only in the form of a synthetic copy of the natural original. Not many people will be thinking of Homer's epics when they use a sponge. But in the first song of his *Odyssey*, that great poet actually wrote a literary monument to the mortal remains of this simple marine creature: "Heralds and busy squires were … washing the tables with porous sponges." (Od. 1, 111, Loeb Classical Library edition). However, this absorbent spongin fiber structure that supports large numbers of individual stinging cells on the seabed is not just used for cleaning. The Greek heroes of antiquity used it to line their helmets and leg armor to prevent abrasions, and if despite this they were still rubbed sore, the fibers' high iodine content helped to avoid infection. The iodine and their absorbency made sponges an essential item in medicine until well into the 16th century: they were made into ash for internal use, and soaked in opium, hemlock, or mandrake juice for external application beneath the nose, although this form of anesthesia often led to severe poisoning. *Spongia officinalis* finally began its most successful career in the 19th century as a bath sponge, so that the sponge fishing centered on Kálimnos rose to become the most profitable concern on the Greek islands. Today, Póthia still bears witness to this wealth. Now, however, the Golden Age is over for several reasons. Over-fishing, increasing pollution levels in the Mediterranean Sea, and a fungal infection have decimated stocks to such an extent that each year the boats have to travel farther and farther to fill their holds. It is simpler and safer to offer cheap imports for sale in the stores, for the work of the sponge fisherman is not without its dangers, even today. He has to dive down to depths of between 180 and 240 feet (60–80 meters) to find this marine treasure. A fully trained diver can stay down on the seabed for an hour or more. If his equipment lets him down and he has to come up to the surface too quickly, he runs the risk of the dreaded bends as a result of excess nitrogen in the blood. Decompression chambers on the islands and helicopters to transport the divers quickly have indeed increased their chances of recovery, but as people can earn just as much if not more in the tourist trade, more and more sponge fishermen are giving up their old traditional occupation.

Even just a hundred years ago, the fishermen were greeted as heroes when they returned fit and well. A visit to the Nautical Museum at Póthia gives the best idea of the conditions under which a sponge fisherman carried out his risky occupation. He could not move in the rubberized diving suit. The heavy helmet restricted his vision, and the infinitely long cord that provided him with stifling air via a pump threatened to ensnare him if he made a wrong move, interrupting the air supply. And the purpose for which he put up with all these hardships hardly looked alluring when he finally brought it to the surface. It requires a great many measures to transform the black-green, slimy, shapeless mass into that clean, soft, golden-yellow luxury item that comes into its own only in a bubble bath. The museum can tell you all about that, too. On board ship, the catch is then left for a day to decompose, before the unwanted invertebrates are beaten and rinsed out of the spongin fiber structure. Further cleaning and rinsing processes using various acid and bleaching additives are carried out on land. The final bleaching with chlorine is for the sake of appearance only. The sponge can be used, and will last, in its natural yellow-gray. The best bath sponges are produced by a sponge variety with a spherical, circular, slightly frayed shape, which is why the individual pieces have to be "trimmed" before being sold. Other types are coarser, have large pores, and are less soft and less valuable, thus being more suitable for cleaning. Despite these hardships, sponge fishing on Kálimnos has survived so far. And once again next spring, a small fishing fleet will sail out of port, the sponge fishermen will leave their families to return in the autumn and again transform the harbor of Póthia into a lunar landscape with their sponges.

Historic diving suit in the Nautical Museum in Póthia

ΚΡΗΤΗ

Above: in the narrow alleyways of the old part of the harbor town of Khanía in northwest Crete you can eat almost anything you could wish for in cozy surroundings.
Background: the palm beach of Váï on Crete's easternmost point is a honey pot for bathers.

CRETE

King Minos' breakfast
The olive tree
Cold pressed
Rich in olive oil
Not just olive oil
Cretan mountain tea
"Mountain jewels"
Domesticated and wild
Cooking in Cretan
Citrus fruit
Wine

ikos Kazantzakis, the Cretan author, gets right to the heart of the matter when he states that the Cretan landscape is like good prose: it is uncluttered, powerful, restrained, and expresses the essentials in simple terms. High mountain ranges, sheltered valleys, and wide plateaus provide clear, clean water, guaranteeing the continued existence of many precious plants (including 140 species that are found only on Crete) and helping to preserve natural livestock farming. The climate and soil create good conditions for citrus trees, vines, and an estimated 30 million olive trees. The people of Crete seem to be close to nature, are healthy, and live in peace – and each year up to two million vacationers try to share in this idyll. The Greek myths reflect the length of time that Crete has enjoyed the reputation of being something special. Legend has it that as a boy, Zeus grew up in the safety of the Cretan mountains, and that later, as the king of Olympus, he abducted and seduced Europa, the beautiful Phoenician daughter of the king, here. Yet the real significance of Crete for Western culture at the time when the myths were set down in writing was not at all obvious, because the tangible heritage left by the Minoan settlement, the first advanced culture of the West, consisted at best of ruins.

Again and again, the inhabitants of Crete have found that life is not always simple when home is an island steeped in legend and situated on a strategically important crossroads for sea trade routes. Demoted to the Mycenaean province after the fall of the Minoans, Crete was not able to assert itself again as an independent *polis* until well into the 8th century B.C., but even after that it remained rather quiet around the island for centuries. As a Roman province, Crete formed an administrative unit with the area of present day Libya, and as part of the Byzantine Empire it was by no means secure for the 150 years of the Arab–Islamic "Saracen" intermezzo. With the fall of Constantinople in 1204, Crete fell to the Venetians, who ruled the island until 1645, calling it Candia. The Cretans spent the following 250 years as part of the Ottoman Empire and did not become part of Greece until 1913. With this great variety of cultural influences, the Cretans have nevertheless managed to retain their independence, not just from other countries, but also from the rest of Greece. Even if they are die-hard Greeks, Cretans have always been themselves and always will be.

The crocheted filigree triangular cloth with its small tassels along the edges is more than just the headdress of the Cretan national costume. Old men in the countryside also wear it as a sign of a certain resistance to modern-day life.

Above: reconstructions such as this one are hotly disputed by archaeologists today, yet despite such reservations, they do indicate a sort of Minoan sense of space in the ruins of Knossos.
Background: view of the northern storeroom and one of the cultic basins in the Palace of Knossos.

KING MINOS' BREAKFAST

Richly decorated pottery such as this spouted vessel (around 1800–1700 B.C.) from the Old Palace of Knossos were used only by members of the upper classes.

Both cups and spouted vessel are in the middle Minoan Kamares style, which differs clearly from the pottery of the pre-palace era in its distinctive use of several colors. Often the décor works in perfect harmony with the shape of the vessel. The larger, bulbous cup comes from Knossos, the small beaker from the Palace of Festós. Advanced pottery skills would be required to make such thin-walled vessels.

Not much is known about the everyday life of the Minoans. Despite the many archaeological finds, it has been difficult to establish a reliable picture of the life of the people of Crete 4000 years ago. We follow the traces of the first advanced culture in Europe with fascination, we admire the buildings or the works of art, and believe that we can find instances of significance with regard to cult preserved in fresco fragments and seals, because our expectations fuel our interpretation. But what were the Minoans doing when they weren't worshiping their gods, burying their dead, watching dancing girls, or celebrating other festivals? What materials did they use to make the luxurious garments shown on the murals and statues? The women on the frescos look as though they were wearing make-up: what did they use for their beauty and body care? What delicacies did the members of the feudal upper class eat, and what food made up the diet of the peasants, servants, civil servants, or craftsmen? We are often left with nothing but assumptions and inferences, because written sources that could perhaps help further are not easy to come by. But it has been possible to draw up an astonishingly comprehensive list of the foods that we know have been in existence since 2000 B.C., (many of them having arrived in the Aegean area even 4000 years earlier with settlers from the Middle East). In addition to sheep, goats, pigs, and cows, this list would include hares and wild boar, seafood, and various types of poultry, as well as barley and wheat, lentils,

In the form of a white bull, Zeus abducts Europa as she picks flowers, taking her across the sea to Crete. And thus a reality from the distant past is reflected in the Greek myth: the significance of the bull in the Minoan's clearly cult rituals.

chickpeas (garbanzo beans), and fava beans. By way of fruit, they had pears, apples, figs, wine grapes, and pomegranates. We can also mention a number of spices and herbs, plus olives, honey, milk, dairy products, and eggs. But even so, we still wouldn't know with any degree of certainty what was a delicacy or what was poor-man's food to the Minoans. We would still learn nothing about table manners and very little about how things were made, which is only to be regretted in light of their highly developed skills of dressmaking, pottery, and goldsmith work. Until we find a "cookbook," such a list will be rather lacking in flavor.

THE THREADS OF ARIADNE

While on Crete, Europa bore Zeus three sons. When it came to discussing which of them should rule over the island, Minos outdid not only his brothers, but also all other rivals by citing his good relations with Poseidon. He asked the god to give him a bull, promising to sacrifice it to him. When he broke his promise, Poseidon punished him by making Minos' wife, Pasiphae, mother of his eight children, fall in love with this bull. With the support of Daedalus, that ingenious Athenian, this passion was consummated, and Pasiphae gave birth to the bull-headed Minotaur. At the request of the cuckolded King Minos, Daedalus built a labyrinth, in which the Minotaur was henceforth housed. King Minos meanwhile extended his command of the seas (clearly the disagreements with Poseidon had been settled), and started a campaign of

vengeance against Athens, where one of his sons had been murdered. Athens was defeated and from then on had to pay tribute to King Minos. Every nine years Athens had to send seven young men and women to Crete, to the labyrinth of the Minotaur. The third group of victims to come to Crete included Theseus, son of the king of Athens, with whom Ariadne, daughter of King Minos, fell head over heals in love. To save him from the Minotaur, she gave him a ball of wool (after all, the Minoans were also famous for their wool processing), and Theseus was able not only to slay the monster, but also to leave the labyrinth unscathed. Together with Ariadne, he set off for home, but on the way, and only at Athena's instigation, he marooned her on Naxos as she slept. Ariadne then committed suicide out of grief, or (according to other sources), married Dionysus.

THE OLIVE TREE

This evergreen tree (*Olea europaea*) with its lance-shaped leaves and their shimmering silvery-white undersides is an oft-described emblem of Greece. The foliage is replaced in a two-year cycle. In June, small, creamy white flowers open on its branches. If successfully pollinated by the wind in the last quarter of the year, or even in January depending on the variety, it ripens to produce blue-black fruits. This undemanding tree thrives on poor, limy soils, can survive with only 8 inches (200 millimeters) of rain a year, and copes with temperatures ranging from as low as 54 °F (12 °C) during the flowering season up to 104 °F (40 °C) as the fruit ripens. It produces its first crop after about eight years, being most productive after between 60 and 100 years. It is calculated that during this period, each tree produces an average of 132 pounds (60 kilograms) every year, with years of bountiful harvests alternating with those of lower yields. Nowadays, this natural cycle is controlled by specific pruning of the branches to produce more even yields.

The best varieties of olives cultivated on Crete are *koronéiki (Olea europaea* var. *Mastoides), throumboliá (Olea europaea* var. *Media oblonga)*, and *tsounáti (Olea europaea* var. *Mamilaris). Koronéiki* is far and away more resistant than the common olive tree, and thrives at altitudes of over 1500 feet (500 meters). Its fruits are rather small, but all the more aromatic for that. *Throumboliá* has been cultivated for longer than the *koronéiki* on Crete, but has now been replaced by the latter in many regions. It grows at altitudes of up to 2100 feet (700 meters), and its olives produce a mild oil, well-balanced in terms of flavor. *Tsounáti* can withstand greater fluctuations in temperature, and its fruits also guarantee production of a high-quality oil. An olive tree can live for several hundred years. With the passing of time, the wood inside the trunk dies away, until finally the trunk is hollow and takes on an oddly perforated appearance.

People were obviously aware of the value of the olive tree from very early on. According to mythology, when both Athena and Poseidon wanted to assume the patronage of Athens, the Olympian gods were swayed by an olive branch. When both candidates were asked to present the city with a gift representing something most useful, the divine jurors found Athena's olive tree won hands down over Poseidon's saltwater spring.

The great significance of olive trees in antiquity is borne out by the fact that adversaries in armed conflict made a point of zealously uprooting as many of their opponents' trees as possible. Even though they do not produce any actual food – in the strict sense, only grains, pulses, and meat count as food – such destruction deprived all classes of the population for many years, not only of a readily available, year-round, valuable food supplement, but also of medications, various body care preparations, and fuel. Furthermore, olive trees lent their owners increased status, and thus the purposeful, systematic destruction of their property also had a psychological effect.

OLIVE BRANCHES

Whether begged or brought, whether desired for this life or the next – the olive branch is a symbol of peace. This is perhaps because people only take the trouble to plant it if they anticipate a fairly long lasting period of peace, because you have to wait at least eight years for it to bear fruit. Victors may have been honored with the branches of a certain olive tree in Olympia, but whether it is Greek burial rites, Noah's dove, the Roman Pax or Christian catacomb paintings, the message conveyed by the olive branch is ultimately the same, and this lasting symbol needs no words to get the message across.

HOLY OIL

You can still see them today on the edges of the streets: small, miniature churches, places of refuge, inviting passersby to stop and rest. Inside are small icons and a glass of olive oil, sealed with a pierced cork disk through which a wick extends into the oil, and a packet of matches. Anyone stopping in can light the wick and ask for protection. The olive oil "nourishes" the flame as a symbol of the Holy Spirit. It not only "feeds" the Eternal Light in the iconostasis of the churches, but also of the domestic altars, as well as representing an essential nutritional element,

alongside bread, water, and wine in close connection with the physical existence of humankind. And in the liturgy, all these elements are given symbolic meaning, leaving no doubt that the human soul hungers for Christendom in the same way as the human body is dependent upon food. Thus the everyday life of the believer is present in the church and the religion is closely interwoven with everyday domestic life through the olive oil, bread, and wine. When someone dies, their body is anointed with oil, and the olive oil flame burns so that the soul can find its way to God.

Fruits ripened on the tree have to be harvested with care, because their soft flesh is extremely sensitive to pressure. Background: Even if they no longer bear fruit, people seldom cut down olive trees.

A common concomitant of olive cultivation, at least in areas that have opened up to tourism, is the great selection of utensils made of olive wood. These popular souvenirs have proved to be very useful in the kitchen.

Olive oil soaps used to be made on Lesbos, in the Peloponnese region, and in Attica, as well as on Crete. The fact that they are very kind to the skin contributes to gentle body care.

COLD PRESSED

Ninety-five-thousand families cultivate 30 million Cretan olive trees. Cretan olive growing thus accounts for 30 percent of total Greek production, ahead of the Peloponnese with 26 percent. Cretan olive oil is the only one to have a protected mark of origin, comparable to the French *Appellation d'Origine Contrôlée*. Since 1993, olive oil has also been produced organically on Crete, and is thus subject to strict conditions with regard to the planting distances and the use of fertilizers and pesticides, among other things. The oil from organically and traditionally cultivated olives is also subjected to ongoing intensive quality control procedures. The critical quality criteria for olive oil include taste and odor classifications. Similar to wine, these depend on the variety, cultivation area, and vintage, and also on the care taken when harvesting and processing the olives. Again, like wine, these properties are subjected to a sensory test. Whereas in the past it was thought that the crop would produce the best quality oil when fully ripe (from October to January, depending on the variety and cultivation area), it is now picked just prior to that, when the oil content of the fruits has already reached its peak. This slightly pre-ripe stage gives the finished oil the ability to keep for a long time, provided it is correctly stored. The olives should be harvested swiftly and reach the nearest oil mill without any further loss of time.

The following processes have essentially remained almost unchanged for thousands of years. Millstone wheels grind the olive and their stones into a pulp, which is then piled onto filters in thin layers and pressed with increasing pressure. Finally the oil is separated from the water. Visitors to the Cretan Olive Museum at Kapsaliana can still admire numerous historical devices from the 19th century. Since then, mechanical mills have dispensed with the horses and donkeys; hydraulics has replaced manpower at the screw press, and is being superceded in its turn by centrifugal force.

In the Agia Triada monastery in northwestern Crete, the monks cultivate not only an olive grove, but also a citrus plantation and a herd of goats.

The Olive Museum of Kapsaliana keeps alive the hard daily life of the olive tree farmers …

… with an oil mill and screw press from the 19th century.

MARINATED OLIVES

Soft, ripe olives from Chalkidikí.

Mild *glikiá* olives with soft flesh.

Round, juicy *volos*.

Firm, green *prásini* preserved in oil.

Almond-shaped *kalamón* (Peloponnese).

Throúmba from Thásos olives.

Overripe olives for stews.

Ripe *prásini* in oil and vinegar.

OLIVE OIL QUALITY CATEGORIES

1 *Exeretikó parthéno eleólado* (extra virgin olive oil): the best cold-pressed olive oil from the first pressing (without the effect of additional heat; the natural friction heat is no more than 176 °F (80 °C).) For frying, it should be heated to a temperature no higher than 338 °F (170 °C). (Maximum acidity (oleic acid) 1 g/100 g oil).

2 *Eklektó parthéno eleólado* (fine virgin olive oil): cold-pressed olive oil from the second pressing; for broiling, baking, and frying. (Maximum acidity (oleic acid) 1.5 g/100 g; EU guidelines: 2 g/100 g oil).

3 *Imi-fino parthéno eleólado* (semi-fine virgin olive oil), *Kinó parthéno eleólado* (ordinary virgin olive oil): cold-pressed olive oil from the third pressing; for cooking vegetable stews and soups, more rarely for salads. (Maximum acidity (oleic acid) 3.3 g/100 g).

4 *Wiomiohanikó parthéno eleólado* (lampante virgin olive oil): an inferior olive oil, unsuitable for consumption.

5 *Rafinarisméno eleólado* (refined olive oil): pomace oil. Although it is suitable for consumption after being refined, it is less aromatic.

6 *Eleólado* (pure olive oil/olive oil): blend of virgin and refined oil.

LÁKHANO ME KHIRINÓ
White cabbage with pork

1 medium white cabbage
1 generous cup/250 ml Greek extra virgin
olive oil
2 lbs/1 kg pork, diced
1 large onion, finely chopped
2 tomatoes, skinned, seeded and coarsely diced
Salt
Freshly ground black pepper

Cut the white cabbage into 8 pieces, remove the stalks, and cut the rest into reasonably thick strips. Wash and thoroughly drain the cut cabbage. Heat the olive oil in a pan and brown the diced meat on all sides. Remove the meat and set aside. Add the chopped onion to the pan, and brown in the oil. Add the strips of white cabbage to the pan and braise for a few minutes, stirring constantly, until they wilt. Add the diced tomatoes and return the browned meat to the pan. Season with salt and pepper. Add 2 cups/500 ml water, slowly bring to a simmer, then lower the heat, cover, and leave to simmer over a low heat for about 50 minutes. As soon as the meat is cooked, season to taste with pepper and serve while still warm.

RICH IN OLIVE OIL

Thoroughly coated in olive oil, any ingredient retains its individual aroma and flavor, while still being in harmony with other ingredients. Vegetables and meat are prepared, divided into pieces, and then cooked slowly over a moderate heat, all of which demands careful attention and application. In the past, women cooked at the domestic hearth *laderó fagitó*, "oily food," which was different from the simple fried meat enjoyed by the men out in the open.

SÉLINO ME ARAKÁ
Celery with peas

2 lbs/1 kg blanched or white celery pieces
Juice of 1 lemon
1 scant cup/200 ml Greek extra virgin olive oil
2 large onions, finely chopped
1 large potato, coarsely diced
1¼ cups/200 g shelled peas
1 tbsp finely chopped dill
1 tsp sugar, combined with the juice of 1 lemon
Salt and freshly ground pepper

Precook the celery for 10 minutes in water and lemon juice, then strain. Fry the onions in oil, add the potato and celery, together with 2 scant cups/400 ml water, cover, and simmer for 15 minutes. Add the peas and dill and cook for a further 15 minutes. Add the sugar and lemon mixture, season with salt and pepper, and briefly bring to a boil. Serve warm.

BAKALIÁROS ME PRÁSA
Stockfish with leeks

2 lbs/1 kg stockfish
1 generous cup/250 ml Greek extra virgin olive oil
2 lbs/1 kg leeks, thickly sliced
1 lb/500 g tomatoes, skinned, seeded, and coarsely diced
2 tbsp finely chopped flat-leaved parsley
Salt
Freshly ground black pepper

Soak the stockfish for at least 12 hours, changing the water at regular intervals. Heat the olive oil in a pan and sauté the leeks. Add 1 scant cup/200 ml water, season with salt and pepper, and cook for about 15 minutes, then add the tomatoes. Place the stockfish on top of the vegetables and sprinkle with the parsley. Cover and simmer over a low heat for about 25 minutes, checking frequently with a fork to make sure nothing is sticking. Serve while still warm.

ANGINAROKOÚKIA
Artichokes with fava beans

10 artichokes, leaves and choke removed
Juice of 1 lemon
1 generous cup/250 ml Greek extra virgin olive oil
2 bunches of scallions, finely chopped
2 lbs/1 kg fava beans, shelled
1 bunch dill, finely chopped
Salt and freshly ground black pepper
1 tsp all-purpose flour combined with the juice of 1 lemon

Rub the artichoke hearts with the lemon juice. Sauté the onions. Add the artichoke hearts, quickly followed by the fava beans and dill. Add 2 generous cups/500 ml water and season. Cover and simmer over a low heat for about 1 hour. Thicken with the flour and lemon, and briefly bring to a boil. Serve hot.

NOT JUST OLIVE OIL

Although even in pure olive oil, aromas of apples, almonds, lemons, or pepper can enhance the flavor, the addition of spicy ingredients has a long tradition, possibly sharing its origin with the perfume industry. Indeed it is known that olive oil was used for this purpose even by the Minoans. Because flowers and leaves release their aromatic substances into oils and fats, herbs and spices preserved in oil provide a very convincing reminder of a fleeting or only seasonal fragrance.

AROMATIKÓ ELEÓLADO
Spiced olive oil

1 nutmeg, grated
1 tsp cloves, finely crushed
2 cinnamon sticks
15 poppy leaves
2 generous cups/500 ml Greek extra virgin olive oil

Thoroughly combine the nutmeg and cloves, place in a clean, dry bottle, together with the cinnamon sticks and poppy leaves. Fill the bottle with olive oil, seal tightly and leave in a cool, dark place for 2–3 weeks.

Nowadays, this oil is mainly used in the production of sweet or hearty pastries, or is served drizzled over bread as an appetizer. In days gone by, it was applied as a liniment to cure headaches and rheumatism.

HOLY OLIVE OIL TO PROTECT AGAINST THE 'EVIL EYE'

Nearly every village has them, the *xematiástres*. If a child has a crushing headache, or if an adult is struck down with sudden, acute pains, then call the *xematiástres*, who will come immediately. With the tacit approval of the Greek Orthodox Church, which has in this case clearly Christianized an old pagan ritual, the women solemnly pour holy olive oil into a spoon, murmur prayers and repeatedly cross themselves. They then give the spoon of olive oil to the sufferer to drink, making the sign of the cross on his or her brow with their fingers. And in most cases, a few moments later, the Greek Orthodox miracle has happened: the aches and pains have gone – and the network of religious–social bonds between the women of a village community has once again proven itself in everyday life.

Sunflower oil with rosemary

Olive oil with sage

Corn oil with red chiles

OIL AS YOU LIKE IT

Preserving herbs in oils is based on the principle of absorption, or *enfleurage à froid*. That may sound rather off-putting, but the times of this being a trade secret held only by "fragrance makers," "barbers," or pharmacists are of course long past. All it means is that the aromatic substances have been released through a cold process, whereas in the case of maceration or *enfleurage à chaud*, this is done by applying moderate heat. In Greece you can of course buy ready-prepared flavored oils, some of them top quality, and the variety of flavors, such as "olive oil with fennel," or "olive oil with coriander, lime, and black pepper" comes as quite a surprise. It can, however, be much more exciting to experiment with making your own, and as no special equipment is required, apart from a couple of empty bottles with tight-fitting tops, your imagination need know almost no bounds. It is, however, advisable to observe a few fundamental rules. Whichever oil you are using as a base should be of top quality. It may be advisable to make your first experiments using oils with less marked aromas of their own, such as sunflower or grapeseed oil, for example. The herbs must be fresh and their aromas fully developed. Wash them carefully and dry them thoroughly with paper towels. Carefully remove any wilted or damaged leaves. The bottles must also be scrupulously clean. It is extremely important that they are absolutely dry inside before adding the chosen herbs or spices and slowly pouring a thin stream of oil into them. The tightly sealed bottles should be left to stand in a cool place, away from direct sunlight, for at least two weeks. For more intense aromas, after this initial two-week period transfer the oil to new bottles with fresh herbs, and repeat this process several times. As the quality of flavored oils decreases over time, make quantities sufficient to cover your actual needs and store the bottles in a dark place such as a closet (unless you wish to use bottles made of dark glass). Aromatic oils can also be used for cooking and sautéing, but they are usually used to best advantage in salads and sauces.

Olive oil with bay leaves and garlic

Sunflower oil with dill

Olive oil with rosemary

Olive oil with chiles, rosemary, thyme, and bay leaves

397

NIKOS KAZANTZAKIS

"Zorbás taught me to love life and not to fear death." With these words, Nikos Kazantzakis (1883–1957) honors not a fictional character, but the worker Georgis Zorbás, whom he met in 1916 during an ultimately unsuccessful attempt to run a brown coal mine on the Peloponnese. The novel *Alexis Zorbás* (*Zorba the Greek*, 1946) thus contains autobiographical elements, although the author chose to set the book in his home of Crete. The book would go on to make Kazantzakis very famous, Zorbás immortal, and an awareness of the Cretans more transparent. Like no other modern Greek author, Kazantzakis conjures up in his novels the history, culture, and landscape of Greece in atmospheric pictures. Despite long absences abroad, the awkward Cretan's ties to his home have remained stronger than those to Orthodox Christianity, which he examined critically (the official Church would say too critically) in his novel *The Greek Passion* (1948–1954). Other works are: *The Last Temptation of Christ* (1951–1955), *Freedom or Death* (1953), *God's Pauper: St Francis of Assisi* (1956), and *Report to Greco* (1961). At the Marengo fort in Iráklion, there is only a simple gravestone in memory of the author, with the inscription: "I hope for nothing, I fear nothing, I am free."

CRETAN MOUNTAIN TEA

Cretan mountain tea can be found in almost every Greek household. When the weather turns cooler and the first signs of an impending cold or cough manifest themselves, when the limbs ache, or when you just feel under the weather, a tea made from the dried stalks of *Sideritis cretica* has a beneficial and curative effect. The twigs are broken into pieces, which are then put into a pan of boiling water. They are left over a low heat for at least five minutes to infuse rather than to simmer, and then strained straight into cups. The addition of cinnamon sticks enhances the flavor still further. The Cretan ironwort is a medium-high shrub that has an upright form, with opposing, wooly leaves growing on straight, relatively non-branching stalks. The plant manages to survive on sites with hot, dry summers. Its small, yellow flowers are rather unobtrusive. The botanical name *Sideritis*, derived from the Greek word *síderos*, meaning iron, indicates this plant's areas of application in ancient medicine. It was used externally for its anti-inflammatory and astringent properties in the case of "wounds from iron struck into limbs," and internally for its ability to strengthen the body's powers of resistance. When the Venetians discovered the tea, they called it *malotira*, because it "draws out the illness."

Break the stalks into pieces. Pour over boiling water, cover, and quickly bring to a boil. Leave to infuse to the desired strength, then strain into cups.

This special variety of ironwort, *Sideritis cretica*, thrives in the highlands of Crete and is considered particularly effective and aromatic among mountain tea connoisseurs.

"MOUNTAIN JEWELS"

Above: *folia Origanum dictamnus* are available from any Cretan herb store.
Background: horsemint (*Mentha longifolia)* is one of the best-known and most versatile herbs.

Don't be deceived by the unassuming external appearance of many a Cretan herb store (as shown below), because its range can easily exceed your expectations. If, for example, you are looking for that legendary hop marjoram that thrives only on Crete, you are sure to find it. By this we mean *Origanum dictamnus*, also known as Cretan dittany. The name is derived from the Greek *óros* (mountain), *gános* (jewel), Dhíkti (a mountain range in Crete), and *thámnos* (bush, bunch, twig), and describes a bushy plant about 8 inches (20 centimeters) tall with circular, wooly, gray-white leaves on thin stems. In summer, pendant, hop-like heads develop from red bracts, between which open small, pink, labiate flowers. Cretan dittany thrives at altitudes of 5,300 feet (1,600 meters).

Ancient Greek–Roman medicine attributed it with almost magical powers as a medicinal plant. In the 4th century B.C., Theophrastus extolled its versatility, but laid particular emphasis on its beneficial effect for women in childbirth. According to a story attributed to Aristotle, Cretan wild goats, injured by a poisoned arrow, ate this herb, after which the body eliminated the poison completely and the wound healed. This fabulous story must have also made an impression on Dioscorides, when he recommended the plant especially for healing spear wounds. Hippocratic medicine used Cretan dittany externally as a poultice on ulcerated wounds or as an infusion forgall bladder complaints and tuberculosis. Whatever the injury or atrophy, folk medicine attributes an aphrodisiac effect to a tea made from *Origanum dictamnus* and still recommends it as a painkiller for menstrual complaints and during childbirth. Modern pharmacology, however, has yet to find proof of any remedial effect of that sort.

It may thus not have such a curative effect, yet there is no denying that it does have a wonderful effect, because it has for centuries been one of the numerous ingredients combined by Christian monks in many monasteries to flavor their own homemade pick-me-up. In the 19th century, some of the recipes were "secularized," so you may well come across *Origanum dictamnus* in a herbal liqueur without realizing it.

The hard *kefalotiri* cheese can be made from untreated goat's or sheep's milk or a mixture of the two. It has a 40–45% fat content and comes in various degrees of ripeness. The fully ripe cheese is also grated for many dishes.

DOMESTICATED AND WILD

The nymph (or goat, depending on the source) Amaltheia fed goat's milk to the infant Zeus when Rhea was forced to take him to Crete to escape the persecution of his father, Cronos. This plainly shows not only the importance of the goat as a source of milk throughout Greece and especially Crete, and the appreciation of goat's milk as an element in the diet, but also gives an idea of the admittedly undefined, but at any rate long period in which it featured in mythology. In actual fact, there is proof that goats, *katsíka*, are one of the oldest domesticated animals. The earliest traces of settlement on Crete date back to 6000 B.C., and the people who settled there clearly brought goats and sheep with them from the Middle East, as well as domestic pigs, which also existed on the Greek mainland, and more developed varieties of grain. Although on Crete a definite reference to a "milk economy" survives from the time around 2000 B.C. – in the form of a seal actually depicting goatherds with milk churns (on the Greek peninsula, a thousand-year-old vessel has been found that would be suitable for making cheese) – there is definitely good reason to date its origins much farther back in time. It actually makes good sense that animals that provide "byproducts" such as milk, wool, or pulling power, would not be considered primarily as meat suppliers and be taken out of milk production early, however much the meat may be appreciated. Another point is that goats are not such prolific breeders as pigs, for example. Even if the animals' milk-producing capacity at the start of the history of goat rearing is in no way comparable with current yields, the value of the milk in the context of food was ranked more highly than that of meat.

A good 300,000 goats (and twice as many sheep) are kept on Crete, so that in purely statistical terms, there is half a goat for every inhabitant. It is claimed that the herdsman would know each of their animals by name.

Goat rearing, which has been going on for 8000 years on Crete, has led to goats being ubiquitous throughout the island. They cover great distances on their annual treks from the winter pastures in the valleys to the summer meadows in the mountains, nibbling at anything of interest to them along the hedgerows on the way. Yet the fact that these animals are so willing to accept a broad range of plants as fodder, so that even on barren plains they can still find enough to eat – a fact that makes goat rearing easier – also has negative consequences for the vegetation, because unlike sheep, goats actually feed down to the roots of the plants.

THE INVISIBLE CRETAN WILD GOAT

The domestic goat originated from the wild form, *Capra aegagrus,* the bezoar goat, from which the sub-species *Capra aegagrus cretica* has survived on the island as the Cretan wild goat. *Kri kri* or *agrími,* as the Cretans call them, have retreated into the steep slopes around the Samarian Gorge, escaping the gaze of the tourists who file past each year in single lines to savor the magnificent natural spectacle of the romantic solitude of the mountains. These creatures are clever enough to let themselves be seen only when they are quite sure that peace has returned. Their habitat demands of them all the agility that you would expect of members of the goat family. They owe their long survival here in no small way to extreme caution and ever-alert distrust. People who actually experience this for themselves sometimes complain how difficult it is to get sufficiently close to the animals unnoticed. Why this proximity is so important to them is one of the best-kept secrets on Crete. Hunting Cretan wild goats has long been banned, for with a stock of only a few hundred animals, it is rightly feared that this wild species could die out completely. However, careful foresight has

The best place to admire Cretan wild goats is in the wild reserves of Khanía.

been demonstrated by setting up reserves on suitable islands off the north coast of Crete. Cretans extol the virtues of wild goat's meat as the healthiest in the world, and go into ecstasies about its natural thyme fragrance. It is generally braised with onions to make *stifádo,* or fried in plenty of olive oil and seasoned with nothing but salt, pepper, and the juice of a lemon to make *tsigaristó.* Of course, the meat that nowadays goes into the pot as wild goat is actually no more wild than purely feral domestic goat. You can never get close enough to the real wild goats while remaining entirely unobserved.

AGRÍMI STIFÁDO
Braised wild goat

3½ lbs/1½ kg wild goat's meat
1 generous cup/250 ml Greek extra virgin olive oil
1 generous cup/250 ml white wine
1 lb/500 g small onions, peeled
2–3 bay leaves
2–3 cloves
1 tbsp tomato paste
Salt
Freshly ground black pepper

Bone the meat and cut it into small pieces. Heat the olive oil in a pan and brown the meat all over. Lower the heat, add enough water to cover the meat, cover the pan, and simmer for about 45 minutes. Add the white wine and bring to a boil, removing any scum that is produced. Add the bay leaves and cloves, and season with salt and pepper. Put the whole peeled onions in the pan, cover, and cook for a further 30 minutes, adding hot water if necessary. Finally stir in the tomato paste, and continue to braise until the meat is tender. This dish is best served with freshly baked white bread to dip in the sauce.

COOKING IN CRETAN

Like anywhere else in Greece, Crete has its naturalized recipes as legacies of various occupying forces. You have to allow the differences between general Greek and specifically Cretan cuisine to linger on your tongue, as they develop only gradually. You are more likely to find them away from the tourist trail. Sometimes it is the special aroma of Cretan olive oil, sometimes the raisins with their waft of bay leaf, then again perhaps goat's milk cheeses such as *mizíthra* and *anthótiros*, which have retained reminders of the great variety of herbs in the mountain meadows.

KOKKINISTÓ MOSKHÁRI
Veal in tomato sauce

1 scant cup/200 ml Greek extra virgin olive oil
1 onion, finely chopped
2 lbs/1 kg veal, coarsely diced
1 scant cup/200 ml brandy
2 lbs/1 kg tomatoes, skinned and finely diced
2 tsp tomato paste, combined with a little water
½ tsp dried oregano
1¼ cups/200 g raisins
¾ cup/100 g pine nuts
2 cloves of garlic, crushed
Salt and freshly ground black pepper

Preheat the oven to 400 °F (200 °C). Fry the onion and meat in hot olive oil. Add the brandy, tomatoes, tomato paste, and oregano, and pour in 2 scant cups/400 ml water. Simmer for 10 minutes, then transfer to a casserole dish, and bake for 1 hour. Ten minutes before the meat is cooked, stir in the raisins and pine nuts. Transfer to plates, sprinkle with a little crushed garlic and a few drops of olive oil, and serve with rice or baked potatoes and *tzatzíki*.

HUNGIAR BEYENTI
Chicken with eggplant purée

1 scant cup/200 ml Greek extra virgin olive oil
1 onion and 2 cloves of garlic, finely chopped
1 chicken (approx. 2–3 lbs/1½ kg), cut into
8 pieces
1 generous cup/250 ml dry white wine
2 lbs/1 kg tomatoes, skinned and diced
5 pale green peppers, cut into strips (from Greek or Turkish delicatessens)

ARNÁKI ME RÍZI
Ragout of lamb with rice

2 lbs/1 kg shoulder lamb, coarsely diced
5 onions, coarsely chopped
3 zucchini, coarsely chopped
2 carrots, sliced
½ celeriac, very finely chopped
1 bunch flat-leaved parsley, finely chopped
2 cups/400 g rice
Salt
Freshly ground black pepper

For the egg and lemon sauce:
2 eggs, separated
Juice of 2 lemons

Put the diced meat in a large pan, add sufficient water to cover, then slowly bring to a boil and lower the heat. Cook for 15 minutes, then add the onion, zucchini, carrots, celeriac, and parsley, and season with salt and pepper. Simmer until the ingredients are soft and the juices have reduced slightly. Meanwhile, bring some salted water to a boil in a pan, add the rice, and cook. For the egg and lemon sauce, beat the egg whites into stiff peaks. Then fold in the egg yolks, followed by the lemon juice, and combine this mixture with a little of the meat juices. Season with salt and pepper. Transfer the ragout to a bowl and serve with rice, freshly baked white bread, and the egg and lemon sauce.

2 tsp tomato paste, combined with a little water
½ tsp dried oregano
Salt and freshly ground black pepper

For the eggplant purée:
5 large eggplants
1 generous cup/250 ml béchamel sauce (see recipe on p. 108)
4 tbsp/50 g grated kefalotíri cheese
Juice of ½–1 lemon
Salt and freshly ground black pepper

Preheat the oven to 350 °F (180 °C). Soften the onion and garlic and sauté the chicken pieces in the hot oil. Add the wine, then the peppers, tomatoes, and tomato paste. Season with oregano, salt and pepper, and simmer for 10 minutes. Transfer to a casserole dish, add enough water to cover the chicken, and bake for 45 minutes. Cool slightly, then remove the bones from the chicken and return the meat to the sauce. For the purée, roast the eggplant in an oven at 400 °F (200 °C) until the skin blisters. Remove from the oven, leave to cool, and take off the skin. Dice the eggplant and purée in a blender together with the béchamel sauce, *kefalotíri* cheese, lemon juice, salt and pepper. The purée can be served warm around the chicken meat or separately cold.

DÁKOS
Barley biscuits, tomatoes, and sheep's milk cheese

1 lb/500 g tomatoes, skinned, very finely chopped
2 cloves of garlic, crushed
½ tsp dried oregano
Greek extra virgin olive oil
8 paximádia biscuits (see recipe p.76)
1 cup/100 g crumbled sheep's milk cheese
Salt

Combine the tomatoes with the garlic, oregano, and a little olive oil and season to taste with salt. Spread over the biscuits, scatter with the crumbled sheep's milk cheese, and drizzle with olive oil. Leave to stand for the flavors to permeate. Barley biscuits are also good broiled or baked until brown on top.

CITRUS FRUIT

Crete and Cyprus are considered the citrus garden of the eastern Mediterranean, even though they are actually situated on the northernmost edge of what is known as the "citrus belt," which goes all around the earth. On Crete's northern coast thrive *portokália* (oranges; *Citrus sinensis*), *mandarínia* (Mediterranean mandarins; *Citrus deliciosa*), and *lemónia* (lemons; *Citrus*); Cyprus grows grapefruits (*Citrus* x *paradisi*), and *pergamóndo* (bergamot oranges; *Citrus bergamia*). In spring the heavy, pleasantly bitter-sweet scent of thousands of citrus flowers hangs in the air. On humid summer evenings, the vast quantity of water that the trees require seems to make the surroundings cooler and the heat more bearable. Citrus fruits from Crete are available almost all year round and have led to oranges being used in salads, an innovation unheard of in northern Greece, perhaps inspired by the menus of the better quality hotels. The best variety grown on Crete is the late-ripening Californian "Newhall," a navel orange closely related to the variety known as 'Navelina' in Spain, with which it is often confused. Navel oranges are really an artificial product, because the small additional fruit that forms between the fruit segments and seals the "navel" where the flower was once attached has been specifically bred to develop the seeds of the main fruit, making the latter seedless. Including the yield from various Spanish Valencia varieties, which have also been established here successfully, Greek orange production comes to an average of 990,000 US tons (900,000 tonnes) per year. They are mostly exported, so the exact time of harvesting is important. Citrus fruits won't ripen after they have been picked, which means they have to be fully ripe when harvested, as otherwise their quality and hence their position in the market are impaired. In this connection, it

Crete mainly grows navel oranges to be eaten fresh.

is chiefly "inner values" that are decisive for the fruit's time of optimum edibility: sugar and acid content, both in relation to each other and the juice content. All four components must be assessed. Using the changing color of the rind as the only external indicator is unreliable, because it depends on weathering. With oranges, this happens only after the first five autumn nights below 54.5 °F (12.5 °C). It could therefore be the case – although admittedly this seldom happens in the Mediterranean – that the oranges are at the optimum harvesting stage, but still green. If the flavor, juice content, and color of the orange are now perfect, then great care must be taken when harvesting and subsequently handling them to make sure that the oil cells in the rind remain in perfect condition. Otherwise the rind will become spotted, and the fruit cannot be sold. For this reason, citrus fruits intended to be eaten fresh and for export are still best picked by hand. They are then carefully cleaned with chemicals, rinsed, dried, and washed again. Fruits in the "Extra" and "I" quality categories are laid in shallow, padded crates, whereas fruits in the lower categories have to share a net with many others.

Whether they have "golden" or pink flesh, the smaller grapefruits are different in botanical terms from the ordinary grapefruit. These fruit are sometimes called pomelos.

Limes and lemons are also grown on Crete, although production is falling slightly at present.

Ever-new combinations of fruits can be used for fruit salad (and by the way: green oranges aren't necessarily unripe, it's just that the weather wasn't cold enough).

FROUTOSALÁTA
Fruit salad

Fresh fruit, depending on the season (such as
*   oranges, apples, pears, bananas, pomegranates,*
*   sweet melons etc)*
2 tbsp honey
1 tsp sugar
1 scant cup/200 ml dry white wine
1 scant cup/100 g chopped walnuts (optional)
1 tsp ground cinnamon

Peel the fruit, cut it into small pieces, and put in a bowl. Dissolve the honey and sugar in the wine and pour over the fruit. Leave to infuse for an hour, then sprinkle with the cinnamon and chopped walnuts (if using).

LIKÉR APÓ PORTOKÁLI
Orange liqueur

5 unwaxed or well-scrubbed oranges
5 unwaxed or well-scrubbed mandarin oranges
6 generous cups/1½ liters brandy
4 cups/1 liter ouzo
2⅔ cups/600 g sugar
2 scant cups/400 ml water

Finely peel the oranges and mandarins, avoiding any pith. Put the zests and two-thirds of the brandy in a glass container with a tightly fitting lid and leave in a cool, dark place for three weeks for the flavors to permeate. Make a sugar and water syrup and leave to cool. Pass the brandy through a strainer into another glass container, and thoroughly drain the fruit zests. Pour in the syrup, ouzo, and the remaining brandy, and transfer the liqueur into smaller bottles.

Above: The bananas grown on Crete may be small, but are all the more aromatic and sweet for that. Background: Unlike Crete, where oranges are the main emphasis of citrus production, the grapefruit predominates on Cyprus.

405

WINE

Of all the Greek islands, the popular and most visited vacation island of Crete produces by far the most wine. After all, the island in the south of Greece can look back on an especially long tradition, if historians are right in their supposition that Crete was home to the very first vineyards anywhere in the Mediterranean region. The fact that one of the oldest wine presses in the world was discovered in the remote Minoan estate of Vathypetro supports the idea of this being an extremely long-standing wine-growing region. The geological and geographic conditions on Crete are still perfect today for wine grapes to thrive. The Dhíkti mountains protect the growing areas against the African winds, while at the same time the minimal fluctuations in temperature throughout the year and the reliable sunshine guarantee the island's fertility.

Because so far Crete has remained clear of phylloxera, the vines do not have to be grafted onto American rootstock. The Cretan winegrowers process four quality grapes in particular, all of which date back to antiquity. The white Vilana, the main grape variety in the Peza appellation, is indigenous and produces fresh, lively, slightly floral white wines with soft apple aromas. The red Mandelaria grape produces pleasantly acidic wines with a full-bodied, tannin-rich aroma, whereas the Kotsifali gives Cretan red wine its spicy aroma. In the Archanes and Peza appellations, growers have successfully experimented in the last several years with red wines blended from both varieties. The red Liatiko grape is also worth a mention. As an appellation, it produces the powerful red Sitia wine. The mythical and once famous sweet Malvasia grape, on the other hand, has unfortunately long since disappeared.

As private wine retailers, the Minos and Lyrarakis wineries are outstanding on Crete, while the winemaking cooperatives of Archanes, Peza, Sitia, and Heraklion should also be mentioned. Here the wine is produced not by international standards, but by traditional Greek production methods. Careful processing is the priority. The grapes are hand picked in small bunches, the juice is extracted using pneumatic presses, and in the fermentation process, cooling the musts in stainless steel tanks achieves the desired fruit aromas.

ARCHANES WINE-GROWERS COOPERATIVE

Vin de Prince: the Archanes Cooperative near the Palace of Knossos produces a rosé as a medium-dry table wine that makes a popular alternative to the region's white wines.

Armanti: the dry wine at Archanes is also a rosé with 12% vol. Served at a temperature of 50 °F (10 °C), it goes particularly well with light appetizers, salads, and with seafood.

Archanes: the red Archanes is a blend of the Kotsifali and Mandelaria grapes, which complement each other particularly well. It is the Archanes Cooperative's top quality wine. The wine reveals its powerful nose best at a serving temperature of 64 °F (18 °C). It has an alcohol content of 12.5% vol.

Vin de Prince: with an alcohol content of 11.5% vol., the medium-dry Vin de Prince made from the Vilana grape is one of the region's lighter white wines. This, together with its freshness produced by a hint of fruity acids, give it a pleasing taste. This wine is best served at a temperature of 50 °F (10 °C) and goes particularly well with sophisticated Cretan *mezés* dishes such as fungi, flaky pastry rolls, or piquantly spiced chicken, all served warm.

PEZA WINE-GROWERS COOPERATIVE

Creta Nobile: the Peza Cooperative also has a dry red wine made from the Kotsifali and Mandelaria grapes. Served at 64 °F (18 °C), this wine, with its soft vanilla aroma, goes especially well with game dishes.

Creta Nobile: this dry white wine is made from the indigenous Vilana grape. It has a fresh taste and is an excellent accompaniment to fish and pasta dishes. It is best served at a temperature of 54–57 °F (12–14 °C).

Xerolithisa: this 12% vol. white wine is also made from the Vilana grape, which is Crete's most important white wine grape variety. It gives the wine a hint of a floral taste.

Xerolithia also has a sparkling character. It goes well with white meat and seafood. It is best when served at a temperature of 46–50 °F (8–10 °C).

Peza Liktos: this wine comes from one of the appellations awarded the V.Q.P.R.D. quality mark. Peza Liktos, – names for the ancient regional capital – made from the Vilana grape, is a particularly dry wine in comparison with the Peza Cooperative's other white wines. It has a well-balanced body and is an ideal accompaniment to salads, fruit, and nouvelle cuisine fish dishes. Serve at a temperature of 46–48 °F (8–9 °C) to get the best out of the wine.

SITIA WINEGROWERS COOPERATIVE

Sitia: situated in the far east of Crete, the Sitia appellation produces this dry O.P.A.P. red wine from the Liatiko grape. Full in flavor, it is best served with meat dishes and with cheese.

Sitia: the white quality wine from the Vilana and Thrapsathiri grapes has delicate and fruity aromas. Served at 50–54 °F (10–12 °C), it is an ideal accompaniment to seafood.

Myrto: this white table wine from Sitia is captivating with its dark yellow color and fresh taste. Its slight acidity combined with youthful liveliness and sparkle makes the Myrto white an ideal wine to drink as an accompaniment to white meat dishes prepared with light sauces.

Myrto: the red Myrto produced by the Sitia Cooperative is a recognized table wine. It is distinguished by its bright red color and is dry in flavor and subtly spicy. In order to develop its

flavor to the full, serve at a temperature of 61 °F (16 °C). It is a perfect accompaniment to light meat dishes with spicy sauces.
The association has produced the wine for the Sitia region since 1933. The technically modern production plant has now reached a capacity of 10,000 bottles per day.

MINOS WINERY

Minos Palace: made from 80% Kotsifali and 20% Mandelaria grapes grown in the Peza region, the Minos Winery, founded in 1932, makes a dry red wine. The wine is first aged for nine months in oak casks, so that this quality wine finally achieves a powerful red color and an aroma of dried fruits such as raisins and plums. This wine can be kept for 4 years.

Minos: the Vilana grape is blended with smaller quantities of Thrapsathiri and Rozaki to produce this light Cretan white wine. This pale yellow drop has a well-balanced flavor and a

lingering citrus aroma. The Minos Winery's wine cellar, which is only a couple of miles from the first Minoan wine press, now has a total capacity of 1,560,000 gallons (6,000,000 liters).

Minoiko: this red Minoiko is the Minos Winery's best wine and is produced from 80% Kotsifali and 20% Mandelaria grapes. It is aged in oak barrels for twelve months in the ventilated wine cellar to achieve its distinctive character. A year after the grapes are harvested, thus in the December of the following year, the wine is poured into numbered bottles. Only a limited number of bottles of Minoiko are sold. A vintage seldom produces more than 20,000 bottles. It has a ruby-red color, a rich aroma of raisins, plums, and cinnamon, and lingering, soft vanilla notes.

LYRARAKIS WINERY

Kotsifali–Syrah: when harmoniously blended with the Syrah grape, the Cretan Kotsifali grape produces a deep red wine with a velvety taste. This goes very well with broiled meats, game and with tangy cheeses.

Dafni: this white wine is made from the rare Cretan grape of the same name. After being fermented under controlled conditions, it attains its full flavor and distinctive bouquet when served at 54 °F (12 °C).

Vilana: for its quality white wine, the Lyrarakis Winery grows the Vilana grape in selected vineyards in the Alagni mountain region at altitudes of over 1600 feet (500 meters). This produces a light wine with delicate floral and fruit aromas. Served at 54–55 °F (12–13 °C), it is excellent for seafood, cheese, and light meat dishes.

Plyto: like Dafni, Plyto has also become one of Crete's oldest and rarest grape varieties, and is therefore grown with care by the Lyrarakis winegrowers in the vineyards in Alagni. The dry white wine it

produces is fresh and its bouquet and taste have lingering, complex fruit notes. Served at a temperature of 54–55 °F (12–13 °C), Plyto is an ideal accompaniment to seafood, fish, veal, and young soft cheeses.

ΚΥΠΡΟΣ

Agía Kyriakí Khrissopolítissa – church and ruins. Background: the Troodos mountains, with Mt.Olympus reaching a height of 6403 ft (1951 m), are famed for their Byzantine churches.

CYPRUS

When the then king of Jerusalem, Guy de Lusignan, acquired the island of Cyprus in 1191, he made a wise choice. Cyprus has been an important port of call along the ancient sea routes linking East and West since time immemorial. The island, which is situated between three continents, was once regarded as the gateway to Syria, Israel, and Asia Minor. Cyprus's history goes back to the Neolithic period and the island's architecture can be traced back 9000 years. In 1400 B.C., Greek traders settled on the island. The Mycenaeans and Achaeans brought with them Greek culture and their Hellenistic heritage. According to Homer, Aphrodite, the goddess of love, emerged from the sea, crowned with foam, between Paphos and Limassol. Thanks to its strategically advantageous position and favorable agricultural conditions, various conquerors have fought to gain control of Cyprus. The most famous of these include Alexander the Great, Cleopatra and Caesar, and Richard the Lionheart of England. The last queen of the Lusignan family of Franconia handed the island over to Venice in 1489. In 1571 the island came under Ottomon rule, which lasted around 300 years. In 1878, Cyprus was taken over by the British, and since 1960 this independent sovereign republic has been a member of the United Nations and the British Commonwealth. In the summer of 1974, Turkish troops occupied about two fifths of the island, effectively splitting Cyprus into two. The northern section, which measures around 1332 square miles (3450 square kilometers), has the name of Turkish Republic of Northern Cyprus, but is not internationally recognized as a sovereign state. Visitors from southern Cyprus can make day trips to the northern sector.

Anyone wishing to stay there longer has to enter the northern sector via Turkey. The southern sector, with its capital of Lefkossia, is relatively affluent thanks to year-round tourism and a thriving export trade in bananas, citrus fruits, grapes, and wine. The wine-growing tradition south of the Troodos mountains dates back to the Crusades. The island's turbulent history has also left its mark on the island's cuisine. Garlic and olive oil, caraway, cinnamon, and coriander are the main spices used for seasoning. Popular foods include pastries filled with ground beef, cheese or a mixture of pumpkin, grains of wheat, and pine kernels. The favored cooking method of Cypriots is over a charcoal grill. Oriental influences, stemming mainly from Syria, distinguish Cyprus cuisine from its Greek counterpart. The island's inhabitants enjoy their food and dine well, and like to take their time over a meal. "Kopiaste" – come and sit down – as they say by way of hospitable invitation. And it is an invitation well worth accepting.

Right: on Cyprus, donkeys help with daily tasks by providing a valuable transport service.

DRINKS

Whether by the pool or at the bar, Cypriot drinks go down well anywhere. The island's most traditional drink is Commandaria, named after an Order of the Knights of the Cross and whose origins can be traced back to the crusaders. This brown high-quality dessert wine is produced north of Limassol by the Solera method. It is made from Xynisteri and Mavron grapes gathered from specific areas of the Troodos mountains, which are dried in the sun before being processed. The best vintages can be up to a hundred years old and have an excellent flavor: unbelievably sweet, aromatic and concentrated. Sultan Selim had a particular fondness for Commandaria, which may well have been one of the underlying reasons for the Ottoman invasion in 1570. This fondness finally led, quite literally, to the Sultan's downfall when he died after injuring his head in a fall after over-imbibing.

Another traditional drink on Cyprus is Zivanía, an aperitif made from spirits of wine. The island also exports several liqueur wines, which were formerly known as Cyprus sherry. Since 1995, this label has no longer been permissible within the EU. One legacy of the British is brandy sour, which has become Cyprus's national drink and is enjoyed by tourists at the Amathus Beach Hotel and beyond. The hotel's head barman (illustrated, center) makes a specialty known as an "Ouzo Special," a long drink in which ouzo is mixed with Sprite and sweetened with a few drops of grenadine. Lager is also popular as a refreshing drink. Carlsberg and Keo, a very popular and pleasant tasting lager, are brewed on the island.

No compromise is allowed in the making of "sherry" at the SODAP winery.

BRANDY SOUR

Originally introduced to Cyprus by the British, brandy sour quickly became the island's national drink. It is a refreshing long drink and is made from one quarter of Cypriot brandy, one quarter of lemon or lime syrup, a dash of angostura bitters and topped up with soda water. It is served in a tall glass over crushed ice, the moistened rim of which is dipped in sugar. Nuts or raw slices of carrot are often served as an accompaniment.

Beer is a popular drink on Cyprus.
Carlsberg as well as the full-flavored Keo
beer are brewed on the island.

Commandaria:
the island's favorite
dessert wine.

Filfar: a bitter
orange liqueur,
good as a digestif.

Náma: one of the
island's good
quality liqueurs.

Zivanía: a firewater
which is drunk as
an apéritif.

The chefs at the Al-Halili restaurant are expert at cooking over charcoal. The restaurant is popular with visitors to the nearby mosque.

Background: the Umm Hazam mosque is situated on Larnaca's salt lake. The lake dries up in summer, but in winter flamingos gather around the water's edge.

GRILLING

Whether you are preparing squid, lamb, swordfish, steak or pork chops, cooking over charcoal provides a quick and healthy alternative to the usual, very time-consuming cooking methods involving oil and sauce. At the weekend, on vacations, or to celebrate family parties, grilling in the mountains is one of the Cypriots' favorite pastimes. The island's residents do not even seem to mind having to drive a long way to their destination if, at the end of it, they can enjoy the atmosphere and cuisine of one of the popular grill restaurants. One such restaurant lies by a salt lake near one of the most important holy sites of the Islamic world. The Umm Hazam mosque, nearly 3 miles (4 kilometers) outside Larnaca, contains the tomb of Mohammed's foster mother, Hala Sultan Tekke, as well as the mother of King Husayn, who was once detained by the British in Lefkossia. Since the division of Cyprus very few pilgrims make their way here.

HANINS – INNS OF THE PAST

Large courtyards and simply furnished rooms with an open fire – this is what a typical hanin looks like. According to Cypriot chroniclers, they served the needs of merchants and their animals, providing them with a place to stay. Within their walls, indefatigable tradesmen transacted their business. Even during the Middle Ages, there were different categories of hanins, some of them large enough to accommodate entire caravans along with their animals.

The origins of these ancient inns date back to classical times when pilgrims came to Cyprus to pay homage to the famous Temple of Aphrodite. The word *hanin* (*han* in Turkish) first appeared in 1571, however, during Turkish rule. The hanins date back to this time and bear testimony to the island's past culture. There are a large number of them in Lefkossia within the demarcation line, which has been guarded by UN troops since 1974, with the result that visitors can only see them from a distance. One such inn, the Pantgarou Hanin, has inspired the Cypriot saying "this place is like the Hanin Pantgarou," implying a little disparagingly that people seem to come and go from somebody's house just as they like.

SOUVLÁKI ME LAKHANIKÁ
Vegetable kebabs

16 button mushrooms
2 bell peppers, deseeded, cored and cut into eighths
3 tomatoes, cut into large chunks
2 onions, peeled and cut into eighths
3 zucchini, cut into thin lengthwise strips
2 eggplants, cut into thin lengthwise strips
⅔ cup/150 ml olive oil
1 tsp dried thyme
1 tsp oregano
Juice of 1 lemon
Salt and freshly ground black pepper

Put the vegetables in a bowl, season with salt and pepper, and add the thyme, oregano, and two thirds of the olive oil. Cover the bowl and stand in the refrigerator for 20 minutes. Then, roll up the strips of zucchini and eggplant and divide the vegetables between 8 skewers. Place on a charcoal grill and cook for 10 minutes, turning occasionally. Arrange the skewers on plates. Mix the lemon juice with the remaining olive oil, pour over the kebabs and serve.

XIFÍAS STA KÁRVOUNA
Swordfish grilled over charcoal

2 lbs/1 kg swordfish steaks
A scant ½ cup/100 ml lemon juice
A scant ½ cup/100 ml olive oil
2 green bell peppers, cut into large pieces
4 small onions, peeled and halved
A few fresh mushrooms, cleaned
1 bunch parsley, finely chopped
1 small onion, finely diced
Salt and freshly ground black pepper

Dice the swordfish steaks into 1–1½ inch/2–4 cm cubes, place in a bowl, season with salt and pepper and pour over half the lemon juice. Leave to marinate for one hour. Skewer the fish, alternating with pieces of bell pepper, the onion halves and mushrooms. Cook over the charcoal grill for 15 to 20 minutes, turning frequently. Mix the olive oil with the remaining lemon juice and use this to baste the kebabs several times during cooking. Arrange the kebabs on a plate and sprinkle with diced onions and chopped parsley just before the kebabs are served.

KOTÓPOULO ME RÍGANI
Chicken with oregano

2 lbs/1 kg chicken breasts, cut into
    2 inch/5 cm pieces
4 tbsp/50 ml olive oil
2 tsp dried oregano
Salt
Freshly ground black pepper

Place the chicken pieces in a bowl, season with salt, pepper and oregano, and pour over the olive oil. Cover the bowl and marinate in the refrigerator for two hours. Spear the chicken onto kebab sticks and place over a charcoal grill. Cook for 15 to 20 minutes, turning frequently. This dish goes well with a fresh salad and tzatzíki.

Freshly prepared grilled dishes are available on Cyprus until late in the evening.

MEAT DISHES

SIKOTÁKI MOSKHARÍSIO
Calf's liver

1 lb/500 g calf's liver
4 tbsp/50 ml olive oil
1 large onion, finely diced
2 garlic cloves, crushed
4 tbsp/50 ml dry white wine
A scant ½ cup/100 ml chicken or vegetable stock
3 tomatoes, peeled and diced
Salt and freshly ground black pepper

Cut up the liver into small pieces. Heat the oil in a saucepan, add the liver, onions, and garlic and sauté quickly. Pour in the wine and stock, add the tomatoes, and season with salt and pepper. Reduce the heat and cook until the liquid has thickened.
This dish goes well with rice or pilau.

ARNÍ STON TAVÁ
Lamb cooked in a clay pot

2 lbs/1 kg lamb (on the bone)
4 tbsp/50 ml olive oil
2 lbs/1 kg onions, sliced
1 lb/500 g tomatoes, peeled and diced
1 tsp caraway
1 cinnamon stick
1 scant cup/200 ml red wine
2 tbsp/30 ml red wine vinegar
Salt and freshly ground black pepper

Preheat the oven to 300 °F (150 °C). Dice the lamb into small pieces. Heat the olive oil in a saucepan, sauté the onions until transparent and

brown the meat well. Add the tomatoes, caraway, cinnamon stick, wine, and vinegar and season with salt and pepper. Bring to a boil briefly, then remove the saucepan from the heat.
The *tavá* is a traditional Greek clay pot, but you can use any type of clay pot instead. Put all the ingredients in the pot and place it in the oven. Leave to cook slowly for 2 hours until the meat is tender. Give the contents of the pot a stir every 30 minutes. Serve the lamb straight from the oven, still in the clay pot, and sprinkle with a little caraway. Rice and yogurt are popular accompaniments to this dish.

VODINÓ PAFÍTIKO
Beef à la Paphos

2 lbs/1 kg neck beef
1 generous cup/250 ml olive oil
4 bay leaves
Oregano
2 lbs/1 kg small potatoes
Salt and freshly ground black pepper

Preheat the oven to 320 °F (160 °C). Divide the meat into 4 portions and place in an oven-proof dish. Season with salt, pepper and oregano, pour over half the olive oil and add 2 bay leaves. Add just under half a cup/100 ml of water, place in the oven and cook slowly for at least 2 hours. Meanwhile, peel the potatoes, season with salt, pepper and oregano, and place them in another ovenproof dish. Add the remaining olive oil, bay leaves, and another scant half cup/100 ml of water. Place in the oven a good hour after the meat, cooking the two together for the last hour.
This dish is often accompanied by a fresh salad and *tzatzíki*.

AFÉLIA
Pork fillet in red wine

3 lbs/1½ kg pork fillet
6 small onions, chopped
1 scant cup/200 ml dry red wine
2 tbsp coriander seeds
A scant ½ cup/100 ml olive oil
Salt and freshly ground black pepper
Marinating time: 6 hours

Season the pork fillets with salt and pepper and place in a bowl. Add the wine and sprinkle the coriander seeds over the meat. Marinate in the refrigerator for 6 hours. Heat the olive oil in a saucepan and sauté the fillets along with the onions. Pour in the marinade mixture and just enough water to cover all the ingredients. Season with salt and pepper, cover the pan and cook over a low heat for one hour, until the meat is tender.

SEFTALIÁ
Grilled ground meat rolls

1 lb/500 g caul
2 lb/1 kg of ground beef and pork, mixed
3 onions, finely diced
½ bunch parsley, finely chopped
1 tsp dried or 2 tbsp fresh mint
3 tbsp breadcrumbs
½ tsp cinnamon
Salt
Freshly ground black pepper

The Anassa complex in the west of the island boasts five restaurants. The culinary skills of their chefs are among the best on the island. Here they present their favorite dishes.

Soften the caul in a bowl of warm water. Season the other ingredients with salt and pepper and knead well. Carefully open out the caul on a flat work surface and trim off any thick parts. Cut into 4×4 inch (10×10 cm) squares and place some ground meat mixture at one edge of each square, fold the end and sides over the meat, then roll up firmly. Thread the sausages onto two flat skewers or a double spit and cook over a hot charcoal fire for 15 to 20 minutes, turning the skewers every 2–3 minutes. The meat will be moist and the outside golden brown.

PERDÍKI ME SÍKA
Partridge with caramelized figs

4 partridges (or 4 quail)
Olive oil
⅔ cup/150 ml Commandaria or Mavrodaphne (red liqueur wine)
½ cup/125 ml dry white sherry

1½ cups/350 ml orange juice
1 tbsp orange zest
⅔ cup/150 ml vegetable stock
4 bay leaves
4 sprigs fresh thyme
4 cinnamon sticks
Salt and freshly ground black pepper

For the figs:
1 generous cup/125 g confectioner's sugar
A scant ½ cup/100 ml orange juice
1 tsp orange zest
8 fresh figs, peeled
4 slices of toasted bread, cut into triangles

Clean and draw the poultry and cut each in half. Heat the olive oil in a skillet and sauté for 2–3 minutes on each side. Set the poultry aside. Using the same skillet, heat some more oil, then add the poultry, the wine and sherry and flambé. Douse the flames with the orange juice and add the orange zest, stock and herbs.

Season well, cover the pan and simmer for 15 minutes. Prepare the figs: Caramelize the sugar in a saucepan, add the orange juice and zest. Simmer for 10 minutes, then add the figs, tossing them in the orange syrup until they are completely covered and caramelized. In another skillet, fry the toast triangles in olive oil before draining on paper towels and dividing between four plates. Serve the partridge or quail with the sauce, figs, and orange syrup.

Kléftiko meat is strongly seasoned with oregano and wrapped in aluminum foil.

The portions are placed next to one another in the preheated oven.

The oven is sealed with clay to make it airtight so that the meat becomes crisp on the outside and tender inside.

KLÉFTIKO

There is ample grazing for numerous flocks of sheep in the foothills of the Troodos mountains.

KLÉFTIKO
Roast lamb

4 lamb fillets, each weighing 8 oz/250 g
Juice of 1 lemon
1 tbsp marjoram, finely chopped
1 tbsp thyme, finely chopped
2 lb/1 kg small potatoes
1 scant cup/200 ml olive oil
3 large tomatoes, sliced
3 bay leaves
Salt
Freshly ground black pepper

Preheat the oven to 300 °F (150 °C). Sprinkle the lamb fillets with lemon juice. Mix the majoram, thyme, salt and pepper together and sprinkle over the meat. Brush oil over four large pieces of aluminum foil, lay a fillet in the center of each and wrap the foil around it. Place the wrapped fillets in a clay pot that has a lid, cover, and place in the oven. Leave to bake for about 3 hours. Meanwhile, peel and wash the potatoes and carefully make a few cuts in each one. Place in a roasting pan, sprinkle with salt and pepper, pour the olive oil over them and dot with butter. Place the sliced tomato on top of the potatoes, then season once more with a little salt and pepper and add the bay leaves. About an hour before the lamb is ready, put the potatoes in the oven and roast until they are golden brown. Serve the lamb fillets in the center of a plate with the potatoes and tomatoes arranged around them and garnish with a few fresh herbs.

A fresh country salad is a good accompaniment to this dish.

Before the Greek struggle for independence began in 1821 in protest against centuries of Ottoman rule, the mountains of Cyprus and Greece were full of wild bands of robbers. These men were universally feared, and not just on account of their cattle-stealing activities. These *kleftes* (robbers), with their growing sense of national consciousness, eventually became militant and successful freedom fighters, who later played an important role as guerrilla fighters in the Greek civil war. From then on, *kleftouria* has represented a way of life supporting the belief that a hunger for freedom and self-determination is a justifiable reason for breaking laws. Since the robbers and rebels were obviously not able to satisfy their appetites for long on meat they had produced themselves, the *kléftiko* has gone down in history as the dish most famously associated with them. There is no way of proving for certain whether they really did prepare their meat in a well-hidden and buried clay oven, but one thing is for sure: the clay oven had to be made airtight and sealed for many hours, if not days, before the *kléftiko* meat was ready.

It is still prepared in the same way today. *Kléftiko* is made from lamb, kid, or beef from older animals since the meat is supposed to be hard and tough. It is cut into portions and rubbed with lots of lemon juice, then seasoned with salt and oregano. Then off it goes into the pot. For the dish to succeed, it is important to preheat the clay oven with charcoal to a low temperature. To prevent it being exposed straight away to high temperatures, broken bits of clay are placed over the hot coals. Only then is it safe to put the pot containing the meat into the oven. Bay leaves are used to improve the flavor of the meat. It tastes even better if it is doused occasionally with beer or wine before the clay oven is finally sealed with yet more clay. The meat is ready to serve after three hours, but tastes even better, if you can leave it in the oven for 48 hours. By then, it will be crisp on the outside and very tender inside. Thickly sliced sautéd potatoes and fresh bread make perfect accompaniments to *kléftiko*.

Kléftiko is regarded as a delicacy on Cyprus and is served with bread and potatoes.

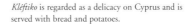

Steamed artichoke hearts, seasoned with salt and pepper, served with vegetables or meat.

Boiled chicken served with little bowls of hot or sweet sauces.

Carrots, celery root, and onions – not boiled, as they are on the Greek islands, but steamed.

Red beets with walnuts, a nourishing as well as refreshing combination, perfect for hot days.

Roast beef: this reflects the British influence on Cypriot cuisine

Paphos cheese, made from pure sheep's milk, tastes salty, but it is milder than the Greek *féta*.

MEZÉS CULTURE

Cypriot *mezés* have nothing in common with the Greek appetizers found on the mainland or elsewhere in the Aegean. *Mezédes* in Cyprus do not have to be ordered, they simply appear on the table. They keep on appearing until waved away by the diner! How long this takes is a matter for the gourmet and his stomach. Some people can manage up to 30 *mezédes* in one sitting. In days gone by, Cypriot tavern keepers often used to make a name for themselves with their *mezédes* before they risked serving other dishes. Cypriot *mezédes* are neither starters nor appetizers, but individual dishes, one following the other, offering such a wide diversity of choice that it is possible to get to know the entire spectrum of Cypriot cuisine in a single evening. They offer the foreign visitor the best and most direct opportunity to become acquainted with the cuisine of the eastern Mediterranean region. At a traditional *mezés* evening, every Cypriot dish is simply declared a *mezés*. The selection of dishes available and the way they are prepared varies between mountain village and coastal resort. The Cypriots living in the mountains

YAKHNÍ RECIPES

The Cypriots are as fond of *yakhní* as the Italians are of pasta. All the ingredients are steamed in tomato juice, tomato paste or with fresh tomatoes. The classic version is made as follows: Cook some lamb with onions, tomato juice, and water. Add broad beans or fava beans when the meat is almost cooked, season with salt and pepper to taste, and leave the saucepan uncovered while the sauce reduces. Another refreshing variation is to wash, dry, and remove the stems from some okras and sauté them in oil. Sauté onions and garlic and cook for 15 minutes with tomato paste, one bay leaf and water. Then put everything together in a saucepan and cook over a low heat for about 40 minutes.

favor offal (variety meats), kid and other meat specialties, whereas various kinds of fish, crabs, and shellfish are also served on the coast. One way in which Cypriot *mezés* differ from the Greek *mezédes* is the menu-like sequence, characterized by the size of the plates. Cheese, sausage, olives, and tahini paste are served on the smallest plates in the house. Medium-sized plates are brought out next, bearing pickled vegetables, for example, or meat patties, offal, salads or smoked meat creations. Some of the most popular fish *mezédes* include grilled octopus, stuffed squid, or sepia with leek and shrimp, to name but a few. Delicious and hearty meat dishes include beef sausages with garlic, veal with garlic and cayenne pepper, or pasties stuffed with spicy ground meat. And even if you simply cannot eat another thing, you should still make room for some delicious fruit or sweet little cakes.

The 7 Georges tavern in Paphos, where George the chef uses only fresh meat and vegetables supplied from his own animals and garden.

LÓUNTZA

"Just say the word *lóuntza* and your mouth will start to water. It is pure poetry for the palate." This is how Archbishop Makarios III, the first President of the independent Republic of Cyprus in the mid 1960s, described this type of ham, which is as unique as the Cypriot language. *Lóuntza* is ham that comes from the back of the pig. Once every bit of fat has been removed, it is laid in salt for 4 to 5 days. If it is undergoing an 8-day wine treatment, the Cypriots call it "roasting" the ham. Only pure, dark Cypriot wine may be used for the marinade to prevent the *lóuntza* becoming too sour. Then it is seasoned with a coating of herbs consisting of black pepper, *artisiá* (cumin), ground cloves, and coriander. The meat is left to hang for 3 to 8 days. The longer it hangs, the stronger the taste. It is suitable for all occasions and is served cut into thick slices. *Lóuntza* can also be smoked in a wood oven with wood from fruit trees, in which case the meat is baked for three hours before being seasoned with basil, marjoram, and lemon-scented geranium leaves.

TSAMARÉLA

The *lóuntza* is not without its competitors: *tsamaréla*, for instance, is a ham made from mountain goats fed solely on fresh grass from mountain pastures. *Tsamaréla* is made in the late summer when the animals return to their stables. Only the fillet parts of the animal are used. The salted meat is first left to dry in the sun. It is then placed in a large cauldron of boiling water for a minute to kill off any bacteria or germs. The *tsamaréla* is seasoned with dried oregano and left to smoke in the baking sun for 24 hours before it is finally ready. The *tsamaréla* will then keep for several months.

KHIROMÉRI

Khiroméri in Greek means "side of the pig," meaning the leg of the pig. Like *lóuntza*, it is preserved and smoked. It is laid in red wine for 21 days, a slightly more costly process as the wine must be continually renewed. The leg of pork is frequently turned and weighted in order to extract the water content. Every 2 to 3 days, it is removed from its wine bath and aired, before it is

ARABIC CYPRUS

Artisiá is the name the Cypriots give to Arabic cumin, but they are also familiar with its Greek name *kimino*. The name reflects its Arabic origins. The Ancient Greeks imported cumin from Central Asia and planted it in the gardens of ancient Greece. Theophrastus classified the spice as a kitchen herb because, at that time, it was not the seeds but the leaves that were used for seasoning. Later on, it became an important herb for the monks in Byzantine monasteries, especially during their regular "water-only days." During these fasting days, they would mix it with aniseed and add it to water, producing a spiced water drink. The Ancient Greeks favored cumin as a seasoning for seafood dishes, but on Cyprus it is more commonly used in meat dishes, introducing a sophisticated and slightly sensuous oriental flavor.

eventually hung up to dry like *lóuntza*. In the past, Cypriots, like the Greeks, would mainly eat pork during the winter months. That is why *khiroméri* was only produced in the winter when pork meat was plentiful. This is still the case today. You do not cut into the *khiroméri* until Easter when Lent is over.

Lóuntza: meat from the back of the pig is cut into equal pieces and cleaned of all fat.

The meat is rolled in salt to season it and to draw out the moisture.

The meat is then left to marinate for one week in Cypriot red wine.

Finally, the *lóuntza* is tossed in a mixture of herbs and hung up to dry.

Background: *loúntza* in the smoke chamber. Above: *loúntza* sliced at the butcher's.

Background and above: *khiroméri* is the Cypriot verson of Parma ham. It is served in large slices.

Tsamaréla is the only ham in the entire Mediterranean region to be made from goat meat.

Left: a Cypriot woman stirring the whey. Above: *arnarí* is a variation of the cheese without the mint leaves.

KHALOÚMI

What goat cheese is to the Greeks, *khaloúmi* is to the Cypriots. This seductive cheese is not entirely a Cypriot invention, however, but is actually Arabic in origin. It is made from a mixture of sheep's, goat's, and cow's milk, sometimes from 100 percent sheep's or goat's milk, and the end product is the result of a complicated series of steps. First, the milk is heated slowly in a large cauldron over a very low heat. Then, the obligatory rennet is added, a kind of ready-made yeast, which comes from the mucous membrane found in the stomach of young kids and contains the important enzyme chymosin. It helps young animals to digest their mothers' milk, but is used in cheese-making to coagulate the milk. The milk must then be left to rest until it begins to solidify. The solid mass is then squeezed by hand over a large saucepan until all the whey is removed and only the solids remain. Next, the cheese is divided into portions and placed in special molds. The leftover whey is heated once more, the cheese portions are cut in two down the middle and carefully put back into the warm whey. As soon as the whey begins to boil, the lumps of cheese are scooped out again and laid on a wooden board. Once the *khaloúmi* has cooled down, the process is repeated. The process is not complete until the cheese begins to float on the surface of the whey. The entire pan of whey is removed from the heat and left to cool for 5 minutes. The next step is to set out large plates containing salt and fresh mint leaves, then toss each *khaloúmi* cheese first in salt, then in the mint. This gives the cheese an unexpected flavor. A second cheese is then placed on top of the first, creating a sort of *khaloúmi* sandwich. This stack of cheeses is then stored in jars or clay pots filled with brine until the cheeses are completely covered.

Khaloúmi contains 43% fat, a maximum 45% liquid, 22% protein and 2–3% salt. Four ounces (100 grams) contains 300 kcal. If you want the cheese to keep longer, it has to be left completely covered in a container for at least 40 days. During this time, it is apparently unpalatable and is said to be "playing hooky." This process hardens the cheese to some extent so that it can, with care, be grated over pasta dishes or baked. *Khaloúmi* cheese can be stored for up to three months at 35–39 °F (2–4 °C) and for over a year at –0.4 °F (–18 °C). Once defrosted, it should be left to stand at room temperature for half an hour before being used. One of the special features of *khaloúmi* is the fact that it does not melt. It can, therefore, be fried, boiled, or broiled. It is ideal as an appetizer, a main course, or as a dessert course accompanied by fruits. *Khaloúmi* always tastes surprisingly fresh.

The cheese is scooped out of the tub by hand while it is still warm.

It is a bit crumbly, but after being lightly kneaded, it is pressed carefully into little molds.

The mold gives *khaloúmi* its typically rounded shape.

THE CAROB TREE

This sole tree of the *Ceratonia* genus is native to the eastern Mediterranean region. Its dark brown, bean-like pods can be picked in autumn and either eaten fresh, or processed into other products. Sometimes known as St. John's bread, it was familiar to ancient Babylonians around 1000 B.C. and was distributed as bread for the poor. Even in those days, it was known to help regulate the digestion and thought to be useful against diarrhea.

The carob tree has gained fame on account of the weight of its seeds. The Arabs used its seeds, which weigh 0.18 grams, to weigh gold and gemstones. The word "carat" comes from the Latin for carob (*Ceratonia*). The carat as a unit of weight was later standardized as 200 milligrams, or 0.2 grams. The carob contains around 40% sugar, 10% protein, and the minerals calcium and iron, which is why it was used for food in times of need. It can even be used to make a type of substitute coffee. More recently, the pods have been used for cattle fodder. Carob tends to be known on Cyprus as *kharoúpi* and is used to make an unusual sweet delicacy. *Kharoúpi-pastéli* is made from boiled carob syrup. The syrup itself is used to enhance desserts, although you are only likely to find this in a few Cypriot villages. The resin of the carob tree is also used in the manufacture of paper and a few alcoholic drinks.

This is the only species of *Ceratonia* native to the eastern Mediterranean region. Its fruit, which resembles bean pods, can be picked in the autumn and eaten fresh.

The pods are boiled over an open fire and stirred constantly.

The resulting mixture is tipped out to cool on a stone slab.

Then it is thoroughly kneaded and rolled into a long shape.

The syrup mass changes color as it cools.

This sweet confectionery is cut into small portions and sold. The *kharoúpi-pastéli* is packed in bags, ready for sale.

The syrup is good with ice cream.

BECCAFICOS

Lawrence Durrell, a great expert on Cyprus and author of numerous books on Greece during the 1950s, had said everything there was to say about Cyprus, but even he had not heard of beccaficos until 1957. The first mention of these small birds – sparrows, warblers, and blackcaps (*silviidae*), as they are known – was in his book *Bitter Lemons*. In it he relates, almost incidentally, of his first culinary encounter with these small creatures, describing how they were served up to him as an appetizer with a glass of wine and meant to be eaten whole. Beccaficos are without doubt Cyprus's most exotic delicacy and the one most shrouded in secrecy. Even today, it is difficult to find out much about them and it would be rare to find them mentioned on any restaurant menu. In reality, however, most Cypriots like nothing better than to return home from a day's hunting with a bag of these tiny birds. The main season for beccaficos is September when the birds can be caught all over the place by means of lime twigs. Sometimes, other birds, such as ortolans (*Emberiza hortulana*) and flycatchers (*Muscicapidae*), get caught at the same time. The fact that this practice is enveloped in secrecy, of course, is due to the fact that trapping songbirds is strictly prohibited on Cyprus. Despite all the conservationists, however, this tradition is still upheld with great enthusiasm.

Every small boy on Cyprus knows how to catch and eat beccaficos. Eleven-year old Ben recommends: "You have to leave them whole. Sometimes, you can just remove the little stomach. Then pull off the feathers. Put them in boiling water for 8 minutes, then season with wine vinegar and salt. Have a glass of wine with it or, if your father lets you, a sip of cognac."

This eating of little birds in Greek-speaking countries dates back to the time of Aristotle. The bird markets of Athens must have been full of birds and poultry in those days. These birds would never have formed part of the main menu for a big evening meal, but were more popular as a snack between meals. They reflected the host's wealth and prestige and were sometimes bred in captivity in citizens' gardens. It would be nice to think that beccaficos could enjoy such a comparatively gentle fate.

An enviable occupation! Rose pickers are careful that only the best petals are used.

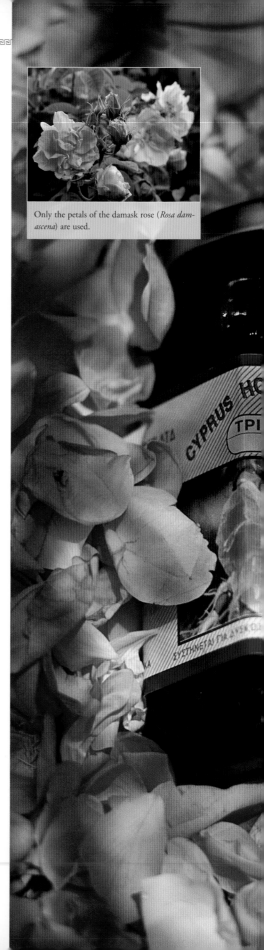

Only the petals of the damask rose (*Rosa damascena*) are used.

ROSES FOR APHRODITE

Even today, there is no denying the effect that the perfume of roses and the magic of love has on people. Their symbolic significance is as old as time and closely associated with the goddess Aphrodite. It was in her honor that "Aphrodisia" festivals used to be celebrated on Cyprus, secret initiation ceremonies about which very little is known, since those participating were sworn to silence. One thing we do know, however, is that they were celebrated in April when everything was in bloom. Young girls adorned themselves with roses, sang and danced, fasted, and planted trees for the beautiful goddess in her temple gardens. Even though the mystique surrounding Aphrodite has long since disappeared, a bouquet of roses is still an expression of love beween a man and a woman.

Rose perfume and rose water are still manufactured on Cyprus as a memorial to the goddess of love. In May, the rose-growers pick around half a million petals from the damask roses cultivated in their fields. The best time to gather them is while the leaves are still damp with morning dew. These flowers of love, from which oil of roses is distilled, fill the whole area with an intense perfume. The island's inhabitants, however, also use essence of roses to make rose water, rose liqueur, and rose brandy. Three hundred rose heads weigh about 2 pounds (1 kilogram) and this is enough to make 4 pints (2 liters) of rose water.

Rose water and rose perfume have many different uses in Cypriot kitchens. Sweet dishes, such as *daktila*, *bouzékia*, *loukoúmi* as well as the Cypriot version of *baklavás* are all flavored with rose water. Alternative medicine has long since recognized the therapeutic qualities of rose oil. It has antiseptic properties, and is good for treating wounds, gum inflammation and herpes. It is thought to have a soothing effect in times of trouble and sadness. Cypriot women use rose water to protect their faces from the sun and grandmothers insist that their granddaughters wash with rose water.

The rose petals are first cleaned with lots of water to remove any dirt or insects.

Women sort the rose petals as only the best ones can be used.

After washing and sorting, the petals are mixed with sugar and lemon juice.

Boiling the petals produces a crystalline mass.

APHRODITE

Wherever she wandered, sweet-smelling roses grew at her feet. Many ancient myths have been woven about the birth of this goddess. Cronos, ruler of the Titans, is said to have cut off the genitalia of Uranus with a mighty blow of his sickle, whereupon they fell into the sea and were shrouded in white foam. From this foam emerged the most beautiful female figure ever born: Aphrodite. Then, from the depths of the sea arose a huge scallop shell, into which Aphrodite climbed and drifted over the water for many days. She was first sighted from Kithira, a small island between the Peloponnese and Crete. Since then, the island's inhabitants have venerated her and given her the name of "Kythereia." She first set foot on land on Cyprus, however, where she was awaited by the three Graces. These three daughters of Zeus remained with Aphrodite until she was grown up and received by the gods on Mount Olympus. She was accompanied by nereids and two of her children. There was scarcely a god who did not propose marriage to Aphrodite! In the end, she had to offer her hand to Hephaestus, the ugliest of all the gods on Olympus. She did not remain faithful to him for long, however. The most famous of all her numerous love affairs with mortals began on Cyprus. Even as a child, she had developed a penchant for the young Adonis: because of his great beauty, she had placed him in Persephone's care when his mother Myrrha died. Persephone also came to love Adonis and was later reluctant to give him his freedom. Adonis became a hunter and was killed one day by a great wild boar. Since then, Adonis as well as Aphrodite have been venerated on Cyprus. Jealousy on the part of Hera and Athena led to a beauty contest from which Aphrodite emerged the winner. It was this contest which eventually led to the Trojan War.

ROSE TARTLETS

1½ cups/150 g ground almonds
⅔ cup/150 g sugar
10 egg whites
1 scant cup/200 ml rose water
¼ cup/30 g all-purpose flour
8 oz/250 g puff pastry

Preheat the oven to 300 °F (150 °C). Place the ground almonds, sugar, and 3 egg whites in a bowl and mix together well. Stir in the rose water and flour and continue to stir for a few minutes. Beat the remaining egg whites until stiff and fold into the mixture. Roll out the pastry into a thin sheet and cut out small rounds, placing them into small, greased tartlet molds. Fill each mold with almond mixture. Sprinkle with sugar and bake until light brown. Leave to cool before tipping out of the pastry molds.

Rose petals are turned into jam, wine, liqueur, rose water, and rose brandy.

Cypriot bananas taste so sweet because they are ripe when picked.

Siesta time: a fresh sea breeze helps cool you down after work.

SIRÓPI APÓ PORTOKÁLI
Orange syrup

4 cups/1 liter orange juice
3½ cups/750 g sugar
½ cup/125 ml lemon juice
Zest of 1 unwaxed orange
4 leaves of fresh basil

Pour the orange juice into a saucepan, heat over a medium heat and dissolve the sugar in the juice. Add the lemon juice, orange zest, and basil and top up with a scant cup/200 ml water. Stirring constantly, simmer until the liquid has thickened into a syrupy consistency. Remove the basil leaves, pour into a clean bottle and seal.
Orange syrup will keep for a long time and can be used to flavor desserts, alcoholic drinks or can be diluted with water to make a soft drink. Grapefruit syrup is also very popular on Cyprus. To make this, merely replace the orange juice with grapefruit juice.

Popular export products: orange juice and lime juice from Cyprus.

SWEET BANANAS

A carpet of banana leaves, blue plastic coverings, impenetrable pathways and mysterious rustlings in the background – anyone wandering through the banana plantations in southwest Cyprus may be forgiven for thinking they are in the tropics. Bananas (*Musa paradisiaca*), which originate from southeast Asia, grow in the warmest part of the island. This fruit has been cultivated for more than 3000 years, but despite all attempts to make it more resistant by means of hybridization, the banana plant will only grow in places where the sun gives off enough light all year round and temperatures do not drop below freezing. In winter, the plantation workers wrap the plants in insulating plastic covering to protect them from cold, wind, and rain.
Every April, they cut the leaves off the old banana plant. The previous year's mother plant is pruned right back because a new little banana plant is already shooting up from the bottom and it is this which will produce new fruit. During the summer, irrigation systems make sure the trees get their 26,000 US gallons (100,000 liters) of water per week. When the farmers start counting the 12 to 16 little bananas on each plant, they treat it with the sort of care and tenderness that they would show a pregnant woman. During the harvest period, which runs from October to January, the farmers are almost as proud as if they had produced their own offspring. One of their secret tips is that bananas should be stored for a few days with an apple, as this will give them an extra special flavor.

KÉIK ME BANÁNA
Banana cake

4 bananas, peeled
1 tbsp cognac
1 generous cup/125 g flour
1 tsp baking powder
1½ tsp vanilla essence
1¼ cups/250 g butter
1 generous cup/250 g sugar
4 eggs

For the sauce:
1 cup/200 g butter
1 cup/200 g brown sugar
1⅔ cups/400 ml light cream

Preheat oven to 350 °F (180 °C). Place the bananas in a saucepan, pour in 3 tbsp water and the cognac, and bring to a boil. Mash the bananas. Sift the flour and baking powder into a bowl, add the bananas, and mix well. Beat the butter, sugar, vanilla essence, and eggs in a mixer until creamy, then add the banana mixture. Pour the cake mixture into a well-greased square baking pan. Bake for one hour until the cake turns brown.
To make the sauce, melt the butter in a saucepan and dissolve the sugar in it, heating until the sugar caramelises. Add the cream and bring to a boil briefly. Turn out the banana cake and cut it into slices. Place one slice on each plate and drizzle a little sauce over it.
This dessert is utterly delicious, hot or cold.

Some of each type of seasonal fruit is preserved as jam or bottled.

This is done by stretching a cloth over a saucepan of boiling water, placing the vegetables on the cloth, and allowing them to cook in the rising steam. Fruit, on the other hand, should be on the firm side if the resulting *glikó* is to be served as an accompaniment to coffee. Once the bottles have been properly prepared, they are placed in a water bath and sterilized. Olives undergo a different procedure. They are not precooked by steaming, but mixed thoroughly with any other desired ingredients, including either lemon or vinegar. They must then be covered and stored in a cool place.

GLIKÓ MELITZANÁKI
Baby eggplants in syrup

2 lb/1 kg small, soft eggplants (approx. 2 inches/ 5 cm in length)
Almonds, one for each eggplant
4 cups/1 kg sugar
2 cups/500 ml cold water
2 tbsp fresh lemon juice
2 vanilla beans, 5 cloves

Cut off the eggplant stalks and make an incision in one side of the fruit. Stand in cold water for 24 hours, changing the water frequently. Drain and press one almond into each cut, then bind it together with kitchen string. Place the sugar, water, vanilla beans, cloves, and eggplants in a saucepan and boil for about 6 minutes. Leave to cool and stand for 24 hours. Remove the eggplants and undo the string. Bring the syrup to a boil, add the eggplants, and boil until the syrup thickens. Keep skimming off any froth that forms. Finally, add the lemon juice. Leave to cool and pour into preserving jars.

PRESERVES

Although people's fates no longer depend to the same extent on whether their harvest is good enough to see them through the winter, individual preferences for preserved fruit and vegetables have meant that the art of preserving has in fact survived despite the advent of deep freezers and imported fruit. The main preservatives are still sugar and salt. Anything sweet is covered in a warm sugar solution of 1¾ cups (400 grams) sugar or more per 4 cups (1 liter) water, whereas non-sweet products require a salt solution of about 1 lb (500 g) sea salt to 1 US gallon (3.7 liters) of water. This is topped by a layer of herbs and spices. Before bottling any fruit or vegetables, they must first be carefully checked to make sure that only the very best gets into the pantry. Then, the fruit or vegetables must be thoroughly cleaned and lightly scored so that they do not burst during cooking. Small varieties of fruit can be mixed with nuts or spices. Vegetables are blanched first.

Eggplants can also be pickled for use as a winter vegetable.

Pickled onions can be served as an appetizer or are a basic ingredient for seasoning sauces.

Sliced zucchini is useful as a type of chutney to go with hearty vegetable dishes.

Olives are preserved uncooked in a mixture of vinegar, lemons and garlic, seasoned with all kinds of herbs.

Preserved apricots can be a dessert or an ingredient in cakes.

Quince *glikó*: Its citrus flavor and fibrous skin harmonize to produce a distinctive delicacy.

Grape juice surrounding almonds on a bit of string: soutzoúko

SOUTZOÚKO

When you see the word *soutzoúko*, do not immediately assume it is some kind of Japanese martial art! *Soutzoúko* has nothing whatsoever to do with sports. On the contrary, the word implies the pleasures of eating. *Soutzoúko* time is synonymous with grape harvest time. While the winegrowers are busy tending their barrels, the cooks back at home are busy with the fresh grape must. In the same way that *petimézi* are made in Chalkidiki, *soutzoúko* (see page 215) and *epsima* are made on Cyprus. When times were hard, *soutzoúko* was given to young children as a substitute for fruit. The older generation think of *soutzoúko* as a delicious candy, rich in vitamins, to be eaten during the Cypriot winter months. It will keep for a long time after it is made. The old folk prefer the strands cut into small pieces, mixed with raisins and almonds, along with a glass of zivanía, a Cypriot schnapps. Youngsters just bite a piece off the 1-foot-long (30 centimeters) candy sausage.

Making *soutzoúko* is surprisingly simple. The main ingredient is grape must. The grape juice

Epsima is grape syrup with rose-scented geranium leaves. Diluted with water, it makes a truly refreshing drink.

The *soutzoúko* workshop produces enough supplies for a whole year.

is first poured into a large cauldron along with the sugar and brought to a boil. It is then cooked over a low heat and watched constantly to make sure that the sugar does not crystallize. People used to add a bit of chalk to draw the acid content from the grapes. When the mixture begins to thicken, any foam that has formed is ladled off and the grape juice is strained through a fine linen cloth. The grape juice is mixed with a little gluten flour in a proportion of 7:1 and brought back to a boil again until the mixture thickens. Now comes the key to the whole operation: shelled almonds, threaded onto unbreakable thread like a string of pearls. These strings of almonds are dipped again and again into the hot syrup, which builds up in layers around the almonds until a sausage of solidified candy, about 1 inch/2–3 cm thick, has formed along the string. The strands must now be hung up to cool and dry. *Soutzoúko* should have the consistency of wine gums. If stored in the refrigerator, it will keep until the following spring.

Loukoúmi can be found piled high at markets all over Greece. It is usually sold loose. The dusting of powdered sugar keeps it from drying out.

LOUKOÚMI

Two things that have brought fame to the Cypriot village of Lefkara. One is its highly regarded embroidery work, much prized from the time of the Venetians right up to the present day, and the other is *loukoúmi*. The embroidery business has survived various ups and downs, but the *loukoúmi* tradition is an economic miracle on Cyprus that has stood the test of time. *Loukoúmi* is one of the sweetest, softest and most sensual of all temptations, its hint of the oriental finding great appreciation among European palates.

Loukoúmi is a jelly-like, fruit-based confectionery, similar to Turkish delight, although it is unrelated to what the Greeks call *toúrkiko méli* (Turkish honey). This – as its name suggests – is boiled honey, to which nuts, spices and egg white are added and which takes on a milky appearance when cooled. Its consistency is quite hard. *Loukoúmi*, on the other hand, is soft and as transparent as jelly.

The oldest *loukoúmi* maker on the island conducts his nearly hundred-year-old business from Lefkara. He was one of the first people at the beginning of the 20th century to represent Cypriot *loukoúmi* cooperatives at London trade fairs. Nowadays, when he offers his customers a *loukoúmi*, it is a matter of honor. The recipe remains his greatest secret. The one thing we do know for sure is that fine cornstarch is heated in a large cauldron with sugar, nuts and water, before ethereal oils are added for flavoring. The most commonly used oils are rose, then bergamot, orange, mint, and lemon. Once the mass has cooled, it is rolled out on a marble surface and cut into bite-sized pieces before being dusted with powdered sugar. This "seals" the *loukoúmi* and prevents it from drying out.

Loukoúmi is a favorite accompaniment to the afternoon cup of coffee or, prettily gift-wrapped, may be taken along as a present for the hostess.

PEANUTS

Hardly any alcoholic drink is served on Cyprus without a variety of nuts to accompany it. The term "nuts," however, refers to anything that is salty and crunches as you bite into it. Even sunflower seeds fall into this category – not to mention peanuts. What a good thing that there is no shortage of these on Cyprus, or else many people would die of thirst!

The peanut plant is a low-growing bush, that is native to South America. It feels very much at home, however, in the dry soils of Cyprus. After flowering, it hides its head in the sand, in other words, the flower stems bend toward the earth, thereby pressing the fruit into the soil. Consequently, when the peanuts are harvested in September, the first task is to clean their shells. After that, they are laid to dry in the sun for a few days. Two and a half acres (1 hectare) of land yields up to half a ton (500 kilos) of peanuts. This guarantees the farmers a good income since there will always be a demand for cold drinks on Cyprus.

The peanut is not really a nut at all, but a pulse, which is more closely related to the pea and bean.

After harvesting, the nuts are placed on large sheets to dry out. It is all hands to the deck for this job.

CYPRIOT WINE

The floor mosaics in Paphos on the southwest coast of Cyprus are a good indication that winegrowing took place on the island even in classical times, and that this is the site of one of the oldest winegrowing traditions in the world. Cypriot viniculture was flourishing even in the days when the island was occupied by the crusaders, after Richard the Lionheart had seized it in 1191. Wine cultivation came more or less to a standstill, however, during the centuries of Ottoman rule. It was not until Britain assumed control in 1878 that winegrowing was resumed in grand style. It has withstood almost unscathed all the subsequent political turmoil and changes in rulers and has improved considerably, particularly in recent years.

The main reasons that grape vines thrive here are the limestone soil and the ideal Mediterranean climate with its long summers, rainy winters, and 330 days of sunshine a year. Winegrowers begin harvesting in the second half of August. This continues until the beginning of November in some of the higher vineyards. Another factor in its favor is that Cyprus has so far been untouched by any outbreak of the disease phylloxera.

It is still largely native grape varieties that are cultivated, for instance the black Mavron and the dark, somewhat lighter and tarter Ophtalmo for red and rosé wines; delicate and fruity white wines, on the other hand, are produced from the aromatic Xynisteri grape. A blend of Xynisteri and Mavron grapes grown to the north of Limassol produces the famous Commandaria wine. Cypriot vintners have been experimenting for several years with twelve other varieties of grape, including some international favorites. The main wineries on Cyprus are Etko, Keo, Loel, and Sodap, all situated in the Limassol area. Some smaller vineyards also deserve a mention, such as Nikolaides, Fikardos, and Pelendria. One very special winegrowing estate is at the Khryssorroyiátissa monastery in the Troodos foothills, which has its own vineyards (illustration right). This is where Pater Dionissos, ensconced within the historic monastery walls, devotes himself to the art of winemaking, thereby financing the upkeep of the monastery. It has withstood several crusades and invasions since it was founded in 1152 by the hermit Ignatius. Whether he really was ordered to do so in a dream, or whether he did it in honor of an icon, as legend suggests, remains a mystery.

Pater Dionissos produces his wine within the shelter of the historic walls of the beautiful Panagía-Khryssoroyiátissa monastery.

Monastere: a dry red wine with a strong, full-bodied flavor.

Agios Andronicos: a top-quality dry white wine.

Agia Marana: a very popular rosé wine, best served at 50 °F (10 °C).

Agios Ilias: a very good, dry and light wine.

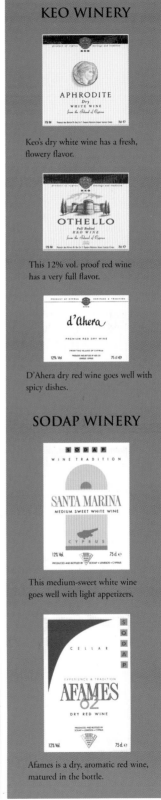

KEO WINERY

Keo's dry white wine has a fresh, flowery flavor.

This 12% vol. proof red wine has a very full flavor.

D'Ahera dry red wine goes well with spicy dishes.

SODAP WINERY

This medium-sweet white wine goes well with light appetizers.

Afames is a dry, aromatic red wine, matured in the bottle.

DONKEY SANCTUARY

The donkey (*yaídros* in Greek) is the domestic animal equivalent of the small runabout car: it is cheap to run, easy to maneuver and, with a little imagination, can be loaded up as much as you like. It has ever been a favorite domestic animal in mountainous countries like Cyprus. Nowadays, in the age of combine harvesters and roads, the donkey has become redundant. Despite this, people are not quite as ready to dispense with them as they were with their companions of the field, the ox and the farm horse. Could this be because a donkey once carried a personage of no little significance for the Greek Orthodox Church on His journey to Jerusalem? Whatever the reason, something special has been thought up for the donkey: In 1994, a sanctuary for old donkeys was set up on Cyprus in the small mountain village of Vouni. For even though no one, with the exception of

ÁGIOS GEÓRGOS

Of all the saints, St. George has ever been one of the most popular and George has always been a very special name in Greece and Cyprus. Greece has even had kings of that name. To the Cypriots, St. George was not just a saint, he was the man who gave them water. This was indeed a special feat as Cyprus had always suffered from a shortage of water even in classical times. As far as Cypriots are concerned, the slain dragon represents a powerful man who had brought the island's entire water supply under his control. George came along and overthrew this water potentate. Since that time, St. George has been regarded as the patron saint of Cyprus. Seven small churches were built in his honor in the southern part of the island. This region is still known as "The Seven Georges." The name *Geórgos* is still considered a very honorable name, which is why so many men are called by it. If a hotel or restaurant is named after St. George, you can expect to encounter hospitality and excellent Cypriot cuisine there.

the old farmers in the mountains, would actually want to be seen with a donkey any more – as this would be a sure sign that they could not afford a car – people often do still inherit donkeys. The solution to the question of what to do with them is usually found at the knacker's yard, in other words, the end of the road for the donkey. But now there is also the alternative of the donkey sanctuary. It was founded by the "Friends of the Cyprus Donkey" society and modeled on refuges in other Mediterranean countries with similar donkey histories. It currently provides room for about 80 animals, which are cared for by two permanent employees. Every eight weeks, the saddler comes along, as well as a pedicurist, and even a dentist visits once in a while. It is a lucky donkey that finds itself adopted by sponsors. If you wish, you can adopt a donkey at a cost of about $7–10 per year per person. A donkey needs 36 sponsors to survive for one whole year. Most of them have managed this and can now enjoy a pleasant retirement.

These donkey grandmothers and grandfathers live out their days in roomy, well-equipped apartments with a variety of occupational therapy alternatives. Their pleasure at seeing visitors is obvious.

CONTENTS TO APPENDIX

GLOSSARY

A

Afródes – sparkling wine

Ágouro krasí – immature or young wine

Akhnistó – steamed, steaming

Aláti – salt

Ambelónas – vineyard

Arní – lamb

Astakós – lobster, rock lobster or spiny lobster

Avgó – egg

Avgolémono – egg and lemon sauce – a standard sauce in Greek cooking, either served with vegetable and meat dishes or used to thicken soups

B

Bakaliáros – white fish, usually preserved in salt, but can also be used fresh

Baklavás – baklava, a flaky pastry, filled with nuts and soaked in syrup

Biskotákia – cookies, biscuits

Bobóta – cakes made with corn flour – shape and flavoring vary according to region

Bougátsa – a sweet pie with a creamy filling, sprinkled with cinnamon and powdered sugar

Briám – the classic Greek vegetable stew

Brizóla – chop, cutlet

D

Dolmadákia – grape leaves stuffed with various fillings and eaten as an hors d'oeuvre

Dríino varéli – oak barrel

E

Elafrí krasí – light wine

Eleólado – olive oil

Epitrapézio – table wine

Erithró or *kókkino* – red

Erithrós ínos – red wine

F

Fasoláda – the traditional Greek bean soup

Fayitó – food, meal, dish

Féta – feta, a firm, crumbly cheese made from ewe's milk, matured in brine

Foúrnos – oven

Froúta – fruit

G

Gála – milk

Galaktoboúreko – a cake made of flaky pastry with a creamy filling and syrup

Galopoúla – stuffed turkey, the traditional Christmas dinner

Gávros –- sardine, anchovy

Géfsi – taste, flavor

Glikó tou koutalioú – a type of jam made from fruit boiled in syrup

Gouroúni – pig

I

Inapothíki – wine cellar

Inopíisi – wine production

Inopiós – wine producer

Inopolío – wine bar, wine merchant's shop

Ínos – wine (classical Greek *oínos*)

Isorropiméno krasí – well-balanced wine

K

Kafés – coffee

Kadéfi – a cake made of fine threads of pastry, chopped nuts and syrup

Kapnós – tobacco

Karavídes – crayfish

Kástana – chestnuts

Katsíka – goat

Kéik – cake

Keftés – meatball

Khalvadópita – a type of nougat, made from almonds and sugar paste, pressed between wafers

Khalvás – halva, a sweet made from sesame seeds or wheat semolina

Khilopítes – homemade, almost square cut noodles

Khimós – juice

Khína – goose

Khirinó – pork

Khórta – wild greens, such as dandelion or nettle leaves, that can be used in salads

Khróma – color

Kivótio – wooden box

Kóliva – steeped wheat, raisins, pomegranate seeds and nuts, wrapped in small paper bags and handed out at religious ceremonies on memorial days

Kotópoulo – chicken

Kouloúri – sesame bread in the shape of rings, one of the 'staple foods' of Greece

Kounéli – rabbit

Krasátos – marinated in wine

Krasí – wine

Krasí me polí sóma – full-bodied wine

Kréas – meat

Kréma – cream

Kritharáki – orzo, pasta in the shape of thick rice grains, which are cooked like risotto rice, in other words with only as much water as they can absorb

Krókos – saffron

Ktíma – estate (where wine is produced)

L

Lagós – hare

Lakhaniká – vegetables

Lefkó – white

Lefkós ínos – white wine

Litouryá – bread symbolizing the body of Christ, taken to church on holy days, consecrated and distributed to worshippers

Loukánika – sausage

Loukoumádes – cakes made of yeast dough in the shape of doughnuts

Loukoúmia – a sweet, cubes of jelly flavored with lemon or rosewater and dusted with powdered sugar

M

Makaronáki – noodles, macaroni

Manitária – mushrooms

Marináto – marinated

Mayirítsa – the classic Greek Easter soup made from the offal of the Easter lamb and traditionally eaten early on Easter Sunday morning after the midnight church service

Melitzána – eggplant, aubergine

Ménta – mint

Mezés – small dishes of fish or meat, served one after the other – a variety of these dishes may make a whole meal

Mídia – mussels

Mílo – apple

Moskhári – beef, veal

Mousakás – moussaka, the well known Greek baked dish containing eggplants

N

Neró – water

O

Omeléta – omelet

Ortíkia – quails

Óspria – legumes, pulses

Oúzo – quite simply the national drink of Greece – a spirit distilled from grape residues and flavored with aniseed

P

Pagotó – ice cream

Paleó krasí – old wine

Pané – breaded, covered with bread crumbs

Pastéli – a candy bar made of sesame and honey, sometimes also containing almonds, depending on the region

Patáta – potato

Péstrofa – trout

Petimézi – concentrated, jellied grape juice, used in a variety of sweet dishes

Piláfi – rice

Pipéri – pepper

Piperiá – sweet pepper, paprika

Píta – flat, flaky pastry pie with various fillings, often cheese, vegetables or meat

Portokáli – orange

Potíri – glass

Próvato – sheep

Psári – fish

Psitó – roasted, grilled, broiled

Psomí – bread

R

Retsína – retsina, traditional wine, usually made from the Savatiano grape variety, with added pine resin

Revaní – orange cake coated with syrup

Revíthia – chick peas or garbanzo beans

Rígani – oregano

Rízi – rice

Rodákino – peach

Rofós – sea perch, grouper

S

Saganáki – gratinated with tomato and cheese

Salákhi – skate, ray

Saláta – salad

Salépi – salep, a thick drink made from an orchid extract and sold mainly on the streets of large cities

Salingária – snails

Sáltsa – sauce

Sardéla – sardine

Síko – fig

Sikotákia – liver

Sintayí – recipe

Skháras – grilled, broiled

Skórdo – garlic

Sokoláta – chocolate

Soupiés – cuttlefish

Souvláki – meat kebab

Spanáki – spinach

Sparángia – asparagus

Spória – roasted sunflower seeds, sold and eaten in the street as a snack between meals

Stafídes – raisins

Stafíli – grape

Stifádo – a goulash, containing whatever kind of meat you like

T

Thalassiná – seafood

Tiganitó – fried

Tirí – cheese

Tónnos – tuna

Tsipoúro – a strong marc brandy, distilled only from wine-making grape varieties and not from dessert varieties

Tsouréki – a traditional Easter bread made from yeast dough

Tzatzíki – a garlic and yogurt sauce served with meat dishes and deep-fried vegetables

V

Vanília – a sticky vanilla syrup, which is enjoyed mainly in summer, together with a glass of water

Varí krasí – heavy wine

Vatrákhia – frogs

Voútiro – butter

Vrastó – boiled

X

Xifías – swordfish

Xirós – dry

Y

Yakhní – a stew, usually made with vegetables, that gets its typical flavor from tomato sauce

Yaoúrti – yogurt

Yemistó – stuffed, filled

Yíros – slices of meat cooked on a large rotating spit

COOKING TECHNIQUES AND BASIC INGREDIENTS

Adding liquid: Topping up the amount of liquid required for the cooking process as necessary.

Béchamel sauce: To every 2 cups/500 ml liquid (stock and milk), use 3 tablespoons each of butter and flour, as well as cream, eggs, grated cheese and ham according to taste. Melt the butter over a low heat, add the flour and cook for a minute or two without letting the flour brown. Pour in the liquid while stirring constantly and simmer gently for about 10 minutes, stirring often. Reduce the temperature further and stir in any other ingredients and seasonings, as desired. Do not allow to boil any further once the added ingredients have amalgamated. Serve warm, or as required.

Blanching: Cooking raw ingredients for a few moments in steam, or pouring boiling liquid over them and then plunging them in cold water. This makes them easier to skin or peel. Vegetables become a little softer and any toxins are neutralized.

Braising: Sautéing (see separate entry) over a high heat in hot fat, then adding just enough liquid to cover and continuing the cooking process with any other ingredients, at a simmer, in a covered pan, either on the stovetop or in the oven.

Breading: Coating food with a mixture of flour, egg and breadcrumbs, then frying it in hot fat so that a crust forms, sealing in the juices.

Caramelizing: Browning sugar in a saucepan, usually without the addition of any fat, until it begins to foam. Remove from heat and add any water extremely carefully, then continue cooking over a low heat until it thickens.

Cooking au gratin: Giving a dish a topping so that a brown crust forms when it is broiled under a high temperature or baked in the oven.

Deep-fat frying: Cooking food immersed in hot fat over a very high temperature.

Filleting: Removing the bones from fish, usually after skinning.

Fish stock: Boil approx. 2 lbs/1 kg saltwater fish in 4 cups/1 liter salted water, together with lemon juice, slices of lemon, a little sugar, lemon balm and sage. Add a small amount of wine, bring to a boil, strain, and leave to cool.

Glazing: Covering pastries or cookies with a sugar-based coating, or covering meat dishes with a light sauce.

Glazing with apricot jam: Giving cakes or pastry a coating of apricot jam. Not only does this add a distinctive flavor, but also prevents them drying out.

Larding: Enhancing the flavor of meat or fish by means of strongly flavored ingredients, such as bacon. Cuts are made in the surface of the meat or fish and the desired ingredients inserted into them.

Light meat stock: About 4 lbs/2 kg prepared marrowbones, 2–3 large carrots peeled and cut into chunks, 2 large onions quartered, 3 celery stalks cut into pieces, 2 bay leaves, parsley stalks, and thyme. Place all the ingredients in a large saucepan or stockpot, cover with about 10 cups/2.5 liters water, and simmer gently for about 3–4 hours. Strain into a pan and allow to become quite cold so that the fat can easily be removed.

Marinating: Using vinegar or lemon juice to add piquancy to meat, fish and salad dishes, usually with the addition of salt and aromatic herbs. Wine can also be used, especially in a marinade for meat.

Phyllo pastry: A type of flaky pastry that forms the basis for many Greek specialties, such as *píta* and its many variations. For preparation, see page 146.

Poaching: Sliding raw eggs into boiling salted water and cooking slowly over a low heat until the egg white has set.

Puréeing: Processing food into a smooth pulp.

Ragout: A dish consisting of small, cooked fish or pieces of meat in a spicy sauce.

Residual juices: The juices left in the pan after braising meat or fish. By adding a little extra liquid and bringing to a boil, these juices make a good sauce.

Sauce mousseline: Stir 2 tablespoons cornstarch or flour into 1 cup/250 ml vegetable stock and bring to a boil, stirring continuously. Then, over a moderate heat or in a bain-marie and stirring continuously, alternately mix in a total of 3 egg yolks and 4 tbsps/50 g butter, which has been chilled in the refrigerator and cut into small pieces. Season with salt, pepper, and lemon juice. Beat ½ cup/125 ml cream until peaks form, and stir in shortly before serving.

Sautéing: Browning the ingredients, usually meat, quickly on all sides in hot fat, stirring or turning constantly in order to seal in the meat juices.

Sifting: Passing food through a fine sieve or strainer.

Simmer: To cook in liquid at a temperature below the boiling point 167–203 °F (75–95 °C).

Sodium bicarbonate: A cooking ingredient which has the effect of reducing the cooking time needed for pulses, which otherwise require very long cooking times.

Steaming: Cooking over steam in a covered saucepan.

Stock: Seasoned liquid in which meat, fish or vegetables have been cooked.

Sweating: Cooking prepared vegetables in a little oil or fat over a low heat in a covered pan to release the flavors before adding to soups, casseroles or sauces.

Thickening: Soups or sauces can be thickened or made creamy by adding flour, egg yolk, or starch-containing ingredients, such as semolina or potatoes.

BIBLIOGRAPHY

Greece – further reading

Ariès, Philippe/Duby, Georges et al (publisher): *A History of Private Life Vol. 1: From Pagan Rome to Byzantium.* Harvard University Press, Cambridge MA 1989

Athenaeus, C. B. Gulick (translator): *Deipnosophists.* Loeb Classical Library, Oxford 1928

Bellingham, David: *An Introduction to Greek Mythology.* Grange Books, Rochester 1996

Bernal, Martin: *Black Athena: The Afroasiatic Roots of Classical Civilization.* Rutgers University Press, Piscataway 1991

Bernal, Martin: *The Fabrication of Ancient Greece, 1785-1985.* Free Association Books, London 1987

Biers, William R.: *The Archaeology of Greece: An Introduction.* Cornell University Press, Ithaca 1996

Boardman, John: *Athenian Red Figure Vases: the Classical Period – a Handbook.* Thames and Hudson, London 1989

Boardman, John: *Athenian Black Figure Vases.* Thames and Hudson, London 1974

Boardman, John: *Greek Sculpture: the Archaic Period.* Thames and Hudson, London 1978

Boardman, John: *Greek Sculpture: the Classical Period.* Thames and Hudson, London 1987

Boardman, John: *The Greeks Overseas.* Thames and Hudson, London 1999

Boardman, John: *Athenian Red Figure Vases: the Archaic Period.* Thames and Hudson, London 1974

Boardman, John: *The Oxford History of Greece and the Hellenistic World.* Oxford Paperbacks, Oxford 2001

Braudel, Fernand, et al: *Memory and the Mediterranean.* Alfred A. Knopf, New York 2001

Calasso, Roberto: *The Marriage of Cadmus and Harmony.* Vintage, New York 1994

Camp, John M.: *The Archaeology of Athens.* Yale University Press, New Haven 2001

Cavafy, Constantine P., et al: *Before Time Could Change Them: The Complete Poems of Constantine P. Cavafy.* Harcourt, New York 2001

Collins Pocket Guide: Fish of Britain and Europe. Collins, London 1997

Cormack, Robin: *Byzantine Art.* Oxford University Press, Oxford 2000

Cotterell, Arthur: *The Mythology Library: Classical Mythology.* Lorenz Books, New York 2000

Davidson, James: *Courtesans and Fishcakes.* Fontana Press, London 1998

De Crescenzo, Luciano: *The History of Greek Philosophy.* Pan Books, London 1989–1991

Dinsmoor, William Bell: *The Architecture of Ancient Greece: an Account of its Historic Development.* B. T. Batsford Ltd, London 1950

Durrell, Lawrence: *Bitter Lemons of Cyprus.* Faber and Faber, London 2000

Durrell, Lawrence: *The Greek Islands.* Faber and Faber, London 2002

Durrell, Lawrence: *Prospero's Cell.* Faber and Faber, London 2000

Ehrenberg, Victor: *Society and Civilization in Greece and Rome.* Harvard University Press, Cambridge MA 1974

Faroqhi, Suraiya, et al: *An Economic and Social History of the Ottoman Empire Vol. 2.* Cambridge University Press, Cambridge 1997

Faroqhi, Suraiya: *Subjects of the Sultan: Culture and Daily Life in the Ottoman Empire.* I. B. Tauris, London and New York 2000

Finley, M.I.: *The Ancient Economy.* Chatto & Windus, London 1973

Finley, M.I.: *The Classical Greeks.* Penguin, Harmondsworth 1989

Finley, M.I.: *The World of Odysseus.* Pimlico, London 1999

Fullerton, Mark: *Greek Art.* Cambridge University Press, Cambridge 2000

Gage, Nicholas: *Eleni.* Harvill Press, London 1997

Gage, Nicholas: *Greece: Land of Light.* Bulfinch Press, New York 1998

Gage, Nicholas: *Hellas: A Portrait of Greece.* Efstathiadis Group, Athens 1992

Grant, Michael and Hazel, John: *Who's Who in Classical Mythology.* Routledge, London 2001

Graves, Robert: *Greek Gods and Heroes.* Dell Publishing Company, New York 1965

Graves, Robert: *The Greek Myths* complete edition. Penguin Books, London 1992

Gruben, Gottfried, Waterhouse, Richard (translator), Hirmer, Max (photographs): *Greek Temples, Theatres and Shrines.* Thames and Hudson, London 1963

Hafner, German: *Art of Crete, Mycenae, and Greece.* Harry Abrams, New York 1968

Haritopoulos, Stathis: *Aayion Oros. Macedonia's Holy Land.* Stathis Haritopoulos, Thessalonika 1997

Hemingway, Ernest: *The First Forty-Nine Short Stories.* Simon & Schuster, Riverside 1995

Homer: *The Odyssey.* Harvard University Press, Cambridge, MA and London 1995

Homer: *The Iliad.* Harvard University Press, Cambridge, MA and London 1999

Howatson, Margaret C.: *Oxford Companion to Classical Literature.* Oxford University Press, Oxford 1997

Jongh, Brian de: *The Companion Guide to Greece.* Boydell Press, Woodbridge 2000

Kazantzakis, Nikos: *Freedom or Death.* Faber, London 1995

Kazantzakis, Nikos: *The Greek Passion.* Transaction Publishers, Somerset NJ 2000

Kazantzakis, Nikos: *The Odyssey: A Modern Sequel.* Pocket Books, London 1986

Kazantzakis, Nikos: *Zorba the Greek.* Scribner, New York 1996

Keeley, Edmund (editor) and Sherrard, Philip (editor): *George Seferis: Collected Poems.* Anvil Press Poetry, London 1982

Keeley, Edmund (translator), et al: *C.P. Cavafy.* Chatto & Windus, London 1990

Kenyon, Davies, John: *Democracy and Classical Greece.* Fontana Press, London 1993

Kerènyi, Karl: *Gods of the Greeks.* Thames and Hudson, London 1961

Kerènyi, Karl: *The Heroes of the Greeks.* Thames and Hudson, London 1974

Làskari, Ninétta: *Kerkyra: mia matia mesa ston chrono, 1204–1864.* I. Sideres, Athens 1998

Latacz, Joachim: *Homer: His Art and his World.* University of Michigan Press, Ann Arbor 1998

List, Herbert, et al: *The Monograph.* Schirmer/Mosel, Munich 2000

Mango, Cyril A.: *Byzantine Architecture.* Faber/Electa, London 1986

Matthaiou, Anna: *Aspects de l'alimentation en Grèce sous la domination ottomane: des règlementations au discours normatif.* P. Lang Frankfurt Am Main 1997

McLoughlin, Marlene: *Across the Aegean: An Artist's Journey from Athens to Istanbul*. Chronicle Books, San Francisco 1996

Meier, Christian, et al: *Athens: A Portrait of the City in its Golden Age*. Pimlico, London 2000

Meier, Christian: *The Political Art of Greek Tragedy*. Polity, Cambridge 1993

Miller, Henry: *Colossus of Maroussi*. Minerva, London 1991

Murray, Oswyn: *Early Greece*. Fontana Press, London 1993

Murray, Oswyn, et al: *The Oxford History of Greece and the Hellenistic World*. Oxford University Press, Oxford 1991

Osborne, Robin: *Archaic and Classical Greek Art* (Oxford History of Art). Oxford University Press, Oxford 1998

Ostrogorski, Georgije: *History of the Byzantine State*. Rutgers University Press, Piscataway 1986

Pausanias: *Description of Greece*. W. Heinemann, London; Harvard University Press, Cambridge, MA 1965–1969

Petrou, Nikos: *Images of Dadia*. Koan, Athens 1994

Pettifer, James: *The Greeks*. Penguin, Harmondsworth 2000

Plato: *Symposium*. In Volume III of the Complete Works. W. Heinemann, London; Harvard University Press, Cambridge MA 1967

Pliny the Elder: *Natural History*. 10 volumes. Heinemann, London; Harvard University Press, Cambridge MA 1966–1968

Ritsos, Yannis: *Exile and Return: Selected Poems 1967–1974*. Anvil Press Poetry, London 1989

Runciman, Steven: *Mistra: Byzantine Capital of the Peloponnese*. Thames and Hudson, London 1980

Sacks, David, et al: *A Dictionary of the Ancient Greek World*. Oxford University Press, Oxford and New York 1997

Sacks, David, et al: *Encyclopedia of the Ancient Greek World*. Constable, London 1995

Schoder, Raymond V.: *Ancient Greece from the Air*. Thames and Hudson, London 1974

Schwab, Gustav: *Gods and Heroes of Ancient Greece*. Pantheon, New York 2001

Seferis, George: see Keeley and Sherrard

Smith, R.R.R.: *Hellenistic Sculpture*. Thames and Hudson, London 1991

Smith's Smaller Classical Dictionary. Wordsworth, Ware 1996

Snodgrass, Anthony M.: *An Archaeology of Greece: The Present State and Future Scope of a Discipline* (Sather Classical Lectures, Vol. 53). University of California Press, Berkeley and Oxford 1992

Storace, Patricia: *Dinner with Persephone*. Granta, London 1997

The Royal Horticultural Society: *Encyclopedia of Herbs and Their Uses*. Dorling Kindersley, London 1995

The Royal Horticultural Society: *Encyclopedia of Garden Plants*. Dorling Kindersley, London 1996

The Royal Horticultural Society: *Encyclopedia of Gardening*. Dorling Kindersley, London 1992

Theophrastos: *Enquiry into Plants*. W. Heinemann, London; Harvard University Press, Cambridge MA 1976–1990

Toynbee, J.M.: *Animals in Roman Life and Art*. Johns Hopkins University Press, Baltimore 1996

Tripp, Edward: *The Handbook of Classical Mythology*. Collins, London 1988

Vassilikos, Vassilis, et al: *And Dreams are Dreams*. Seven Stories Press, New York 1996

Webster's New Geographical Dictionary. Merriam-Webster, Springfield MA 1984

Xenophon: *Hellenica* volumes I and II. W. Heinemann, London; Harvard University Press, Cambridge MA 1968

Travel

Baedeker's Athens. AA Publishing, Basingstoke 2000

Baedeker's Greece. AA Publishing, Basingstoke 2001

Baedeker's Greek Islands. AA Publishing, Basingstoke 2000

Barber, Robin: *Blue Guide Athens*. A & C Black, London 1999

Barber, Robin: *Blue Guide Greece*. A & C Black, London 2001

Barber, Robin: *Blue Guide Rhodes and the Dodecanese*. A & C Black, London 1997

Boleman-Herring, Elizabeth, Patrick Leigh Fermor and Clay Perry: *Vanishing Greece*. Conran Octopus, London 1995

Bowman, John: *Frommer's Greece*. Frommer's Travel Guides, New York 2001

Bradford, Ernle and Francis Pagan: *The Companion Guide to the Greek Islands*. Boydell Press, Woodbridge 1998

Brewer, David: *The Greek War of Independence: The Struggle for Freedom from Ottoman Oppression and the Birth of the Modern Greek Nation*. Overlook Press, Woodstock 2001

Cameron, Pat: *Blue Guide Crete*. A & C Black, London 2002

Chandler, Richard: *Travels in Greece*.

Daly, Kathleen: *Greek and Roman Mythology A to Z*. Facts on File, New York 1992

Daniel, Geoff. *Landscapes of Cyprus*. Sunflower Books, London 1998

Dodwell, Edward: *Klassische Stätten und Landschaften in Griechenland: Impressionen von einer Reise um 1800*.

Dörfler, Hans-Peter and Gerhardt Roselt: *The Dictionary of Healing Plants*. Blandford, London 1989

Dubin, Marc: *Cyprus, The Rough Guide*. Rough Guides, London and New York 2000

Ellingham, Mark, et al: *The Rough Guide to Greece*. Rough Guides, London and New York 2000

Fermor, Patrick Leigh: *Mani: Travels in the Southern Peloponnese*. Penguin, Harmondsworth 1989

Fermor, Patrick Leigh: *Roumeli: Travels in Northern Greece*. Penguin, Harmondsworth 1988

Geldard, Richard G. and Astrid Fitzgerald: *Traveler's Guide to Ancient Greece*. Quest Books, Wheaton Il 2000

Gouffier, Choiseul and Marie Gabriel Auguste: *Voyage pittoresque de la Grèce*. Tilliard, Paris 1782, 1809 and 1882

Harris, Andy: *A Taste of the Aegean: Greek Cooking and Culture*. Pavilion Books, London 2000

Jongh, Brian de: *The Companion Guide to Mainland Greece*. Boydell Press, Woodbridge 1996

Jongh, Brian de: *The Companion Guide to Southern Greece: Athens, the Peloponnese, Delphi*. Boydell Press, Woodbridge 1996

Kizilos, Katherine: *The Olive Grove: Travels in Greece.* Lonely Planet, London and Oakland 1997

McNeal, R.A. (editor): *Nicholas Biddle in Greece: The Journals and Letters of 1806.* Penn State University Press, University Park PA 1993

Parlama, Liana (editor), Stampolidis, Nicholas (editor): *Athens: The City Beneath the City; Antiquities from the Metropolitan Railway Excavations.* Harry N. Abrams, New York 2001

Schneider, Andreas: *Insight Compact Guides: Crete.* Insight Guides, London 1995

Stoneman, Richard: *A Literary Companion to Travel in Greece.* J. Paul Getty Museum, Los Angeles 1994

Stoneman, Richard (editor): *A Luminous Land: Artists Discover Greece.* J. Paul Getty Museum, Los Angeles 1998

Willett, David, et al: *Lonely Planet Athens.* Lonely Planet Publications, London and Oakland 2001

Willett, David, et al: *Lonely Planet Greece* 4th edition Lonely Planet Publications, London and Oakland 2000

Willett, David, et al: *Lonely Planet Greek Islands.* Lonely Planet Publications, London and Oakland 2000

Cookery

Baumann, Hellmut: *The Greek Plant World in Myth, Art and Literature.* Timber Press, Portland 1996

Dalby, Andrew and Sally Grainger: *The Classical Cookbook.* British Museum Press, London 2000

Dalby, Andrew: *Siren Feasts: A History of Food and Gastronomy in Greece.* Routledge, London 1996

Debelius, Helmut: *Mediterranean and Atlantic Fish Guide.* Conch Books, Hockenheim 1997

Dowell, Philip and Adrian Bailey: *The Book of Ingredients.* Mermaid, London 1988

Frimodt, Claus: *An Illustrated Guide to Shrimp of the World.* Huntington, New York 1987

Frimodt, Claus: *Multilingual Illustrated Guide to the World's Commercial Coldwater Fish.* Fishing News Books, Oxford 1995

Herbst, S. T., *New Food Lover's Companion.* Barron's Educational Series, New York 2001

Howe, Robin. *Greek Cooking.* Andre Deutsch, London 1998

Jones, D., *The Pocketbook Guide to American Cooking in England.* Glencoe House Publications, Burton upon Trent 1998

Kochilas, Diane: *The Food and Wine of Greece.* St. Martin's Press, New York 1993

Kochilas, Diane: *The Glorious Foods of Greece: Traditional Recipes from Islands, Cities, and Villages.* William Morrow & Company, New York 2001

Kremezi, Aglaia: *The Foods of Greece.* Stewart, Tabori & Chang, New York 1999

Kremezi, Aglaia: *The Foods of the Greek Islands: Cookery and Culture at the Crossroads of the Mediterranean.* Houghton Mifflin, Boston 2000

Labensky, S., et al: *Webster's New World Dictionary of Culinary Arts.* Prentice Hall, Upper Saddle River 1999

Liacouras Chantiles, Vilma: *The Food of Greece.* Simon & Schuster, Riverside 1992

Maitland, Peter S.: *Guide to Freshwater Fish of Britain and Europe.* Hamlyn, London 2000

Migdalski, Edward C., et al: *The Fresh and Salt Water Fishes of the World.* Knopf, New York 1976

Mirams, Peter, et al: *Ingredients.* Könemann, Cologne 2000

Ortiz, Elisabeth Lambert: *The Encyclopedia of Herbs, Spices and Flavourings.* Dorling Kindersley, London 1992

Polemis, Aphrodite: *From a Traditional Greek Kitchen.* Book Publishing Company, Summertown 1992

Rombauer, I. S., et al: *Joy of Cooking.* Simon & Schuster, Riverside 1999

Santorinio-Santorinaki, Jill: *Food of the Gods: Traditional Greek Country Cooking.* Mardin Publishing, Aleppo 2001

Sarianides, Georgia: *Best of Greek Cuisine.* Hippocrene Books, New York 1997

Souli, Sofia: *222 Recipes: The Greek Cookery Book.* Toumbis, Athens 1989

Stavroulakis, Nicholas: *The Cookbook of the Jews of Greece.* Kuperard, London 1995

Stobart, Tom: *Herbs, Spices and Flavourings.* Overlook Press, Woodstock 2000

Taste of Greece, Anness Publishing Ltd., London 1997

Wilson, Anne: *Greek Cooking.* Könemann, Cologne 2000

Wilson, Anne: *Meze: Mediterranean-style Eating.* Könemann, Cologne 2000

Wines and beverages

Clarke, Oz: *Oz Clarke's Encyclopedia of Wine.* Little, Brown, London 1999

Dominé, André (publisher): *Wine.* Könemann, Cologne 2001

Foulkes, Christopher: *The Color Atlas of Wine.* World Publishers 1995

Foulkes, Christopher: *Larousse Encyclopedia of Wine.* Larousse Kingfisher Chambers, London 2001

Johnson, Hugh: *Hugh Johnson's Pocket Wine Book 2002.* Mitchell Beazley, London 2001

Johnson, Hugh: *Modern Encyclopedia of Wine.* Simon & Schuster, New York 1998

Johnson, Hugh and Jancis Robinson: *The World Atlas of Wine.* Mitchell Beazley, London 2001

Priewe, Jens: *Wine: From Grape to Glass.* Abbeville Press, New York 1999

Ray, Jonathan. *Everything You Need to Know about Wine.* Mitchell Beazley, London 1999

Robinson, Jancis: *The Oxford Companion to Wine.* Oxford University Press, Oxford 1999

PICTURE CREDITS

Key:
l. = left, r. = right, c. = center, a. = above, b. = below, ill. = illustrations, sm. photo = small photo

© Tandem Verlag GmbH, Königswinter

Photography: Günter Beer
55 b.r., 59 b. (all shells except for the hard clam, 4 ill.), 94 b.l., 166/167 (6 ill.: lemon balm, sage, oregano, rosemary, basil, thyme), 300/301 (background)

Photography: Saša Fuis
34 a.l., 250 (bay)

Photography: Peter Medilek
130 a. (background)

Photography: Zeva Oelbaum
368/69 (background)

Photography: Werner Stapelfeldt
1, 2/3, 6 (3 ill.), 7 (5 ill.), 8, 10/11 (2 ill.), 13, 14/15 (5 ill. except 14 b.), 16/17 (4 ill.), 20/21 (5 ill.), 22/23 (all except 22 b.l., 22 a,r., 5 ill.), 24 b.l. (sm. photo), 24/25 (background), 25 a.r., 26, 27, 28 (9 ill.), 29 (9 ill.). 30/31 (7 ill.), 32 (2 ill.), 33 a., 34 (4 ill.), 35 (4 ill.), 36/37 (2 ill.), 40/41 (13 ill.), 42 (4 ill.), 43 (all except background, 3 ill.), 44/45 (6 ill.), 46 (5 ill.), 47 (2 ill.), 48 b. (background, sm. photo), 49 a.l., 49 a.c., 49 a.r., 50/51 (all except labels, 7 ill.), 53 a.r., 54/55 (all except 55 a.r., 4 ill.), 56 (3 ill.), 57 a. (beer), 58 (2 ill.), 59 a., 60 a.l., 60 a.r., 62/63 (8 ill.), 63 (sm. photo), 64/65 (2 ill.), 67, 68 (2 ill.), 69 a., 69 b. (background), 70, 71 (sm. photo), 72/73 (8 ill.), 74/75 (background), 76 a., 77 (2 ill.), 78 (6 ill.), 79 (3 ill.), 80/81 (19 ill.), 82/83 (background), 84 (sm. photo), 84/85 (background), 85 l. (2 sm. photos), 87 b.r., 88/89 (5 ill.), 90/91 (8 ill.), 94 (Rhoditis), 96 a., 97 b. (background, sm. photo), 98 b., 99 a., 99 b., 100/101 (2 ill.), 104/105 (all except 105 a.r., 7 ill.), 106 a., 106/107 (background), 108 (4 ill.), 109, 110 a.l., 110 b.c., 112 a., 114, 115 (5 ill.), 118 b.l., 122 (sm. photo), 122/123 (background), 124 a.l., 124 b.l., 124/125, 125 r. (3 ill.), 126 (background), 127 (5 ill.), 128 b.l., 128/129 (background), 129 a.l., 129 a.r., 130

a.r. (sm. photo), 130 b.c., 130 b.r., 131 (2 ill.), 132/133 (2 background photos), 133 b. (sm. photo), 135, 136/137 (7 ill.), 138, 139 (background), 140/141 (8 ill.), 142 (2 ill.), 143, 144/145 (all except 144 a.r., 5 ill.), 146, (10 ill.), 147 (4 ill.), 148 a. (background), 148 b. (4 ill.), 149 (5 ill.), 150 (3 ill.), 151 (3 ill.), 152 (3 ill.) 153 (2 ill.), 154/155 (6 ill.), 156/157 (all except 157 b.r., 4 ill.), 158/59 (background), 159 (sm. photo), 161, 162/163, 164 (8 sm. photos), 164/165 (background), 166/167 (background), 170 a., 172 a.r. (sm. photo), 172/173 (background), 173 b.l., 173 b.c., 173 b.r., 174 a., 174 c., 175 (3 ill.), 176/177 (5 ill.), 178, 179 (7 ill.), 180/181 (background), 181 (sm. photo), 183, 184/185 (13 ill.), 186/187 (6 ill., 188 a., 188 b. (background), 189 (7 ill.), 190 a.l., 190 b.r., 191 a.r., 191 a c., 191 a.l., 192/193 (12 ill.), 194/195 (all except 194 b.c., 195 b.r., 15 ill.), 196/197 (background), 197 (sm. photo), 199, 200/201 (all except 200 b.l., 8 ill.), 203 (sm. photo), 204/205 (20 ill.), 206, 209, 210/211 (all except map, 12 ill.), 212/213 (all except 213 a.r., 213 a.c., 5 ill.), 214/215 (7 ill.), 216/217 (all except labels, 5 ill.), 218 a.l., 218 a.r., 218 b., 219 a. (sm. photo), 220/221 (13 ill.), 222/223, 224/225 (background), 225 (sm. photo), 227, 228/229 (7 ill.), 230/231 (9 ill.), 232 (6 ill.), 233 (2 ill.), 234/235 (7 ill.), 236 b.c., 236/237 a., 236/237 b., 242/243 (5 ill.), 244/245 (7 ill.), 246 (4 ill.), 247 (6 ill.), 248/249 (8 ill.), 250/251 (background), 6 sm. photos (cardamon, juniper berries, wild roses, medlar leaves, wormwood, hyssop), 251 a.r., 251 b.r., 252 (sm. photo) 255, 257 (2 sm. photos), 258 (3 ill.), 259 (30 ill.), 260 (2 ill.), 261 (5 ill.), 262/263 (all except 262 b.l., 6 ill.), 266/267 (12 ill.), 268/269 (all except 269 b.r., 7 ill.), 270 (sm. photo), 271 a.l., 271 b., 272 (5 ill.), 273 a.l., 274 (sm. photo) 275 b., 275 c.r., 280/281 (background), 281 (3 sm. photos), 284/285 (8 ill.), 286/287 (6 ill., cigarettes), 288/289 (all except 289 a.r., 3 ill.), 292 a., 293 a.r., 296/297 (background), 299, 300 (4 ill. in panel), 302/303 (background), 303 b.l., (sm. photo), 303 a.c., 304/305 (all except 305 a.l., 305 a.r., 11 ill.), 306 (sm. photo), 306/307 (background), 308/309 (all except "Lazári", 20 ill.), 311 (4 ill.), 312 a., 313 (sm. photo), 314/315 (all except 315 a.r., 6 ill.), 316 b., 318/319 (background), 319 (sm. photo), 321, 322 a.r., 322 b.c., 323 r. (4 ill.), 324/325 (background), 325 r. (3 ill., bottles), 326 (2 ill.), 328 b.r., 328 b.l., 329 (5 ill.), 330/331 (2 ill.), 332/333 (6 ill.), 334/335 (6 ill.), 336 (2 ill.), 337 (all except b.r., 3 ill.), 338/339 (background), 339 (sm. photo), 341, 344/345 (all except 344 b.l., 345 a.r., 5 ill), 348/349 (all except 349 a.r., 3 ill.), 350/351 (5 ill.), 353 (sm. photo), 354 a., 355 (3 ill.), 356 b.l., 358 b.l., 358 a.c., 358/359 (background), 359 r. (3 ill.),

360 (4 ill.), 361 (3 ill.), 362 (sm. photo), 362/363 (background), 363 a.r., 363 b.r., 364/365 (background), 365 (sm. photo) 367, 368/369 (all except background, 4 ill.), 370 (2 ill.), 372/373 (background), 378/379 (9 ill.), 380 (5 ill.), 382/383 (4 ill.), 384/385 (background), 385 (sm. photo), 387, 390/391 (5 ill.), 392 (3 ill.), 393 (9 ill.), 397 b.r., 398 a.r., 398 c.r., 398 b., 399 (3 ill.), 400 (2 ill.), 401 a., 402/403 (2 ill.), 404/405 (all except lemon, 6 ill.), 408 (sm. photo), 408/409 (background), 411, 412/413 (7 ill.), 414 a. (background, sm. photo), 415 b., 416 (5 ill.), 417 (2 ill.), 418/419 (6 ill.), 420 (7 ill.), 421 (2 ill.), 422 (4 ill.), 423 (5 ill.), 424, 425 (5 ill.), 426/427 (all except 427 a.r., 8 ill.), 428/429 (all except 428 a.r., 429 a.r., 429 b.r., 7 ill.), 430/431 (5 ill.), 432/433 (9 ill.), 434 (3 ill.), 435 (3 ill.), 436 (sm. photo), 436/437 (background), 438, 439

Photography: Ruprecht Stempell
166/167 (3 ill.: mint, camomile, coriander), 250 (5 ill.: fennel, aniseed, cinnamon, cloves, pepper), 274/275 (background), 404 b. (lemon)

Photography: Heinz Troll
18/19 (background), 33 b., 42/43 (background), 53 a.l., 53 b.l., 57 b.r., 60 b.r., 61 (2 ill.), 71 (background), 74 (sm. photo), 82 a.l., 82 b.l., (sm. photo), 83 r. (4 ill. one beneath the other), 85 b.r., 87 l., 107 a.r., 107 b.l., 110/111 (background), 112 b., 113 (2 ill.), 116/117, 118/119, 120/121 (2 ill.), 165 b.r., 168/169, 171 (2 ill.), 172 b.l., 173 a.r., 174 b.l., 190 b.l., 191 b.r., 194 b.l., 195 b.r., 202 b.r., 203, 208, 213 a.r., 213 a.c., 237 a.r., 237 b.r., 238/239, 241 r., 256/257 (background), 264/265 (3 ill.), 269 b.r., 270 (background), 271 a.r., 273 (all except a.l., 4 ill), 276, 277 (2 ill.), 278/279 (10 ill.), 289 a.r., 290/291, 292 r., 294/295 (all except 294 l., 8 ill.), 302 a.l., 303 b.r., 305 a.r., 310 b.l., 312 a., 313, 317, 322 a.r., 322 b.r., 324 b.l. (sm. photo), 327, 342/343 (background), 346 (all except a.r., 3 ill.), 347 (2 ill.), 352/353 (background), 354 b.r., 356 a.r., 356 a.l., 357 (2 ill.), 372/373, 374 (5 ill.), 375 (5 ill.), 376/377, 381 a.l., 381 b., 394/95, 401 b., 415 a.l., 415 a.r., 429 b.r.

Graphic design: Rolli Arts, Essen: 69, 139, 188, 211

Maps: Studio für Landkartentechnik, Detlev Maiwald, Norderstedt: 5, 12, 38, 66, 92, 102, 134, 160, 182, 198, 226, 254, 298, 320, 340, 366, 386, 410

© AKG, Berlin
389 a.l. (2 sm. photos), photos: Erich Lessing: 280 a.l., 280 b.l., 337 b.r.

© Arcturos (Civil Society for the Protection and Management of Wildlife and Natural – Environment/Life Project "Lycos"), Greece
293 b.r.

© Helmut Baumann, Zurich
129 u.r.

© Bildarchiv Staatliche Museen Preußischer Kulturbesitz, Berlin
157 b.r., 240 b.l., 297 (sm. photo), 363 a.l., 363 b.l., photo: Ingrid Geske-Heiden: 14 b., 76 a., photo: Johannes Laurentius: 86 b.l., photo: Reinhardt Saczewski: 162 b.l., photo: Lutz Braun: 294 l., photo: U. Hoffmann: 388/389 (background), photo: Félicien Faillet: 429 a.r.

© Bildarchiv Steffens/Bridgeman Art Library
305 a.l. (sm. photo), 345 a.r., 389 b.r.

© Klaus Bötig, Bremen
75 a.l. (sm. photo), 349 a.r., 414 b.r.

© The Bridgeman Art Library, London
105 a.r., 371 b. (sm. photo), 381 a.r.

© Cinetext, Frankfurt
200 b.l.

© Flora Foto, Langenhagen
166/167 (3 ill.: centaury, wild mallow, dill)

© Heather Angel, England
428 a.r. (sm. photo, background)

© Hulton Archive, London, England
52

© Ikan-Unterwasserarchiv, Frankfurt
342 (3 sm. photos), 343 (3 sm. photos)

© Yiorgos Karahalis, Piraeus, Greece
240/241 (background)

© laif, Cologne
Photo: Velissarios Voutsas/On Location: 74/75 (background), 126 a.l., 241 a.l., 252/253 (background)

© Marianthi Milona, Cologne
310 a.

© Okapia, Frankfurt
Photo: O.Cabrero i Roura: 370 a., photo: H.P. Fröhlich: 370 b. (background), photo: Wolfgang Buchhorn: 427 a.r.

© Nikos Petrou, Athens, Greece
170 b.l.

© Photo Press, Munich, photo: Bartsch
388 b.l. (sm. photo)

© Konstantinos Pittas, Illoupolis Attkis, Greece
82/83 (background), 94/95 (all grapes except Limnio, Savatiano, Malagousia, Rhoditis, 10 ill.)

© Scala, Florence, Italy
307 a.r. (sm. photo)

© Semper Idem Underberg
22 b.l., 22 a.r.

© Sipa Press, Paris, France
Photo: Argyropoulos: 86 a.l.

© Marion Steinhoff, Dortmund
75 r.

© Stock Food, Munich
Photo: S. & P. Eising: 33 b.r., photo: Robert Kanngießer: 83 a.l. (sm. photo), photo: TH Foto-Werbung: 166/167 (3 ill.: common yarrow, St. John's Wort, lime blossom), 250 (eucalyptus), photo: Maximilian Stock LTD: 166 (scented geranium), 396 (3 ill.), 397 (all except b.r., 3 ill.), photo: Karl Newedel: 250 (cumin)

© Studio Kontos, Athens, Greece
24 a.r. (2 sm. photos), 25 a.l., 25 b.l., 240 a., 262 b.l., 328 a.r., 344 b.l., 389 a.r., 398 a.l.

© Heinz Troll, Thessaloniki, Greece
95 (Malagousia, plus background), 207 (4 ill.), 219 (background), 219 b. (sm. photo), 315 b.r., 316 a., 324 a.l. (sm. photo), 359 a.l., 406/407 (background)

The publishers would like to thank the following wineries, wine cellars, distilleries, and cooperatives for their contributions:

Achaia Clauss: Patras, Peloponnese
Antonopoulos: Vassiliko, Peloponnese
Archanes: Heraklion, Crete
Asimina Fragou: Spata, Attica
John Boutari & Son: Thessaloniki, Macedonia
Cosmetatos: Athens, Attica
Creta Oylmpias: Athens, Attica
Gerovassilou: Epanomi, Macedonia
Hatzidakis: Pyrgos Kallistis, Santorini
Hatzimichalis: Atalantis, Central Greece
Katogi: Métsovo, Epirus
Keo: Lemesos, Cyprus
Kir-Yianni: Yianakohori, Macedonia
Kourtakis: Markopoulo, Attica
Lazaridi: Adriani Drama, Macedonia
Lyrarakis: Heraklion, Crete
Markovitis: Naoussa, Macedonia
Minos: Heraklion, Crete
Monte Royia: Khryssorroyiátissa monastery, Cyprus
Oenoforos: Selinous, Peloponnese
Papaioannou: Nemea, Peloponnese
Parparoussis: Patras, Peloponnese
Peza: Heraklion, Crete
Samos Coop: Malagari, Samos
Semeli: Stamata, Attica
Sigalas: Baxedhes Oia, Santorini
Sitia: Heraklion, Crete
Sodap: Limassol, Cyprus
Spiropoulos: Mantinia, Peloponnese
Tsantalis: Agios Paulos, Chalkidikí
Vassiliou: Koropi, Attica
Zitsa: Ioannina, Epirus

INDEX OF ILLUSTRATED
WORKS OF ART

ACKNOWLEDGEMENTS

The editor would like to thank the following persons and institutions:

Achaia Clauss Winery, Peloponnese
Agnes Tsara, Macedonia Palace, Thessaloniki
Angeliki Perdikari, Greek Press Ministry, Athens
Anna Schönebeck-Sych, Ithaca
Antonopoulos Winery, Peloponnese
Archäon Gefsis, Maria Karaméri, Athens
Boutaris Winery, Macedonia
Boutla Ioanna, Pílion, Thessaly
Chandris Hotel, Chios
Chris Tsolakis, Cyprus
Christian Herrmann, Cologne
Cosmetatos Winery, Cephalonia
Cronus Airlines, Frankfurt, Frau Partsch
Cypriot Central Tourist Office, Frankfurt
Cypriot Chamber of Trade, Cologne
Cyprus Airlines, Frankfurt, Mrs Lazaridou
Darzentas Mathäus, Santorini
Date Cooperative, Peloponnese
Dimitris Katsouras, Tsantali, Chalkidiki
Dimitris and Michalis Mavrikos, Rhodes
Dr. Josef Schnelle, for the Athos chapter, Chalkidiki
Dr. Sabine Wollnik Kursche, Cologne
Evangelou Sotiris, chef at the Macedonia Palace, Thessaloniki
Fish specialist, Papazoglou, Athens University
Fragou Winery, Attica
Giorgos Nikolaidis, A.S.M., Macedonia
Greek Central Tourist Office, Frankfurt
Greek Press Ministry, Athens
Günter Beer, Cologne
Haitoglou Bros. S.a., Thessaloniki
Hatzimichalis Winery, Attica
Heinz Troll, Thessaloniki
Hotel Anassa, Maria Constantinidou, Cyprus
Hotel Athens Plaza, Athens
Hotel Evdokia, Giorgos Tsounos, Ikaría
Hotel Macedonian Palace, Thessaloniki
Hotel Palladion, Nikos Sourelis, Ioaninna
Hotel Paphos Amathous Beach, Cyprus
Hotel Skites, Ouranópolis
Ilias Milonas, Meliki
Ioannis Stamatakis, Skopelos
Irini Androutsou, Ouranópolis
Kai Hasse, beef producer, Cologne
Katerina Yiannouka, Macedonia
Kitro concern Promponas, Cyclades
Terkenlis confectioners, Thessaloniki
Konstantinos Stoupas, chef at the Aegle, Corfu

Kostas Drosinos, Ouranoupolis
Kostas Pistolas, Thrace
Kostas Trikalopoulos, Macedonia
Kotsolis, milk bar, Athens
Koulinos Travel Bureau, Cologne
Kourtakis, Mrs Terti, Attica
Loukoumi concern, Krambidou, Cyprus
Makis Efraimidis, Boutari, Macedonia
Markos Kafouros, Santorini
Mary Skinner, Friends of the Cyprus Donkey, Cyprus
Mike Dinos, Skopelos
Molho Bookstore, Thessaloniki
Mrs Konstantinidou, Metaxa, Athens
Music Restaurant, I Stoa ton athanaton, Athens
Nikolaides Bros Winery Ltd., Cyprus
Nikos Yiannakis, boat builder, Chalkidiki
Nikos Katsanis, Chalkidiki
Nikos Sarantos, chef at the Athens Plaza, Athens
Oenoforos Winery, Peloponnese
Pamela Ahrens, Thessaloniki
Panagiotis Drakakis, Chalkidiki
Panagiotis Georgiadis, Thessaloniki
Panagiotis Papageorgiou, date cooperative, Peloponnese
Pandelis Taptas, Ouranópolis
Pangiota Milona, Macedonia
Panos Deligiannis, Athenorama, Athens
Pantelis Lambadarios, Aegina
Paoloa Maier, Pílion
Papaioannou Winery, Peloponnese
Pater Athanasios, Agias Triadas Monastery, Crete
Pater Dionyssos, Khrysorroyiatissa Monastery, Cyprus
Pater Epiphanios, monastic republic of Athos
Pavlos Protopapa, Anopolis, Crete
Peter Simon, Cologne
Petroula Lütz, Cologne
Restaurant Aegle, Maria Gisdakis, Corfu
Restaurant Al Halili, Cyprus
Restaurant Baroulko, Lefteris Lazarou, Piraeus
Restaurant Bosporon Megaron, Thessaloniki
Restaurant Dafne, Athens
Restaurant Esai, Manos Chronakis, Ioannina
Restaurant Kritikos, Ouranópolis
Restaurant Mirovolos Smirni, Thessaloniki
Restaurant Monastiri, Ioanna Darkadaki, Crete
Restaurant Selini, Santorini
Restaurant Tamam, Eva Sirri, Crete
Samos Winery, Giorgos I. Roussos, Samos
Semeli Winery, Attica
Seven Georges, Cyprus
Sinodis Taptas, Thessaloniki
Sotiris and Katerina Basvekopoulos, Macedonia
Spyropoulou, Peloponnese

Tasos Andreou, Hunters' Association, Ioannina
Taverna 1912, Lesbos
Taverna Arap Memis, Kos
Theodosis Theodosiou, Cyprus
Thomas and Maria Harisouda
Tstantalis Winery, Athos
Vassilakis & Sons S.A., Corfu
Vassiliou Winery, Attica
Vasso Kritaki, Chios

The photographer would like to thank the following people and institutions for their helpful assistance:

Macedonia
  Boutaris winery, cooperative in Meliki, Soulis Furs in Kastoria
Chalkidiki
  Hotel Skites in Ouranópolis, Restaurant Kritikos in Ouranópolis, Tsantalis Winery, Pater Ephanios, Agion Oros
Ikaría
  Hotel Evdoxia
Thessaloniki
  Ouzeri Astistoteleus, Agrolab, Tepketidis the confectioners, Prof. Gertsis of the American Farm School, the Loumidis coffee store, Haitoglou, Loula Siouti, the Mirovolos Smirni taverna, the Tiropolio cheese store, the Status bar in Epanomi, the Papanikolaou family in Eanomi, "Kechris Otelios" retsina producer, the Gerovasiliou winery, the Molho bookstore
Epirus
  The Prassini Akti tavern in Ioannina, the Ioannina Hunters' Association, Hotel Paladio Ioannina, Panagiotis Purnaropoulos in Preveza, Restaurant Esaei in Ioannina, the saffron cooperative in Krokos, the I Gastra restaurant in Ioannina
Skopelos
  Ioannis Stamatakis, Kostas and Michalis Dinos
Central Greece
  Albatros taverna in Galaxidi, the I orea Ellada restaurant in Galaxidi, the apple cooperative in Zagora
Peleponnese
  Kalamata Fig Cooperative, the Georga pig farming center in Alt Epidaurus
Athens
  Daphne's restaurant, Archeon Gevsis restaurant, Baroulko restaurant in Piraeus, the Mextaxa distillery, Rembetiko I Stoa ton Athanaton, the Kotsolis confectionery store
Santorini
  Selene restaurant, Roussos winery, the Bonatsa taverna in Perivolos
Kos
  Arap taverna

Crete

Tamam estiatorio, Monastyri restaurant, Panayiotis Kontoyianis herb store in Rethymon

Corfu

Aegle restaurant

Cyprus

Mezedion 7 saint Georges in Paphos, Hotel Anassa, Amatheus Beach Hotel, SODAP wine producers, SEDIGEP Agriproducts Cooperative, Al Hallil tavern in Larnaca, Kafkalia LTD Agros, Adelfi Nikolaidi LTD Anogira, Rosewater and Pottery in Agros

Rhodes

Michalis Mavrikos in Lindos

Aegina

Lambadaros family firm

Ithaki

Mrs Schönebeck-Sych

Cephalonia

Centilini winery

Chios

Estiatorio Messaionas in Mesta

Lesbos

1912 taverna in Molivos, Elsa Eglesopoulou, Ouzo Kouroumichali in Petra, Ouzo Mini

Naxos

Palatia restaurant, the Promponas family

Heinz Troll would like to thank the following persons for their kind assistance with the food photography

Elina Steletari for props, organization and her good spirits, **Christos Raptis** for her help with the photography, **Dimitra Barda** for the styling in Macedonia Palace, **Irene Fotiadis**, **Nikos Katsanis** and **Sotiris Evangelou** for making available their great skill as internationally renowned cookery experts in the making of this book.

The publishers extend special thanks to:

Dr. Ioanna Mylonaki for her advice on all matters relating to Greek language and culture, **Anastasia Sioutis** for reading the recipes and her numerous tips regarding Greek food and eating customs, **Aicha Becker** for the index and for helping wherever assistance was needed, **Berthold Bartel** for the final reading, **Mareile Busse** for correction input, **Martina Gäbelein** for photo scans, **Maria Netsika** for consultation on matters of wine, **Paola Maier** for advice on herbs, **Agni Tsara** of the Macedonia Palace Hotel for her assistance in carrying out the photographic work, **Lisa Georgoula** for translations and advice on fish matters, **Petra Sparrer** for reading the Cyprus material, **Elke Teubler** for the appendix layout.

INDEX OF DISHES

Page numbers for illustrated dishes are shown in bold

ENGLISH RECIPE INDEX

Page numbers for illustrated dishes are shown in bold

GREEK RECIPE INDEX

Page numbers for illustrated dishes are shown in bold

INDEX OF KEY WORDS